This document is c... any fair dealing for the purposes of priv... Designs and Patents Act 1988, no part of ... mitted in any form or by any means, e... electrical ... ing or otherwise, without th... ddressed to

Parts of this text hav...
© The Association...

Lynn Brewer – Educ... aining Consultant for SEND; Guy Jarvis – ... al Officer, Lancashire Outdoor Education; ... SU; Steve Boocock – Chief Executive, Wil... indlehurst – Head of Primary PE, Scho... h – Head Teacher, Astley Park School, C... Katie Towner and the team at Swim England; Professor Jo Harris; Ron Tulley – England Boxing; Sue Trotman – One Dance UK; Eileen Marchant – Quality Assurance/Proofreader; Simon Leach, Simon Roche and Hazel Allen – afPE

At the time of publication, the UK is in the midst of a Covid-19 pandemic. This is fast changing and readers should refer to gov.uk for updated guidance.

Editor: Christopher Stanners
Proofreader: Craig Smith
Project management team: Craig Smith and Charlotte Galbraith
Designer: Saima Nazir
Cover photos: © Simon Leach, Alan Edwards Photography and Robert Kneschke/Shutterstock.com
Inner photos unless otherwise stated: © Leweston School and Raglan School
Indexer: Paul Douch

Published in partnership with:

UK
COACHING

Room 117 Bredon
University of Worcester
Henwick Grove
Worcester WR2 6AJ
Tel: 01905 855 584
Email: enquiries@afpe.org.uk
Website: www.afpe.org.uk

UK Coaching
Chelsea Close
Leeds
LS12 4HP
Tel: 0113 274 4802
Email: communication@ukcoaching.org
Website: www.ukcoaching.org

93577
Produced by Coachwise Ltd, the trading arm of UK Coaching.

Foreword

The year 2020 will be remembered as one of challenge, difference and change.

Very few people will have experienced anything close to this before and we will be debating the impact on young people for years to come. Young people and schools are having to be adaptable and there will no doubt be change on the horizon for them.

Never has physical education, school sport and physical activity (PESSPA) been more important for helping the nation's young people move towards a brighter future.

I have frequently talked about the power of sport and physical activity from a wider perspective, but also a personal one. When I was growing up as a wheelchair user my parents encouraged me to be active, not because it was a pathway to elite sport, but because it would be good for my long-term mental health and fitness and allow me to live in a largely (at the time) inaccessible world.

In school I had great people around me who were passionate about their teaching to ensure that I developed new skills, built my resilience, was safe and that I also had fun.

The lessons I learnt in school have continued way beyond my sporting career and into 'retirement' and will be important for years to come. Without that positive early learning I would not have been able to take the many opportunities that I have experienced along the way.

The power of PESSPA in changing young people's lives is immense, but it must be taught safely to ensure all children and young people feel safe. It is also essential that the workforce feels secure and confident in their teaching.

This is exactly what is enabled in the 10th edition of *Safe Practice: in Physical Education, School Sport and Physical Activity*. The Association for Physical Education (afPE) have once again provided an essential resource for all those involved in the teaching of PESSPA.

It is an essential reference for everyone at all levels and is a definitive guidance document for all aspects of the subject, and has been written in collaboration with a wide range of partners to ensure accuracy and current best practice are at the heart of the book.

Cvey Thompson

Baroness Tanni Grey-Thompson DBE, DL

Contents

Introduction

About this resource

This resource is organised into four chapters, each of which addresses a key aspect of teaching safely or teaching safety.

Chapter 1 focuses on essential health and safety law pertinent to both employers and employees. It provides a useful background to explaining how the guidance in this resource has been developed.

Chapter 2 is a comprehensive overview of the most pertinent areas of interest of the Physical Education, School Sport and Physical Activity (PESSPA) workforce. The chapter sections cover a range of topics for consideration when planning a PESSPA offer for students. In some sections generic guidance is provided on a principles basis, followed by specific guidance for activities, where appropriate.

Chapter 3 focuses on the importance of learning about being safe and feeling safe, in and through the context of PESSPA. It provides examples of objectives, outcomes and tasks to support staff to promote effective learning about pertinent areas of safe practice. It is not a scheme of work but when considered alongside statutory requirements such as the home national curriculum, it may help staff to embed appropriate content into their schemes of work which are used when planning for each student's PESSPA career.

Chapter 4 outlines some of the most frequently asked questions addressed to the Association for Physical Education (afPE) health and safety team. The questions cross reference useful background information within the main body of the resource. Key learning points are also drawn out.

Relevant case law formulates the rest of this chapter and follows a similar format. Cross reference is made back to pertinent sections within the main body and key learning points are outlined which can be used when planning a PESSPA programme.

Web links appear throughout the resource and, in some cases, the home page is outlined acknowledging the fact that the sub sections and specific pages of websites change frequently. This ensures that the link will remain current, although in places a specific search may then be needed to navigate to the exact page.

Glossary of Terms

accident	An event that results in harm/injury.
aquatic activities	For example, swimming, water safety activities, lifesaving, diving and open-water swimming.
British Standards (BS)	Advisory and not regulatory standards of quality for goods and services produced by the British Standards Institute (BSI) group. Where any personal protective equipment (PPE) is involved in an injury, these standards are considered to be a benchmark.
case in point	Use of case law and information from legal inquiries and hearings to illustrate key principles and help readers to apply the theory to actual situations.
case law	Law established by the outcome of former court cases and based on decisions that judges have made.
Clubmark	Cross-sport accreditation scheme for community sports clubs, used in England, Northern Ireland, Scotland and Wales. An accredited club is recognised as a safe, rewarding and fulfilling place for participants of all ages, as well as helping parents and carers know that they are choosing the right club for their young people.
coaches	Those who are qualified to coach specific sports.
code of conduct	This sets out the expectations placed on individuals (eg by the school) in a specific context or situation.
combat activities	Activities that are characterised by one-on-one combat in which a winner is determined against a set of rules.
competence	Appropriate and relevant experience, expertise and/or qualifications to undertake specific responsibilities.
concussion	A brain injury that can occur after a blow or other injury to the head or body that involves the brain being shaken against the inside of the skull. Concussion is known to have potential dangers both at the time of injury and in later life.
contingency planning	A course of action planned to respond effectively to a significant future event or situation that may or may not happen (eg deterioration in weather conditions).
cool-down	Helps the body and mind recover safely and effectively after taking part in PESSPA activities.
cover supervisors	Adults employed to supervise groups doing pre-prepared work. They may not have any expertise in physical education, school sport and physical activity (PESSPA).
curriculum gymnastics	Movement challenges that develop body management and locomotor skills, and help students acquire precision of movement and quality of response in the context of balancing, inverting, climbing, rolling, jumping, landing, transferring weight, stepping and managing the body in flight.
developmentally appropriate	How appropriate a PESSPA activity/task is for the physical, social or emotional maturation of the child or young person.
direct supervision	Involves a member of staff working alongside students or support staff in order that they can intervene at any time, as necessary.
disability	Under the Equality Act 2010, a person has a disability if the person has a mental or physical impairment, and the impairment has a substantial and long-term adverse effect on the person's ability to carry out normal day-to-day activities.
duty of care	A legal obligation to ensure the safety and/or well-being of others.
dynamic risk assessment	Carried out before an activity or event and while it is taking place, identifying and responding to unforeseen issues, such as an unsafe response to a task, sudden illness, changes in climatic conditions or ineffective officiating. Sometimes referred to as ongoing or continuous risk assessment.

early years foundation stage (EYFS)	Sets the standards for the learning, development and care of a child from birth to five years old. All schools and Ofsted-registered early years providers must follow the EYFS, including childminders, preschools, nurseries and school reception classes. The EYFS only applies to schools and early years providers in England. There are different early years standards in Scotland and Wales. Scotland – the Early Years Framework pre-birth – eight years old. Wales – Early years outcome framework, for children 0–7.
education, health and care plan	A plan for students with specific special educational needs and disabilities (SEND) that considers what would help the individual to access PESSPA within the curriculum and as part of an extracurricular programme.
employee	Within this text it means the school staff – both teaching and non-teaching – contracted to provide a specific service within the school organisation.
employer	Within this text it refers to the school authority – the Board of Governors, Trust, local authority or proprietor that has legal responsibility for education in a school or group of schools.
European Standards (EN)	Advisory and not regulatory standards of quality for goods and services. Where any PPE is involved in an injury, these standards are considered to be a benchmark.
forethought	An element of competence for teaching safely that involves forward planning, anticipating what may happen, and thinking about where harm is likely.
generic risk assessment	Considers the general principles that apply to an activity, wherever it may take place. A generic risk assessment is usually the starting point and is generally provided in a written format by the employer, governing body of sport or similar organisation.
governing body of sport	Independent, self-appointed organisation that governs its sport through the common consent of the sport.
hazard	Something with the potential to cause harm.
head teacher (HT)	The most senior teacher, leader and manager of a school.
health-related physical activity (HRPA)	Physical activity associated with health enhancement and disease prevention.
hidden disability	An invisible or hidden disability is one that is not easily visible and immediately apparent. This may include disabilities including autism and mental health.
higher duty of care	That held by a professional with specialist expertise, experience, qualifications or responsibility whose level of expected care is based on those with the same expertise within the same profession.
higher level teaching assistant (HLTA)	Does all that regular teaching assistants do, and has an increased level of responsibility. For example, HLTAs might teach classes on their own, cover planned absences, and allow teachers time to plan and mark. Under the direction of a teacher, HLTAs often plan, prepare and deliver learning activities with individual students, groups, and also assess, record and report on students' progress.
incident	An adverse event resulting in an undesired situation or 'near miss' where no injury occurred, but there was the potential to cause injury.
Key Stage 1	Students aged 5–7 years (now covered by the Foundation Phase in Wales, which includes students aged 3–7).
Key Stage 2	Students aged 7–11 years.
Key Stage 3	Students aged 11–14 years.
Key Stage 4	Students aged 14–16 years.
must	Used only where the situation described relates to a statutory requirement, or where the employer sets out what must be followed by the employees.
National Governing Body (NGB) of sport	This is a governing body of sport that has submitted a whole sport plan, which details how it will use Sport England investment to help it increase the number of people playing its sport and nurture talent.
near misses	Incidents that have occurred in a PESSPA session, in which an individual could have suffered harm but fortuitously did not.

negligence	May be defined as 'careless conduct which injures another and which the law deems liable for compensation' – Frederick Place Chambers (1995) *Negligence at Work: Liability for Injury and Disease*. St Albans: XPL Publishing. ISBN: 978-1858110-31-8.
organiser's event risk assessment	An event risk assessment, completed by the organiser, that takes account of venue issues and the organisation of the planned event.
parent	The Education Act 1996 under section 576 defines a 'parent' in relation to a child or young person as the biological parents of a child, whether they are married or not as anyone, who although not a biological parent, has parental responsibility for a child, or a person with day-to-day care.
personalised learning	Involves matching the tasks to the students to enable progress at appropriate pace within lessons, over a series of lessons and throughout a programme of study – sometimes referred to as differentiated learning.
personal protective equipment (PPE)	Any device worn or held by an individual for protection against one or more health and safety hazards. The most common forms of PPE used in schools include mouth guards, shin pads, helmets, padding and swimming goggles.
PESSPA activities	Include all practical learning contexts that are part of physical development activities, physical education lessons, organised sport and/or physical activity sessions beyond the curriculum, both in school settings and the community.
PESSPA sessions	Include physical development activities, physical education lessons, organised sport and/or physical activity sessions beyond the curriculum both in school settings and the community.
PESSPA subject leaders	All those responsible for managing physical education in an educational establishment.
physical activity	A broad term referring to all bodily movement that uses energy. It includes all forms of physical education, sports and dance activities. However, it is wider than this as it also includes indoor and outdoor play, work-related activity, outdoor and adventurous activities, active travel (eg walking, cycling, rollerblading, scootering) and routine, habitual activities such as using the stairs, doing housework and gardening.
physical contact	In a safeguarding context, this is 'intentional bodily contact' initiated by an adult with a child, child on child or adult on child.
physical education	Planned, progressive learning for all students that takes place within the school curriculum and involves both 'learning to move' (ie becoming more physically competent) and 'moving to learn' (eg learning through movement and the development of a range of competencies beyond physical activity, such as cooperating with others). The context for the learning is physical activity, with children experiencing a broad range of activities, including sport and dance.
post-primary	Term used in Northern Ireland for 'secondary'.
professional learning	Teachers engage in this to stimulate their thinking and professional knowledge, and ensure their practice is critically informed and up to date.
programmed aquatic activities	Activities with formal structure, supervision, control and continuous monitoring from the poolside. (Also see unprogrammed aquatic activities.)
progression	Staged development of knowledge, skills and understanding in accordance with confidence, ability and successful prior experience.
protected characteristics	The Equality Act 2010 sets out the following characteristics as protected characteristics: age, disability, gender reassignment, marriage and civil partnership, pregnancy and maternity, race, religion and belief, sex, sexual orientation.
quality mark	afPE's benchmark and industry standard for high quality PESSPA in schools for students aged 5–16 years.
regular and approved practice	Practice that is common and widely practised as safe as opposed to an idiosyncratic practice adopted by individuals or organisations.
remote supervision	This type of supervision (as opposed to direct or close supervision) usually occurs when, as part of planned activities, a group works away from the supervising staff, but is subject to stated controls. Staff, even though not physically present, remain fully responsible for the safe management of the young people and this is a reasonable practice based on the rigorous assessment of risk.

risk	The likelihood of harm occurring from a hazard.
risk assessment	A judgement about whether a situation is safe within established practice and procedures, or whether additional precautions are required.
risk-benefit analysis	Comparison of the level of risk against the benefits. It aims to balance acceptable risk with appropriate challenge and, in doing so, considers whether the benefits of participation outweigh the likelihood of harm or injury occurring.
risk management	Risk management is the process of identifying, quantifying and managing the risks that an organisation faces.
risk protection arrangement	An alternative to commercial insurance for all academy trust and multi academy trust schools to opt in to. This is managed by the Department for Education (DfE) to protect academy trust schools against losses due to any unforeseen and unexpected event.
safe exercise practice	Physical activities that are developmentally appropriate, and performed with appropriate control and correct joint alignment while minimising any undue stress associated with high impact.
safeguarding	Action that is taken to promote the welfare of children and protect them from harm.
safe practice in PESSPA	Where the risks for those involved in PESSPA sessions are deemed to be acceptably managed.
scheme of work	A written long- or medium-term plan that informs lesson planning, fulfils the statutory requirements of any curriculum, and meets local circumstances and needs. A scheme of work typically comprises detail such as progressive learning targets, essential techniques and skills, suggestions for assessment, suggested requirements for prior learning, cross-curricular learning, and relevant safe-practice information.
school sport	Structured learning that takes place beyond the curriculum but within school settings. The context for learning is physical activity that has the potential to develop and broaden the learning that takes place in physical education, and form vital links with community sport and activity. Sometimes referred to as extracurricular or out-of-school-hours learning.
school staff	A collective term for the group of people – both teaching and non-teaching – employed within the school.
second impact syndrome	Second impact syndrome (SIS) is a very rare condition in which a second concussion occurs before the first concussion has properly healed. SIS can result from even a very mild concussion that occurs minutes, hours, days or weeks after the initial concussion.
should	Used in this resource to illustrate regular and approved practice.
staff	A collective term for all who are involved in the delivery of PESSPA whether on the school roll or visiting coaches.
STEP framework	A framework for making adjustments to the learning environment in terms of space, task, equipment and people in order to provide appropriate differentiated challenge for all students in relation to achieving learning outcomes.
students	All children and young people attending school.
support staff	A term used for all adults without qualified/registered teaching status (QTS) who contribute to the teaching of students in schools (eg HLTAs, cover supervisors, physical education apprentices, volunteers and sports coaches). Support staff do not include trainee teachers.
teacher	Within this text it refers to the adult delivering the lesson or session to a class or group whether on the school roll, a visiting coach or volunteer.
trainee teachers	Those undergoing training that leads to qualified/registered teacher status (QTS).
unprogrammed aquatic activities	Sessions in water without a session structure but with supervision and continuous monitoring, in most cases from the poolside (also see programmed aquatic activities).
venue risk assessment	A risk assessment completed by the manager/owner/host that identifies the hazards, evaluates the risks and establishes appropriate controls to make the venue safe for the purpose for which it is being offered or hired out to the user group.
visiting coach	An external contributor to teaching PESSPA whether as a volunteer or in a paid capacity.
warm-up	Prepares the body and mind safely and effectively to take part in PESSPA activities.

Chapter 1:

Health and Safety Law and Responsibility

Section 1: Introduction

1.1.1   Physical education, school sport and physical activity (PESSPA) consists of practical activities involving a range of movement challenges such as changing speed, moving in different directions, moving with or around objects or people, or using equipment to help develop movement skills.

1.1.2   The very nature of PESSPA activities involves elements of inherent risk to participants. Those risks range from minor trips, slips or collisions through to catastrophic equipment failure. The challenge for those providing such activities is to manage those risks effectively to reduce the probability of harm occurring and the seriousness of any potential injury to an acceptably low level whilst maintaining appropriate challenge.

1.1.3   Where risk is effectively managed, the delivery of the activity will be considered to be safe. However, it is important that providers, participants and their parents/carers where appropriate, are aware that a safe activity will never be risk free.

1.1.4   Effective risk management can only be achieved where providers and participants are made aware of and appropriately apply their health and safety responsibilities. These responsibilities are informed by a combination of statute law, case law, statutory and non-statutory guidance, activity specific best practice and the policy and procedures adopted by organisations.

1.1.5   Although all involved in PESSPA activities will have a role as far as health and safety is concerned, the primary responsibility, both under the criminal and civil law, will generally lie with the employer. The employer in the education sector is determined by the category of the school and may be the Governing Body, the maintaining Local Authority or Trust.

1.1.6   The Health and Safety responsibilities of the employer cannot be devolved to the head teacher or leadership team within a school or to an external provider, however tasks to fulfil those responsibilities can and are routinely devolved to school level. Head teachers may be appointed as premises managers for their schools and could be required, for example, to arrange for the testing of safety equipment such as the fire alarm system, typically this takes place annually. Tasks may also be delegated from the head teacher to the leadership team, to subject leaders, other school staff and to commissioned third party providers such as coaches or swim schools. Such tasks may include the routine inspection and maintenance of PESSPA equipment which may take place annually, termly or even daily, depending on the nature and use to which the equipment is put. It is important to remember that although tasks are delegated, the responsibility is non-delegable.

1.1.7   In carrying out any health and safety task devolved to them, it is essential that employees follow the appropriate policy or procedure adopted by the employer. A failure to do so may result in them being held personally liable for any injury that occurs as a result of that failure. Although it is worth noting it is likely that the employer would be held vicariously liable for an injury which results from a breach of policy, even where the act of the employee is sufficient to be deemed criminal.

1.1.8   Effective health and safety practices are integral to good management, as such the Leadership team within a school must ensure that school staff are aware of the employer's current policy and are taking appropriate steps to put that policy into practice. All are expected to know and apply the school policy, report any concerns to the leadership team via the adopted procedures, and take reasonable steps to control any existing risks of which they become aware. Any changes to the employer's PESSPA policy or procedure should be presented to governors for adoption and communicated to staff, students and parents.

1.1.9   The employer will have responsibility for all activities over which they have control. This includes all day-to-day health and safety issues within the curriculum as well as any school organised extra-curricular activities and extended activities which take place at weekends or during the holidays.

1.1.10   Where a school hire their premises to user groups, those groups become responsible for the safety of participants, except where any injury results from negligence on the part of the employer, for example a failure to maintain the building to an appropriate standard. The hirer, whether that is the employer or the Governing Board, will also be liable if the hiring agreement states that the premises are safe for a specific purpose that turns out not to be the case.

1.1.11   Where premises are known to have a particular defect or to be unsafe for a particular activity, it is essential that those planning to use the premises are advised of the defect or unsafe aspect. Before proceeding with the planned activity a risk assessment would need to be undertaken by the group leader before advising all participants of the group of the safety issue and the action to be taken to avoid accidents and injury.

1.1.12   Health and safety law requires employers to appoint someone competent to help them meet their health and safety duties. A competent person is someone with the necessary skills, knowledge and experience to give sensible advice about managing the health and safety risks at the school.

1.1.13   This duty may be devolved to school level along with other health and safety responsibilities. Where the responsibility is devolved, the Leadership team can choose to contract with their Local Authority via a service level agreement where this is available or with an external company.

1.1.14   It is however important to note that the advice provided should not take precedence over the employer's adopted policy or procedures. Further, the existence of such an agreement does not absolve the employer, the Leadership team, individual employees or visiting staff of their responsibilities under the law. It is therefore essential that employers, employees and visiting staff are able to identify their respective roles.

1.1.15   In a PESSPA context this will be understanding what areas are covered by the school Health and Safety Policy under identified responsibilities and whole school health and safety arrangements and what areas are needed in greater detail in the PE or Physical Activity Policy. This could include, for example, subject specific support on undertaking a risk assessment, training employees (and where necessary visiting coaches) and using equipment.

1.1.16   Health and safety legislation does require schools to manage the risk from PESSPA activities sensibly, but this does not have to be complex. In most cases this will involve making sure that equipment is suitable for the students involved, that grounds are properly maintained and effective supervision for students is in place. Managing the risks sensibly means that the schools and relevant teaching staff keep up to date with guidance and standards applicable to the activities they are leading and ensuring skills are developed progressively and safely.

1.1.17   Where schools use a range of adults to provide PESSPA activities, whether school staff, visiting coaches or volunteers, they should ensure that all those individuals are aware of the school health and safety policies, procedures and practice and are implementing those within provision to the same standard.

Section 2: The Role of the Employer

1.2.1   The employer bears the central responsibility for health and safety in law. In most sectors the identity of the employer is usually a very straight forward matter however the same cannot be said of the education sector where the identity of the employer varies in accordance with the category of school.

1.2.2   The following table identifies the employer in each category of school.

1.2.3   **Table 1: The employer in each category of school**

In England and Wales	
The local authority (LA) is the employer in:	• community schools • community special schools • voluntary controlled schools • maintained nursery schools • student referral units.
The governing body or the board of trustees is the employer in:	• foundation schools • foundation special schools • voluntary aided schools • academies • free schools • University Technical College (UTC).
The proprietor is the employer in:	• independent schools.
In Scotland	
The LA is the employer in:	• the majority of schools that are state owned.
The governing body, or equivalent, is the employer in:	• the few grant-aided schools that are independent of LAs, but that are supported financially by the Scottish Government.
The proprietor, Board of Trustees or equivalent is the employer in:	• independent schools.
In Northern Ireland	
The Education Authority* is the employer in: *Until recently there were five Education and Library Boards. These have now been amalgamated into the one body.	• controlled schools (nursery, primary, special, post-primary and grammar schools).
The Council for Catholic Maintained Schools (CCMS) is the employer in:	• Catholic maintained schools (nursery, primary, special and post-primary).
The Board of Governors is the employer in**: ** Arrangements for employment can vary. In some cases in these schools, the Education Authority is the employer for ancillary staff, while the governing body is the employer for teaching staff.	• voluntary schools (grammar) • integrated schools (primary and post-primary).

1.2.4 The statutory responsibilities of employers for health and safety under the law are primarily set out under the Health and Safety at Work etc Act 1974 (HaSaWA). However, employers should be aware of regulations and guidance issued under the Act including what is referred to as the "six pack" regulations. This is a group of regulations including the Management of Health and Safety at Work Regulations 1999, which expand upon the employer's duties under the 1974 Act.

1.2.5 The main duties of the employer to the employee are set out under section 2 of the 1974 Act. This indicates that the employer must ensure as far as is reasonably practicable the health, safety and welfare of all employees while at work.

1.2.6 The employer must also ensure they have a written Health and Safety policy which they must ensure is brought to the attention of their employees. Procedures must be initiated to ensure that there is a satisfactory implementation of the policy by all such staff. Further, the policy must be reviewed regularly. Within schools the review may be done on an annual basis in-line with other policies, although there is no requirement that it is carried out this frequently. A review of policy and procedures may also take place following a major incident.

1.2.7 Although visiting coaches may not be bound by the employers policy through an employee relationship, employers should ensure that the expectations are brought to the attention of visiting coaches and consideration should be given to including observance of its principles via the contract of service.

1.2.8 Employers also have a legal duty under Section 3 of the 1974 Act to ensure that, so far as is reasonably practicable, others not in their employment are not exposed to risks to their health and safety. In schools this is commonly interpreted as including students, but it may also include visiting coaches. Further, self employed visiting coaches will be under this same duty when working with students. This duty may include providing appropriate instruction in relation to safe practice and developing policies in relation to behaviour for example. It is however important that the leadership team is able to demonstrate not only the development of policy and procedure but the extent to which these are communicated, applied and monitored.

1.2.9 It is a criminal offence for the employer to fail to discharge the statutory duties under health and safety law. The Health and Safety Executive (HSE) have the power to investigate dangerous practice and to prosecute where appropriate. Although many cases result in a fine for the employer, individuals can in certain situations, be subject to a custodial sentence.

Section 3: The Role of the Employee

1.3.1   Although the employer holds the main responsibility for health and safety, employees also have duties under the 1974 Act and the regulations and guidance issued under it. Section 7 places a duty on employees to take reasonable care for their own health and safety and that of any other person that may be affected by their acts or omissions while at work. Further, employees are required to cooperate with their employer and any arrangements that are in place to enable the employer to meet their own statutory duties. In essence this means that the employee is required to follow policy, procedure or guidance issued by the employer in relation to health and safety.

1.3.2   In summary:

1.3.3   In the majority of cases the employer guidance will be drawn from and make reference to national guidance, whether general or activity specific. However, there may be cases where local circumstances mean that the employer's guidance differs from that issued nationally.

1.3.4   Where employers produce policy, directives or guidance, these must be followed and applied by employees within the organisation, in the same way that laws and statutes must be applied. Further it must take precedence over national guidance including that issued by the Association for Physical Education.

1.3.5   A failure to follow the employer's policy, directives or guidance may constitute a criminal offence under the 1974 Act and result in a formal HSE investigation and subsequent prosecution against those involved. Where a prosecution is successful a fine or custodial sentence may be imposed. Further, employees may also be subject to disciplinary procedures and visiting staff have contracts terminated.

1.3.6   As outlined above, the main duties rest with the employer, not leadership teams or school staff. Staff will only become personally liable if they ignore clear, direct, instructions about serious risks and depart from regular and approved practice. Where sensible and proportionate steps have been taken by a school and its staff, it is highly unlikely that there would be a breach of health and safety law involved.

1.3.7   Visiting coaches are not generally employees of the schools they work with. More commonly they are employed by a local sports club or foundation but may also be self-employed. It is essential that employers and employees understand their statutory duties will still apply regardless of the involvement of the external coach. This means that if the coach is using school based equipment it will still require regular checks and maintenance from school staff.

1.3.8   While there is no employment relationship to force visiting coaches to comply with school policy, schools would be strongly advised to set out clearly as part of a contract of services, the expectations on the visiting coach to work to the school policies along with a suitably worded indemnity and insurance requirement.

Section 4: Negligence

1.4.1   In addition to statutory requirements set out in the previous section, the approach to health and safety, in particular the professional standards expected and what is considered safe practice, is informed by the law of negligence. Negligence is a civil wrong where the actions of an individual fall below the expected standard and as a result foreseeable harm is caused. Where a claim for negligence is successful, compensation may be payable.

1.4.2   Although negligence claims are increasing in society in general, they remain relatively rare in the area of PESSPA when compared against the sheer numbers of students participating in activities. Where claims are made, they will generally be made against the employer as the concept of vicarious liability dictates that the employer will be responsible for the acts or omissions of their employees made in the course of their employment. Vicarious liability may also apply in the context of non-employees such as visiting coaches where specific conditions are met.

1.4.3   Most claims are made by student's parents on their behalf due to the fact they are unable to make a claim in their own right as a child. Once a student reaches the age of 18 years, they have a right to make a claim in relation to any injury they sustained as a child. Although this right to claim subsists until the student reaches the age of 21, the Courts have on occasions extended the deadline. The importance of good record keeping can therefore not be under estimated.

1.4.4   Injuries will occur in PESSPA simply because of its active nature although many of these may be 'no-fault' accidents. In order to succeed in a claim for negligence however, it is necessary to establish the existence of the following factors:
- a duty of care
- the actions of those owing the duty fell below the expected standard (breach of duty)
- that damage (harm or injury) has been caused
- that the damage caused was reasonably foreseeable.

1.4.5   The term "duty of care" describes the legal obligation to safeguard others from harm. It can apply to organisations and individuals; both in their personal and professional lives. A duty of care will exist where organisations or individuals have care of or responsibilities towards others, provide others with services or affect others by their activities.

1.4.6   In a school for example, a duty of care will exist between the employer and the staff, between staff and between staff and students. A duty of care will also exist between a Governing Body and service users, where the Governing Body provides community services or facilities from the school premises.

1.4.7   Where a school provides activities after school, at weekends or in the holidays, they will retain a duty of care to the students. Where open activities are advertised by the school to a broader range of participants a duty of care will be owed to all, whether or not they are students of the school.

1.4.8   Where third party organisations hire the school for the provision of activities such as Cubs, Rainbows or external sports teams the duty of care will rest with the third party organisation regardless of whether or not the participants are also students at the school.

1.4.9   The key factor in deciding where the duty of care rests is whether the event was organised and controlled by the school. If staff or leadership teams are in any doubt about the particular arrangements in their schools they are strongly advised to seek advice from a legal advisor.

1.4.10   Where a school uses a third party provider for the provision of curricular or extra-curricular PESSPA such as swimming for PE, the school will retain the duty of care for the students who participate. It is therefore essential that all school staff involved in the management of third party providers satisfy themselves that they are following safe practice.

1.4.11   In deciding whether a duty has been breached the Court will consider whether the actions of those owing the duty fell below the standard which would be expected of a reasonably competent person performing that task. Essentially this means whether others in the same profession, working at the same level, would have acted in the same way; ie are the actions regular and approved practice in the profession? Action is regular and approved if it is common and accepted across a wide geographical area as being safe. The standard applied will take into account factors such as whether the action was taken in an emergency, the level of risk created, the seriousness of potential injuries that may be caused and the costs of taking preventative measures.

KEY LEARNING: Any visiting coaches involved in PESSPA sessions, whether working alongside or at a distance (remotely) from the class teacher, are expected to show the same standard of care. In a school-organised activity, which is delivered by an external agency, on or off site, the school's duty of care to students continues whether or not the teacher is involved in the delivery of the session.

1.4.12   Where a duty is owed by a professional in a situation where they would be expected to exercise specialist expertise, for example between a Doctor and a patient, that duty, will be subject to a higher standard than that of a reasonably competent person, as the professional is expected to have a greater insight and awareness of the consequences of their actions. This is commonly referred to as a higher duty of care.

1.4.13   Teachers may be deemed to have specialist knowledge where they specialise in a particular PESSPA activity, lead higher-risk PESSPA activities (such as trampolining or outdoor adventurous activities) or have qualifications to teach in a specialist environment or with specific student groups such as those with additional needs. It is therefore important for those working within a specialism to keep up to date with current knowledge through training.

1.4.14   Even where a breach of duty is found to have occurred negligence will only be found if the breach led to an individual suffering harm which was reasonably foreseeable or likely. Harm may be physical or mental but must be foreseeable. The more remote the likelihood of the particular harm the more unforeseeable it will be.

1.4.15   Defending claims of negligence relies on good record keeping which demonstrates both compliance with the requirements of health and safety law and a commitment to appropriate professional standards.

Ongoing preparation for defending any allegations of negligence might include maintaining a 'portfolio' of support information. This could comprise documents including:

- policy and guidelines
- schemes of work and lesson plans
- instructions provided to students
- registers of attendance (detailed enough to illustrate what content would have been missed through non-attendance)
- assessment records
- medical information
- risk assessments
- equipment maintenance reports
- minutes of meetings highlighting discussion of safe practice
- professional learning records
- emergency action procedures
- special educational needs and disabilities (SEND) register
- extra-curricular club registers
- accident management and reporting systems and analysis
- health and safety audits
- school procedures – fire safety/first aid/evacuation/critical incidents.

KEY LEARNING: Local Authorities, Governing Bodies or Trusts remain liable for any negligent act relating to their services and programmes, including where these are contracted out to a third party to use technical expertise not necessarily available within the direct workforce of the school staff.
Where the external agency is found to be negligent, it is the school authority that would be in breach of its duty of care to the students.

The school must continuously **monitor and manage** that whoever carries out duties on its behalf does so without fault, and not simply rely on a pre-check of competence.

Section 5: Competence

Competence and the PESSPA Workforce

1.5.1   Anyone teaching a PESSPA session needs to be competent to do so safely.

1.5.2   A head teacher, as the manager technically deploying staff, must ensure that those delivering PESSPA sessions are competent, and carries responsibility on behalf of the employer should any staff be placed in a situation where they do not have the skills to fulfil the requirements of the deployment safely.

1.5.3   Staff, whether a qualified teacher, other member of school staff, visiting coach or volunteer, would be judged by the same standard as more experienced colleagues to avoid inexperience being frequently used as a defence against an allegation of negligence. Head teachers (HTs), on behalf of the employer, should be aware of this when deploying a range of staff.

1.5.4   The same level of competence **applies at all times** whether in lesson time or out, on or off site, in term time or holidays where the activity is part of a school organised programme.

1.5.5   If specialist staff are used to lead activities (such as those at residential activity centres or for higher risk activities in school), the activity provider or instructor are responsible for the technical aspects of the experience, however school staff would maintain overall **duty of care** for the students, and clarity of roles and responsibilities in such situations is essential. This is outlined in the first part of this section.

1.5.6   Part of this duty requires the employer to ensure that students are taught by competent staff to fulfil the demands of the tasks to which they are deployed. If any staff are not competent to undertake the responsibility placed on them by the employer, or by the employer's representative (eg a head teacher), the employer may be prosecuted. The employer will almost always be vicariously liable for the negligence of the staff. A possible exception is where that negligence is capable of constituting a criminal offence.

1.5.7   Where staff feel they do not have an appropriate level of confidence, knowledge or expertise, they should discuss the issue with their line manager in order to determine what should be done to maintain safe situations in lessons.

1.5.8   Competence to **work alone** in teaching PESSPA includes the ability to progressively develop techniques and skills; know whether a situation is safe and if not make it safe; apply the rules of a sport; control and organise the class; and use knowledge of the students to provide appropriate challenge and support.

1.5.9   Poor behaviour management, or inadequate group-management skills by staff may adversely affect the standard of safety in any PESSPA situation.

The Health and Safety Executive (HSE) highlights four means of demonstrating competence:

- hold a relevant qualification
- hold an equivalent qualification
- have received appropriate in-house training
- be competent through experience.

These are not totally discrete. Qualifications, experience and training overlap to produce expertise in a particular field or aspect of PESSPA.

A checklist to assist with assessing competence to teach PESSPA

The Teacher	Yes/Evidence/Date	No/Evidence/Date
Understands the importance of applying forethought in their planning		
Can teach the relevant techniques, tactics or compositional skills safely, accurately and at a level that is appropriate to the ability, confidence and previous experience of the students involved		
Provides appropriate progressive practices to enable and support student improvement		
Effectively applies the safety issues relevant to the specific activity		
Has a secure knowledge of, and can appropriately apply, the rules of the activity if a sport		
Knows or is able to quickly judge the abilities, confidence and particular needs of the students		
Has well-developed observational and analytical skills to ensure that what is going on is safe, and amend or stop anything that is deemed unsafe		
Has effective class control		

1.5.10   **Forethought** or forward planning involves reasonable anticipation of what may happen, and requires those teaching lessons to think about where harm may be likely by considering:

- what they want students to learn
- how they will support students to achieve desired outcomes
- how to organise the lesson prior to physical engagement in the activity.

1.5.11 **Knowledge of the students**. It is important that all staff have relevant knowledge of the students they teach. Where the member of staff is not the usual adult responsible for the students (eg they are a visiting coach or replacement competent person), it is essential that they are provided with key information about the students with whom they will be working. This should include:

- **medical information (on a need-to-know basis)**
- **behavioural information**
- **previous experience/prior learning**
- **group confidence and competence**
- **any special educational needs and disabilities (SEND)**
- individual needs or specific personal circumstances that might affect a student's performance, health or emotional well-being, such as a recent bereavement.

This information helps staff to pitch the challenge of the activity more accurately for all students, and to ensure that expectations are appropriate and within their ability.

1.5.12 Students with additional needs such as **visual, hearing, motor or cognitive impairment** should be considered and catered for appropriately to enable them to participate safely. All staff, regular or visiting, need to be fully aware of the implications of the ability and needs of any student in order to provide a worthwhile and safe learning opportunity.

1.5.13 **Observation and analysis skills**. Staff delivering PESSPA need to check constantly whether the activity taking place is safe, and **if not, to intervene or stop it** in order to make it safe. This requires them to have expertise to make adjustments (eg to technique, skill, task, space, intensity, equipment) in order to make it safe. For example, staff should be confident to identify the onset of fatigue, which might impact on students' concentration levels. This is particularly important in activities such as swimming, gymnastics, trampolining and sustained running.

1.5.14 **Higher-risk** activities include adventurous activities, aquatic activities, athletics throwing events, combat sports, contact sports, aspects of gymnastics, trampolining and working with free weights in a fitness room. Those leading sessions in schools in these contexts should hold recognised and current qualifications (eg governing body of sport qualifications). In the absence of such qualifications, it is strongly advised that significant, recent and relevant experience or training is required to demonstrate an individual's competence to teach these activities safely.

1.5.15 **PESSPA awards, qualifications for specific activities**

The standards of expertise, discipline, relationships and risk management expected of all who work with students need to be consistent with providing a safe working environment. This level of competence applies to all who contribute to PESSPA activities as part of a school-organised programme, and at all times when they are delivering the activities (eg during activities which take place inside and outside of lessons; on or off the school site; in term time or holidays).

Some governing bodies of sport and other awarding organisations require qualifications to be revalidated periodically. This is not simply to endorse previous requirements, but to inform learners of changes and developments that may have occurred in the interim period. Guidance should be obtained from the relevant governing body of sport, awarding organisation or LA, the Education Authority in Northern Ireland or an expert consultant.

1.5.16 **Ongoing professional learning**

Primary teachers with little or no ITE in physical education may lack confidence. Where this is the case, they should undertake appropriate professional learning before being allowed to teach a full range of activities. HTs must be satisfied that all those who are required to teach PESSPA are able to do so in a safe manner, with a sound understanding of the needs and stages of development of all the students in their charge.

1.5.17 **Use of support staff in PESSPA**

For a number of reasons, students may be taught in schools by adults who are not qualified teachers. Generally, in maintained schools, these are referred to as **'support staff'** – a term used for all adults, other than trainee teachers, without QTS who contribute to the teaching of students in schools. Support staff include regular staff on the school roll such as classroom assistants, teaching assistants, cover supervisors, learning mentors and volunteer parents, as well as visiting staff, whether occasional or regular contributors, such as coaches, and physical education apprentices.

1.5.18   **Cover supervisors** are suitably trained school support staff who **supervise** students carrying out pre-prepared tasks when teaching staff are on short term absence. The cover supervisor's main function is to manage a learning environment, ensuring that students remain engaged. Careful thought should be given before allowing cover supervisors to supervise practical lessons for absent physical education staff unless they can demonstrate the necessary competence to deliver the activity and this has been evidenced through qualifications, recent relevant knowledge and experience. Where the school leadership are not satisfied that the requirements around competency have been satisfied, the cover supervisor should only be permitted to cover a classroom based lesson.

1.5.19   **Assessing the suitability of visiting coaches in PESSPA**

The school procedures for engaging visiting coaches should address three essential questions:

- Is **it legal** to engage this person? This will be determined by the requirements of a broad range of legislation that sets out whether particular individuals are prohibited from working with children and young people. The relevant **vetting** and background checks need to be completed carefully. (Please refer to **Chapter 2, Section 2: Safeguarding.**)
- Is **it safe** to employ this person? **Safe recruitment** procedures include checking and confirmation of disclosure certification, qualifications and authenticity of identity, and a relevant governing body of sport coach licence (where relevant).
- Is **it effective** to engage this person? This will be determined by the expertise the person brings to the school, how their expertise may **add** to the professional learning of the school staff, how the quality of student learning experiences will be improved, and whether the PESSPA programme will be beneficially broadened.

1.5.20   In undertaking a **competence assessment of visiting coaches**, it is good practice for class teachers to **directly supervise them during the initial phase of teaching**. Direct supervision involves the coach working alongside a class teacher in order that the teacher can intervene at any time, as necessary. At a later stage, **distant supervision** might be appropriate, according to their competence and the level of responsibility assigned. This would allow the coach to work at some distance from a class teacher, possibly out of sight, in a different facility or even off site. However, frequent monitoring by the class teacher would be part of good management. (Where physical education and sport premium funding for primary schools is being used to employ external staff in curriculum time, the visiting coach should always teach alongside the class teacher to satisfy the criteria of this funding.)

The level of supervision required for such staff should be determined by a thorough competency and risk assessment. They can be judged on the **national standards** for higher level teaching assistants (HLTAs) or, alternatively, on competences specific to PESSPA to determine the eventual level of direct or remote supervision required.

Table 2 provides guidance for headteachers and other managers to use to recruit, induct, and assess the competence of external support staff.

Table 2: Best practice guidance on the effective use of individual and agency coaches in physical education, school sport and physical activity (PESSPA)

1 Safe Recruitment	Date/Signature/ Comments
a **Arrange a face-to-face interview** with each coach to confirm that they are at least 18 (ie an adult), confirm their identity using original documents (passport, driving licence, recent service provider bill confirming current home address) and discuss any relevant issues arising from their application.	
b **Make the decision about whether the coach's role is eligible for a Disclosure and Barring Service (DBS) check.** If the coach will be engaged in regulated activity, request access to an enhanced DBS disclosure certificate including information from the barred list. If the coach will not be in regulated activity, although there is no right to access information from the barred list, an enhanced disclosure certificate should nevertheless be required (regardless of whether the coach will be supervised by school staff or not). If disclosure is required, the employer should see the original disclosure certificate and record the number. (Do not photocopy it without the applicant's consent.) Decide if portability applies and is acceptable.	
c **Check qualifications** – see the originals. Accept a Level 2 award as the normal baseline qualification for each PESSPA activity the coach is expected to teach, diverting from this standard only if the coach is observed prior to acceptance and demonstrates good coaching qualities and is working towards a Level 2 qualification, where appropriate.	
d **Check the coach's training in, and experience of, working with children and young people** (eg attendance at safeguarding, health and safety or concussion awareness and management workshops).	
e **Explore the coach's motivations for working with children, and attitudes towards children and young people**.	
f **Check original reference(s)** – investigate any gaps in coaching employment and any conditional comments in the reference(s).	
g **Check, if relevant, with the appropriate governing body of sport that the coach is currently licensed to coach**. (A qualification cannot be rescinded, but a governing body of sport licence to coach can be if any poor practice or abuse issues have arisen.)	
h **Ensure correct employment status and employment rights are made known to the coach.** Provide a written summary and include in contract as appropriate.	
i **Ensure the coach is fully aware of what, if any, insurance provision is made by the school** and what aspects he/she needs to provide for him/herself (according to employment status) re: 　i　employers' liability (compulsory by law) – legal liability for injuries to employees (permanent/temporary/contracted for services) arising in the course of employment 　ii　public liability (essential but not compulsory through law) – to meet the responsibility for "third-party" claims against the activities of the individual/group and legal occupation of premises 　iii　professional liability (desirable) – legal cover against claims for breaches of professional duty by employees acting in the scope of their employment (eg giving poor professional advice) 　iv　hirers' liability (desirable) – covers individuals or agencies that hire premises against any liability for injury to others or damage to the property while using it 　v　libel and slander insurance (optional) – cover against claims for defamation (eg libellous material in publications) 　vi　personal injury, accidental bodily injury or deliberate assault (desirable) – arranged by individual or employer 　vii　miscellaneous – a variety of types of insurance such as travel (compulsory or required for best practice) or motor insurance (compulsory – minimum of "third party") – check personal exclusions and excesses individual carries. (For more information regarding insurance, see **Chapter 2, Section 2**.)	

21

j	**Set out a clearly defined role, identifying any limits of responsibility, lines of supervision, management and communication, and specialist expertise needed** (eg children with individual special needs), and ensure that the coach is appropriately qualified/experienced to undertake the role.	
k	**Determine an agreed period of probation**, and monitor the coach's performance and attitude closely during this period.	
l	**Check that all of the above have been addressed by the agency or school before a self-employed or agency-appointed coach begins work.**	
m	**Agree an appropriate induction package that must be fulfilled**. This should include information about how safeguarding or other concerns should be reported (within the school and, where relevant, to the appropriate sport's governing body).	
	2 Induction	
a	The HT or their representative presents the coach with a summary of relevant school policy and procedures, including risk assessments, emergency evacuation, referral and incentives, behaviour management, first aid, managing suspected concussion, safeguarding procedures and information about the ethos of the school – how staff work with children and young people (such as looking for success in young people, rewarding achievement).	
b	Identify a member of staff to manage induction into school procedures who will:	
	i arrange a meeting with the SEND designated person and class teacher(s) as appropriate to pass on specific information about students	
	ii monitor and assess the competence of the coach through observations and discussions with students and other staff	
	iii determine the coach's role in contributing to the overall assessment of students.	
	3 Qualifications, Experience and Qualities Necessary for a Coach to Work Alone	
a	Expect a Level 2 award as the normal baseline qualification for each activity the coach will be teaching. Divert from this standard only if the coach is observed prior to acceptance, demonstrates good coaching qualities and is working towards a Level 2 qualification, where appropriate, or where a coach holds a recognised multi-games qualification and will be teaching generic skills to a basic level. NB: In addition to activity-specific qualifications, afPE's good practice expectation is that coaches supporting curriculum-time PESSPA should hold or be working towards a 1st4sport/afPE Level 2 or 3 qualification in supporting physical education and school sport.	
b	Check previous experience in working with small/large groups.	
c	Check behaviour management skills.	
d	Check:	
	i the quality of their relationships – the way the coach cares for and respects students, acts as an appropriate role model and promotes the ethos of school	
	ii how they develop knowledge of the students – their levels of confidence, ability, individual needs, medical needs and behaviour	
	iii their student management skills – how they match students' confidence, strength and ability in pair and group tasks, maximise participation, have strategies for effective student control and motivation, apply the school's standard procedures and routines (eg safeguarding, emergency action, managing suspected concussion, jewellery, handling and carrying of equipment)	
	iv their knowledge of the PESSPA activities – appropriate level of expertise to enable learning to take place in the activities being delivered, use of suitable space for the group, differentiated equipment, differentiated practice, evident progression and application of rules	
	v their observation and analytical skills – providing a safe working and learning environment, ability to identify faults and establish strategies for improvement	
	vi they have a clear understanding of risk-management principles and can apply them appropriately.	

	4 Day-to-day Management of the Coach	
a	Check that the coach has received a summary of school and subject procedures, and understands what is required (including clear guidelines in relation to handover of responsibility at the start and end of lessons/sessions).	
b	Ensure the coach receives relevant information on students/groups (eg medical conditions that may impact on participation, illness, family bereavement, behaviour issues, students recovering from injury, including concussion).	
c	Monitor promptness.	
d	Establish regular review and evaluation of the coach's work.	
e	Determine who assesses students' work.	
f	Ensure the coach is supported and valued, and accepted as a member of staff.	
g	Monitor the dialogue and relationship between class teacher and coach.	
	5 Monitoring Quality and Effectiveness	
a	Ensure direct monitoring of the coach for an agreed period – use the criteria set out in 3 on the previous page.	
b	Set up continual indirect monitoring to ensure students make progress and enjoy lessons.	
c	Ensure that students are engaged in consistent high quality learning, using challenging and stimulating activities that support them to achieve their potential, not just activities that keep them "busy, happy and good", and that sessions have an educational focus and are not used simply for "talent spotting".	
	6 Identification and Provision of Continuing Professional Learning	
a	Evaluate the coach's abilities against appropriate standards.	
b	Arrange attendance on afPE/UK Coaching's "Adults Supporting Learning" (ASL) induction course.	
c	Agree essential qualifications and desirable qualifications – plan and provide for a personal development programme beyond governing body of sport coaching qualifications to enable the coach to proceed from emerging to established, and advanced ratings.	
	7 Dealing with Inadequate Performance by the Coach	
a	Proactively monitor the coach's work, as set out in 5 above.	
b	Intervene immediately if a coach's performance is inadequate and poses a health and safety risk to the students or has the potential to impact on their welfare. Consider arrangements to inform or consult with the relevant governing body of sport when significant concerns arise.	
c	Review the situation with the coach after any lesson in which their performance is technically inadequate.	
d	Agree and provide supportive continuing professional learning to improve inadequate aspects of performance.	
e	Monitor for improvement.	
f	Terminate a short-term contract if little or no improvement occurs, or initiate competency procedures if a longer-term contract exists.	
g	Terminate a longer-term contract where competence does not improve.	

Adapted from Whitlam, P. (2016) 'Best practice guidance on the effective use of individual and agency coaches in physical education and sport'.

Section 6: Policy Writing for PESSPA

Why PESSPA Policy and Procedures are Needed

1.6.1   Clear policy is useful within a school to enforce standards and expectations. For example, policy regarding acceptable clothing, footwear, jewellery and personal protective equipment (PPE) can be set out in school communications such as a prospectus, newsletter, school website or in letters to parents.

1.6.2   When parents choose to send their children to the school, it is useful for them to know exactly what is required in physical education, school sport and physical activity (PESSPA). Equally, when students arrive for PESSPA without the correct kit or equipment, the policy can be used to remind them and their parents about the requirements they "signed up to". Students might also become involved in influencing policy that directly affects them as part of learning about safety.

1.6.3   Policy and established procedures provide order, and a secure learning and work environment for students and staff. Policy should be relevant to a school's particular circumstances and help to ensure that students feel safe, are safe, and learn how to be safe during any PESSPA session.

1.6.4   Accidents occasionally happen in PESSPA. Many cannot be anticipated and arise from **unforeseen** circumstances. Other accidents could have been **foreseen**, and as such, lessons can be learnt from them, which can in turn inform future policy.

1.6.5   When an accident, incident or "near miss" occurs, **analysis** should consider not only the immediate causes but also the origins of the causes and whether or not **management systems (policy and procedures)** were sufficient.

1.6.6   In the event of an accident or incident at a school, policy and procedures are **likely to be requested** as part of the portfolio of evidence required for any investigation.

1.6.7   Analysis can lead to improvements in safety standards through upgrading **documented policy and procedures**, improving communication, conducting thorough risk assessments and by ensuring that all staff involved in teaching the PESSPA programme consistently apply the required safety standards. In essence, subject leaders should constantly ask, in relation to safety standards in PESSPA.

Characteristics of PESSPA Policy and Procedures

1.6.8   **Case law** indicates that the policy and procedures should be:

- in written form
- specific to the school
- reasonably comprehensive
- regularly reviewed (typically annually)
- regularly communicated
- consistently applied by **all staff** contributing to the PESSPA programme.

Table 3: An exemplar PESSPA policy

Please note this table is designed to be adapted to meet individual school needs. The generic template is loaded with content for the practitioner to shape to best fit your school and curriculum offer. Safe practice is about applying the principles to your specific needs. This template is best used as a reflective tool and not just adopted in its entirety. For example, there may be individual variations on where PESSPA equipment can be stored in each setting, ie playground, outside store or designated area. Schools will need to make individual decisions on where this should be based on safe practice principles concerning safe storage.

PLEASE NOTE: This example physical education, school sport and physical activity (PESSPA) policy provides a typical range of generic headings and statements that schools may find useful when writing their own PESSPA policy. It should be adapted to meet the specific requirements of individual schools. Simply lifting the policy and adopting as it stands is not the most effective use of the template.

Due to the rise in the number of engagement programmes and initiatives to increase physical activity, many schools now produce a separate physical activity policy to outline relevant opportunities and reporting mechanisms.

Example Primary PESSPA Policy

Our intention at Anytown primary school is to ensure that PESSPA is experienced regularly, in a safe and supportive environment, as it is a unique and vital contributor to a student's physical development and well-being. PESSPA is the only subject whose primary focus is on the body; it uniquely addresses the physical development aim of the curriculum and makes a significant contribution to the spiritual, moral, social and cultural development of young people. Through Anytown's high quality physical education programme, our students will become physically literate and develop the knowledge, skills and motivation necessary to equip them for a healthy, active lifestyle and lifelong participation in physical activity and sport.

Aims:

The school's aims for PESSPA are for our students to:

- participate and develop physical competency in a wide range of physical activities that provide appropriate challenge with acceptable risk
- build confidence and resilience to try hard and make progress across all activities
- enjoy learning in and through the subject across the domains of physical skills, creative and thinking skills, and social, personal and leadership skills, and be able to apply those skills across their wider learning and beyond school
- be highly motivated and understand how to plan, organise and lead their own healthy, active lifestyles as well as influence those around them
- develop their physical well-being through increased stamina, strength and suppleness, and recognise the positive impact on their emotional well-being and health from engaging in physical activity on a regular basis
- be involved in learning about risk management, and their responsibility in this, in order for them to participate independently in physical activity in later life.

Implementation – Curriculum:

All students are entitled to a progressive and comprehensive physical education programme that embraces current Statutory Orders of the national curriculum (country-specific) and takes into account individual interests and needs.

Our curriculum will provide activities to promote a broad base of movement knowledge and skills, placing students in cooperative, collaborative and competitive situations that aim to cater for the preferences, strengths and needs of every student. We will develop their creative and expressive abilities, and provide situations where students work independently, in pairs and in groups. They will be encouraged to appreciate the importance of having a healthy body and begin to understand the factors that affect health and well-being. Our curriculum embraces the Statutory Orders of the National Curriculum 2014 and Early Years Foundation Stage (EYFS) Guidance (England). It is inclusive, and every student has equal access irrespective of their age, gender and cultural or ethnic background.

While retaining its unique contribution to a student's movement education, PESSPA has considerable potential to contribute to much wider areas of learning. It is considered important for PESSPA to be integrated into the whole school's planning for the development of students' literacy, numeracy, science, geography, Personal, Social and Health Education (PSHE) and computing skills.

In the **EYFS**, teachers should:

- plan activities that offer appropriate physical challenges, and provide sufficient space, indoors and outdoors, to set up relevant activities
- give sufficient time for students to use a range of equipment and, whenever possible, teach half the class in each session
- provide resources that can be used in a variety of ways or to support specific skills
- introduce the language of movement to students, alongside their actions
- provide time and opportunities for students with physical disabilities or motor impairments to develop their physical skills, working as necessary with physiotherapists and occupational therapists
- use additional adult help, if necessary, to support individuals and to encourage increased independence in physical activities.

During **Key Stage 1 (England)**, students should be taught knowledge skills and understanding through dance, gymnastics and games activities.

Key Stage 2 (England) students should have access to all components of the National Curriculum Programme of Study (athletics, dance, games, gymnastics, outdoor and adventurous activities and swimming).

The school provides all students with their entitlement of at least two hours of high quality physical education a week. This is delivered through 2–3 lessons in a typical week.

Students have access to a broad and balanced curriculum programme of study. A copy of the long-term curriculum map from year 1 to year 6 is attached as Appendix [please insert your appendix number].

PESSPA is rarely cancelled. The school values regular and frequent lessons to develop children's skills and abilities. In the event of weather conditions making it unsuitable to complete the activity planned, alternative arrangements would be made. These include class-based activities around the planned activity (eg evaluating and improving work based on watching video clips from the previous week's learning) or rescheduling the activity for another day. If a suitable indoor space is available, the activity could be taught inside with modification or adaptation, still allowing the learning intentions to be achieved.

On no account is PESSPA used as a sanction.

Implementation – Out of School Hours Learning:

The aims of the out of school hours learning (OSHL) programme are to **extend** and **enrich** the work being done during curriculum PESSPA and to provide some students with opportunities to **enable** them to develop the skills they need to access curriculum PESSPA. The programme will reinforce the importance of keeping physically active in order to lead a healthy lifestyle.

At Anytown school, all OSHL opportunities are developed in consultation with students, and the programme will:

- provide a balance of competitive and non-competitive activities through intra- and inter-school events
- provide specific movement/general physical activity clubs, which develop health and fitness, such as Change4Life clubs
- ensure that every student is offered the opportunity to attend a minimum of one OSHL activity each week
- ensure that the school regularly participates in school sport partnership (SSP) and county-wide events that promote competitive opportunities and physical activity.

To ensure the quality and sustainability of the OSHL programme, the school will:

- employ a range of qualified and experienced auxiliary coaching staff and implement quality assurance through the subject leader
- ensure that the subject leader takes responsibility for forging strong local community club links (club coaches visit school/students attend club taster days/clubs advertise on noticeboard)
- inform students and parents of the range of OSHL opportunities.

A timetable of Anytown school's OSHL activities can be found in Appendix [please insert your appendix number].

Curriculum Planning – Planning and Preparing the Physical Education Programme:

All our PESSPA lessons will be planned and structured to contribute to safe learning situations. Good practice equals safe practice. In the planning stage, we think through the following process:

- "This is what I want students to learn. This is how I plan for learning to take place, and ask, 'Is the learning experience safe?'"
- Students' learning needs are assessed against the scheme of work we use. Safe practice is embedded in the learning process and implemented in every lesson.

At Anytown school, class teachers teach PESSPA not only to develop and maintain students' skills and understanding of the subject but also because the teachers know their students' personal, social and health needs, and make appropriate cross-curricular links wherever possible.

Our long-, medium- and short-term plans, plus other useful PESSPA resources, are stored on [insert relevant place for your school] drive, and these are regularly updated by the PESSPA subject leader. Teachers need to plan their own learning objectives and outcomes to suit the needs of the particular class, and these are made clear to students. It is important that explicit learning about safety is annotated on the plans where appropriate and teachers monitor students' understanding of safe-practice principles and ability to apply them effectively. Teachers should also conduct their own risk assessments, and plan differentiated learning tasks and assessment opportunities and ensure these are noted on their short-term plans.

Each lesson should include a warm-up and cool-down relevant to the main activity and learning environment/weather conditions. All students should be physically active for sustained periods of time in every lesson.

Progressively, they should learn about the components of fitness and how to perform warm-up and cool-down exercises, paying attention to the principles of safe exercise practice.

The use of visual aids and ICT is strongly encouraged to enhance learning.

Swimming takes place at Anytown pool for all Year [...] and [...] students, for [...] weeks of the year. Lessons are planned and delivered by the pool provider's swimming instructors, but class teachers are strongly encouraged to assist with and support the sessions. The instructors will provide assessments at the end of each term and deliver a session, in school, on water safety.

Time Allocation for PESSPA:

At Anytown school, PESSPA is delivered throughout the whole day, and a timetable showing when each class is either outside or indoors is displayed in the staff room. All classes have at least two hours of PESSPA each week. In KS1, this is divided into shorter lessons to strive towards every child having an active PESSPA lesson every day. In KS2, every child has three lessons of PESSPA each week, made up of two shorter lessons and one longer lesson. The longer lesson is planned to enable the development of more complex skills, knowledge and understanding, such as compositional work using gymnastics apparatus and applying strategies through playing games. All class teachers will seek opportunities to develop the learning through a cross-curricular approach.

Leadership and Management:

The subject leader is responsible to the head teacher and will ensure that the following tasks associated with the role are considered and carried out where appropriate:

- developing good classroom practice
- managing the budget and PESSPA and sport premium based on the needs identified through the monitoring and evaluation of the subject, staff audit and the whole-school development plan
- posting reports on the school website about the allocation of the PESSPA and sport premium and its impact
- auditing, ordering and reviewing the efficiency of equipment, learning resource and accommodation management to ensure students are well taught and protected
- attending courses to further their own professional development and providing information, support and appropriate continuing professional learning for colleagues
- monitoring classroom practice and planning, auditing needs for continuing professional learning to ensure high quality delivery and impact on the children is achieved
- making all resources available to all staff, including health and safety policy, schemes of work, assessment materials and resources to support learning
- carrying out risk assessments in line with employer procedures
- extending relationships and contacts beyond the school and in the local community
- keeping up to date with and implementing any national, employer and SSP developments as appropriate.

Teaching and Learning:

The organisation of PESSPA in the school promotes learning through physical activities and sport. Lessons are blocked in units of work that are age-appropriate and aim to promote physical skills and competency, a greater depth of understanding and application of these skills and the ability to perform reflectively.

The structure of the [.........] developmental scheme of work will promote teaching and learning as it provides both continuity and progression. This scheme of work specifies progression of fundamental movement skills and sport-specific skills, knowledge and understanding.

The planning and delivery of each unit of work in the scheme will be adapted by individual teachers to provide appropriate challenge for all students, to extend those who are more able and provide appropriate levels of support in order for all students to make progress.

Monitoring of Standards of Teaching and Learning:

Subject monitoring and evaluating will be carried out by the subject leader with support from the school leadership team where appropriate. The school will utilise the following strategies and measures in order to evaluate standards in PESSPA:

- observation of teaching and learning, including support staff and coaches, to assist in the identification of strengths and development needs
- assessment of student progress and achievement
- student interviews
- self-evaluation of the subject in relation to PESSPA and sport premium.

Additional PESSPA and sport premium funding is being accessed here to release the subject leader to ensure that this monitoring is carried out in accordance with best practice and this policy.

Staff Development:

Appropriate professional development for all staff will ensure secure PESSPA subject knowledge, consistency and awareness of health and safety procedures. This is exemplified in the new teachers' standards. Staff should be comfortable and competent in the area of activity being taught in PESSPA.

Opportunities for the development of all Anytown school staff will be provided in order to enhance the quality of PESSPA within the school. This can be seen in the school's PESSPA Premium Action Plan – Key Indicator 3 in Appendix [please insert your appendix number].

Assessment and Recording:

Students' work will be assessed throughout each unit of work using formative and summative assessment methods. Students' progress will be monitored by the individual class teacher who will use these methods to set realistic targets for individual students, based on their strengths and weaknesses. At the end of each unit, an indication of the progress that they have made will be recorded. This will allow an overview of all progress made over the academic year. The attainment target for PESSPA sets out the knowledge, skills and understanding that students of different abilities and maturities are expected to have by the end of each key stage.

Assessing Progress:

At Anytown school, the following summative assessments are carried out by the class teacher:
[Input your assessment process and year groups.]

At Anytown school, we also assess the children by:

- watching them work, talking to them about what they are doing and listening to them describe their work
- gathering feedback from students to inform teachers and students of what has been successful and allowing them to set their own future targets
- using ICT to develop portfolios of children's work in PESSPA to show their progression and quality of performance.

Recording and Reporting:

At Anytown school, we record the results of the [complete with your school assessment process]. This allows the school to track student progress against national expectations.

Significant achievements or weaknesses may be noted in lesson evaluations and used to:

- inform future planning by the current teacher or a new class teacher
- form part of the statutory annual reporting process, and in discussions with parents
- help children as a basis for future target setting
- provide information to ensure continuity of progression throughout transfer between classes and key stages.

Equal Opportunities, Gifted and Talented, and Inclusion:

Every student has equal access to national curriculum PESSPA. At Anytown school, learning experiences are differentiated to meet the specific needs of individuals and groups of students, including those who have diverse SEND, gifted and talented students and those who have English as an additional language. A "can-do contract" will be devised through discussion between teachers, support staff, parents and, where relevant, specialist medical staff.

Lesson planning, delivery and assessment aim to ensure that students are provided with appropriate and effective opportunities to actively participate and succeed in the whole range of learning opportunities offered within and outside the curriculum.

Any classroom support provided must extend into PESSPA lessons as appropriate. Teachers and adults other than teachers (AOTTs) working with children will be made aware of any students who have special educational needs or medical conditions. The special educational needs coordinator (SENCO) will liaise with staff to ensure all students' needs are met in relation to teaching and learning in PESSPA.

Differentiation:

PESSPA at Anytown school will comply with the three basic principles for inclusion in that it will:

- set suitable learning challenges
- respond to students' diverse learning needs
- strive to overcome potential barriers to learning and assessment for individuals and groups of students.

Actions necessary to respond to an individual's requirements for curriculum access will be taken in the form of greater differentiation of tasks and materials, consistent with school-based intervention aligned to current accepted practice.

Safety Issues – Safe Teaching, Teaching Safety:

Anytown school follows the PESSPA guidance provided by the Association for Physical Education (afPE). This is a comprehensive guide to safe practice and managing risk in PESSPA and should be referred to regarding any aspect of health and safety.

A copy of the current edition of the afPE *Safe Practice* in PESSPA is located in the staffroom.

Risk Assessment/Managing Risk:

Good teaching and therefore safe teaching in PESSPA are achieved where a balance between appropriate challenge and acceptable risk is maintained and the likelihood of injury occurring is minimised. Anticipating possible risks can help in the planning of effective risk management strategies. A logical and structured approach to preparation, referred to as **"forethought"**, is an essential part of effective teaching, managing and learning.

Where this process reveals a risk that cannot be sufficiently managed, then the planning needs to be reviewed.

During the thorough risk assessment of the school, which is carried out on a termly basis (in line with the statutory requirements under the Management of Health and Safety at Work Regulations 1999), significant risks will be reported to the head teacher.

Risk assessments for the hall and outside area for PESSPA can be found in Appendix [please insert your appendix number].

Teachers are also encouraged to carry out dynamic risk assessments prior to every PESSPA lesson. This will involve a quick overview of the teaching environment and equipment, which is then matched with the planned lesson content to assess whether it is safe to proceed or an alternative approach should be used.

Support Staff:

These include classroom assistants, teaching assistants, HLTAs, learning mentors, visiting coaches, sports apprentices and volunteer parents but not trainee teachers.

Additional support staff will be used during curriculum and non-curriculum time in order to:

- support the delivery of high quality PESSPA
- enrich or enhance an activity students are undertaking
- provide training opportunities for staff linked to PESSPA and sport premium key indicator 3
- provide additional opportunities for OSHL.

All adults supporting learning (ASL) and coaches will receive appropriate access to relevant training and support to ensure their knowledge and understanding of delivering curriculum PESSPA are in line with current statutory requirements and recommended good practice.

No ASL should operate independently. They may work alone if competence has been monitored but will be managed effectively by the teacher, who remains legally responsible for the students in their care, whether through direct or indirect supervision of the ASL.

External Sports Coaches:

The head teacher will always maintain responsibility for safe recruitment procedures, disclosure certification, possession of a governing body of sport licence, where relevant, and confirming authenticity of all ASL and coaches.

[Refer to your employer guidance on employing external coaches.]

The class teacher will always maintain overall responsibility for what is taught and the conduct, health and well-being of the students.

PESSPA Kit:

Students should wear clothing that is **fit for purpose** according to the PESSPA activity, environment and weather conditions.

Indoor and outdoor clothing

A [...] for indoor sessions:

[Insert your school requirements for indoor PESSPA clothing.]

A [...] for outdoor sessions:

[Insert your school requirements for outdoor PESSPA clothing.]

Long hair worn by students should always be tied back with a suitably soft item to prevent entanglement in apparatus and to prevent obscuring vision.

For classroom-based movement in a limited space or **playground activity** (eg "wake and shake" type activities), it is acceptable for children to remain in their school uniform. During this type of activity, children work within a small area or on the spot, and safety concerns linked with slips, trips and falls are reduced.

In **hot weather**, protection from the sun is advisable; therefore children can wear caps and loose, light clothing. Parents will be advised to provide sun cream protection for their children to apply.

Religious and cultural clothing

To maximise safe and meaningful participation, the school and staff will use sensitive management when dealing with any concerns arising from the wearing of certain items of clothing specific to religious requirements.

Clothing for PESSPA – staff

Clothing and **correct attire** for a particular PESSPA activity represent important features of safe practice that apply in equal measure to both staff and students. Staff should always endeavour to **change** into appropriate clothing for teaching PESSPA. On the rare occasions that this proves difficult or impractical, a change of footwear and removal of jewellery, at the very least, should always be undertaken.

Personal effects, including jewellery and cultural or religious adornments

Personal effects, such as jewellery (including body piercings), religious artefacts, watches, hair slides, and sensory aids (including glasses) should be **removed** to establish a safe working environment.

Ongoing risk assessment needs to determine what action will be appropriate. Staff should always try to avoid complete exclusion from a lesson due to a student being unable to remove personal effects.

Disclaimers from parents about the wearing of any item of jewellery by a student will be declined. Such indemnities have no legal status. The duty of care remains firmly with the school on such matters.

Changing Provision:

This principle is about ensuring **dignity, decency and privacy**, where needed, be it for reasons of physical development or other individual needs.

As Anytown school lacks purpose-built changing rooms, when changing for PESSPA, KS1 and lower KS2 students will change together in their classrooms, whereas upper KS2 students will change in separate areas. Staff are present during changing times to ensure children are safe at all times.

Equipment and Resources:

The majority of PESSPA equipment is stored in the [...] (eg PESSPA store on the playground, with the exception of smaller equipment, which is kept in the hall). All equipment is catalogued and a list is available from the PESSPA subject leader. The suitability of equipment is regularly reviewed to ensure it is appropriate to the range of ages, abilities and needs of children in order to enhance learning.

Students are encouraged to:

- look after resources
- use different resources to promote learning
- return all resources tidily and to the correct place (with staff supervising)
- learn any safety procedures relating to the carrying or handling of resources.

All other resources are located in the staffroom or with the PESSPA subject leader.

Any damage, breakage or loss of resources should be reported to the PESSPA subject leader as soon as possible. Any piece of apparatus where damage is observed that could cause injury must be isolated from use and reported. No groups or individuals should be able to access the resource until such time as it is made safe.

The school's detailed plans are attached as Appendix [please insert your appendix number] and are also available on the school's website.

Link Governor:

As governors are responsible for the spending of this funding and ensuring it meets the requirements of the conditions of grant, it is best practice to have a nominated governor or trustee with whom the PESSPA subject leader liaises on all matters to do with the primary PESSPA and sport premium.

Our PESSPA and sport link governor is [add name of governor].

Review of policy: <date> (Remember that policies should inform practice. Therefore, a review of every two years is optimal, or if any incidents or significant changes occur.)

Policy agreed by   Staff: **Date:**

                                      Governors: **Date:**

Next review date:

Section 7: Risk Management

1.7.1   Managing risk is the key to safe practice. It is the process of applying established safety principles, deciding whether these are sufficient for the situation and, if necessary, applying additional safety measures to ensure the environment and activity are acceptably safe.

1.7.2   This approach is promoting a form of risk-benefit analysis. The benefits of appropriate challenge, progression and improvement can be realised within a safe learning environment where the benefit outweighs the risk of injury.

1.7.3   Risk assessment is central to safe practice. It involves managing the risk, or possibility, of injury by:

- deciding what to risk assess – the physical education, school sport and physical activity (PESSPA) programme as a whole or each activity, facility or special event
- identifying the hazards that could cause harm (injury)
- judging whether or not existing safety precautions are sufficient to provide a safe learning environment
- deciding whether any significant risk of harm remains
- identifying who could be harmed by any significant risk
- reducing or controlling any remaining significant risk of harm to an acceptable and reasonable level by some additional form of corrective action or control measure
- recording the findings on a risk assessment and implementing them
- informing participants, staff and any other relevant people about changes (additional controls and procedures) that have been implemented to make any situation safer
- reviewing and updating the risk assessment regularly.

 Risk assessment: A judgement about whether a situation is safe within established practice and procedures, or whether additional precautions are required.

1.7.4   **Myth: Risk assessment is too complicated for me to do.**
Carrying out a risk assessment should be straightforward. It is about focusing on real risks and hazards that cause real harm and, more importantly, taking action to control them. A sensible approach to health and safety in schools means focusing on how real risks are managed.

1.7.5   **Does health and safety legislation place any barriers on participation in PESSPA?**
No – health and safety legislation should not be used as a reason to prevent participation in PESSPA. Health and safety legislation does require schools to manage risks associated with PESSPA activities sensibly, but this does not have to be difficult. In most cases, it will involve making sure that equipment is suitable for the students involved, that grounds are properly maintained and the right level of supervision for students is in place.

1.7.6   Managing risks sensibly involves schools and relevant teaching staff keeping up to date with guidance and standards applicable to the activities that are taught.

1.7.7   Good practice is safe practice, with the balance of appropriate challenge and acceptable risk well managed. Guidance on safe practice in PESSPA is always available to afPE members.

1.7.8   It must be understood that even when PESSPA is well managed, the physical challenge and competitive nature of some activities may occasionally lead to injuries.

KEY LEARNING: When developing learning opportunities, the focus should be on controlling the real risks, not eliminating all risks. Health and safety is about doing things safely, not finding reasons not to do them. This is often defined as **risk-benefit analysis** – a comparison of the level of risk against the benefits of undertaking an activity. It aims to balance acceptable risk with appropriate challenge and, in doing so, considers whether the benefits of participation outweigh the likelihood of harm or injury occurring.

1.7.9   There are three main types of risk assessment:

- **Generic risk assessment** is based on general principles that apply to an activity wherever it might take place. This will generally be the starting point of any risk assessment and is usually provided in a written form by the employer, governing body of sport, activity provider (eg outdoor adventurous centre) or similar organisation. Generic guidance needs to be amended to be appropriate to a school's particular needs and will inform both the ongoing risk assessment and the written site- or activity-specific risk assessment.
- **Site- or activity-specific risk assessment** is usually carried out for each location, facility or activity, with specific consideration of the people involved, the circumstances and the planning of the situation/event. This is usually in a written form and reviewed periodically.
- **Ongoing risk assessment**, sometimes referred to as dynamic risk assessment, is continuously carried out before and while an activity or event is taking place. It involves taking into account and responding to unforeseen issues, such as an unsafe response to a task, sudden illness, changes in the weather or ineffective officiating. This expertise evolves over time and is applied during the activity, in forward planning and also to inform future risk assessments. Ongoing risk assessment is unwritten and represents the dynamic process where staff remain vigilant, constantly reassessing the precautions they have put in place.

1.7.10   Events need to be as safe as necessary, not as safe as possible.

1.7.11   The risk assessment template on the pages that follow illustrates a typical range of generic issues. This should be adapted to meet your specific school requirements.

Written risk assessments should be reviewed on a regular basis, typically annually, but also following a near miss or injury. All staff involved in PESSPA should know the location of, and read, written risk assessments.

- This form should be adopted to meet your specific needs. This means amending, deleting or adding questions to column 1.
- Indicate in column 2 where the question in column 1 has been actioned appropriately, and is therefore considered 'safe'.
- Use column 3 where the question in column 1 still requires action to be taken, and therefore is considered to be 'unsafe'.
- Use column 4 where action is required to identify who may be harmed by the acknowledged risk.
- Use column 5 to list the action needed, over and above what is already in place, to reduce the risk to an acceptable level.
- Use column 6 for dating and signing, to demonstrate when appropriate action has been taken to make the issue safe.

Table 4: An example risk assessment for PESSPA

PESSPA Issues 1: Safe Exercise Practice – Clothing, footwear – Personal effects – Preparation	Appropriate Action 'Safe'	Action Required 'Unsafe'	Who Affected? (Student, Staff, Visitor)	Control Measures to Reduce the Risk to an Acceptable Level	Checked By: (Sign and Date)
a. Are there any times when group sizes or teacher/student ratios make a situation unsafe?					
b. Is the clothing appropriate for each activity?					
c. Is the policy to remove jewellery and other personal effects applied consistently?					
d. Is your policy around the use of fitness trackers applied consistently?					
e. Are the school policies on physical contact (supporting) and substantial access (1:1) known and applied effectively?					
f. Are there any concerns about Disability Act requirements for access and involvement in PESSPA for those with cognitive, visual, hearing or motor impairment?					
g. Do the students know and safely apply departmental routines and procedures?					
h. Are there safety issues about participation in any specific activity?					
i. Are there any other student-related safety concerns that require attention? (List them here):					
j. Is the student led 'warm-up' monitored by staff?					
k. Do written schemes of work/other guidance set out safety issues to be followed?					
l. Do lessons provide appropriate and effective warm-up and cool-down?					
m. Is student led warm-up monitored by staff?					
n. Are there any other preparation-related safety concerns that require attention? (List them here):					

PESSPA Issues 2: Group Management – Competence – Safeguarding – Safe exercise practice – Insurance – Personal protective equipment (PPE)	Appropriate Action 'Safe'	Action Required 'Unsafe'	Who Affected? (Student, Staff, Visitor)	Control Measures to Reduce the Risk to an Acceptable Level	Checked By: (Sign and Date)
a. Do all staff have adequate qualifications, experience, confidence, competence to fulfil their teaching commitments safely?					
b. Is some system in place to monitor that qualifications are current, particularly for higher risk environments/activities?					
c. Does anyone require some form of professional development or support for reasons of safe teaching?					
d. Do staff adequately supervise students at all times?					
e. Are there any times when additional supervision is required but not provided?					
f. Are there any times when students are not supervised that give cause for concern?					
g. Is relevant information (including medical) always passed on to visiting staff before they lead a group?					
h. Are there any control/discipline/ behaviour problems by any student/group with any adult teaching them that causes safety concerns?					
i. Is the system secure to ensure that student medical conditions are known by any adult teaching an individual (including visiting staff)?					
j. Are staff observation and analysis skills adequate?					
k. Is staff clothing or personal effects appropriate for teaching PESSPA?					
l. Do all staff demonstrate appropriate teaching positions in relation to participants?					
m. Do all assistants/support staff know the limits of their role/ responsibility?					
n. Is effective communication between teacher and support staff evident?					
o. Do all adults teaching groups have appropriate insurance cover where needed?					
p. Have disclosure certificates been seen for all support staff?					
q. Are there any other staff-related safety concerns that require attention? (List them here):					

r.	Are group numbers always known/checked?					
s.	Is a register check taken for every lesson?					
t.	Do staff regularly scan or do head counts at the beginning/during/end of lessons?					
u.	Are group organisation/management procedures safe and consistently applied?					
v.	Are demonstrations accurate and safely performed?					
w.	Are students with visual, hearing, motor or cognitive impairment catered for appropriately to enable them to participate safely?					
x.	Are there any activity-specific safety concerns?					
y.	Are there any other class organisation-related safety concerns that require attention? (List them here):					
z.	Does the demand/challenge in sessions match students' abilities, needs and confidence?					
aa.	Are appropriate teaching styles used to ensure safety?					
bb.	Is progression based on ability?					
cc.	Is regular and approved practice used at all times?					
dd.	Are physical support and manual handling techniques known and applied where appropriate?					
ee.	Is intervention appropriate to individual student needs?					
ff.	Are tasks differentiated to meet individual abilities and confidence?					
gg.	Are rules consistently applied in games?					
hh.	Do staff know the limits of their involvement in games, practices and demonstrations involving students?					
ii.	Are there any activity-specific safety concerns?					
jj.	Are there any other teaching-related safety concerns that require attention? (List them here):					

PESSPA Issues 3: Procedures and Routines – First aid – Digital technology – Parental consent – Emergency action	Appropriate Action 'Safe'	Action Required 'Unsafe'	Who Affected? (Student, Staff, Visitor)	Control Measures to Reduce the Risk to an Acceptable Level	Checked By: (Sign and Date)
a. Is the head teacher appraised of all activities offered within and beyond the formal curriculum?					
b. Are parents informed and involved as necessary about PESSPA situations?					
c. Is movement to the work areas safe and orderly?					
d. Is access to each facility safely managed?					
e. Are first-aid equipment, procedures and responsibilities known by staff and (where appropriate) students?					
f. Are notices providing safety information evident, clearly positioned, effective, shared and applied?					
g. Are emergency evacuation procedures known?					
h. Are there any other procedures/routine-related safety concerns that require attention? (List them here):					
i. Is the policy on digital imagery known and applied?					
j. Have requested permissions been obtained from parents, or have they been informed of any off-site visits and activities?					
k. Is a register check taken for every session (secondary), and where applicable primary?					
l. Are emergency procedures to address potential incidents during lessons and visits set out, known and applied by all?					
m. Are accident procedures to address potential incidents during lessons and visits set out, known and applied by all?					
n. Can first aid support be summoned and provided quickly?					
o. Are contingency plans to address potential incidents during lessons and visits set out, known and applied by all staff?					
p. Are there any other emergency/contingency-related safety concerns that require attention? (List them here):					

PESSPA Issues 4: Equipment	Appropriate Action 'Safe'	Action Required 'Unsafe'	Who Affected? (Student, Staff, Visitor)	Control Measures to Reduce the Risk to an Acceptable Level	Checked By: (Sign and Date)
a. Is equipment used for the purpose it was designed?					
b. Is all equipment in good condition?					
c. Is equipment of an appropriate size, type, weight, quality and suitability for the age, build, strength of students?					
d. Have students been taught to carry, move, place and retrieve equipment safely?					
e. Is supervision of carrying/siting of equipment managed where appropriate?					
f. Do staff check equipment before use by participants?					
g. Do staff regularly check equipment before use and report any faults found?					
h. Is equipment easily accessed and safely stored?					
i. Are routines for collection, retrieval, changing of equipment known and applied by staff and students?					
j. Are there any other equipment handling, carrying, siting concerns in any activity?					
k. Is there an annual gymnastic, play and fitness equipment inspection check by a specialist company?					
l. Is any improvised use of equipment allowed?					
m. Is all required safety and rescue equipment present?					
n. Are there any other equipment-related safety concerns that require attention? (List them here):					

PESSPA Issues 5: Transport for PESSPA	Appropriate Action 'Safe'	Action Required 'Unsafe'	Who Affected? (Student, Staff, Visitor)	Control Measures to Reduce the Risk to an Acceptable Level	Checked By: (Sign and Date)
a. Are school vehicles checked for roadworthiness before use?					
b. Is a reputable coach/taxi company used?					
c. Is a clear policy applied where any form of transport is used?					
d. Are embarkation points safe?					
e. Are seat belts always used?					
f. Are booster seats available where required?					
g. Is there always a check on numbers leaving and returning onto the transport?					
h. Are driver requirements and responsibilities known and applied?					
i. Are there any concerns about supervision whilst driving?					
j. Is there a procedure for dismissing students after an event away from school that is understood, accepted and applied by all staff, students and parents/carers?					
k. Is there an emergency contact system in place?					
l. Are procedures in place in the event of a transport problem arising?					
m. Are there any other transport-related safety concerns that require attention? (List them here):					

PESSPA Issues 6: Teaching Facility	Appropriate Action 'Safe'	Action Required 'Unsafe'	Who Affected? (Student, Staff, Visitor)	Control Measures to Reduce the Risk to an Acceptable Level	Checked By: (Sign and Date)
a. Are changing rooms safe?					
b. Are changing rooms secure when not in use?					
c. Are work areas free of hazards?					
d. Is there a clean, non-slip floor providing security of footing?					
e. If there is a swimming pool, is water clarity good?					
f. Is there sufficient space for group size/activity?					
g. Are there any activity-specific safety concerns?					
h. Is storage adequate and safe?					
i. Is lighting safe and adequate for activities?					
j. Are there any access issues for those with disabilities?					
k. Are operating procedures known/ applied?					
l. Are fire regulations applied?					
m. Are safety signs in place?					
n. Is the facility secured when not in use?					
o. Are there any concerns about equipment?					

PESSPA Issues 7: Away Fixtures	Appropriate Action 'Safe'	Action Required 'Unsafe'	Who Affected? (Student, Staff, Visitor)	Control Measures to Reduce the Risk to an Acceptable Level	Checked By: (Sign and Date)
a. Student information/ consent form					
b. Parents/carers informed?					
c. Staffing issues (including match officials)					
d. Assembly/embarkation/ disembarkation					
e. Transport/journey					
f. Venue (host risk assessment known?)					
g. Supervision issues					
h. Reciprocal arrangements in place for the safety of students? – ie first aid provision, emergency supervision					
i. Emergency action/ contingency plans					
j. First aid provision					
k. Weather/clothing/ personal protection issues					
l. Clear dismissal arrangements known by parents and students?					

EXEMPLAR FACILITY ASSESSMENT: Gymnasium
Date: Assessors:

PESSPA Issues	Appropriate Action 'Safe'	Action Required 'Unsafe'	Who Affected? (Student, Staff, Visitor)	Control Measures to Reduce the Risk to an Acceptable Level	Checked By: (Sign and Date)
• Changing room safe? Wire grilles above benches loose and broken with sharp edge – cutting injuries likely		✓	PSV	Needs repair.	
• Work area hazard free? Ceiling tiles broken and out of place – could fall and injure		✓	PSV	Needs replacing urgently.	
• Secure footing?	✓				
• Sufficient space for group size/activity?	✓				
• Any activity-specific safety concerns?	✓				
• Storage adequate and safe? Small store – window broken – glass shards on floor and equipment – danger to staff and could be trampled into gym floor and become danger to users		✓	S	Needs sweeping and replacing urgently.	
• Lighting safe and adequate for activities?	✓				
• Access issues for those with disabilities?	✓				
• Operating procedures known/applied?	✓				
• Fire regulations applied? Trampoline blocks near fire exit. Bolts on other (most likely to be used) fire exit – may prevent small students reaching and escaping		✓	PSV	Trampoline must be moved to alternate storage position. Fire doors must not be locked other than by push bar mechanism – needs altering immediately.	
• Safety signs in place?	✓				
• Equipment concerns? Large store – bows and arrows loose in corner; trampettes not disabled/locked		✓		Bows and arrows must be removed immediately to prevent unauthorised use. Trampettes must be locked/disabled immediately to prevent unauthorised use.	

Chapter 2:

Principles for Developing the PESSPA Learning
Experience

Section 1: Qualifications and Professional Learning

Qualifications Landscape

2.1.1   As outlined in **Chapter 1**, it is essential that anyone leading a class in physical education, school sport and physical activity (PESSPA) is confident and competent to do so. It is worth reinforcing that the Health and Safety Executive (HSE) has outlined four means of demonstrating competence: **hold a relevant qualification; hold an equivalent qualification; have received appropriate in-house training; be competent through experience**. Head teachers (HTs) must satisfy themselves that whoever is teaching a class has been deemed competent to do so using one or more of these criteria. Where leaders are looking for the most relevant qualifications in specific activities, they need to keep up to date with the qualifications listed on the Association for Physical Education (afPE) and relevant governing body of sport websites, and choose the most appropriate one to suit their **school context**.

2.1.2   The Chartered Institute for the Management of Sport and Physical Activity (CIMSPA) has introduced development standards, which will allow coaches to demonstrate that they have the expertise to work in a particular learning environment. For schools that employ the services of coaches, although a coach may demonstrate that they have achieved the relevant standard (eg as outlined in CIMSPA [2019] "Working in the school environment: Out of curriculum"), it is still incumbent on employers to satisfy themselves of the **technical** expertise of the coach for the activities they are teaching.

  For information on CIMSPA's standards, see https://www.cimspa.co.uk/

2.1.3   When utilising any coach who can demonstrate that they have met the standard, leaders should note that the CIMSPA standards are specific to an extracurricular context. It should also be noted that safety standards (and therefore competence criteria) remain the same whether during curriculum time or extracurricular time.

2.1.4   If a coach is needed to provide the expertise to teach curricular or extracurricular activities at a level to suit particular students, then the coach's competence for that context needs to be verified. This would most commonly be through the coach holding a relevant Level 2 coaching award. In addition, they would be expected to have the teaching skills listed in afPE's "Guidance on the effective use of coaches in physical education and sport".

  To access the afPE guidance, visit http://www.afpe.org.uk/physical-education/
guidance-on-the-effective-use-of-coaches-in-pe-a-sport/

2.1.5   The teacher has the common law duty of care for the class, but the coach also has a duty of care under both common law (as the expert) and health and safety law (as a person legally required to avoid placing others in unsafe situations). It becomes a joint responsibility where both are present. As outlined previously, the employer's responsibility is not displaced by the employment of the coach.

  For more information on the legal duty of care, see **Chapter 1, Section 4**.

2.1.6   A Level 2 qualification in the activity being delivered is widely recognised as the minimum expectation for any coach to be involved in either curricular or extracurricular delivery. This qualification needs to be one that is suitable for teaching in an education setting; thus, the syllabus needs to include relevant content for this context. Some Level 2 awards are designed only for those working in community or leisure settings.

2.1.7   Within the maintained sector, anyone who does not hold qualified teacher status (QTS) or is not progressing along a school-based training programme is labelled "support staff". Such staff need to demonstrate the appropriate competence for whatever curriculum delivery they are deployed to do. Similarly, in the academy and independent sectors, while the label of support staff does not apply, the statutory demonstration of competence as set out by the HSE and the management responsibility stated in the Health and Safety at Work etc Act (HaSaWA) 1974 section 3, and possibly section 7, apply to ensure that competence is demonstrated at the level of learning at which a "class" is working.

---

afPE Position Statement

afPE's position is that anyone with QTS is recognised as having met the relevant Teachers' Standards and thus is assumed to have the relevant expertise to teach curriculum physical education, such as gymnastic activities, without a specific coaching qualification. However, additional professional learning is strongly advised in order to maintain competence as the student level of skill and challenge increases and, therefore, level of risk. Higher risk activities may also require an activity appropriate National Governing Body (NGB) of sport Level 2 qualification even for those with QTS. Examples include swimming, gymnastics, trampolining, athletics (when using standard equipment) and specific outdoor and adventurous activities.

afPE strongly recommends that any coach deployed by the school leadership to lead a curricular or extracurricular activity holds a minimum of a Level 2 qualification in that activity as an indication of expertise to lead a group and not simply assist a more expert leader.

To access the afPE guidance, visit http://www.afpe.org.uk/physical-education/ guidance-on-the-effective-use-of-coaches-in-pe-a-sport/

Physical Education, School Sport and Physical Activity Awards and Qualifications for Specific Activities

2.1.8   Primary school staff who hold QTS are not legally obliged to hold activity-specific qualifications or awards in order to teach specific PESSPA activities unless required to do so by their employer. In the secondary sector, physical education teachers holding QTS are also strongly advised to hold specific qualifications to teach high risk activities such as trampolining. Some local authorities (LAs), school trusts or school governing bodies establish their own policies and insist on specified levels of training, experience or qualifications before allowing staff to teach PESSPA activities that involve greater risk (eg trampolining). Staff should be aware of **local employer requirements** and ensure that they meet these before teaching the activities concerned. (See the afPE Position Statement above.)

2.1.9   Examples of potentially **higher risk** activities include adventurous activities, aquatic activities, athletic throwing events, combat sports, contact sports, aspects of gymnastics, trampolining and working with free weights in a fitness room. Those leading curricular or extracurricular sessions in schools in these contexts should hold recognised and current qualifications (eg governing body of sport qualifications). In the absence of such qualifications, it is strongly advised that significant, recent and relevant experience or professional learning is required to demonstrate an individual's competence to teach these activities safely (see **Chapter 1, Section 5**).

2.1.10   Some governing bodies of sport and other awarding organisations require qualifications to be revalidated periodically. This is not simply to endorse previous requirements, but to inform learners of changes and developments that may have occurred in the interim period (eg as in the British Gymnastics "Refresher" Trampolining award). Guidance should be obtained from the relevant governing body of sport, awarding organisation or LA, the Education Authority in Northern Ireland or an expert consultant.

2.1.11   The standards of expertise, discipline, relationships and risk management expected of all adults working with students need to be consistent with providing a safe working environment. This level of competence applies to all who contribute to PESSPA activities as part of a school-organised programme, and at all times when they are delivering relevant activities (eg during activities which take place inside and outside of lessons, on or off the school site, in term time or holidays).

2.1.12   Employers need to keep up to date with any redesigned qualifications and ensure they guarantee the technical expertise that would be expected of the member of staff leading the lesson within a school setting.

2.1.13   Schools can receive credit for their high quality PESSPA provision. afPE's **Quality Mark** recognises high quality PESSPA in schools, and evaluates the competence of the PESSPA workforce and the work they do through PESSPA to make a difference to students' learning within the subject and more widely across the curriculum. Safeguarding and the promotion of health and safety are important aspects of the Quality Mark criteria, as well as the effective deployment of competent support staff.

 For more information on the afPE Quality Mark, visit http://www.afpe.org.uk/physical-education/afpe-quality-mark-for-pe-a-sport/

Ongoing Professional Learning for Staff

2.1.14   Health and safety law includes a **requirement** that employees **receive the professional learning** necessary for them to fulfil the demands of the work they are deployed to do by managers. Professional learning opportunities in safe-practice procedures are therefore a necessity and an entitlement where any lack of confidence or competence is evident. Otherwise, alternative staffing arrangements need to be made. Those involved in delivering PESSPA need to undertake professional learning in order to keep abreast of what is acceptable and safe. This is exemplified in England by the Education Inspection Framework (2019), which outlines the importance of **subject** continuous professional learning.

 For more information on the Education Inspection Framework, visit www.gov.uk/government/publications/education-inspection-framework

2.1.15   A rolling programme of professional learning in relation to safe practice, evidenced through a personal or collective **training log**, would indicate that the required qualifications and experience, relevant to the PESSPA programme being offered, remain current.

2.1.16   Primary teachers who lack confidence in teaching PESSPA should undertake appropriate professional learning before taking responsibility for a full range of activities. As outlined at the start of this section, HTs must be satisfied that all those who are required to teach PESSPA are able to do so in a safe manner, with a sound understanding of the needs and stages of development of all the students in their charge. afPE has developed a range of qualifications for the primary environment that help to ensure effective leadership and high quality support.

2.1.17   **Primary staff** with QTS can now access the afPE and Sports Leaders UK:
- Level 5 Certificate in Primary School Physical Education Specialism
- Level 6 Award in Primary School Physical Education Subject Leadership.

2.1.18   **All staff** contributing to a school PESSPA programme can also access the Level 5 Certificate in order to increase their competence in promoting learning through PESSPA activities.

 For more information on these qualifications, see http://www.afpe.org.uk/physical-education/level-56-professional-vocational-qualifications-primary-school-specialism-and-subject-leadership-in-pe-school-sport/

2.1.19   Coaches supporting PESSPA provision in schools can also access these qualifications:

- Level 2 Certificate in Supporting Learning in Physical Education and School Sport
- Level 3 Certificate in Supporting the Delivery of Physical Education and School Sport
- Level 3 NVQ Diploma in Supporting the Delivery of Physical Education and School Sport
- Level 5 Certificate in Primary School Physical Education Specialism

 For more information on these qualifications, see https://www.afpe.org.uk/physical-education/vocational-qualifications/

- Level 3 Certificate in Supporting Physical Development and Physical Activity in the Early Years

 For more information on this qualification, see http://www.afpe.org.uk/physical-education/level-3-certificate-in-supporting-physical-development-a-physical-activity-in-the-early-years/

- Level 3 Award in Supporting the Delivery of Dance in Physical Education and School Sport

 For more information on this qualification, see https://www.afpe.org.uk/physical-education/level-3-award-in-supporting-the-delivery-of-dance-in-physical-education-and-school-sport/

 See **FAQ 19** in **Chapter 4** and **Case Law 51** in **Chapter 4**.

2.1.20   The 2013 Supreme Court decision (Woodland versus Essex County Council 2013 – see **Chapter 1, Section 4**) established in common law that the school employer (LA, governors or trust) retains the responsibility for students even where a school-based activity is provided through a third party, such as an individual coach or coaching agency. This is because the agency or coach provides the teaching service **on behalf** of the school employer, and the responsibility for the care of students **cannot be delegated**. The HT, as manager of the school, technically deploys all staff, whether on the school roll or visiting, and as such, it is their duty to actively ensure that anyone teaching or coaching any PESSPA activity in a school context is competent to fulfil the demands of the tasks to which they are deployed.

2.1.21   School support staff and visiting coaches can add to the quality of a PESSPA programme through their expertise, encouragement and support. In addition, teachers can develop their own knowledge by **learning from support staff** and visiting coaches who have particular expertise in a specific PESSPA activity. This can be achieved if:

- provision is made for teachers to **work alongside more expert school support staff and visiting coaches** whenever possible
- more expert school support staff and visiting coaches are committed to imparting information through such a joint working arrangement.

2.1.22   The use of school support staff and visiting coaches can also help to broaden the PESSPA programme, increase the quality of learning and challenge, and provide greater flexibility in staffing.

Section 2: Safeguarding

Introduction

2.2.1   Safeguarding is action that is taken to promote the welfare of children, and protect them from harm. The concept is enshrined in statute based on the principle that the health, safety and welfare of the child are paramount. The definition provided in the most recent statutory guidance suggests that this should be achieved by:

> *protecting children from maltreatment; preventing impairment of children's health or development, ensuring children grow up in circumstances consistent with the provision of safe and effective care; and taking action to enable all children to have the best outcomes.*
>
> Department for Education (DfE) (2019) "Keeping children safe in education: Statutory guidance for schools and colleges", https://assets.publishing.service.gov.uk/government/uploads/system/uploads/attachment_data/file/835733/Keeping_children_safe_in_education_2019.pdf

2.2.2   All who work with students have a duty to ensure the health, safety and well-being of those in their care and, within the law, may do what is reasonable in all circumstances for the safeguarding or promotion of students' welfare. Staff have a duty to **pass on concerns** about possible abuse (including suspected cases of female genital mutilation [FGM]) to the designated safeguarding lead (DSL) within their organisation or school.

2.2.3   There is no requirement to find evidence to support any concern, nor to have to be certain that significant harm may have, or has, occurred in order to report the concern. Where required, schools need to work with social care, the police, health services and other services to promote the welfare of children and protect them from harm.

2.2.4   Schools are required to have clear safeguarding **policy and procedures**. Employers must ensure that all staff are aware of and apply the necessary policy and procedures relating to the prevention of **intentional and unintentional harm to their students**. Within physical education departments, subject leaders need to check that the relevant school policy and procedures adequately cover the physical education, school sport and physical activity (PESSPA) context and, where they do not, discuss how these might be added from the relevant physical education documentation.

For further information regarding schools' responsibilities for safeguarding, see:

Ofsted (2019) "Inspecting safeguarding in early years, education and skills settings: Guidance for inspectors undertaking inspection under the common inspection framework", https://assets.publishing.service.gov.uk/government/uploads/system/uploads/attachment_data/file/828763/Inspecting_safeguarding_in_early_years__education_and_skills.pdf

DfE (2019) "Keeping children safe in education: Statutory guidance for schools and colleges", https://assets.publishing.service.gov.uk/government/uploads/system/uploads/attachment_data/file/835733/Keeping_children_safe_in_education_2019.pdf

HM Government (2018) "Working together to safeguard children: A guide to inter-agency working to safeguard and promote the welfare of children", https://www.gov.uk/government/publications/working-together-to-safeguard-children--2

Understanding Intentional Harm

2.2.5   Safeguarding in some schools may be limited in scope to protecting students from **deliberate harm**, including self-harm, physical, emotional or sexual abuse, neglect, bullying (including online or cyberbullying), racist abuse, harassment, discrimination and the potential for abuse of trust by adults working with children and young people. *The Teachers' Standards in England* (DfE, 2012), for example, state that teachers, including head teachers (HTs), should safeguard children's well-being, and maintain public trust in the teaching profession as part of their professional duties.

For more on *The Teachers' Standards*, see the DfE guidance at www.gov.uk

2.2.6   All staff need to know about **indicators of intentional harm**, the school's systems for reporting causes for concern, and how to deal with students **disclosing** information about intentional harm to themselves or others.

2.2.7   It is important that PESSPA staff are aware of the general **signs and symptoms** of intentional harm, such as non-accidental bruising, and identifiable changes in the mood or personality of students who may be affected by any such harm.

For information about identifying signs of abuse or neglect, and recognising signs of child grooming or exploitation, see the National Society for the Prevention of Cruelty to Children (NSPCC) website: https://www.nspcc.org.uk/what-is-child-abuse/spotting-signs-child-abuse/

2.2.8   In the **Case Law** section of **Chapter 4**, **Case Law 24** presents present four cases (24a, b, c and d) concerning safeguarding and "abuse of trust". They were all brought under the principle of "**abuse of a position of trust**". It is an offence under the Sexual Offences Act 2003 for a person over the age of 18, such as a teacher, to have a sexual relationship of any kind with a child under 18 where that person is in a position of trust in respect of that child, such as in teaching, even if the relationship is consensual.

2.2.9   PESSPA staff should also be aware of specific PESSPA-related incidences of intentional harm, such as staff intentionally:

- overplaying and overtraining talented students, using inappropriate training methods and imposing physical punishment for not carrying out a task or for being last to complete a task as **forms of physical abuse**; this is particularly important as exercise is a positive experience to be encouraged, not one to be undertaken as a consequence of a lack of success
- depriving students of rehydration during physical activity in hot weather or adequate clothing during cold weather
- encouraging or allowing violent play.

Safeguarding Students by Preventing Violent Play

2.2.10   Injuries can occur in sport because of bad luck, careless acts or unacceptable violence on the pitch. Dangerous play in sport represents unacceptable risk. Acts of violent conduct committed **outside the laws and spirit of the game** can also constitute assault.

2.2.11   Violence in sport is not confined to adult participation. It is thus relevant to staff, coaches and managers in school situations.

2.2.12   Staff who teach, encourage or accept **over-aggressive play** may face disciplinary action if their players go beyond the rules and spirit of the game. Exercising control of a team is the responsibility of the team manager and one they cannot afford to ignore. A club can be held vicariously liable for injuries caused by such play.

2.2.13   It is therefore important that schools have a procedure for monitoring students' fair play in competition. Where violent or reckless play occurs outside the rules and spirit of the game, immediate corrective action should be implemented during the game.

2.2.14   Staff should also encourage students to report any occasion when they feel threatened or intimidated as a result of violent or reckless play.

2.2.15   Further investigation will be needed after any incident to establish whether the player involved has a propensity for violent or reckless play, or whether the incident in question can be deemed to have been an isolated one. This will determine whether that player is selected in future. Where there is the probability of repetition, the team manager selecting the player may be judged to condone violent play.

2.2.16   It is good practice to design a "fair play" **code of conduct** and develop it in collaboration with students. This code should be communicated to and agreed by students, staff and parents. It should outline the expectations on all concerned, and make clear any sanctions that might be imposed on those failing to respect its requirements.

2.2.17   **Examples of case law** that concern incidents of **not following the rules/codes** of conduct are presented in **Case Law 25-27** in **Chapter 4**.

2.2.18   Poor behaviour by parents and other spectators at sports events and matches can be a concern for schools and have a detrimental effect on students. Several governing bodies of sport provide guidance on parental behaviour. The NSPCC Child Protection in Sport Unit (CPSU) in its tool kit "It's our game not yours" provides useful information to help organisations manage these concerns by:

- encouraging positive parental participation through clear communication, information and expectations
- handling challenging parental behaviour by promoting codes of conduct for parents, and developing a clear process to respond to concerns or complaints
- promoting values such as respect and listening to each other, ensuring a designated safeguarding officer is known to all, and reminding parents to be positive role models for their children
- establishing sanctions for parents by monitoring behaviour, and carrying through to barring individuals from attending, while ensuring that the child's participation is not affected.

Understanding Unintentional Harm

2.2.19   In addition to addressing the prevention of intentional harm, schools have a duty to ensure that students are safe and feel safe through protection from **unintentional harm**. Fundamentally this is about poor teaching/coaching practice. Many of these issues are central to safe teaching and form part of relevant school policy and procedures. However, in PESSPA contexts, there are a number of more specific aspects of safeguarding that should be considered, and good practice indicates that these should be documented in PESSPA procedures and risk assessments.

2.2.20   **Table 5, pages 58-63**, provides a checklist of aspects of safeguarding issues that are relevant to PESSPA and directs the user to where relevant information can be found in this resource.

2.2.21   The essential outcome is that intentional harm receives an effective response and is eradicated, and unintentional harm is avoided so that students **feel safe and are safe** within the broader consideration of safeguarding.

Vetting and Barring – the Disclosure and Barring Service Process

2.2.22   School appointment procedures, including those for visiting coaches and other volunteers who will be in "regulated activity", must include **vetting** to ensure that the person appointed is not barred from working with children and young people.

2.2.23   The Protection of Freedoms Act became law in May 2012. A key purpose of this legislation in relation to safeguarding is to clarify checking procedures and reduce the number of applications for checks, while still maintaining safe standards of protection.

Eligibility to request a check

2.2.24   In order to request a check, managers need to ensure they are legally entitled to apply for one. It is an offence to obtain a check to which they are not entitled. This can lead to prosecution of both the individual and the registered body. A registered body is an approved organisation the DBS service has registered to assist with carrying out DBS checks. These are usually large organisations such as local authorities, the NHS or organisations that submit more than 100 applications to check applicants. In order to be eligible for an enhanced check, an applicant must be in work that is currently defined as regulated activity relating to children or adults.

 For more information on the Protection of Freedoms Act, see https://services/.parliament.uk/bills/2010-11/protectionoffreedoms.html

2.2.25   **For most appointments in schools** and settings working with children, an enhanced Disclosure and Barring Service (DBS) check with barred list information will be required as the majority of staff will be engaging in regulated activity. For those who will not be in **regulated activity**, a DBS check is not a requirement, but is considered to be good practice.

2.2.26   For more information, refer to safer recruitment guidance. For example, in England, the statutory guidance is "**Keeping children safe in education**", last updated 1 October 2019.

 https://assets.publishing.service.gov.uk/government/uploads/system/uploads/attachment_data/file/835733/Keeping_children_safe_in_education_2019.pdf

https://www.gov.uk/government/publications/keeping-children-safe-in-education--2

Current definition of regulated activity for children

2.2.27   The scope of work that is regulated activity for children is:

- unsupervised activities – teaching, instructing, caring for or supervising children or providing advice or guidance on well-being or driving a vehicle only for children

or

- working for a limited range of establishments ("specified places") with opportunity for contact (eg schools, children's homes, childcare premises).

2.2.28   These types of work are only considered to be regulated activity if they are done regularly. "Regularly", in this case, is defined as at least once a week or more, or four or more days in a 30-day period, or overnight.

2.2.29   The following types of care are considered to be regulated activity even if they are only carried out once:

- **personal care**, such as:
  - physical help with eating or drinking due to illness or disability
  - physical help with toileting, washing, bathing or dressing due to age, illness or disability
- all forms of **healthcare** relating to physical or mental health including palliative care and procedures similar to medical or surgical care.

Defining 'Supervision'

2.2.30   When appointing **support staff** to a PESSPA programme in schools, a number of recommended checks, observations and assessments should be carried out in addition to the DBS checking procedure. These will include confirming the identity of the person, their actual qualifications, competence, relevant courses attended and current licence to coach from a governing body of sport.

 Chapter 1 Table 2 Best practice guidance on the effective use of individual and agency coaches in physical education, school sport and physical activity (PESSPA).

2.2.31   A set of nationally recognised professional standards for those coaching children are being established by the Chartered Institute for the Management of Sport and Physical Activity (CIMSPA) on behalf of Sport England – "**Minimum deployment requirement guidelines for the deployment of sports coaches outside of curriculum time**". More information can be found at www.cimspa.co.uk

2.2.32   The minimum deployment requirements are being developed to help drive the quality of coaching delivered to children. There is an expectation that schools will encourage and support coaches to access further training that would allow them to go beyond minimum requirements and meet additional recommendations for out of curriculum hours work. One of the expectations both during the transition period and following this is that all coaches will have an enhanced DBS check.

 Minimum requirements in the transition period are as follows:

- Minimum age 18
- CIMSPA-endorsed training based on professional standards for coaching, coaching children, coaching in the school environment and safeguarding technical standard, or Governing Body Level 2 (or above) qualification in the activity being delivered
- Any additional technical standard required for the activity being delivered (eg gymnastics)
- Enhanced DBS check
- Appropriate insurance.

2.2.33   If the HT or employer establishes that the newly appointed support staff member will not be working in regulated activity, and that the scope and frequency requirements are not met, they do not need to request a DBS check.

2.2.34   If they are appointing or managing an individual or agency coach, the situation is different. If the coach will be engaged in regulated activity, the HT or employer will have to request access to an enhanced DBS disclosure certificate including information from the barred list.

2.2.35   If the coach will not be in regulated activity, although there is no right to access information from the barred list, an enhanced disclosure certificate should nevertheless be requested (regardless of whether the coach will be supervised by school staff or not). If disclosure is required, the employer should see the original disclosure certificate and record the number. (This should not be photocopied without the applicant's consent.) The employer can then decide if portability applies and is acceptable.

2.2.36   The minimum age at which a DBS check can be requested is 16.

Arrangements for the Self-employed

2.2.37   Current legislation in England does not allow self-employed individuals to apply for a DBS check on themselves. Where a self-employed person (eg educational consultant, sports coach) needs to obtain a DBS check, they have the following options:

- **Contracting organisations** – if an organisation contracts a self-employed person for the delivery of a service, this organisation may apply for the DBS certificate on the self-employed person's behalf.
- **Endorsement organisations or umbrella bodies** – some professional bodies apply for DBS checks on behalf of their members (eg governing bodies of sport). The government provides a database of DBS umbrella bodies.
- **Disclosure Scotland** – the government's own advice suggests that a "basic check" can be obtained from Disclosure Scotland (the sister organisation of the DBS), whether an individual lives in Scotland, England or Wales.
- **Subject access request** – this is an option where the local police force provides a certificate with similar information to a DBS certificate at the cost of £10. Since local arrangements vary for obtaining an application form, it is advised that applicants telephone the police and ask to speak to the data protection team. In order to complete the form, two sources of identification must be provided, one with a name and a photograph (passport or driving licence) and the other with a current address (a recent utility bill or bank statement), and a cheque or postal order for the appropriate sum.
- **A recruitment agency** can apply for a DBS check for self-employed people who register with it. The agency would be eligible to ask an exempted question as it would be the agency assessing the individual's suitability. The agency could countersign the application form.

Disclosure and Barring Service Update Service

2.2.38   The DBS update service was introduced in June 2013. It allows applicants to keep their DBS certificates up to date online, and employers to check a certificate online. For a small annual subscription of £13 (free for volunteers), an applicant can move from role to role without the requirement to undertake a new check as long as they are within the same workforce, where the same type and level of check is required. Applicants sign up to the service voluntarily.

2.2.39   If an applicant has previously signed up to the update service, employers and other organisations can check their DBS certificate status online and receive a result straight away. This could significantly reduce the amount of time a new employee has to wait before taking up their post, or be convenient for coaches who work across a number of settings. There is no registration process or fee for employers to check a certificate online, but employers must:

- be legally entitled to carry out a check
- have the applicant's permission.

 For more information on the DBS update service, see https://www.gov.uk/dbs-update-service

---

 FAQ 22 relating to the update service can be found in the **FAQ section of Chapter 4**.

2.2.40   Volunteers and coaches should never be used to replace teachers within the school curriculum, and always require some level of supervision as the class teacher remains responsible for the children in their group. (See **Chapter 1, Section 4, page 14.**)

2.2.41   In the case of **trainee teachers salaried** by a school or college, the school must ensure that all necessary checks are carried out. If the school decides that these trainee teachers are likely to be engaging in regulated activity, an enhanced DBS certificate (including barred list information) must be obtained.

2.2.42   Where **trainee teachers** are **not salaried**, it is the responsibility of the initial teacher education (ITE) provider to carry out the necessary checks. Schools should obtain written confirmation that this has been done.

2.2.43   It must, however, be remembered that **trainee teachers are not fully competent to teach** until they are **"signed off"** as having reached the required level of competence against the teachers' standards (TS). This being the case, until that time, they should not be given full, unsupervised responsibility within a practical PESSPA setting for any group, and are therefore unlikely to be deemed to be in regulated activity.

Levels of check

Enhanced check

2.2.44   Every check typically undertaken by the school/employer is an enhanced check. This check contains details from the Police National Computer of all spent and unspent convictions, cautions, reprimands and final warnings, which have been filtered in line with relevant legislation. It also checks if any information is held by local police forces.

 Information on filtering can be found at https://www.gov.uk/government/collections/dbs-filtering-guidance

Barred list check

2.2.45   For some roles (teaching, instructing or assisting children in an unsupervised regulated activity), an additional level of check may be required. In this case, a request can be made to check the applicant against the relevant barred list.

Child barred list

2.2.46   Eligibility for a child barred list check requires the applicant's job role to be in regulated activity with children. A role is considered to be in regulated activity with a child if the employee meets any of the criteria in the current definition of regulated activity with children.

Disqualification

2.2.47   Under government regulation, all teachers and support staff, and those who supervise activities out of school hours with students up to the age of eight, such as childminders and nursery staff, can be disqualified from their employment if they have committed a serious violent or sexual crime, or have been banned from working with children.

2.2.48   Staff within this category can be asked to go through the process of declaring this information.

2.2.49   Where a staff member is affected, they may be suspended and will need to apply to have the disqualification waived. Anyone who is disqualified (or disqualified by nature of association) should not be employed. In these cases, it is understandable that the employer should suspend them until the waiver is granted. Making a decision to employ a person who has been disqualified is an offence.

Procedures Across the UK

2.2.50   The procedures already outlined are as set out by the DBS and apply in **England and Wales**.

2.2.51   In **Northern Ireland, AccessNI** provides the information required to consider a person's suitability for a post working with children and vulnerable adults. It will issue the necessary DBS information.

2.2.52   In **Scotland**, the **Protecting Vulnerable Groups (PVG) Scheme**, managed by Disclosure Scotland, makes decisions about who is barred from working with children.

2.2.53   For further information please visit the CPSU website (www.thecpsu.org.uk). This unit was founded in 2001 to work with the UK Sports Councils, governing bodies of sport, Active Partnerships (previously known as county sport partnerships) and other organisations to help them minimise the risk of child abuse during sporting activities.

2.2.54   In Scotland, there is a similar partnership between Children 1st (www.Children1st.org.uk) and **sport**scotland (www.sportscotland.org.uk).

Safeguarding Considerations when Planning for Students to Stay with Host Families – Sporting Events or Tours Abroad

2.2.55   The most significant distinction between exchange visits and other educational/off-site visits is that children will spend most of their time with host families and are not, therefore, under the direct supervision of teachers, staff or accompanying adults. Parents must be made fully aware that teachers and accompanying adults will therefore not always be in a position to exercise the same degree of supervision that they would on other educational/off-site visits.

2.2.56   It should also be clearly explained to parents that children will be very much part of the exchange family and, as such, they are likely to be invited to join in any activities that the family undertakes. These might include skiing, cycling, swimming, horse riding or adventurous activities. The school has limited control over the manner in which any such activities might be undertaken, and parents should clearly understand this.

2.2.57   The importance of careful selection of host families cannot be overstated. This will normally be the responsibility of the host school or perhaps a placing agency.

2.2.58   The host school or placing agency should be asked to confirm what steps they have taken to confirm the suitability of host families, with a view to ensuring the welfare of children who are to be placed with those families.

2.2.59   It should be clearly established whether criminal background or other checks can be undertaken. Parents should be advised of the extent and limits of any vetting procedures and should also be made aware that overseas host families are not subject to English law.

2.2.60   Where an English school is acting as the host, there are certain safeguarding requirements that must be considered. If the school directly places visiting children with host families then the school bears responsibility for ensuring, as far as is reasonably possible, that the host family will provide a safe and suitable home.

2.2.61   As part of that responsibility, the school must carry out an enhanced DBS check and a children's barred list check on the adults who are to provide care for the visiting children/young people. Such checks must be carried out in respect of every host family in such circumstances in line with the statutory guidance – DfE (2019) **"Keeping children safe in education: for schools and colleges (DfE) Annex E: Host families – homestay during exchange"**. https://www.gov.uk/government/publications/keeping-children-safe-in-education--2

The Outdoor Education Advisers' Panel National Guidance information provides further supporting documents on exchange visits and homestays: https://oeapng. info/3689-exchange-visits-and-homestays/

Safeguarding Considerations when Planning for Students to Stay with Host Families – Residential Events in the UK

2.2.62   Procedures should be the same as existing in-school arrangements, and minimum operating standards should be applied in the same way. If a central residential venue is used, then accreditation, safeguarding policies, procedures and good-practice guidance should be in place, but it is wise never to make assumptions.

2.2.63   The vetting of host families in the UK is mandatory. If the school is responsible for making the arrangement, and the host family is being paid, then the school can be seen as the regulated activity provider. Such a provider would be committing an offence if it knowingly allowed a person to carry out a regulated activity while barred.

2.2.64   Even where the family was not being paid, the school must carry out an enhanced DBS check and a children's barred list check on the adults who are hosting students and therefore providing care for the children/young people.

Use of Supplements in Physical Education, School Sport and Physical Activity

2.2.65   In recent years, the use of sports supplements by young athletes has increased dramatically. In the past, their use may have been focused on talented sports students. However, today, overt, widespread advertising has made these products obtainable, and appear more desirable for many young people.

2.2.66   The use of sports supplements should **never be recommended** to students by school staff.

2.2.67   Claims are made that the variety of chemicals in these products, such as minerals, vitamins, caffeine, creatine and glutamine, promote body development and, subsequently, enhance sports performance.

2.2.68   While the risks associated with taking vitamin supplements are relatively low, there is some concern that young athletes may then progress to taking more dangerous substances under the impression that they are as harmless as vitamins and minerals. However, overdose with vitamins and minerals cannot be ruled out, and some vitamins can be toxic when taken in vast quantities (such as iron and vitamin A) and may interact with other vitamins or drugs.

2.2.69   Sports supplements have not yet been tested on young people. Studies on adults indicate that many supplements provide no benefit to physical capacity or performance. As supplements are not classified as drugs, there is no regulation in their manufacture, often resulting in contamination with other chemicals, such as banned substances, during the manufacturing process. In addition, there are no formal guidelines for dosage so there could be adverse side effects if too much is inadvertently taken.

2.2.70   Protein powders are a commonly used supplement in the form of shakes, bars and capsules, and claim to promote muscle growth, and aid metabolism, hence assisting with weight loss. Again, these are **not recommended for young people** due to the lack of research into their long-term effects.

2.2.71   Where staff are asked about the use of sports supplements, or they become concerned that students may be putting themselves at risk through the use of such substances, they should provide students with clear information:

- There is no clinical evidence that a young person who already eats a healthy, well balanced diet comprising plenty of fruit and vegetables, and keeps hydrated before, during and after exercise will improve their physical capacity or performance further by taking supplements.
- If used alongside a healthy diet, supplements will be excreted by the body as being "surplus to requirements".
- Supplements can place young people at risk and cause serious health problems.
- Higher risk supplements have been found in some products – these include androstenedione and other "prohormone" precursors of testosterone, yohimbine and products containing cava. Tests on the effects of these products on the body have shown evidence of:
  - headaches
  - hair loss
  - raised cholesterol
  - stress on the liver
  - high blood pressure
  - heart palpitations
  - hallucinations.

Anti-doping

2.2.72   UK Anti-Doping (UKAD) – www.ukad.org.uk – provides information for schools, parents and sporting bodies to promote "clean sport" and to help athletes comply with the world anti-doping code.

2.2.73   UKAD has an accreditation process for schools that involves training for staff and students to promote a "clean" approach to competition, and discourage the use of banned substances. Areas such as nutrition, physiotherapy and strength and conditioning are also covered, with the aim of educating potential "athletes" early in their sporting careers.

 For more information, visit www.ukad.org.uk/support/clean-sport-accreditation

A Checklist for Safeguarding Issues within a Physical Education, School Sport and Physical Activity Context

Table 5: Checklist for safeguarding issues within a PESSPA context

Indicators of Effective Safeguarding	
Students:	
• feel knowledgeable, comfortable and confident in PESSPA (ie caring ethos, safeguarding context and staff relationships)	
• are appropriately matched (eg in terms of group/team sizes, match ability, physical size, age, maturation)	
• are given consideration in specific situations as to whether they are likely to feel intimidated, threatened or harmed by others during activity	
• are given opportunities to lead aspects of PESSPA sessions	
• wear clothing and footwear appropriate for the activity and conditions	
• remove/make safe jewellery and other personal effects	
• have access to personal protective equipment (PPE) that is adequate for activity demands	
• with cognitive, visual, hearing or motor impairment can access and be involved in PESSPA in line with requirements of the Equality Act	
• with English as an additional language (EAL) are supported to understand safety procedures	
• are knowledgeable about procedures and routines.	
Staff:	
• recruitment procedures are safe and followed for all PESSPA appointments	
• competence to teach activity to the level of student ability is checked and monitored	
• requirement for a licence to coach (this is a requirement of some governing bodies of sport/local authorities) is checked before employment commences	
• observation and analysis skills are effective to ensure safe practice	
• control, discipline and organisational skills are adequate	
• project a positive, encouraging, educational manner	
• establish appropriate relationships with, and respect for, students (and any other adults) who are teaching, training or instructing the same group of students, unsupervised frequently. (This could be once a week or more often, or on four or more days in a 30-day period or overnight, ie in regulated activity)	
• have an enhanced DBS disclosure and a barring check confirmed and accepted by the school	

• who are constantly supervised (not in regulated activity) have an enhanced disclosure accepted by the school if the school has decided to request one	
• satisfy all disqualification checks	
• who are coaches need to be thoroughly vetted before starting work in schools to ensure they are not barred from working with children and young people	
• delivering PESSPA should remove/make safe their jewellery and personal effects	
• professional learning needs are identified and supported with regular training	
• know and consistently apply school procedures to deal with observation or disclosure of possible abuse	
• always supervise young sports leaders	
• avoid one-to-one situations with students wherever possible	
• should know which member of the senior staff has designated safeguarding responsibility.	
Protecting children from deliberate harm:	
• School safeguarding procedures adequately address PESSPA situations.	
• School procedures and codes of conduct are known and consistently applied by all staff and students.	
• Checks are made with all club links/outdoor activity centres/other organisations that are used by the school/signposted to students, and their protocols are known and monitored.	
• Staff have good awareness of contexts and opportunities in PESSPA and sports trips for bullying/racist incidents (including cyberbullying) and monitor these closely.	
• General and PESSPA-specific indicators of neglect, and physical, emotional and sexual abuse are known and regularly monitored by all staff.	
• Staff responses to disclosure of abusive experiences/knowledge are consistent with school reporting policy.	
Medical conditions:	
• Staff know that administration of medicines is a voluntary activity that cannot be enforced.	
• Parents are asked for relevant medical information about their child.	
• Relevant medical information about students is known by the school, regularly updated, and always communicated to the class teacher and other adults teaching the student.	
• PESSPA-related individual education, health and care plans (EHCPs) are in place, where appropriate.	
• Student medications are available to use in different PESSPA locations.	
• School policy on removal/wearing of medical bracelets is known and applied.	
• School policy on medication management is followed.	

• Staff are trained in specific medical situations as necessary (eg administering EpiPens).	
• School-parent agreements on administration of medicines are checked and applied to individuals.	
First aid provision: Provision for first aid must be available at all times for employees, and within a school situation, it is accepted that students are also included in such provision. Appropriate provision comprises:	
• clear, detailed and effective school procedures for managing first aid/emergency situations	
• staff who know and apply these school procedures	
• strategies to address time implications to respond to illness/injury at extremes of the school site	
• an effective emergency contact system	
• a travelling first aid kit being taken on all off-site visits	
• a trained first-aider or appointed person accompanying any group going off the school site, or alternative arrangements	
• agreed reciprocal arrangements for use of the host school's first aid provision, equipment and facilities when injury occurs at away fixtures/off-site events	
• keeping injury records according to school procedures	
• knowing and monitoring recovery and return procedures following concussion	
• discussion of near misses to improve safety standards	
• following school procedures for informing parents and keeping in touch regarding the student's recovery	
• making community users aware of limitations of first aid provision by the school.	
Digital technology:	
• School policy and strategy on Internet safety are applied consistently in PESSPA.	
• All PESSPA staff are trained in Internet safety.	
• Students are reminded about Internet safety during PESSPA sessions and must be safeguarded from potentially harmful and inappropriate online material.	
• A school policy on staff contacting students by phone, email or text is known and applied by all.	
• Parents are involved in any electronic communication about fixtures/visit arrangements, and only via a disclosed list.	
• Photography and filming are used only within a clear learning context, and parents are made aware of such use within school policy.	
• Procedures and protocols to ensure ethics and security of digital imagery are known by all PESSPA staff, applied consistently and communicated to parents.	
• Access to images held by the school is controlled by a password/authentication process.	
• Clear procedures and agreement exist about when and where it is appropriate to use imagery across groups of schools.	

• Staff apply general safeguarding considerations in use of imagery (eg students cannot be identified, consideration of filming angles, general shots, particular care in swimming and gymnastics contexts).	
• School policy is applied on parental consent for digital imagery in education contexts.	
School/department security:	
• All adults involved in the PESSPA programme wear identification and/or are known to students.	
• Facilities not in use are locked, wherever possible, to prevent unauthorised access.	
• Facilities are checked before locking to ensure that nobody is locked in.	
• High risk equipment is disabled/locked, or where preventing access cannot be assured, prohibition signs are in place to prevent unauthorised use.	
• Equipment and facilities are checked periodically for continued safe use.	
• Routes to outside areas are safe and lit at night.	
Drug and substance misuse:	
• Staff are trained in recognising symptoms of drug misuse.	
• School strategies to identify and support students with drug problems are known and applied.	
• Club links are checked for inclusion of anti-doping education and strict application of policies in written and practical procedures.	
• Implications of doping to enhance performance are communicated to students and monitored by staff.	
• School policy on advising about sports supplements is followed.	
Transporting students:	
• School/employer policies on the use of cars, taxis, coaches and minibuses are clear for PESSPA activities.	
• Seat belts are always worn in any vehicle where belts are provided.	
• Child restraints are made available and used where required.	
• The roadworthiness of any vehicle used is checked.	
• Appropriate and current documentation (eg insurance, MOT) is in place.	
• Any driver has DBS clearance that has been checked and approved by the school/local authority.	
• No adult travels alone in any vehicle with an individual student other than their own children, unless required to do so in an emergency.	
• Emergency contact information is either carried by the group leader or held at school, with access ensured at any time.	
• Safe embarkation/disembarkation points are identified and used.	

• There are no distractions for the driver of any vehicle other than in an emergency.	
• Adult supervision ratios are considered pre-journey.	
• Reciprocal arrangements are in place. (Through such an arrangement, the host school would agree to supervise students from a visiting school should an emergency require the supervising teacher from the visiting school to accompany a student to hospital. Another member of staff would be called from the visiting school to go to the host school to take over this supervision.)	
• Accredited/well-known taxi, bus and coach companies are used.	
• Parents are informed if their child is to be transported in another parent's car arranged by the school, and their agreement is obtained.	
• A section 19 standard permit is displayed in the minibus if any form of charge is made by the school.	
• School/employer requirements for driving a minibus are fully met.	
• A minibus driver's legal responsibilities are known and met.	
• The school system for management of minibuses is compliant, effective and ensures safe use.	
• Trailer towing regulations are met.	
• Passenger access/exit is unobstructed when luggage/equipment is carried.	
Health and safety:	
• Good teaching standards are applied.	
• There is good organisation (management) of lessons by the teacher and of the subject by the physical education subject leader.	
• Consistent safety standards are applied across the team of staff delivering the PESSPA programme.	
• School policy, procedures and standards are applied in PESSPA.	
• Written risk assessments and documentation, specific to the school, are reasonably comprehensive and reviewed regularly.	
• All necessary health and safety management documents are accessible to all staff.	
• Students are involved in their own safety at a level compatible with their age, understanding and ability.	
• Potentially hazardous PESSPA equipment (eg trampolines, climbing/traverse walls, resistance equipment, swimming pools) is used safely.	
Use of appropriate physical intervention and support:	
• Exercise is not used as punishment.	
• Stage/age/physical size/experience is matched in contact sports and in dance/gymnastics when lifting/supporting others' weight.	

• No adult participates fully in contact sports, weight-bearing activities or PESSPA activities that involve "accelerating projectiles".	
• Students are informed about how manual support will be given (eg in dance or gymnastics). Manual support is provided using only appropriate techniques, and only when student consent has been given.	
• Spotters in trampolining are well trained, effective and limited in number.	
Overplaying and overtraining:	
• Staff demonstrate awareness of governing body of sport requirements/guidance in this area.	
• Careful consideration is made about the size of court/pitch/hall and type of equipment appropriate for each group of students.	
• Students/teams are matched in terms of comparable age, standard, ability and confidence in early stages of competition.	
• Fixtures are stopped if a significant imbalance in size, age, ability or capability of students is observed.	
• Fixtures are rearranged to reflect better balance and matching of participants.	
• The appropriateness of activities is considered where boys and girls compete or take part together in fixtures or competition.	
• Programming and scheduling ensure that students' participation is not more than one full sports fixture in any given day, or in cases where a student participates in more than one game, their match preparation and training, and levels of fitness and skill are considered appropriate to ensure safe participation.	
Intimate care issues within PESSPA:	
• School policy addresses the PESSPA context adequately.	
• Staff are trained and assessed as competent (eg at manual handling, administration of specific medicines).	
• Gender staffing implications are considered where intimate care applies.	
• Dignity, decency and respect are consistently evident.	
Responding to weather conditions:	
• Measures to reduce overexposure to sun/heat are effective.	
• Rehydration systems are in place.	
• Staff teaching position avoids students looking directly into the sun.	
• Appropriate additional clothing is allowed in cold conditions.	
• Security of footing on playing surfaces is considered.	
• Students are taught a safe response if caught in a sudden thunderstorm.	

Section 3: Special Educational Needs and Disabilities

Student Entitlement

2.3.1   There is widespread agreement that physical activity brings benefits to all who participate, including significant and long-lasting gains to psychomotor and sensory development, physical health, emotional well-being, and social integration for students with special educational needs and disabilities (SEND).

2.3.2   The **Equality Act 2010** makes clear that schools must make reasonable adjustments for students with disabilities, or for an aspect of their disability, that enable them to access as full a programme of education, including physical education, as possible. Examples might be:

- supplying auxiliary aids and services
- providing additional support staff
- ensuring that changing facilities are suitable.

2.3.3   In addition, for students with SEND, organisations must have regard to the Department for Education (DfE) code of practice.

 To access the code of practice, see https://goo.gl/DhDcS7

2.3.4   The Equality Act 2010 defines a disability as "a physical or mental impairment which has a long-term and substantial adverse effect on their (the person's) ability to carry out normal day-to-day activities". Many students who have SEND may have a disability according to this definition. "Long-term" is "a year or more", and "substantial" is "more than minor or trivial".

2.3.5   Sensory impairments such as those that affect sight or hearing, and long-term health conditions such as asthma, diabetes, epilepsy and cancer, are all included in this definition. Students with these conditions do not necessarily have SEND, but the overlap between disabled students and those with SEND is significant. Where a disabled student requires special educational provision, they will be covered by the SEND definition.

(Summarised from DfE/Department of Health (2015) "Special educational needs and disability code of practice: 0 to 25 years", https://goo.gl/DhDcS7)

Education, Health and Care Plan

2.3.6   **Table 6: Supporting students with SEND and medical conditions in PESSPA, pages 70-76**, details a number of specific conditions that students might present, and is designed to support safe inclusive practice within a physical education, school sport and physical activity (PESSPA) programme. There are, however, a number of generic safety considerations that apply regardless of the specific disability or special educational need. This information should be shared with, and understood by, all who contribute to the PESSPA programme.

2.3.7   In all cases and for all conditions, specialist advice, guidance and support should be sought to help plan and develop an **individual education, health and care plan (EHCP)**. The plan should consider what would help the individual to access PESSPA within the curriculum and as part of an extracurricular programme, and might cover issues such as:

- personal health care equipment (eg inhalers, syringes, incontinence pads)
- body splints and aids (eg orthoses, stability footwear)
- valves and shunts
- administration of drugs and treatments
- mobility aids
- daily living aids (eg hoists)
- frequency and duration of professional input
- contraindicated activity for their condition.

2.3.8   The student and their parents are key in developing such a plan alongside teachers, support staff, physiotherapists and medical staff. The outcomes of the plan should focus on ability, ie what the student can do, and would like to be enabled to do, rather than the disability/medical condition. An important part of an EHCP is ensuring that it can be actioned safely. This involves carrying out **risk assessments** that consider the extent to which the activity in question is safe, appropriate and accessible for the individual student. A PESSPA risk assessment should consider whether:

- the activity needs to be modified or adapted (eg in terms of space or equipment) to meet the specific needs/medical condition of the student
- the facility or environment where the activity will take place is suitable (eg if the acoustics and lighting are suitable for the student, the surfaces are sufficiently stable and even, there is suitable access for wheelchair users, there are sufficient accessible emergency exits, if the environment is too "busy and noisy" and likely to cause stress)
- the safety of other participants can be maintained
- any support person is able to manage the student's individual needs, understands their role and is able to fulfil it (eg if they are supporting a student for swimming, they are water confident)
- external staff brought in to deliver parts of the PESSPA programme (eg sports coaches) are working under the direction of a teacher, and have been made fully aware of the needs of the student; the external staff member needs to have the necessary competences required to work with the student in question
- specific evacuation procedures for the student, in the case of an emergency, are safe and dignified.

2.3.9   In the case of **wheelchair users**, consideration needs to be given to whether it is possible and safe for the individual to take a full part in PESSPA situations that involve mixed groups of non-disabled and disabled students. The student should be consulted about how safe they feel. A risk assessment should be carried out to establish the normal routines for the class to ensure the safety of both wheelchair users and ambulant students. This would include consideration of the stability of wheelchairs in activities, who should push a wheelchair, and particular conditions during activities (eg placement of equipment used). Where an activity is obviously not suited to, or safe for, participation in a wheelchair (eg rugby on the field), discuss with the student what alternative activity they might want to do.

Enabling Safe Participation and Inclusion

2.3.10   While students may have the same disability or condition, their abilities will vary, as will their needs. To enable suitable and safe participation, and provide optimum and appropriate inclusion, staff should:

- establish individual students' aspirations within PESSPA
- have some knowledge of their specific learning difficulty, disability, medical condition, or emotional or social difficulties
- fully understand how an individual's condition affects them
- be aware of any constraints on physical activities as a result of the learning difficulty, disability, medical condition, or emotional or behavioural difficulties, or as a result of any medication/ treatment the student might be taking
- be able to provide any necessary emergency treatment/action if physical activities exacerbate the learning difficulty, disability, medical condition, or social or emotional difficulties
- be aware of any personal and family background knowledge about the student that might be significant
- be confident in their approach to teaching students with SEND
- have the knowledge, techniques and strategies necessary for safe teaching
- notice when a student's condition deteriorates by being alert to changes in their ability, attitude, levels of stamina, or how quickly they fatigue
- be able to adapt tasks, or know when to suggest that the student takes a break, or when the student requires additional support or medical input.

2.3.11   Failure to properly address a student's needs may lead to their not being able to complete tasks, a perception of failure, frustration and despondency, and in some cases, disruptive behaviour, which may present risks to the student and others.

2.3.12   In some activities, it is helpful to operate a "buddy system", in which a student "looks out" for a partner with SEND/a medical condition with regard to their requirements for any additional help. A buddy can also be used to inform/alert staff about any concerns associated with the particular student's condition during activity. This system is often operated in swimming activities, but can be applied as a useful safety measure in other PESSPA activities.

2.3.13   Where appropriate, and after consultation with the student, some details of their SEND/medical condition could be shared with other class members so that they understand and respect the individual's needs. This will also make other students aware of any measures they can take to promote a safe environment for the student and themselves (eg to be aware of how to respond if a student experiences a seizure, to make eye contact before speaking to a person with a hearing impairment).

2.3.14   **Teaching styles and tasks** should be varied according to need, and staff should be able to **adapt as required**, using a range of inclusive methods, as well as recognising when specific students may need to be set separate activities, or when the task set is not suitable or safe. Possible examples might include the following:

- A wheelchair user who lacks the strength or coordination to keep up with a fast-paced game of basketball may benefit more from a parallel activity with fewer players and adapted equipment.
- An ambulant student with cerebral palsy affecting one side of their body only (hemiplegia) may enjoy and be more successful playing in a small 3v3 situation rather than a full game.
- A student with autism and hypersensitivity to visual and auditory stimuli may become dysregulated and overly anxious when surrounded by an entire class playing dodgeball. A smaller-sided game may be more enjoyable and enable more learning to take place.

2.3.15   Students with **sensory processing issues**, including many with autistic spectrum conditions, may experience difficulties when sensory stimuli become too much to tolerate (eg a busy swimming pool, the acoustics in a sports hall, a muddy field with wet equipment). An appreciation of these difficulties combined with a flexible and graduated small-step approach, and breaks when necessary, can help to encourage and build up these students' levels of participation.

2.3.16   Students with social, emotional and mental health (SEMH) difficulties may experience a wide range of such conditions that manifest themselves in many ways. These students' behaviours may reflect **hidden disabilities** and may include becoming withdrawn or isolated, as well as displaying challenging, disruptive or disturbing behaviour. The underlying mental health difficulties might include anxiety or depression, self-harm, substance misuse, eating disorders or physical symptoms that are medically unexplained. Other students may have conditions such as attention deficit disorder, attention deficit hyperactivity disorder or attachment disorder.

2.3.17   Certain activities, particularly team sports involving contact, are not suitable for some students with **poor mobility**, or conditions that make bones brittle or limbs prone to injury. Staff should discuss with these students safer alternatives that they would like to develop, and build steady progression, challenge and appropriate supervision of these alternative activities into their planning. Wherever possible and practical, such alternative activities might link with those being undertaken by the student outside the school setting.

2.3.18   All students should be provided with equal opportunities to participate in a curriculum where there are **no barriers to access**. Physical education lessons should aim to provide high quality experiences that challenge all students. Every student must have equal access to PESSPA.

2.3.19   Learning experiences should be **differentiated** to meet the **specific needs of individuals and groups of students**, including those who have diverse SEND. Lesson planning, delivery and assessment should aim to ensure that students are provided with appropriate and effective opportunities to actively participate and succeed in the whole range of learning opportunities offered within and outside the curriculum.

2.3.20   Ongoing positive feedback and reward will be necessary to keep students on task. Developing confidence is fundamental to helping students achieve success, especially if they may become frustrated with some of the challenges they experience, or where they feel overwhelmed by what is expected of them. **Frustrations and challenges** can lead to disruptive behaviour in specific students. However, as self-esteem grows through increased success, disruptive behaviour generally reduces, and this is an **important safe management consideration**.

2.3.21   In many cases, safety can be improved by providing a range of **adapted equipment** (eg yellow balls with bells or buzzers for visually impaired students; balls of different textures, sizes and pace for those with motor skills difficulties; sticks, bats and rackets with shorter handles to aid control).

2.3.22   It is not always possible to pre-empt the effects of external experiences that students bring to a lesson. Historical life traumas, or simply a problem that has arisen in a previous session that day, can have a bearing on a student's state of mind and their ability/willingness to adopt a safe approach to learning. Staff need to be aware of, and sensitive to, the different situations students face and take these into account, as far as possible, in their efforts to create a calm and encouraging environment.

2.3.23   Some students develop **coping strategies**. An example could be time spent watching other students before starting the activity or being last "in the queue", thereby allowing them time to assess what is required of them. Such strategies should be recognised and tolerated by staff, rather than putting pressure on the student to become involved at a pace that is not suitable for them.

2.3.24   More apparent physical concerns may cause a student to be reluctant to take part. For example, the presence of a skin condition such as psoriasis or eczema may result in a lack in confidence and/or unwillingness to change for activity in front of others; students who are overweight or obese may feel self-conscious and embarrassed with their peers. **A consistent approach** that recognises and adapts to individuals' concerns will help to maintain an appropriate and positive climate to support students' full participation in PESSPA activities.

2.3.25   Specific guidance follows, outlining activities that are often used to support students to engage in PESSPA.

Working on trampolines with students with SEND

2.3.26   Trampolining, trampoline therapy and rebound therapy are names given to activities using a trampoline bed that can provide **stimulus and therapeutic benefit** for students with a range of SEND. These activities can help to promote balance, movement, fitness, sensory awareness, communication and relaxation.

2.3.27   These forms of therapy do not constitute trampolining, and the usual qualification requirements for staff teaching trampolining would not apply. However, teachers should be **trained in the particular therapeutic discipline**, particularly when they share the trampoline bed with the student to adjust the effect of weight and speed for control between movements. Staff should also be fully up to date with relevant procedures such as the safe assembly and folding of the trampoline.

2.3.28   The teacher or therapist should assess the need for **safety matting and end decks** when working with non-ambulant students and also those with erratic or impulsive behaviours. Similarly, they should consider whether or not the potential benefit of floor mats would be outweighed by the tripping hazard, and the restriction of access for mobile hoists and wheelchairs.

2.3.29   Very careful risk assessments should be carried out before introducing any students with SEND to any kind of activity using a trampoline. Certain individual students with SEND may be considered able to progress from therapeutic activities to developing recognised trampoline skills. This will also require careful risk assessments and the lead adult delivering the session to have the appropriate trampolining qualifications.

Website link

Rebound therapy: www.reboundtherapy.org
Winstrada: www.winstrada.com

Aquatic activities

2.3.30   Warm water pools, sometimes located in special schools or alternatively in venues such as hotels or leisure providers, provide opportunities for students to exercise in warm water. This is of particular benefit to students with a variety of physical difficulties.

2.3.31   The adult:student ratio should not be determined in accordance with any swimming-specific written guidelines that may exist. A safe ratio can only be determined by carefully examining individual students' abilities, medical profiles and EHCPs in conjunction with relevant medical staff. For example, specialist knowledge and care is required when planning for students who are nil-by-mouth or require thickened drinks. These students should never take any pool water into their mouths due to the risk of secondary drowning.

2.3.32   These activity programmes usually involve multidisciplinary **teaching** by a group of professionals; for example, this might include the class or swimming teacher, learning support/care assistants and a physiotherapist.

2.3.33   Warm water pools tend to be shallow in depth and small in size. It is not always considered necessary for a lifeguard to be present on the side, although this is good practice. There should, however, be a **pool watcher**, as an additional adult present on the poolside, whose sole duty is to observe all pool activities and draw attention to any problems developing in the water.

2.3.34   One person qualified in lifesaving, and therefore able to prevent and respond to a swimming pool incident/emergency with aquatic rescue skills, and perform cardiopulmonary resuscitation (CPR) and first aid should also be present to provide general supervision. Depending on the particular circumstances of the student, a specialist swimming teacher may also be involved in the session.

2.3.35   All staff involved in warm water pool sessions need to be confident and competent to complete any water-based rescue that may be necessary, and should complete regular training to ensure this. Supervision must be provided in accordance with the pool Normal Operating Procedure (NOP) as identified in the Pool Safety Operating Procedure (PSOP).

2.3.36   Staff working closely with individual students in the water will also need to be appropriately trained, and have handling expertise and sufficient knowledge of each individual student's physical and medical needs.

2.3.37   As the pool will be used by students with complex physical difficulties, particular attention should be given to the development of risk-management schemes for:

- moving and handling, which includes all aspects of lifting and carrying of students or transfers between equipment, such as in and out of wheelchairs
- transporting students between the changing rooms and the pool
- entry to and exit from the pool
- dressing/undressing areas and support staff
- emergency equipment and procedures.

2.3.38   Due to the water temperature, it is imperative that regular maintenance of the plant and filtration and sterilisation systems, and a comprehensive programme of water testing are carried out to ensure the safe use of warm water pools.

2.3.39   Further information about working with students with SEND in special needs school pools and swimming pools can be accessed through the links that follow.

Website links

Swim England: www.swimming.org/swimengland

Swimming Teachers' Association (STA): www.sta.co.uk

Halliwick: www.halliwick.org

Managing Students with SEND and Medical Conditions in PESSPA

2.3.40   The points discussed previously in this section should be considered when working with any student with SEND or a specific medical condition. The table that follows provides more specific information and guidance for staff about a number of SEND and medical conditions. The information provided in the table should be used in conjunction with the recommended websites.

Table 6: Supporting students with SEND and medical conditions in PESSPA

Condition	What Do Staff Need to Know?	Advice for Staff Teaching and Supporting PESSPA
Asthma www.asthma.org.uk	• Very common condition affecting many children, caused by a combination of genetic and environmental factors. • Can be triggered by viral infections, allergens (eg dust mites), irritants (eg air pollutants) and the onset of exercise in some instances. • Symptoms include coughing, wheezing, shortness of breath, tight chest. • Mild attack: the student should sit, try to relax, breathe out, and use an inhaler if required. • Severe attack: access prompt medical support. • Exercise is generally beneficial for children with asthma, leading to improved cardiorespiratory fitness and reduced breathlessness at a given exercise intensity.	• Ensure that their inhaler (and spacer) is immediately available when exercising. • Encourage them to use their inhaler (reliever) approximately five minutes prior to warm-up if exercise usually triggers asthma. • Ensure that they warm-up and cool-down thoroughly; this should last at least 10 minutes. • Increase intensity of physical activity gradually. • Discourage participation in physical activity when the air is affected by known trigger elements (eg grass cutting pollens, dust, pollutants such as cigarette smoke, car exhaust fumes, changes in temperature). • Allow them to stop exercising if symptoms occur, and use the reliever inhaler to ease the symptoms until they are ready to resume.
Attention deficit hyperactivity disorder (ADHD) www.addiss.co.uk	• Children with ADHD find it difficult to concentrate and remember instructions. • This can be hard for a student with ADHD to control their impulsivity. • In some cases, medication is used to help students focus.	• Provide and repeat clear, easy-to-follow instructions. • Reinforce desirable behaviours rather than focusing on what is undesirable. • Reward and encourage achievement to retain focus. • Be consistent in approach. • Risk assess activities to ensure that they can be safely managed by staff and students.
Autism/autistic spectrum disorder (ASD)/Asperger's syndrome www.autism.org.uk www.autismeducationtrust.org.uk www.afpe.org.uk for hyposensitivity	• Students display a range of symptoms dependent on where their condition sits within the spectrum. • Those with Asperger's syndrome or high-functioning autism may appear eloquent but still have some of the other difficulties associated with autism. • Those with very mild conditions may not be diagnosed. • Many have difficulty processing everyday sensory information such as sounds, sights, and smells, and will display an oversensitive (hyper) and/or under-sensitive (hypo) reaction to these. Noisy and crowded conditions may therefore cause anxiety. • Unusual sensory-related behaviours that are self-regulatory may also occur. • Some may find interaction and conversation with others difficult, interpreting jokes or sarcasm literally (eg if they were told to "pull their socks up" as an instruction to work harder, they would interpret this in its literal sense). • Collaborative activities with a partner or team may place huge social demands on them. • They like routine and order, and may find change unsettling. • Understanding and appreciating rules, and in particular the complexities of team games, can be very challenging.	• Speak clearly, and allow time for instructions and expectations to be understood. • Prepare students if manual support is required in PESSPA activities – some students are intolerant to touch. • Encourage, and give both verbal and visual prompts. • Prepare students thoroughly for the activity they will be doing by showing photographs, video and demonstrations, and sharing plans. • Be mindful that they might react adversely to noise and multiple activities (eg if sharing a sports hall space, in a busy swimming pool environment or using loud music, they might find it difficult to filter out noise that others would be able to ignore). • Sensory issues will be unique to every individual. They may include difficulties with specific clothing, equipment or the environment. A dialogue with the individual about their sensory issues can help to provide appropriate and safe solutions. • Opportunities to practise a skill individually may provide a welcome relief from social demands. • Be prepared to provide support with spatial awareness if this is needed. • Allow or plan for breaks if sensory or social demands become too much.

Condition	What Do Staff Need to Know?	Advice for Staff Teaching and Supporting PESSPA
Brittle bones www.brittlebone.org	• A condition brought on by lack of collagen – a protein within parts of the body, including the bones, that provides structure and strength. • Bones are prone to fractures.	• Make staff and other students aware of the situation. • Develop a clear understanding of the extent of the condition. • Plan activities that reduce the risk of injury while still enabling activity (eg individual activities rather than activities in large groups or zoned areas with parallel activities).
Cerebral palsy www.scope.org.uk	• Caused by damage to, or failure in the development of, the motor areas of the brain before or during birth, or in the first few years of life. • The number of limbs or amount of the body affected varies (eg one side of the body – hemiplegia, one limb only – monoplegia, two limbs – diplegia, three limbs – triplegia). • May be affected in one or a combination of ways: **Spasticity:** – Increased muscle tone, resulting in restricted movement. – Sudden movements extending the back and neck. – Swallowing and speech difficulties. – In some cases, cognitive development is affected. **Athetoid:** – Involuntary movements and uncontrolled motion. – Speech, hearing and sight may be impaired. **Ataxic:** – Movements are slow and awkward. – Lack of directional control and balance may result in falls.	• Develop a clear understanding of the range of conditions. • Check for understanding of instructions, use demonstration where helpful. • Work with specialists to assess the specific needs of each student, and plan activity accordingly. Physiotherapists will advise on any specific movements or stretches that are to be encouraged or discouraged. • Ensure other students are mindful of space required for wheelchairs or other mobility aids where used. • Allow sufficient time for movement about the area. • Appreciate that the effort required to concentrate and execute any movement will be great and therefore tiring.
Congenital heart conditions www.chfed.org.uk www.bhf.org.uk/heart-healthy/heart	• These are conditions that some children are born with. • There are a range of different conditions. Some never require treatment, others have no cure. • A range of symptoms might be seen, including unexplained breathlessness, tiredness, palpitations, dizziness, fainting or collapsing. • Common medications include diuretics (to reduce excess fluid), anticoagulants (to prevent the blood clotting) and anti-arrhythmic medicine (to control the rhythm of the heart). • Regular physical activity can improve the function of the heart and circulation.	• PESSPA lessons should be adapted to allow students to take part at their own level and pace (eg lower intensity, longer rests). • Students should be encouraged to work to a level where they can feel warm and slightly "out of puff", but can still talk. If they become too breathless to talk, they need to slow down or stop and rest. • The warm-up and cool-down are very important and should be sufficiently long to allow for gradual increase in heart rate and breathing. • Appropriate intensity of dynamic activity (eg walking, running, swimming, dancing) is more suitable than static (isometric) activity – where the pressure is loaded on the heart, and there is a sudden rise in systolic blood pressure, which can be difficult to control. For this reason, static exercises and stretching should also be avoided.

Condition	What Do Staff Need to Know?	Advice for Staff Teaching and Supporting PESSPA
Cystic fibrosis (CF) www.cysticfibrosis.org.uk	• An inherited condition where glands in the body (primarily the pancreas) secrete excessive mucus, leading to blockages, which can prevent food being broken down and absorbed. • Sweating can produce additional mucus in hot weather and after exercise. • Lungs needs to be kept clear and physical activity monitored. • Participation in physical activity is very important for students with CF because it helps clear mucus from the lungs, and improves physical bulk and strength.	• Encourage students with CF to take part in as much physical activity as possible, ideally types of exercise that leave them out of breath, like running, swimming, football or tennis. • Recognise when a student with CF feels unusually tired and lacks energy after a cold or chest infection, to which they are prone.

Diabetes
 	
www.diabetes.org.uk
	• A condition where the amount of glucose (sugar) in the blood is too high because the body cannot use it properly due to either no insulin being produced (type 1 diabetes) or insufficient insulin being produced (type 2 diabetes).
	• In children under the age of 18, type 1 is the most common form, although the number of children affected by type 2 is increasing.
	• Children are encouraged to check their blood glucose level before taking part in physical activity. Where it is lower than recommended, they should have a snack before starting the activity.
		• Encourage physical activity as part of a planned and managed programme as it stimulates the action of the insulin by lowering blood sugar through the use of the sugar in the muscles. Managing diabetes in school is important to make sure a child with diabetes has the same education and experience at school as other students. It is important to manage their diabetes at school as well as it is managed at home, which can involve:
		  – knowing how to react to the onset of **hypo**glycaemia (when the brain is starved of glucose energy), and how to look for and identify early symptoms such as tiredness, loss of alertness, muscle strength, and coordination
		  – recognising signs of **hyper**glycaemia - students will feel ill if blood sugars are too high, and if they have type 1 diabetes, will need to test their blood sugars and, if required, their ketones to determine if they need to correct their sugars with insulin.
		• Be aware of those students who have an insulin pump, and never insist that it is removed.
		• Check that the student has the items they may need close at hand (eg blood glucose testing kit, food, glucose tablets, drinks), and allow them to use these at any time. Diabetes UK advises physical education departments to have some sugared energy drinks available, in preference to snacks, in case they are required.
		• Inform students well in advance about how long and how intense the physical activity session will be so that they can prepare by eating sufficient snacks.
		• Check that the student has carried out a blood glucose check before starting activity.
		• Build up physical activity programmes gradually.

Condition	What Do Staff Need to Know?	Advice for Staff Teaching and Supporting PESSPA
Down's syndrome (DS) www.downs-syndrome.org.uk www.british-gymnastics.org/technical-information/discipline-updates/disabilities/9316-atlanto-axial-information-pack-1/file	• Sometimes referred to as trisomy 21, due to the failure in cell division of chromosome 21, leading to the development of 47 rather than 46 chromosomes. • Every student with DS will have different needs and conditions. • Students with DS may have reduced muscle tone, heart conditions, hearing and vision difficulties, respiratory difficulties, and learning difficulties. • Students with DS may suffer from instability and potential acute dislocation of the atlanto-axial joint. They may experience pain behind the ear or in the neck. There may be a deterioration of posture, manipulative skills, or bowel and bladder control – these symptoms require specialist advice.	• Break down instructions or tasks into short, manageable chunks, and speak directly to the student to check that they have understood. • Use demonstrations, signs and gestures. • Offer frequent praise and encouragement. • Collisions should be avoided. • Jumping or diving into water is not advised. • Proceed with extreme caution when using trampolines – this activity may be high risk due to risk of damage to the atlanto-axial joint. • Specific medical advice should be obtained before gymnastic activities such as jumping from a height, forward and backward rolls and vaulting are attempted, as these activities also risk dislocation of the atlanto-axial joint. • Allow students who may have associated heart conditions to rest if they complain of tiredness.
Dyspraxia www.dyspraxiafoundation.org.uk	• Also known as developmental coordination disorder (DCD). • The condition presents as an immaturity in movement, involving "clumsy" action. • Poor balance and coordination of body parts. • Difficulty with planning and executing gross and fine motor skills. • With numerous opportunities to practise and overlearn, students with dyspraxia can develop good specific movement skills.	• Taking part in PESSPA opportunities that allow for learning of specific movement skills can be extremely beneficial for students with dyspraxia. • Allow sufficient time for them to plan their movements and provide opportunities to practise a skill over and over again. • Give clear instructions, allowing the student to position him/herself safely at each stage. They may require help with placing their hands and feet correctly. • Use cones, marker lines and spots to direct the student back to their work area. • Have a variety of equipment, such as larger bats and slower balls, available to accommodate coordination challenges. • Encourage the development of skills as an individual, rather than incorporating them into team activities. • Think about the activity surface – running on a track may be acceptable, but a rough cross-country course could be difficult.
Epilepsy www.epilepsynse.org.uk www.epilepsyresearch.org.uk www.epilepsy.org.uk	• The effects of epilepsy vary from person to person. • The condition is characterised by seizures originating in the brain as a result of excessive or disordered discharge of brain cells. • Some children may never have a seizure at school. • Participation in physical activity is dependent on each individual's condition.	• Organise a support system, such as a "buddy system". • Be aware that prolonged periods underwater, and environments with strobe or flickering lighting may cause seizures. • Be vigilant when students are working at height (eg in gymnastics or on a climbing wall). • Know how to respond if a seizure occurs. • Be aware of the need to check understanding and repeat instructions when a student's epilepsy presents as brief "absences".

Condition	What Do Staff Need to Know?	Advice for Staff Teaching and Supporting PESSPA
Foetal alcohol spectrum disorder (FASD) www.fasdtrust.co.uk www.fasdnetwork.org www.nofas-uk.org www.afpe.org.uk for hyposensitivity	• This condition occurs as a result of the mother consuming high levels of alcohol during pregnancy, which results in the development of the foetus being affected. • Physical signs around the face include low nasal bridge, short nose, thin upper lips, and minor ear abnormalities. • Symptoms may be similar to those with an autistic spectrum condition or ADHD – fine and gross motor skills tend to be poor, students find it difficult to sit still and concentrate, and there may be associated learning difficulties. • Motivation can be low, there may be the appearance of "daydreaming" or laziness. • Spatial awareness may be poor. • Either under-sensitivity (hypo) or oversensitivity (hyper) (see Autism) may be experienced in relation to any of the senses. • Students can master a task one day, and forget how to do it the next day. • Physical activity can be very beneficial for students with FASD.	• Explain tasks simply and thoroughly with key safety points. • Repeat instructions and reinforce with gestures and demonstrations for clarification. • Allow students to work at their own pace.
Haemophilia www.haemophilia.org/inhibitors	• A hereditary condition that mainly affects boys. • The blood-clotting mechanism is affected, and bleeding following a minor incident may be life-threatening, although levels vary. • By secondary school age, students generally treat themselves with a blood-clotting factor that is injected, usually into existing cannula in their veins. • Participation in PESSPA activities is encouraged as it strengthens joints and muscles, which helps to improve stability and coordination.	• Ensure that the severity of the condition is known and implications understood. • Make provision for participation in individual and small-sided or individual PESSPA activities (eg swimming, badminton). • Ensure that activities such as basketball, netball and athletics are well controlled. • Avoid involving these students in contact sports such as rugby, martial arts or boxing. • Ensure that students carry out a thorough warm-up before activity and that specific medical advice is followed and any necessary medication administered prior to physical activity. • Ensure that full PPE and, in some cases, additional protective equipment such as knee pads and wristbands are worn, when appropriate.
Hearing impairment www.actiononhearingloss.org.uk www.ndcs.org.uk www.mid.org.uk	• Conductive hearing loss is a condition often caused by a build-up of fluid, such as in glue ear, in which sounds cannot pass through the outer or middle ear. • This condition is generally temporary, and can clear up or may require surgery. • Sensorineural hearing loss is a condition caused by a problem in the inner ear or auditory nerve that may affect a person's speech and balance, and is likely to be permanent.	• Ensure that the student can clearly see the member of staff when instructions are given or demonstrations carried out. Be aware that it can be hard for a student to lip-read if the person speaking is on the move. • Establish eye contact before starting to give instructions. • If a student uses a hearing aid, they should always be encouraged to wear it during PESSPA. In some circumstances, a headband may help to secure it. • Be mindful of activities that require good balance, particularly in gymnastics and dance. • Use gestures and visual alternatives to auditory prompts, particularly in relation to a "stop" command when there is danger. • Check understanding regularly.

Condition	What Do Staff Need to Know?	Advice for Staff Teaching and Supporting PESSPA
Hydrocephalus www.headway.org.uk/hydrocephalus.aspx	• Caused by an obstruction in the circulation of the cerebro-spinal fluid around the spinal cord and brain. • The accumulation of this fluid in the brain can lead to a variation in the severity of damage caused by pressure on the brain cells. • In most cases, to relieve this pressure, a valve or shunt is inserted behind the ear just below the skin. • Students struggle to retain information.	• Break down tasks/instructions into small stages for safety. • Talk through tasks, in addition to providing practical demonstrations. • Support students, and be prepared to adapt activities that require judging distance and direction. • Encourage involvement in all activities unless specific individual medical advice states otherwise. This includes contact sports and gymnastics. There is very little problem with shunts being damaged during activity or minor falls. Advice to avoid contact sports, rolling, jumping and twisting is only applicable to a small minority.
Multiple sclerosis www.nationalmssociety.org	• This condition disintegrates the nerve fibres over time in a random way so that progress of the disease can vary and be at different paces. • Those affected may experience spasticity, difficulties with attention and balance, blurred or loss of vision, incontinence, loss of memory, and speech problems. • It is more common in adults, but some students are diagnosed while still at school. • Swimming is a particularly beneficial and safe activity when supported correctly.	• Be vigilant to changes in symptoms, which may vary from week to week. • Provide clear, brief instructions. • Repeat instructions. • Check regularly with the student about the clarity of their vision, and notice signs that vision has deteriorated. • Ensure that students work on even surfaces and are made aware of surface issues that might make them lose their balance.
Muscular dystrophy www.muscular-dystrophy.org	• Relates to a group of conditions characterised by a breakdown of muscle fibres, leading to weak and wasted muscles. • The condition exists on a continuum from severely disabled to only a mild disability. • The condition is progressive, but at variable pace. • The most prevalent type, Duchenne, sees symptoms appear usually before the age of five. • Early signs include difficulty when running, standing and climbing stairs. • Swimming provides appropriate and safe activity.	• Clarify manual handling issues with wheelchair users, and provide guidance on whether the student can get out of the chair for activity. • Be aware of frequent changes in the student's physical condition. • Be led by the individual's capabilities at any given time.
Social, emotional and mental health (SEMH) difficulties www.semh.co.uk	• Students may experience a wide range of social and emotional difficulties that manifest themselves in different ways. These behaviours may reflect hidden disabilities, including underlying mental health difficulties such as anxiety, substance misuse, eating disorders or physical symptoms that are medically unexplained. • Young people with SEMH difficulties may not have a formal diagnosis or SEND categorisation. • A range of responses are required to address different needs. • Many students with SEMH difficulties will lack confidence, and may develop a perceived sense of failure that can lead to refusal to participate in physical activity. This may in turn lead to disruptive behaviour. • Some students prefer to avoid large-group and team games, where they might be overwhelmed or intimidated, whereas others are motivated by these situations. • Physical activity has been shown to improve mental well-being.	• Gauge the "mood" of students. Be aware that they may have been affected by incidents prior to the lesson. • Be flexible in making adaptations as necessary to accommodate the "mood" of the students. • Set achievable targets for each student. • Vary activities frequently to keep students on task and interested. • Encourage an ethos of praise for themselves and each other. • Discuss safety with the students, and encourage them to understand how they can contribute to safe practice. • Allow time for students to cool-down and relax at the end of a lesson. • Encourage students to pursue any particular interests that they show in physical activity.

Condition	What Do Staff Need to Know?	Advice for Staff Teaching and Supporting PESSPA
Spina bifida www.spinabifida association.org	• A congenital condition through which a deformity in the spine causes damage to the nerves that communicate movement and feeling. • At its most severe, there will be a complete loss of motor and sensory function below the area of damage. • The extent of the disability is dependent on the position and severity of the damaged area. • Symptoms are generally paraplegia and a wasting of the lower limbs. • Students with this condition may also have hydrocephalus (see previous page). • Students tend to have little feeling in their lower limbs and are not aware of the pain when they bang into objects or walls (while in their wheelchair).	• Adapt activities to make them safe for students who are using wheelchairs or other mobility equipment. • Provide clear instructions, and repeat them regularly. • Use modified equipment when students are in wheelchairs (eg shorter sticks, slower-paced balls). • Avoid "tagging" the wall as a "safe" zone.
Visual impairment www.rnib.org.uk	• Visual impairments exist along a continuum, from being able to manage with or without support to those who are registered blind and will need specialist support. • Students who have a degree of sight may still struggle with moving objects and people moving quickly in a PESSPA environment. • Students are usually encouraged to be independent with regard to mobility and movement around the facility. • Eye conditions, such as a history of retinal detachment, mean that activities such as trampolining, diving and contact sports should be avoided.	• Be prepared to modify tasks as necessary. • Use modified equipment such as balls with bells, and buzzers attached to goals or targets. • Use brightly coloured tape on walls, floors and surfaces, and brightly coloured equipment. • Provide clear and precise instructions. • Give accurate spatial instructions (eg size of area of pitch or hall, fixed objects within that space). • Remove obvious hazards from the working area. • Provide opportunities to take part in individual personal fitness activities. • Allow the use of glasses or peaked caps if bright light is a problem. • Position the student in the optimum place for vision, taking account of sunlight and glare.

For more information regarding SEND and medical conditions:

The Activity Alliance: disability inclusion sport – previously known as the English Federation of Disability Sport (EFDS): www.activityalliance.org.uk

Governing bodies of sports: There are many different governing bodies of sport that have responsibility for managing their specific sport. They each have a commitment to get more people accessing and participating in sport regularly, and growing their sport. For advice on any areas related to disability and inclusion, please visit each individual governing body of sport website for their current guidance on investment, programmes and support.

Section 4: Parental Consent

Parental Consent for Participation in School Activities

2.4.1   Parental consent is not generally required for participation in curricular activities such as physical education lessons, but consent will be required for optional activities such as after-school clubs and sports fixtures. However, regardless of whether consent is required, it is important that parents are kept informed of school activities in which their children are participating and advised of any additional safety measures that may be implemented, particularly where activities take place off school premises.

2.4.2   Schools may adopt a variety of mechanisms for communicating with parents, including letters home, newsletters, text messaging and social media. It is important to ensure the mechanisms adopted are effective and take account of any communication difficulties parents may have. Identifying reliable lines of communication between school and home can make it easier to secure the support of parents and to enforce procedures that contribute to a safe and well organised programme.

2.4.3   Within education law, an extended definition of "parent" is used that includes natural parents, persons with parental responsibility and persons who have day-to-day care of a child. As such, an increasing number of students will have more than two parents. Schools are required to hold contact details for all parents, which are likely to be updated via annual data collection forms.

2.4.4   While all parents have a right to provide consent in relation to their child's participation, schools are not required to obtain consent from all of them unless specifically requested to do so. Schools can lawfully act based on a single parent's consent. However, where two parents disagree, schools are advised to conclude that valid consent has not been provided.

2.4.5   When consent is required for participation in organised activities, the information provided to parents needs to be as **comprehensive** as possible in order for them to make informed decisions. Parents should be made fully aware of the itinerary, particularly the arrangements for the collection of students after the activity.

2.4.6   Parents should be asked to confirm that they understand the risks involved in an activity and that they agree to comply with the conditions stated. Students should not take part where their parent has crossed out any part of the consent form or amended the wording in any way as this could create difficulties should an emergency arise. Any student not providing a **signed consent form** should not take part in an optional school sport activity.

2.4.7   Should a student be injured taking part in an activity for which consent has not been given, the school will be at risk of legal action. Furthermore, the individual members of staff may face disciplinary action if they can be shown to have acted contrary to their employer's policy.

2.4.8   A consent form is merely an indication that a parent is willing for their child to take part in certain activities offered by the school, based on the information the parent has received. It does not offer an indemnity against a claim for negligence in the event of an injury. As it is not legally possible to exclude liability for death or personal injury by reference to terms in a consumer contract or notice, schools should avoid using such clauses within consent forms and make it clear that the school accepts no responsibility for injuries however they are caused.

2.4.9   Signed consent forms and accurate attendance registers should be stored in accordance with the Data Protection Act 2018 and the school's privacy notice. In the event of a claim being brought for any injury suffered, such documents may be valuable in supporting a defence. When considering the length of time documents should be stored, it should be noted that the three-year limitation period applicable to personal injury claims does not start until a student reaches 18 years of age.

2.4.10   Although there is no set format for consent forms or the frequency with which consent is obtained, staff must observe the requirements of any employer policy (eg the school's educational visits policy). The protocol for consent forms should **not be burdensome** on staff or parents but should ensure good communication, and fully **inform parents** of the schedules and organisation of any optional activities in which their child may be involved.

Waivers and Disclaimers

2.4.11   Parental consent does not mean that parents or students have waived the right to make a legal claim should this be necessary. The right to hold the school body to account is not relinquished.

2.4.12   Schools need to be aware that they cannot sign waivers/disclaimers on behalf of students, neither can they ask parents to sign waivers for students while the students are under the school's duty of care. All staff working in schools must demonstrate this duty of care. Where expected standards are not met, and as a result injury occurs, and this was reasonably foreseeable, then an allegation of negligence on the teacher's part could be made.

2.4.13   The Association for Physical Education (afPE) recommends that schools do not arrange visits for students if a provider insists on the completion of a waiver/risk acknowledgement form. Schools must make their own decision as to whether this is acceptable for the purposes of an educational visit.

2.4.14   Disclaimers from parents alleging the removal of responsibility from teachers in the event of an injury occurring (eg when their child takes part while wearing jewellery, personal effects, or non-policy clothing or footwear) should be declined. Such indemnities have no legal status. The duty of care remains firmly with the school on such matters, as the student may take independent action for compensation when they become an adult, thus nullifying any agreement made in good faith. Schools should work with parents to achieve a solution that does not compromise the safety of the student and others. See **Chapter 2 Section 1.**

Parental Consent for Students to be Transported by the School

2.4.15   Parental consent will not generally be required to transport students to curricular activities such as swimming. However, where students are being transported to extracurricular activities or in a vehicle belonging to another adult or in a taxi, it is recommended that parental consent is obtained. Such consent may also be sought for students being transported in a vehicle belonging to another student of adult age (this could be applied from age 17 and above, given the legal driving age). Parents should be asked to give consent in the knowledge that the adults providing the car have satisfied the conditions set by the school.

2.4.16   Such conditions should include the following:
- The driver has a current clean licence to drive the category of vehicle.
- The car has valid tax, MOT and insurance suitable for transporting students.
- The car is roadworthy.
- The driver ensures that appropriate restraints and car seats are used.
- The driver shall at no time transport a single student, other than their own child, as part of any journey (this does not apply to any 17/18/19-year-old student transporting their peers).
- The driver has never been interviewed, cautioned or convicted of any offence that would render them unsuitable to work with young people.
- The driver shall at no time transport a student or students while under the influence of alcohol or drugs.

See **Chapter 2, Section 4** for further information on transporting students.

Code of Conduct – Parent Information

2.4.17 Another way to maintain good relationships with parents and students is through a **code of conduct**.

2.4.18 It is good practice for schools to agree a code of conduct with parents and students before students participate in sports activities and other educational visits. Codes of conduct set out the **expectations** placed on a student by the school, and are useful documents to make clear to students and parents the standards expected of those taking part. Such a code of conduct could also be developed to include expectations of parents when they are observing any school events. Acceptance of a code of conduct by parents and students will help staff to enforce the necessary authority to carry out their responsibilities.

2.4.19 While codes of conduct are key, in some circumstances, in setting out safe practices, they can also be used as the basis for administering discipline procedures stated within the code. For example, the decision to return a student home early from an event, such as a sports tour, might be made if their behaviour causes concern. The parents and student will have been made aware, through the code of conduct, and agreed to the premise that acceptable behaviour is a condition of taking part and that it will be the school's prerogative to judge the situation and to impose an early return home, if necessary, and at the parents' cost.

2.4.20 Breach of a code of conduct due to poor behaviour can have serious implications for the safety of that individual and others in the group, and should be effectively dealt with.

2.4.21 It is recommended that as part of "**teaching safety**", students are included in the compilation of specific codes of conduct so that they have involvement in the process and more ownership of the outcome. It is considered effective practice for students to be asked to comply with a code of conduct that they have had some responsibility for producing.

2.4.22 An agreed code of conduct should be formalised and sent to parents together with the medical and possibly photographic consent forms where these are required. These documents should be signed by parents and students.

2.4.23 The list that follows gives examples of behavioural standards that might be included in a code of conduct for an **off-site visit, sports tour or residential trip**. This could form the expectations that all parties adhere to. Publishing the code and sharing it widely would be good practice.

2.4.24 Students are required to:
- observe normal school rules
- cooperate fully with all staff at all times
- consult with school staff if in doubt about any issues
- fulfil any tasks or duties set prior to and during the event
- participate fully in all activities and sessions during the event
- be punctual at all times
- ask permission before leaving group sessions or accommodation
- return to the meeting point or accommodation at agreed times
- remain in groups of no less than three students if granted indirectly supervised time
- avoid behaviour that may inconvenience others
- be considerate and respect others at all times
- observe rules relating to the use of mobile phones/smartphones, filming and the use of social media
- behave at all times in a manner that reflects positively on themselves, the party and the school
- abide by the rules, regulations and laws of the school, venue or countries visited
- comply with customs and duty-free regulations when travelling abroad
- not purchase or consume alcohol or tobacco products, or purchase dangerous articles, such as explosives and knives, during a school excursion
- accept that a full written report of any misconduct will be forwarded to the school governors and leadership team, and their parents.

2.4.25   Staff might also explore the development of safe practice codes for the use of the school fitness room, behaviour in the changing rooms and other aspects of physical education, school sport and physical activity (PESSPA) where a code can help to establish expectations.

    See **FAQ 4** in **Chapter 4**.

Managing Medical Information, Needs and Conditions

2.4.26

> *Governing bodies should ensure that their arrangements are clear and unambiguous about the need to actively support students with medical conditions to participate in school trips and visits, or in sporting activities, and not prevent them from doing so.*
>
> DfE (2017) "Supporting students at school with medical conditions", https://goo.gl/ud1Jjg

2.4.27   It is standard practice for schools to request student medical information from **parents** and to update this information regularly. The onus is on the parents to provide adequate information and to inform the school when any medical conditions or the treatment for them change.

2.4.28

> *The governing body must ensure that arrangements are in place to support students with medical conditions. In doing so it should ensure that such children can access and enjoy the same opportunities at school as any other child.*
>
> *The governing body should ensure that its arrangements give parents and students confidence in the school's ability to provide effective support for medical conditions in school... They should ensure that staff are properly trained to provide the support that students need.*
>
> DfE (2015) "Supporting students at school with medical conditions", https://goo.gl/fDwuHv

2.4.29   Some students who have medical needs may also have special educational needs and/or be disabled within the meaning of the Equality Act 2010. More information about special educational needs and disabilities (SEND) can be found in **Table 6**.

2.4.30   A student's education, health and care plan (EHCP) typically details their learning needs although it may mention physical issues (eg where occupational therapy is required). Medical needs are usually more detailed within an individual healthcare plan (IHP), but these may not be in place for all children. All staff delivering PESSPA need to be aware of the information detailed in the individual EHCPs of students they teach.

2.4.31   Where a student has SEND but does not have an EHCP, their special educational needs should be considered and planned for in a PESSPA context.

2.4.32   Schools should have a secure system to inform and regularly update staff about student medical conditions and associated triggers, signs, symptoms, treatments and risks in order for them to take account of such information when planning and delivering a PESSPA session or lesson. Staff should understand how a student's medical condition will impact on their participation, and on maintaining a safe learning environment. This may involve adjusting particular tasks for particular students, such as not asking a student who has poorly controlled epileptic seizures to work at a height in case a seizure occurs with little or no notice. There should be enough flexibility for all students to participate safely according to their own abilities.

2.4.33   The staff member responsible for the students (eg the class teacher) must also inform any support staff, whether on or off site, on a need-to-know basis of any medical conditions existing in the groups they will teach during a visit. This will enable the student's needs to be accommodated within the lesson. Communicating this information to external staff coming into school is not always as effective and reliable as it needs to be. Procedures should be in place to enforce this. Schools will also need to ensure that their procedures for sharing information are compliant with the General Data Protection Regulation 2018 and Data Protection Act 2018.

2.4.34   Schools should consider any reasonable adjustments they might need to make to enable students with medical needs to participate fully and safely in **trips and visits**. This usually includes carrying out a risk assessment in consultation with the student, their parents and any additional medical staff to establish safe inclusion.

2.4.35   The school's medical policy must apply any guidance issued by the employer. It must set out clear guidelines regarding the administration of medicines and be followed by all staff. The policy should clarify:

- the role of the staff – staff cannot be compelled to administer medicines to students nor to supervise the administration of medicines; however, they must not give out medicines or undertake healthcare procedures without student-specific information and appropriate training; a first aid certificate does not constitute appropriate training in supporting students with specific medical conditions
- whether students should be allowed to carry their own medicines and devices, or procedures for accessing them quickly and easily for self-medication – students who can take medicines or manage procedures themselves may still require a level of supervision.

2.4.36   Where there are variations to this policy, or individual needs differ, the outcomes of discussions with all those involved should be recorded within a student's individual healthcare plan in order to guide staff. Arrangements will vary in practice from one school to another.

2.4.37   There are now many students in schools recognised as having asthma, epilepsy, diabetes or conditions that may cause anaphylactic shock. Where these conditions are substantial and long term, they have the potential to fall within the meaning of "disability" under the Equality Act 2010. Schools should be aware of their obligations under the Act to prevent discrimination and to make reasonable adjustments to ensure inclusion.

2.4.38   Governing bodies should ensure that sufficient staff have received suitable training to support students with specific medical conditions, that they are competent to take on the responsibility, and that they can access information and further support as needed.

Section 5: Insurance

Provision of Insurance

2.5.1   School status (see **Chapter 1, Section 2**) impacts on how schools source their insurance. Some local authorities (LAs) continue to provide comprehensive cover and support for LA schools.

2.5.2   Academies and other non-LA eligible schools may choose independent insurance providers, or opt for the government's risk protection arrangement (RPA) scheme (https://goo.gl/3kcRLP), which aims to protect academy trusts against losses due to any unforeseen and unexpected event. As a minimum, the RPA is intended to cover risks normally included in a standard schools insurance policy, where there is no alternative valid insurance policy already in place.

2.5.3   Whatever choice is made, academies and other non-LA eligible schools must ensure that they have adequate insurance cover to comply with their legal obligations.

2.5.4   Staff should **check** with their head teacher (HT) and/or employer to clarify precisely what insurance cover is provided, under what circumstances the cover applies and whether all of their intended activities fall within this remit. This information needs to be shared with any volunteers or visiting staff. All staff need to ensure that they are working within their agreed contract.

2.5.5   The aspects of insurance that need to be considered are set out in the rest of this section.

Employer's liability insurance

2.5.6   Employers are responsible for the health and safety of their employees while they are at work. It is a statutory requirement for employers to insure against liability for **injury or illness that may occur to their employees** while they are working within the remit of a contract, whether permanent, temporary or for specific services. LAs are exempt from this requirement, but need either to act as the insurers or make alternative insurance arrangements to cover the potential liabilities of their employees.

2.5.7   **Schools not maintained by an LA are not exempt** and must therefore comply with these employer requirements.

2.5.8   The **RPA is not an insurance**. However, those schools that have opted for it are exempt by virtue of the fact that the Secretary of State has certified that any claim against an academy from an employee will be satisfied out of monies provided by Parliament. In practice, claims will be met by the RPA from monies provided by Parliament, which means that academies that are relying on the RPA for employer's liability cover are compliant with the law.

2.5.9   The only deviation to the extent of this cover occurs in the case of church academies, where the RPA will cover losses and liabilities incurred by the trustees in respect of the academy trust's operations **on their property**, and allow the trustees to make claims on behalf of an RPA member in respect of losses and liabilities incurred by the trustees relating to trust property made available to the member by the trustees.

2.5.10   Employer's liability insurance applies to employees only and not to students or visiting coaches. Coaches should carefully follow the public liability insurance guidance to ensure they know their rights.

Public liability insurance

2.5.11   Schools should obtain public liability insurance that covers them against claims made by others who have suffered injury or damage to property or person in connection with the school. This would include:

- death or injury to students, volunteers, coaches and other support staff, during school activities on and off school premises as a result of the school's negligence
- injury or damage to third parties (this includes visitors), including that caused through student **negligence** within the scope of the school's provision for their education.

Professional liability insurance

2.5.12   This insurance for staff is advisable. It provides cover against claims for **breaches of professional duty** by employees acting in the scope of their employment, such as giving poor professional advice.

Personal injury insurance

2.5.13   This insurance for staff is desirable. It provides cover against accidental bodily injury or deliberate assault by someone.

2.5.14   Personal injury insurance might be arranged by the employer or may need to be provided by individual members of staff.

2.5.15   **It is a parental responsibility to provide personal injury insurance for students**. Some schools choose to make this facility available collectively to parents, but there is no requirement to do so.

Hirer's liability insurance

2.5.16   This covers individuals or agencies that hire premises against any liability for injury to others or damage to the property while using it.

2.5.17   This type of insurance is recommended due to the increase in initiatives that encourage schools to hire out their premises for community use.

2.5.18   Where hirers do not already have such a policy, schools can organise this on their behalf from their insurers or through the RPA.

Libel and slander insurance

2.5.19   This is an optional insurance. It provides cover against claims for defamation (eg libellous material in publications).

Other types of insurance cover

2.5.20   There might also be a range of **miscellaneous aspects** that require insurance cover, according to the particular roles of individuals. These range from compulsory to merely advisable and may include travel or motor insurance.

2.5.21   Where cover is not provided, it is the responsibility of the individual member of staff to ensure that adequate provision is made where appropriate to their work circumstances.

Transport-related Insurance

2.5.22   The provision and requirements for **transport** insurance **will** vary. Staff need to ensure that:

- commercial transport companies have the appropriate range of insurance cover
- the school minibus insurance policy is appropriate for the journey being undertaken (eg there are additional insurance and licence requirements for travelling abroad that require staff to take the school minibus insurance certificate, or a copy, on their journey)
- they have read the employer's policy on the use of private cars to transport students; local requirements vary considerably – some employers do not allow it (eg the RPA does not cover staff intending to use their own or others' private cars on occasional business use)
- they understand the insurance procedures required to use private cars for school business, and obtain confirmation from other drivers that their insurance covers the risk involved.

Insurance for Physical Education, School Sport and Physical Activity Events

2.5.23   Insurance cover relating to the use of physical education, school sport and physical activity (PESSPA) **facilities** is relevant to the employer or owner of the facility, and should be checked. It should be clearly understood who is financially responsible and under what circumstances, should any claim arise.

2.5.24   It is important that adequate risk assessment of school PESSPA activities and events is made in order that appropriate insurance cover can be arranged where necessary.

2.5.25   The employer's insurance provision needs to cover all PESSPA **events organised by the school**, whether on or off site, in lesson time or outside, in term time or during holidays, provided the HT is fully aware of the events taking place. The HT will then determine whether the governors and/or the employing authority need to be informed. Staff should check what documentation needs to be completed, and ensure that this is in place prior to the event.

2.5.26   All **special events**, such as "one-off" sports trips, or sports tournaments will need appropriate insurance. Staff should check with the HT to clarify what provision is in place and whether any additional cover needs to be arranged. Sports tours arranged wholly by the school are likely to be covered in part by the employer's insurance provision, but some additional aspects of cover might need to be arranged specifically.

2.5.27   Sports tours, ski trips and other excursions arranged as a **package** through a commercial provider usually have a full range of insurance cover built in. Staff need to check carefully the detail of the insurance provided, particularly the levels of compensation offered and any particular exclusions to the cover. Parents should be provided with full details of the insurance cover so that they can make additional arrangements in relation to personal injury cover for their child should they wish to do so.

For more information on this area, see **Chapter 2, Section 15**.

2.5.28   **Overseas trips are now covered by the RPA**. This is a new provision as, until recently, this only covered trips in the UK.

Full details can be found at https://www.gov.uk/guidance/academies-risk-protection-arrangement-rpa and https://www.gov.uk/government/publications/risk-protection-arrangement-rpa-for-academies Enquiries regarding this development can be sent to academies.RPA@education.gov.uk

2.5.29   Appropriate **insurance cover is needed for centrally organised events**, such as **sports festivals**, in which students from a variety of schools take part. It is important that the organiser for the managing agency, such as the local Active Partnership, governing body of sport, schools association or LA, makes clear who is providing essential insurance, and clarifies what schools and even individual parents might need to consider in terms of providing additional cover. The organiser for the managing agency should check that:

- the venue used for the event has its own public liability insurance that covers any accident involving a person due to a fault with the venue
- there is adequate third-party liability to cover any accident arising from negligence by the managing agency, or as a result of a student participant causing injury to another participant or spectator
- parents know that it is their responsibility to take out personal injury insurance for their child should they feel that this is necessary, based on information they have received about the event.

More information regarding insurance requirements and planning a sports event can be found in Association for Physical Education (afPE) (2011) "Safe practice for the School Games – Guidance for local organising committees and schools" at www.yourschoolgames.com

---

For more information on the need for insurance for extracurricular activities, see **FAQ 11** in **Chapter 4**.

For an illustration of the importance of parents taking out personal insurance for their children, see **Case Law 28** in **Chapter 4**.

Section 6: Digital Technology

Digital Imagery

2.6.1 The development of digital technology (eg digital cameras, electronic tablets, portable gaming devices with inbuilt cameras, mobile phones/smartphones and analysis software programmes) has opened up an exciting and highly effective way of **enhancing learning in schools**. A great deal of visual learning currently takes place in PESSPA.

2.6.2 Digital photographs and video clips can provide students with clear images of performances and specific techniques, as well as immediate visual feedback about their own progress. New software enables this process to be managed easily during physical education lessons, school sport and off-site activities. The availability of specific sport, physical activity, fitness and exercise applications ('apps') can add to the variety of tools that staff and students can access on different devices within and outside a lesson.

2.6.3 However, in accordance with the Data Protection Act 2018 (and the General Data Protection Regulations 2018 commonly referred to as 'GDPR') and the principles contained within Keeping Children Safe in Education (2019) (www.gov.uk) certain procedural issues need to be addressed to ensure that schools manage images legally, effectively and securely. This is particularly important since images can now be transmitted and manipulated easily. Schools should be clear about when and who can **photograph students** in school, and how images might be used to promote or support physical education, school sport and physical activity (PESSPA) using various online media.

2.6.4 Guidance issued by the Information Commissioner's Office clarifies that it is not unlawful for parents **to take photos or videos** at school events provided that the personal data obtained is for personal use only (ie that the images are for use in a family photograph album, whether physical or digital). Similarly, it is not unlawful for parents to take photographs in public places without obtaining the prior consent of those in shot.

2.6.5 However, schools are not public places and, given their safeguarding responsibilities towards students and concerns over the inappropriate use of child imagery, schools are able to impose restrictions on parents and students taking images on school premises. In order to avoid any unnecessary conflicts, schools should have a clear policy in place regarding the use of photography on the school site. It is good practice for this policy to be available on the school website and for students and parents to be reminded of it at regular intervals and preferably before significant events such as the school sports day.

 For more information on the Data Protection Act 2018, see http://www.legislation.gov.uk/ukpga/2018/12/contents/enacted

---

2.6.6   Photographs taken for official school use are generally covered by the Data Protection Act 2018. In accordance with GDPR, parents and students must be provided with certain information (referred to as 'privacy information') about how their personal data, including photographs, will be 'processed' by the school. Processing includes all aspects of collecting, filing, storing and sharing the data.

2.6.7   Privacy information will include details about when and why personal data is collected, how it is used and, where it is shared, the legal basis on which this is carried out. A school's privacy information will commonly be contained in a policy or notice which is displayed on the school's website and provided to parents on an annual basis.

 For further information see the Information Commissioner's Office (2016) "Data sharing code of practice", www.ico.org.uk

2.6.8   Schools are reminded that obtaining consent is only one of the lawful expectations for processing data under GDPR and may not always be the appropriate basis. For example, if images of a student are required to be submitted for part of an examination, it would be more appropriate to consider the 'legal obligation' or 'public duty' basis, as relying on consent could possibly interfere with the schools obligation to submit all appropriate assessment data to the exam board.

2.6.9   However, where consent is appropriate, for example where images are being used for media or publicity reasons, schools must be able to demonstrate that it was given positively rather than by implication or default. Consent for the use of images in school is routinely obtained on admission although many schools renew this on an annual basis. Even with such consent, it is still good practice to keep parents and students informed of events where photographs may be taken or videos made. Where consent is refused and there is no other appropriate legal basis for processing the data, the school must cease to do so with immediate effect. A **list of students** who are not permitted to have their photo taken or be filmed in circumstances where consent is required, should be made available to all staff for reference purposes.

2.6.10   Where the use of digital imagery is common to support learning, it is good practice to include relevant details on school admission forms, websites and the school prospectus and to provide reassurance that it will only be used in specific circumstances about which parents and students will be advised.

 For more information on the Data Protection Act 2018, see http://www.legislation.gov.uk/ukpga/2018/12/contents/enacted

2.6.11   Great care should be taken to safeguard students when storing and using digital images in an educational context. The school's Data Protection Policy should set out how this is to be achieved. Schools are free to produce their own policy or adopt one commended to them by their Local Authority/Diocese. The school's Data Protection Officer would generally be responsible for ensuring appropriate arrangements are in place and that they are complied with by staff. Any member of staff using images in PESSPA must have them available for scrutiny and must store them securely in accordance with school policy. Access to the images should be controlled by **authentication mechanisms** (eg password protection, with passwords being changed on a regular basis, and the use of encryption and access permissions).

2.6.12   Whenever new devices are introduced into schools, a risk assessment should take place in relation to their use. For example, where schools decide to issue electronic tablets to students, the foreseeable risks would need to be considered and mitigated as far as possible, including making decisions about whether the tablets can go home with students and what Internet sites the students can access.

2.6.13   All devices and equipment should be security marked and should be signed out and in when used by staff and students. This provides a record of who has been using each device.

Guidelines for Filming

2.6.14   When filming or taking photographs in PESSPA sessions, it is recommended that:

- students know the purpose of the filming and have agreed to it (where appropriate)
- parental consent is sought, if necessary
- where consent is not considered appropriate that another lawful basis for processing is identified
- clutter-free backgrounds are used to focus students' attention on the specific performance issues
- care is taken over the angles chosen for filming, particularly in sensitive sporting situations (ie swimming, gymnastics, trampolining, some athletics events)
- profile shots of students (side on) are used – these are generally more informative and less prone to risk of misuse
- where possible, action shots rather than static pictures of individuals are used
- filming students on poolside is avoided (profile shots or in water are more appropriate)
- care is taken to ensure images cannot be misinterpreted – some specialist sports clothing (eg swimming costumes, close-fitting running wear) can create added risk.

2.6.15   **The publishing** of images refers to when they are distributed beyond a defined group via DVD, a website or other social media sites such as Facebook, Twitter, Instagram, Snapchat and many others. Publishing images has obvious associated risks, particularly for students in PESSPA environments. Many schools have websites for the physical education department, and use their sites to promote their activities. Staff responsible for operating these sites should receive relevant and regular training, and understand how to maintain safe and lawful operating procedures.

Guidelines for Publishing

2.6.16   When publishing PESSPA images, it is recommended that:

- permission is obtained from the students (and parents where required) to use the image(s) as intended
- general-view shots are used to establish the theme
- shots held for a maximum of three seconds are used
- **no individual names of students** are attached to images; generic team names such as 'the under-15 football team' are acceptable alongside a whole or part team photograph as long as no individual names are included
- images show students suitably dressed, including wearing personal protective equipment (if appropriate)
- filmed interviews only show the head and shoulders of the students involved; students should not be identified by name (this includes voice-overs and text-overs)
- group shots are in wide vision.

2.6.17   It is not recommended for staff or students to publish video content to YouTube or other free Internet video-sharing sites. Although effective and far-reaching, these sites generally allow anyone to view and share images and can be extremely difficult to monitor. It is best practice to upload content to secure sites that restrict viewers and operate an 'invite to view' only policy, such as WeTransfer.

2.6.18   Staff and students should be aware of the dangers of distributing any images via email or the large range of social media sites. This leads to a **loss of control** of the images by the user group.

 Further guidance on photographing and videoing children in sport is available from the Child Protection in Sport Unit at https://goo.gl/vm0D5P

 See **FAQ 12** in **Chapter 4** for guidance on specific issues around photography.

Storing Material

2.6.19 Master photographic materials and digital photographs used in PESSPA must be stored in a secure environment and in accordance with the school's Data Protection Policy.

2.6.20 In addition to having a Data Protection Officer to oversee the practices around storage of digital images across the whole school, it is good practice to appoint a staff member from each department to regularly check and delete digital files that are no longer required.

2.6.21 A number of **examination boards** require DVD/digital evidence to be sent to them, labelled with the individual candidate's name and number. Schools are likely to have data sharing agreements with exam boards which will dictate the arrangements for sharing, storing and deleting the data.

2.6.22 Libraries of photographic materials should be managed with care. The storage of unnecessary material is contrary to data protection law and therefore should be avoided. Schools should have in place a retention schedule which sets out the time period that each category of data is retained for. Staff should be aware that materials which form part of the pupil's educational record, which will include images submitted to an exam board, are likely to be required to be retained even when the pupil has finished compulsory education.

2.6.23 The reuse of DVDs that have not been erased can increase the risk of unwanted images being used inappropriately.

Mobile Telephones/Smartphones

2.6.24 Staff using mobile telephones/smartphones during lessons, training sessions or at competitions, for the purposes of either making or receiving calls, is not good practice. The primary responsibility of staff is the supervision and safety of students. Anything that compromises the staff member's ability to maintain a safe environment and give their full attention to the supervision and coaching of the students should be actively discouraged.

2.6.25 There are situations, however, where access to a mobile phone/smartphone will make a positive contribution to the safety and welfare of students and staff, particularly when an emergency occurs. Using a mobile phone/smartphone at sporting fixtures would be an example of this, where an emergency may require a rapid response. Schools should consider **providing mobile phones/ smartphones to all staff** taking part in extracurricular activity both on and off site. These phones should be kept topped up with credit and used as required for matters of safety or security, or for contacting parents. This practice removes the need for staff to feel that they must use a personal phone. Staff using their own phones to contact parents or students expose themselves to their personal mobile number and details being stored and shared without their consent.

2.6.26 Commercial systems are available for mobile phones/smartphones whereby staff can contact parents collectively in the event of an emergency or change in published arrangements. While some cost is involved, such systems contribute to good practice in keeping parents informed about events, training, delays and other relevant information.

Email

2.6.27 There are occasions when a member of staff may email a student or reply to an email from a student for educational reasons, regarding homework or coursework, for example. This is acceptable although parents should be made aware of this practice. Schools may consider whether it is appropriate that **a senior member of staff be copied in** to all communications as evidence of the correspondence. It is important that the school email is always used for this purpose, never a personal email.

2.6.28   Email communication may also be used as part of a disclosed list (having received prior permission from parents to disclose in a group email) where information in relation to training or competitions is disseminated. Sports clubs may also wish to use disclosed lists for sending club information via a designated and suitably trained adult. This person should also have been subject to appropriate selection and vetting processes.

2.6.29   Individuals should be given the opportunity to have their contact details removed from a group email list. This can be achieved by adding a statement at the end of every group email, such as: 'If you wish to be removed from this email list, please contact the administrator.'

The Internet

2.6.30   Students' use of the Internet is common in education and can be extremely beneficial to learning, whether accessed via mobile phones/smartphones or other devices. There is debate about whether students should be self-regulated in their use of the Internet in schools. Many schools 'filter' access on school equipment. It is also possible to monitor Internet use.

2.6.31   Filtering and monitoring are carried out to ensure that students' use of the Internet remains relevant to the learning environment. However, such monitoring could be seen as an infringement of an individual's privacy. For this reason, schools should share with parents the intention, reasons and process whereby such monitoring might be carried out.

2.6.32   Use of the Internet in PESSPA for researching examination material should be carefully managed. Students should be advised to adhere to strict plagiarism policies, which, if compromised, could lead to copyright infringement. At the same time, staff who recommend specific applications or websites should always check their security certificates and safety, and ensure that students are not exposed to malware or viruses through their use.

2.6.33   Staff need to be fully aware of the school policy and protocols, and ensure requirements are followed in PESSPA situations. 'Acceptable use' policies for staff and students, and 'eSafety policies' should form part of the safeguarding suite of information provided, and positive eSafety messages should be promoted at all times. The latest DfE 'Keeping Children Safe in Education' 2019 document includes the directive that students must be safeguarded from potentially harmful and inappropriate online material (www.gov.uk).

2.6.34   Where students use classroom-based **computers** in physical education, they should learn about, and take increasing responsibility for, implementing the standard health, safety and welfare protocols, such as:

- ensuring an adjustable sitting position, setting the eye level at mid-screen height
- taking regular short breaks to rest the eyes and loosen the body
- ensuring the keyboard is positioned appropriately in relation to the screen
- checking for loose wiring that could cause tripping incidents
- ensuring that bags and other items are placed away from the work area to prevent tripping incidents.

Social Media

2.6.35   Social media sites are popular and commonly used by students, as well as adults. An approach needs to be taken by schools to balance their popularity with the possible adverse consequences, such as the potential for instantaneous circulation of mobile phone/smartphone video clips taken in changing rooms while students are in a state of undress, or the tweeting of messages, often automatically, into the public domain. Several local safeguarding children boards (LSCBs) and governing bodies of sport provide advice on good practice.

 For more information on LSCBs, visit:
https://www.gov.uk/government/publications/local-safeguarding-children-boards

2.6.36   Schools need to impose **strict protocols** about the use of mobile devices and social media sites in any school context and include reference to this in the school's required code of conduct for staff and students. Staff must report any concerns within the school's safeguarding procedures.

2.6.37   Other than within the school's published protocols, staff should not communicate with students via social media sites and, where such communication occurs, should include **a third person** (a member of staff) for monitoring and evidential purposes.

2.6.38   It is highly recommended that staff avoid allowing any student to be a 'named friend' unless the school protocols allow this via limited contexts, strict guidelines and parental approvals. In addition, staff should refrain from adding past students to their friends' network. Past students will often be siblings of current students, and be connected to other students via different accounts. This can compromise both staff and students.

2.6.39   Staff should be aware of the increasing practice of **cyber-bullying**, which includes posting upsetting or defamatory remarks about an individual online, and name-calling or harassment using mobile phones/ smartphones. These may be general insults or prejudice-based bullying.

2.6.40   Cyber-bullies use their mobile phones/smartphones and social media platforms to send sexist, homophobic or racist messages, or they attack other kinds of differences, such as physical or mental disability, cultural or religious background, appearance or socio-economic circumstances. In some cases, bullies may physically assault other students, post images of the bullying or fights online, or send recorded messages to other people.

2.6.41   **Fraping** has developed as another form of this practice, in which the perpetrator accesses another person's social media profile and sends messages as if from the owner.

2.6.42   Alternatively, they may set up a "spoof" account which looks as if it belongs to an individual but in relation to which they have no control over the comments or views that are being attributed to them.

2.6.43   In a PESSPA context, comments can be made in the changing areas and other sporting environments. Staff need to be alert to these types of incidents and be prepared to act quickly if they suspect any acts of cyber-bullying.

2.6.44   In some environments, these practices appear to be so commonplace that they have become 'normalised' and not viewed as bullying at all. Schools may wish to take opportunities to discuss these issues with students, such as during assemblies or student council meetings, so that students recognise that such practices will not be tolerated and that sanctions are in place to deal with the perpetrators. Staff should be mindful of the signs that students are victims of these practices, looking out especially for isolated students or noticeable changes in behaviour. All types of cyber-bullying are wholly unacceptable, and, where staff become aware of any aspect of them, they must inform the school leadership team immediately.

Closed-circuit Television

2.6.45   The use of closed-circuit television (CCTV) for security has become fairly common in schools. As a system that processes personal data it is subject to the data protection legislation as well as a Code of Practice issued by the Information Commissioner's Office.

2.6.46   Schools planning to install a new system or alter an existing one should consider the need for a Data Protection Impact Assessment.

2.6.47   Schools need to plan carefully whether and where these cameras should run during the school day. In areas where privacy would be expected, such as changing rooms, they should only be used in extreme circumstances, such as identifying reported bullying or vandalism. Good practice would include informing staff and students where this occurs, and clear signage should be used wherever CCTV is in operation.

2.6.48   It is important that images are viewed in a restricted area and only by staff authorised to do so. The member of staff responsible for this operation should be fully trained in the school's policy, and the Data Protection Act and code of practice.

2.6.49   Recordings should be retained and stored for as short a period as possible, dependent in some cases on the purpose of the filming. School policy should cover how this will be organised and reviewed, as well as being clear about allowing access to recordings by external agencies or individuals whose data has been recorded.

Biometric Information

2.6.50   Schools must notify both parents of students **under 18** if they wish to process students' **biometric information** to use as part of a biometric recognition system (eg fingerprint traits for authentication purposes when paying in the school canteen). As long as the student or parents do not object, the written consent of only one parent is required. Objections from students can be verbal; from parents, they must be written. Where neither parent can be notified (so consent cannot be obtained from either), Section 27 of the Protection of Freedoms Act 2012 sets out who should be notified and who can give consent: http://goo.gl/R0flSP

Electronic Signatures

2.6.51   Some schools choose to communicate with parents by email and text to avoid postage and paper costs, and accept electronic signatures as consent for students to take part in fixtures, trips or events.

2.6.52   Schools considering or using this method of communication may make use of the following options:
- sending electronic notes out, and requesting handwritten letters with signatures back
- offering another level of security by responding to an electronic consent with a confirmation of receipt
- collecting parental consent once a year or once a term for all activities with the 'original' being handwritten; once this is obtained, any additional consent required could be accepted electronically.

2.6.53   Whatever policy and procedure is in place, it needs to be agreed by the school senior management and governors, and communicated clearly to all parties concerned.

Staff Use of Digital Equipment

2.6.54   Staff using school equipment at home should remain vigilant to the guidelines and policies provided, to avoid compromising themselves and their school.

2.6.55   All schools should ensure laptops/tablets have security logins that are regularly changed, and that staff do not store personal data and images on their school laptop, tablet or phone. It is strongly recommended that staff do not allow their families or friends to access their school equipment in case this leads to inappropriate use.

2.6.56   Staff and students should 'lock screen' their laptops or tablets when not in use and ensure their digital hardware is security code-enabled to prevent 'Fraping' and other such 'non-consent'-based incidents from occurring.

2.6.57   The use of digital cameras/camcorders for filming and taking photographs by staff at home is particularly sensitive. If digital files are not deleted, images of a personal nature, including family trips and activities, can be viewed by students when they come to use the same equipment. For this reason, it is not recommended that staff use school equipment for any reason other than educational purposes for their school.

Further Information for Schools

CEOP Command
The National Crime Agency's CEOP Command (formerly the Child Exploitation and Online Protection Centre) works with child protection partners across the UK and overseas to identify the main threats to children both on and offline: http://goo.gl/O5Nqr7

Online Safety Mark
https://360safe.org.uk/Accreditation/E-Safety-Award/

Student Help Advice Reporting Page System
The Student Help Advice Reporting Page (SHARP) System, personalised to each school, is a web-based system that allows young people to anonymously report any incidents that occur within the school and local community: www.thesharpsystem.com

UK Safer Internet Centre
www.saferinternet.org.uk

Section 7: First Aid

Health and Safety Regulations for First Aid

2.7.1   A range of individuals in schools can suffer injuries or be taken ill. It does not matter whether the injury or illness happens in school or elsewhere, it is important to give immediate attention and call an ambulance in serious cases.

2.7.2   In schools, it is the responsibility of the employer to make sure that the Health and Safety (First Aid) Regulations 1981 are met. These require employers to provide:

- a sufficient number of trained first-aiders (where 25 or more people are employed, one such person should be provided)
- appropriate first aid equipment, kits and facilities
- a system for incident and accident reporting.

 For more information on these regulations, see http://goo.gl/gf5DYA

2.7.3   The regulations do not commit employers to provide first aid for anyone other than their own staff, but employers do have health and safety responsibilities towards non-employees. The Health and Safety Commission (HSC) guidance recommends that organisations, such as schools, that provide a service for others should include them in their risk assessments and provide for them.

Providing a Sufficient Number of Trained First-aiders

2.7.4   Head teachers (HTs) are required to assess the first aid needs of their school. What is "adequate and appropriate" will depend on the outcome of this needs assessment and the circumstances of each school. Such an assessment may consider:

- the size and design of the school (eg on different levels or split sites)
- school location and accessibility for the emergency services
- any hazards or dangerous substances on site
- the number of students with special educational needs and disabilities (SEND)
- the number of first-aiders required, giving particular attention to how this might impact on physical education, school sport and physical activity (PESSPA) staff taking students to fixtures and sports events
- accident statistics and whether there are specific areas and/or times of greater than average risk.

For more information, see Department for Education (DfE) (2014) "First aid in schools", https://goo.gl/znQuyY

2.7.5   The findings of a first aid needs assessment will identify the type of training that is appropriate:

- first aid at work (FAW)
- emergency first aid at work (EFAW)
- appointed person (AP)
- other appropriate training, such as the British Red Cross "First Aid for Sports" training (http://goo.gl/M88MKd)
- paediatric first aid or emergency paediatric first aid certificate.

2.7.6   All schools, as a minimum requirement, must have an "**AP**" to take charge of first aid arrangements, including looking after first aid equipment and facilities, and calling the emergency services when required. In practice, most schools would have several "appointed people", in order to ensure one is available at all times. Appointed people are not necessarily first-aiders, and should not undertake treatment for which they are not trained. However, it is good practice for them to have some emergency first aid training, and to be able to take control of all first aid arrangements at all times when required.

Appropriate First Aid Training

2.7.7   EFAW training enables a first-aider to give emergency first aid to someone who is injured or becomes ill while at work. FAW training includes the same content as EFAW and also equips the first-aider to apply first aid to a range of specific injuries and illness. Since 31 December 2016, both EFAW and FAW have included training in the use of an automated external defibrillator (AED) as the Resuscitation Council UK guidelines now state that the procedure for management of a casualty requiring cardiopulmonary resuscitation (CPR) is to request an AED.

EFAW Training Specification	FAW Training Specification
<ul><li>Understand the role and responsibilities of a first-aider.</li><li>Be able to assess an incident.</li><li>Be able to manage an unresponsive casualty who is breathing normally.</li><li>Be able to manage an unresponsive casualty who is not breathing normally.</li><li>Be able to recognise and assist a casualty who is choking.</li><li>Be able to manage a casualty with external bleeding.</li><li>Be able to manage a casualty who is in shock.</li><li>Be able to manage a casualty with a minor injury.</li></ul>	The specification includes **all** components of the EFAW plus the following:<ul><li>Be able to conduct a secondary survey.</li><li>Be able to administer first aid to a casualty with:<ul><li>injuries to bones, muscles and joints</li><li>suspected head and spinal injuries</li><li>suspected chest injuries</li><li>burns and scalds</li><li>an eye injury</li><li>sudden poisoning</li><li>anaphylaxis</li><li>suspected major illness.</li></ul></li></ul>

2.7.8   Where standard FAW training courses do not include content pertinent to children (such as resuscitation procedures for children), the employer should request that they are tailored to meet the needs of those being trained.

2.7.9   FAW certificates are only valid for three years, and need to be refreshed before expiry to avoid having to undertake another full course. Employers can arrange for a refresher course up to three months before the expiry date, and for this reason, schools should keep a record of first-aiders and their certification dates.

2.7.10   Since 1 October 2013, the Health and Safety Executive (HSE) has not approved training and qualifications for the purposes of first aid at work. The flexibility arising from the changes in the regulations gives employers more choice in the first aid training they provide for their employees and who they choose to provide it. An employer will need to undertake varying levels of due diligence (reasonable enquiry or investigation) in order to make their selection. For schools, the updated guidance from the DfE is that they should select what is in their opinion the "best provider". In light of this, they have published "Selecting a first-aid training provider: A guide for employers", which includes a checklist for employers to evaluate the competence of a first aid training organisation. *(Information provided in response to a question to the DfE, February 2016.)*

To download a copy of "Selecting a first-aid provider: A guide for employers", see
https://www.hse.gov.uk/pubns/geis3.htm

2.7.11   The operational aspect of providing such training sits at school level so leaders should ensure training is organised and logs/records are kept so staff can respond appropriately. This would include full consideration of whether first aid situations can be handled effectively in PESSPA situations should they arise.

2.7.12   First-aiders in schools are advised to identify and familiarise themselves with the needs of students with SEND to establish any additional requirements for first aid provision.

2.7.13   Following a review in 2016, the HSE changed its rules regarding blended learning. It now accepts that some elements of workplace first aid training (FAW, EFAW or other) can be delivered remotely via distance-based online methods. Employers are expected to conduct the necessary checks to decide if a blended approach is sufficiently effective and suitable for their staff in comparison to exclusively face-to-face learning. They should make sure that sufficient time is allocated to classroom-based learning and assessment of the practical elements of the syllabus.

2.7.14   A first aid certificate does not constitute appropriate training in managing students with medical needs. Staff should receive training that equips them to deal with the medical needs of students they teach.

Appropriate First Aid Equipment

First aid kits

2.7.15   First aid kits are a legal requirement for every workplace. All staff should be made aware of where the nearest first aid container is located. Each first aid container must be a clearly marked green box with a white cross on it.

2.7.16   First aid kits should be:

- made of suitable material, designed to protect the contents from damp and dust
- easily accessible to staff
- checked regularly to make sure all contents are in stock and in date.

2.7.17   British Standard (BS) 8599 is the standard that the manufacturers of first aid kits have been granted. A risk assessment should be carried out to determine the appropriate contents of every workplace first aid kit and the number of kits needed. This should consider split sites, distant sports fields or playgrounds, and any other additional high-risk areas.

2.7.18   The HSE does not issue a definitive list of what a first aid kit contains. However, it offers a guide to the **minimum provision** in a low-risk environment. (See **Table 7**.) Sufficient quantities of each item should always be available in every first aid kit, with no additional equipment included.

2.7.19   The school should identify in their first aid procedures the person responsible for ensuring that the contents of the first aid kits are in date, discarded if expired, and replaced after use. Extra stock should be kept available for this purpose.

2.7.20   Sterile first aid dressings should be packaged in such a way as to allow the user to apply the dressing to a wound without touching the part of the dressing that is to come into direct contact with the wound.

2.7.21   When mains tap water is not readily available for eye irrigation, at least 900ml of sterile water or sterile normal saline (0.9%) should be provided in sealed disposable containers. Each container should hold at least 300ml and should not be reused once the sterile seal is broken. Eye baths, eye cups or refillable containers should not be used for eye irrigation.

2.7.22   Soap and water, and disposable drying materials, should be provided for first aid purposes. Siting first aid kits near to hand-washing facilities is recommended where possible. Alternatively, wrapped, moist cleaning wipes, which are not impregnated with alcohol, may be used.

2.7.23   Staff should exercise special care to **avoid infection** through the use of disposable gloves and effective hand washing when dealing with blood or other bodily fluids, or disposing of soiled equipment and dressings.

2.7.24   If an employee has received additional training in the treatment of specific hazards that require the use of special antidotes or equipment, these may be stored near the hazard area or kept in the first aid kit.

Supplementary equipment

2.7.25   In addition to the minimum provision of first aid items, there may be a need to have additional products available and stored alongside first aid kits. (See **the list in Table 7**.)

Travelling first aid kits

2.7.26   The contents of travelling first aid kits should be appropriate for the circumstances in which they are to be used. Before undertaking any off-site PESSPA visits, the level of first aid provision needs to be assessed. First aid kits must be taken to all PESSPA events and be easily accessible where the activity is taking place. The minimum recommended items (where no special risk is identified) are listed in **Table 7**.

2.7.27   Transport regulations require a first aid kit to be carried in the school minibus when transporting students to fixtures and events. Items required to be kept on board are listed in **Table 7**.

2.7.28   School staff undertaking specialised outdoor and adventure activities with students should consider attending the relevant first aid course to equip them with the specific knowledge required, such as the mountain first aid course, which includes practice in the use of inflatable splints.

Table 7: First aid kit contents

Standard First Aid Kit (minimum provision)*	Supplementary First Aid Equipment (can be stored with or alongside the standard first aid kit)
• Leaflet giving general advice on first aid • 20 individually wrapped sterile plasters (hypoallergenic if necessary) in assorted sizes • Two sterile eye pads • Four individually wrapped triangular bandages, preferably sterile • Six safety pins • Two large, sterile, individually wrapped un-medicated wound dressings (approximately 13cm x 9cm) • Six medium-sized, sterile, individually wrapped, un-medicated wound dressings (approximately 10cm x 8cm) • Pair of plastic, sterile disposable gloves.	• Blunt-ended stainless steel scissors (minimum length 12.7cm) – when used, consideration should be given to avoiding cross-contamination • Disposable plastic gloves and aprons, suitable protective equipment and appropriate protection against hypothermia – these should be properly stored and regularly checked to ensure they remain in good condition • Plastic disposable bags for soiled or used first aid dressings – employers should ensure systems are in place for the safe disposal of items such as used dressings • Blankets – it is recommended that these are stored in such a way as to keep them free from dust and damp • Suitable carrying equipment for transporting casualties – this is recommended if a school covers a large area or is divided into a number of separate and self-contained working areas.
Travelling First Aid Kit (based on assessment of needs)	Public Service Vehicles (including minibuses) First Aid Kit (based on transport regulations) and for Minibuses Used Not for Reward (based on road vehicles [construction and use] regulations 1986 [as amended]) [PW1]
As a minimum: • Leaflet giving general advice on first aid • Six individually wrapped, sterile adhesive dressings • One large, sterile, un-medicated dressing (approximately 18cm x 18cm) • Two triangular bandages • Two safety pins • Individually wrapped, moist cleaning wipes • Pair of disposable gloves.	• Leaflet giving general advice on first aid • 10 antiseptic wipes, foil wrapped • One conforming disposable bandage (not less than 7.5cm wide) • Two triangular bandages • One packet of 24 assorted adhesive dressings • Three large, sterile, un-medicated ambulance dressings (not less than 15cm x 20cm) • Two sterile eye pads with attachments • 12 assorted safety pins • Pair of rust-free stainless steel blunt-ended scissors • Disposable gloves • Mouth mask for resuscitation.

*DfE (2014) "First aid in schools", https://goo.gl/znQuyY

First Aid Accommodation

2.7.29   The Education (School Premises) Regulations 1996 require every school to have a suitable room (with washbasin and near to a toilet) that can be used to administer medical or dental treatment as required, and for the care of students during school hours. This facility can be used as a "first aid room", although first aid provision may be required in various locations at different times.

Defibrillators

2.7.30   An AED is a machine used to give an electric shock to a person who is in cardiac arrest. Cardiac arrest can affect people of all ages without warning. In the event of a cardiac arrest, swift action in the form of early CPR and prompt defibrillation can help save lives. The British Heart Foundation suggests that after a cardiac arrest, every minute without CPR and defibrillation reduces an individual's chance of survival by 10%. **It is important to understand that defibrillators are not intended for use with heart attack patients**.

 For further information on this, see https://www.bhf.org.uk

2.7.31   The recommended procedure for dealing with cardiac arrest is referred to as the "Chain of Survival". Defibrillation forms a key part of this chain. The four recognised links of the chain are:

- early recognition to prevent cardiac arrest – at this stage, a 999 call to the emergency services is made; the operator can stay on the line and advise on giving CPR and using an AED
- early CPR to buy time – either through mouth-to-mouth resuscitation or compression-only CPR
- early defibrillation to attempt to restore the heart to a healthy rhythm, and blood and oxygen circulation
- post-resuscitation care to stabilise the patient and restore quality of life.

2.7.32   While defibrillation is the third link in the chain, for maximum effect, the two preceding links must have been achieved.

2.7.33   It is becoming increasingly common to see defibrillators available for emergency use in a wide range of public places. The DfE (2015) publication "Supporting students at schools with medical conditions: Statutory guidance for governing bodies of maintained schools and proprietors of academies in England" advises schools to consider purchasing an AED as part of their first aid equipment.

 To access "Supporting students at schools with medical conditions: Statutory guidance for governing bodies of maintained schools and proprietors of academies in England", go to https://goo.gl/fDwuHv

2.7.34   DfE (2019) "Automated external defibrillators (AEDs): A guide for maintained schools and academies" highlights the part that AEDs can play in ensuring the health and safety of students, staff and others, and encourages all schools to consider purchasing AEDs as part of their first aid equipment. However, it also makes clear that the decision to purchase and install AEDs is one for each school to determine.

 To access the DfE guidance on AEDs, see https://goo.gl/JZVEpE

Deciding whether a defibrillator is required in school

2.7.35   In order to establish the need for an AED, a risk assessment should be undertaken by the school. If it is thought prudent to go ahead with the purchase, the risk assessment can also be used to decide how many machines are required.

2.7.36   The Northern Ireland Education Authority (EA) and DfE both provide guidance for deciding the number of AEDs needed.

2.7.37   Schools in England can receive assistance with purchasing AEDs that meet a certain minimum specification, through the DfE's arrangement with the National Health Service Supply Chain.

 Further details about schools purchasing AEDs can be found on page 11 of the DfE guidance: https://goo.gl/JZVEpE

2.7.38   The Northern Ireland Education and Library Boards (NEELB) and Council for Catholic Maintained Schools (CCMS) (2014) "AED guidelines for schools" also recommend AEDs are sourced centrally through ongoing procurement procedures that are available to schools.

 To view Northern Ireland AED guidelines for schools, access http://www.nias.hscni.net/our-services/aed/

Locating defibrillators

2.7.39   To ensure optimum coverage and swift access from anywhere on the premises, schools may decide to have a number of AED machines. The DfE suggests that they should be situated no further than a maximum of two minutes' walk from the areas where they are most likely to be needed. The distance of school playing fields from the main school buildings might be an important consideration in this respect. Locating a machine in the vicinity of the sports facilities and play areas would seem sensible. Schools may also wish to consider using portable machines taken out to sports fields, especially where they are away from the main school site.

2.7.40   AEDs mounted outside require heaters to keep them at the optimum temperature. There are also a number of different options for installing AED cabinets so that they are anti-theft and tamper-proof while still being sufficiently accessible in an emergency.

2.7.41   Both the DfE (2015) and the NEELB (2014) documents provide suggestions regarding sites that might be used by both the school and the community, and the best way to enable access to the AED by all parties during and out of school hours.

Defibrillator training

2.7.42   AEDs are work equipment and, as such, are covered by the HSE (1998) "Safe use of work equipment: Provision and use of work equipment regulations 1998 – Approved code of practice and guidance". Accordingly, training in the use of AEDs should be provided by the employer.

 To access the Provision and Use of Work Equipment Regulations (PUWER) "Safe use of work equipment" code of practice, see http://goo.gl/EupbiP

2.7.43   Staff need a sound understanding of when it is appropriate to use an AED, ie in the case of cardiac arrest when the heart stops beating, and not following a heart attack, when oxygen is prevented from getting to the heart. Where appropriate, staff should also understand the differences between treating adults and children under eight years of age, and that AEDs are perfectly acceptable to use on pregnant mothers when required. Modern AEDs assess the patient's heart rate and will not administer a shock unless it is correct to do so.

2.7.44   In light of these requirements, staff who have undergone a process of structured and organised training are more likely to feel confident and be better equipped to use an AED appropriately and safely in an emergency situation.

2.7.45   The guidance from the NEELB (2014) requires that all AED operatives in schools undertake their approved training course and, in line with the Resuscitation Council UK's recommendations, do not accept a demonstration by the AED manufacturer as being adequate training. Attendance at AED training and subsequent refresher sessions must be suitably recorded.

2.7.46   In all cases, schools that purchase AEDs should inform their local ambulance service of their existence and location, and develop a relationship with the service that can support ongoing training in the use of the defibrillator, potential funding available to purchase them, and additional advice and guidance around their location. Schools should also inform them when the device has been used.

2.7.47   AED training is now included in all standard one or three-day first aid courses so it is unlikely schools would have to organise separate training. Where they do, most commonly, the supplier offers a training session on using the AED at the location.

© RossHelen/Shutterstock.com

Managing and maintaining defibrillator units

2.7.48   It will be necessary to appoint at least two individuals to take responsibility for the ongoing (daily, weekly and other) operating checks on the units. It is essential that devices are always in working order, ready for when they may be required. Modern AEDs are set up to carry out regular self-checks, with problems being flagged up to the user. These must be noticed as promptly as possible, hence the need for daily checks. The Northern Ireland guidance provides a number of templates for use in setting up checking routines.

2.7.49   Action plans should be developed, setting out the resuscitation procedures, assigning responsibilities, and clarifying the order of response. This should also initiate records of incidents and follow-up action taken.

2.7.50   Appointed staff should understand the need to update the software used in the machine. This is in response to new UK and European resuscitation guidelines, which are issued every five years. Suppliers appointed under the arrangements put in place by the DfE (2015) must agree to provide such updates to schools free of charge. The various components of the device (eg pads, batteries) have an anticipated service life. This needs to be noted and the units replaced when necessary.

2.7.51   A very comprehensive table of maintenance responsibilities and checking requirements is included in the NEELB (2014) guidance.

2.7.52   As a minimum, appointed staff should regularly check:

- that there is no visible damage or missing parts through a visual check of the device
- batteries
- pads are in date and sealed
- spare pads are in date and sealed
- all accessory equipment is present and in date (towel, razor, scissors, gloves, paperwork)
- the storage cabinet is secure.

Use of defibrillators and the law

2.7.53   Schools may have concerns regarding the legal risks of trying to resuscitate a casualty. Information from the Resuscitation Council (UK) states:

> *At the present time there are no statutory laws in the UK designed to protect rescuers who attempt to help others. It can be seen, however, that there remains a good deal of protection in the common law principles that are described in this guide.*
>
> *It is, in practice, extremely difficult to envisage (and no precedent has yet been set) how a victim could successfully sue an individual who rendered him aid in an emergency situation. If anyone were to bring a successful claim, it is likely that the rescuer would have to have acted in a grossly negligent fashion and, if this was the case, it would probably not be desirable to introduce legislation to protect him.*
>
> Resuscitation Council (UK) (2015) "The legal status of those who attempt resuscitation",
> https://goo.gl/eZZHnq

Accident and Emergency Procedures

2.7.54   As part of general risk management processes, all schools must have arrangements in place for dealing with accidents and emergencies. **School policy should set out what should happen in an emergency situation.**

2.7.55   Staff must know, and be able to apply, the **school's procedures** for dealing with injuries and other emergencies. Where concerns exist about not knowing the whole-school procedures or how to apply them, staff should consult the HT.

2.7.56　Particular forethought needs to be given to dealing with accidents and emergencies that may occur at the **extremities of the school site** and also during off-site activities that extend beyond the normal school day. In such circumstances, effective and efficient communication through the school's accident report point (ARP), which is usually the school office, or with the school leadership team is essential.

2.7.57　Staff need not be qualified in **first aid**, but all need to have a working knowledge of dealing with accident and emergency situations to the extent that they can **manage** an initial injury effectively and summon an AP or first-aider to take over management of the situation.

2.7.58　First aid organisations advise that, in the event of an accident, a responsible person should **manage** the situation typically by:

- keeping calm
- assessing the situation – making any danger safe and not moving any casualty unless they are in immediate danger
- reassuring any casualties
- ensuring the rest of the group is safe – stopping all activity
- sending for help – preferably by mobile phone/smartphone, walkie-talkie or sending students to the ARP (usually the school office)
- monitoring, treating and managing situations where there is more than one casualty in the order of those who:
  - are unconscious
  - have severe bleeding
  - have broken bones
  - have other injuries
- regularly checking consciousness and informing the paramedic if consciousness is lost (also informing them of any relevant medical issues)
- not trying to do too much
- getting others to help
- asking the students (according to age and ability) what happened if the full incident was not seen
- recording the details as soon as possible after the incident.

2.7.59　If a student needs to be taken to hospital, a staff member or responsible adult should be prepared to accompany them in the ambulance. In all cases, where required, the ambulance should be called immediately and the parents informed. The member of staff or responsible adult should stay with the student. If the parent arrives in time, they may accompany the student in the ambulance. Failing this, the staff member or responsible adult should do so. It is important that parents are made aware of this approach to handling incidents where students require hospital treatment.

2.7.60　Where injury occurs to a student visiting another school, such as during a fixture, if the visiting school has only one member of staff accompanying them, they will hopefully have previously entered into a **reciprocal arrangement** with the host school. Within the scope of such an arrangement, the host school agrees to supervise the remaining students until arrangements can be made for another staff member from the visiting school to arrive. This then enables the visiting staff member to accompany the injured student in the ambulance.

2.7.61　Where possible, staff should not take students to hospital in their own cars. If this becomes necessary, in the case of an emergency, or where a student needs medical attention away from the school, and the parents are not available, an additional staff member or responsible adult should accompany them. Where the immediacy and seriousness of the injury does not allow time to arrange this, the teacher should proceed independently to hospital with the student (Children Act 1989, Section 3, Subsection 5). Schools need to ensure that they understand the local emergency services' cover arrangements and that the correct information is provided for navigation systems.

2.7.62　Where a student has an education, health and care plan (EHCP) or individual healthcare plan (IHP), this should clearly define what constitutes an emergency, and explain what to do, ensuring that all relevant staff are aware of emergency symptoms and procedures. Other students in the school should know what to do, such as informing a teacher immediately if they think help is needed.

2.7.63   On the very rare occasions a major crisis or **critical incident** occurs, staff need to be aware of, and apply, the school's plan for dealing with such instances. School policy should make staff aware of the relevant aspects of such a plan, and PESSPA staff should familiarise themselves with how they would respond, to what would be a small section of the plan, should they ever become involved in a major incident while taking teams to fixtures or festivals or on sports tours.

2.7.64   It is essential that where a school has adopted **standard accident procedures (SAPs)**, school staff and students are aware of them. This will help to ensure they all respond to an emergency in the same way, thus minimising the time spent between the accident occurring and the injured student(s) receiving first aid.

See **Case Law 12** in **Chapter 4**, Felgate versus Middlesex County Council (1994).

Accident and Incident Reporting System

2.7.65   Most accidents that happen in schools or on school trips do not need to be formally reported under the Reporting of Injuries, Diseases and Dangerous Occurrences Regulations (RIDDOR) 2013 set out below. The school health and safety policy should detail its own required reporting procedures and responsibilities.

2.7.66   However, under RIDDOR, some incidents must be reported to the HSE.

2.7.67   Those that come into this category for **employees** are work-related accidents (including those caused by physical violence) that result in:

- death or a specified injury (these include some fractures, injury leading to loss or reduction of sight, serious burns, any loss of consciousness caused by head injury or asphyxia)

- accidents that prevent the injured person from working or performing their normal work duties for more than seven consecutive days.

2.7.68   In addition, any work-related disease (specified under RIDDOR) that affects an employee and is confirmed by a doctor must be reported.

2.7.69   **For students and visitors**, accidents at school or during activities organised by the school are reportable if the accident results in:

- the death of a person, and arose out of or **in connection with a work activity**
or
- an injury that arose out of or in connection with a work activity where the person is taken directly to hospital for treatment.

2.7.70   **An accident would be deemed to be "in connection with a work activity"** if caused by:

- a failure in the way a work activity was organised (eg poor or inadequate supervision)
- the way equipment or substances were used (eg the incorrect use of fitness room equipment, or use of swimming pool chemicals)
- the condition of the premises (eg potholes on a football pitch).

2.7.71   If the accident was attributed to one or more of these criteria, it would be reportable. Consequently, many common incidents in school playgrounds and during PESSPA lessons are not formally reportable.

For more information about RIDDOR, see http://goo.gl/GCEw0y

2.7.72   The following useful aide memoires have been adapted and reproduced with the kind permission of *handsam*.

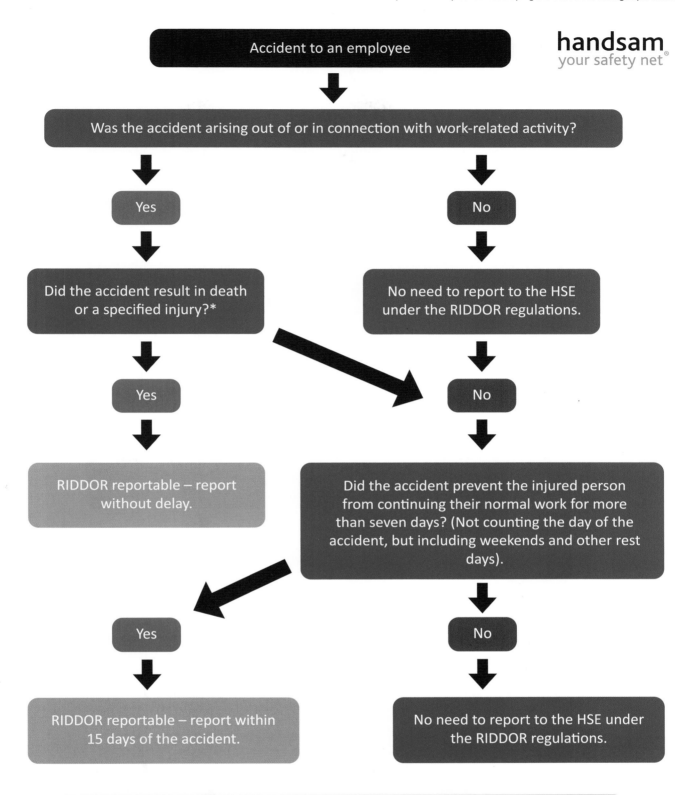

Accident to an employee

Was the accident arising out of or in connection with work-related activity?

Yes → **Did the accident result in death or a specified injury?*** → **Yes** → **RIDDOR reportable – report without delay.**

No → **No need to report to the HSE under the RIDDOR regulations.**

No → **Did the accident prevent the injured person from continuing their normal work for more than seven days? (Not counting the day of the accident, but including weekends and other rest days).**

Yes → **RIDDOR reportable – report within 15 days of the accident.**

No → **No need to report to the HSE under the RIDDOR regulations.**

Reportable specified injuries:

- Fractures, other than to fingers, thumbs and toes
- Amputations
- Any injury likely to lead to permanent loss of sight or reduction in sight
- Any crush injury to the head or torso causing damage to the brain or internal organs
- Serious burns (including scalding), which cover more than 10% of the body or cause significant damage to the eyes, respiratory system or other vital organs
- Any scalping requiring hospital treatment
- Any loss of consciousness caused by head injury or asphyxia
- Any other injuring arising from working in an enclosed space which leads to hypothermia or heat-induced illness, or requires resuscitation or admittance to hospital for more than 24 hours.

Accident to a student or visitor

Did the accident arise out of or was it in connection with work?
ie Was the accident caused by:

- a failure in the way an activity was organised (eg inadequate supervision of learning outside the classroom or a sports activity)
- the way equipment or substances were used (eg lifts, machinery, experiments)
- the condition of the premises (eg poorly maintained or slippery floors, playgrounds or pitches)?

Yes

No

Did the accident result in death?

No need to report to the HSE under the RIDDOR regulations.

Yes

No

RIDDOR reportable – report immediately.

Was the person taken directly from the scene of the accident to hospital for treatment for an injury? (Note: Examinations and diagnostic tests do not constitute treatment and therefore there is no need to report incidents where people are taken to hospital purely as a precaution, when no injury is apparent.)

Yes

No

RIDDOR reportable – report within 15 days of the accident.

No need to report to the HSE under the RIDDOR regulations.

handsam
your safety net®

106

See **Case Law 38** in **Chapter 4**.

 Further guidance for schools on what, how, where and when to report is explained in HSE (2013) "Incident reporting in schools (accidents, diseases and dangerous occurrences): Guidance for employers", http://goo.gl/OKPwYv

2.7.73   The school's reporting procedures will also set out policies in relation to additional requirements that contribute to maintaining records of:

- accidents that result in the person being incapacitated **for more than three consecutive days**; these do not require reporting to the HSE, but do need recording
- other minor incidents that do not fall into the other categories, but where reports and witness statements might help in any future complaint or claim; it is a requirement to keep statutory accident records for a minimum of three years, but it is recommended that schools store their records for a longer period as there are some cases when this information may be requested several years later
- first aid treatment given to students and staff, including details of treatment and after-care monitoring.

 See **Case Law 39** in **Chapter 4**.

2.7.74   It is also useful to record "**near misses**", where an incident occurred, but injury was avoided. These, along with the incident report forms, can be analysed to establish whether any pattern exists to the causes of injury. This is a valuable exercise to carry out within department or staff meetings, and can help to inform future safe practice.

 An example template for a school accident report is included in **Table 8**.

Table 8: Example school accident report form

1 Accident Details		Date:	
Student's name:	Age: yrs mths	Sex:	Height in cm:
Student's health prior to the accident:			
Student's home address: Tel no.:			
Date and time of accident:		Class:	No. in class:
Member of staff in charge:		Other adults present in lesson:	
Type of lesson:		Unit no.:	Lesson no.:
Nature of injury:			
Location:			

In the space above, draw a plan of the location of the accident showing the position of:

- any apparatus, equipment or other people
- the student involved in the accident
- any adults present
- two witnesses.

Give approximate measurements to show the relative relationship of the people to the apparatus and to each other.

Other persons involved: Names of any school staff sent to assist at the scene of the accident:	
Name of person who carried out emergency aid:	
Names of witnesses – indicate both **adults** and **students**:	
Statements obtained from witnesses: *(Circle appropriate response)*	Yes No
Name of person who contacted: • ambulance service: • student's parents:	

2 Post-accident Procedures	Date:

Assessment of the nature of the injury determined that the student should be treated by:
(Circle appropriate response)

school only   hospital A&E department   student's doctor

Treatment at school:

- Name of person who carried out treatment:
- Treatment details (brief):

Treatment at A&E department:

- Approximate time between accident and arrival of ambulance:
- Name of paramedic (if possible):
- Who accompanied student to hospital?
  (Circle appropriate response)   Parent   Staff member   Responsible adult
  - If school staff, state name:
  - Did hospital ask member of staff to sanction any   Yes   No
    action or form of treatment prior to arrival of parents?
    (Circle appropriate response)

(The Children's Act places a duty on school staff to take the emergency action necessary to ensure the health, safety and well-being of children in their care).

  - If **Yes**, specify action or treatment:
- Approximate time parents arrived at hospital:
- Was student admitted to hospital following treatment   Yes   No
  in A&E? *(Circle appropriate response)*
- Did the student receive treatment for identified injuries   Yes   No
  at hospital? *(Circle appropriate response)*

3 Follow-up Procedures	Date:

Completion of employer's accident report form:

- Form completed by:
- Date forwarded to employer:

Compliance with the **Reporting of Injuries, Diseases and Dangerous Occurrences Regulations 2013 (RIDDOR)** requires that, for students and visitors in schools, only certain accidents need to be reported to the **HSE**. They are those accidents that result in:

- the death of a person, where the accident arose out of or **in connection with a work activity**
- an injury that arose out of or in connection with a work activity where the person was taken directly to hospital for treatment.

Risk assessment:

- Risk assessment of the lesson/session reviewed by:
- Date carried out:
- Was a change to procedures recommended?   Yes   No
  (Circle appropriate response)
- What was the nature of the change(s)?
- When and how were these changes implemented?

Contact with parents:

- Who contacted parents to ascertain student's progress?
- How soon after the accident was contact made?
- Brief details of information received:

Student's return to school:

- Date of return to school:
- Date of restart of physical education:

Any restrictions on student's involvement in physical education laid down by medical profession:

Form completed by:

Signed: Date:

Note: Schools may choose to attach additional information to this form (eg employer's accident report form, witness statements, risk assessment form covering activity, photocopy of register covering the four weeks prior to the accident).

Administering Medication at School

2.7.75   School staff are not legally required to administer medication as part of their professional duties – this is a voluntary duty. Those who agree to do so should:

- have a clear understanding of their legal responsibilities
- be protected by an effective system of medication management
- be adequately trained to ensure they have the understanding, expertise and confidence required
- be familiar with normal precautions for avoiding infections
- be issued with written confirmation of insurance cover to provide specific medical support.

2.7.76   In an emergency situation, staff need to be prepared to fulfil their duty of care, but need do no more than is obviously necessary to relieve immediate distress or prevent further harm.

Supporting Students with Medical Conditions

2.7.77   A first aid certificate does not constitute appropriate training in managing students with medical needs. Staff should receive training that equips them to deal with the medical needs of the students they teach.

2.7.78   Students with existing medical conditions will have an IHP, which will outline their needs while participating in out of school activities to avoid an emergency.

2.7.79   Employers must ensure that policies set out clearly how staff will be supported in carrying out their role to support students with medical conditions, and how this will be reviewed. This should specify how training needs are assessed, and how and by whom training will be provided.

 For further information about supporting students with SEND and medical conditions, see **Chapter 2, Section 3**.

Supporting students with anaphylaxis

What is anaphylaxis?

2.7.80   **Anaphylaxis requires immediate medical attention.**

2.7.81   Anaphylaxis is a serious, acute, severe **allergic reaction** that is rapid in onset and may cause death. In most allergic reactions, the resulting chemicals are released locally into the tissues in a particular part of the body (skin, eyes). This means the symptoms of the allergic reaction usually only occur in this area. In anaphylaxis, the chemicals that cause the allergic symptoms (eg histamine) are released into the bloodstream.

2.7.82   It typically causes a number of symptoms including an itchy rash, throat swelling and low blood pressure. The whole body is affected, usually within seconds or minutes of exposure to a certain food or substance, but on rare occasions, the reaction may happen after a few hours. Any allergic reaction, including the most extreme form, **anaphylactic shock**, occurs because the body's immune system reacts inappropriately in response to the presence of a substance that it wrongly perceives as a threat. Anaphylaxis must be treated with an adrenaline pen.

2.7.83   With sound precautionary measures and support from staff, anaphylaxis in students is manageable, and school life can continue as normal for all concerned.

Triggers

2.7.84   Common causes include foods such as peanuts, tree nuts (almonds, walnuts, cashews, Brazils), sesame, eggs, cow's milk, fish, shellfish and certain fruits such as kiwi fruit. Non-food causes of anaphylaxis include penicillin or any other drug or injection, latex (rubber) and the venom of stinging insects (bees, wasps, hornets).

2.7.85   In some people, **exercise** can trigger a severe reaction, either on its own or in combination with other factors such as food or drugs such as aspirin. It is to be noted that the DfE's statutory guidance explicitly states that aspirin must **never** be given to a child under 16 unless prescribed by a doctor or nurse consultant.

Symptoms

2.7.86   The most severe form of allergic reaction is anaphylactic shock, when blood pressure falls dramatically and the patient loses consciousness. This is rare in young children but does occur in adolescence. More commonly, there may be swelling in the throat, which can restrict the air supply, or severe asthma. Any symptoms affecting the breathing are serious.

2.7.87   Common symptoms in children are:

- nettle rash (hives) anywhere on the body
- sense of impending doom
- swelling of throat and mouth
- difficulty in swallowing or speaking
- vocal changes (hoarseness)
- difficult or noisy breathing
- alterations in heart rate
- severe asthma
- abdominal pain, nausea and vomiting
- sudden feeling of weakness (drop in blood pressure)
- dizziness, collapse, loss of consciousness.

2.7.88   A child would not necessarily experience all these symptoms and may use different words to describe how they feel, such as relating a tightness in their chest to "tummy ache".

2.7.89   Even where only mild symptoms are present, the student should be watched carefully. The symptoms may herald the start of a more serious reaction.

Medication

2.7.90   The treatment for a severe allergic reaction is an injection of adrenaline. Pre-loaded adrenaline injection devices containing one measured dose of adrenaline are available on prescription for those believed to be at risk. The devices are available in two strengths – adult and junior.

2.7.91   Adrenaline (also known as epinephrine) acts quickly to constrict blood vessels, relax the smooth muscles in the lungs to improve breathing, stimulate the heartbeat and help stop swelling around the face and lips.

2.7.92   Should a severe allergic reaction occur, an adrenaline injection needs to be administered into the muscle of the upper outer thigh.

2.7.93   Adrenaline injectors are simple to administer. When given in accordance with the manufacturer's instructions, they have a well understood and safe delivery mechanism. It is not possible to give too large a dose using such a device. The needle is not seen until after it has been withdrawn from the patient's leg. In cases of doubt, it is better to give the injection than to hold back.

2.7.94   Medical opinion differs about whether schools should have at least two injection doses available at all times on site. The school policy should be developed in consultation with healthcare professionals.

2.7.95   **An ambulance should always be called.**

What the school should do

2.7.96   Students who are at risk of severe allergic reactions are not ill and neither are they currently, in most cases, to be regarded as disabled. They are normal children, except that if they come into contact with a certain food or substance, they may become very unwell. It is important that such students are not made to feel different. It is important, too, to allay parents' fears by reassuring them that prompt and efficient action will be taken in accordance with medical advice and guidance.

2.7.97   Many schools have decided that it is necessary to draw up individual protocols for students with severe allergies. The school (in consultation with the school nurse or designated school medical support), the child's doctor and (where appropriate) the school authority should agree such protocols with the parents and student. **The risks for allergic students will be reduced if an individual plan is in place**. The identity of these students and details about their allergy and treatment should be known to members of staff and to supply staff taking responsibility for the class they are in.

2.7.98   In addition, a general policy for responding to students with severe allergies must be incorporated into the school's policies on first aid and supporting students with medical conditions. All staff must have at least a minimum level of training in recognising symptoms and the appropriate measures. School procedures must be known to staff, students and parents.

2.7.99   The general policy could include risk assessment procedures and day-to-day measures for food management, including awareness of children's needs in relation to the menu, individual meal requirements and snacks in school. It is important to ensure that the catering supervisor is fully aware of each student's particular requirements. A "kitchen code of practice" could be put in place. It is not, of course, always feasible to ban from the premises all foodstuffs to which a particular child may be allergic.

2.7.100   Where students are sufficiently responsible to carry their emergency treatment on their person, there should always be a spare set kept safely but not locked away, and accessible to all staff. In large schools, it will be quicker for staff to use an injector that is with the child rather than taking time to collect one from elsewhere.

2.7.101   Members of staff are not obliged to give injections, but when they volunteer, they **must** always be trained and named in the school policy. Training should be provided by the local health trust.

Planning for Students with Allergies (eg Anaphylaxis)	
Checklist for Schools	**Checklist for Parents**
• Inform parents to outline any allergies their child has. • Ensure that catering supervisors are aware of an allergic student's requirements and are compliant with the conditions of the EU Allergen Directive, which requires the 14 most prevalent allergenic substances to be identified clearly on all food supplied in schools. • Include food-allergic children in school activities. Students should not be excluded because of their allergy. School activities should be designed and developed to ensure the inclusion of food-allergic students. • Ensure that named members of staff who have volunteered to give injections receive high quality training in managing severe allergies in schools, including how to use an adrenaline injector. • Review health records submitted by parents. • Identify a core team to work with parents to establish prevention and treatment strategies. Arrange staff training (the school nurse should be able to help to arrange this). Ensure all staff can recognise symptoms. • Make sure all relevant staff know what to do in an emergency, and work to eliminate the use of allergens in the allergic student's meals, educational tools, and arts and crafts projects. • Ensure that medications are appropriately stored, and easily accessible in a secure location (but not locked away) central to designated staff members. • Review policies after a reaction occurs. • Recognise the individuality of each child's or young person's needs and reflect this in their IHP. • Ensure that the school has a robust, detailed and regularly reviewed medical conditions policy.	• Notify the school of the child's allergies. • Ensure that there is communication. • Work with the school to develop a plan that accommodates the child's needs throughout the school. • Provide written medical documentation, instructions and medications as directed by the doctor. • Replace medication after use and on expiry. • Educate the child or young person in allergy self-management.

 For more information regarding the EU Allergen Directive, visit the following websites:
http://www.foodallergens.info/Legal/Labelling/Labelling.html
https://www.fsai.ie/legislation/food_legislation/food_information/14_allergens.html

EpiPens

2.7.102   In the past, it was a requirement that in order to use an EpiPen/autoinjector, the user had to have received training. Under the revision of the Medicines Act 2012, this is no longer the case, and any layperson can administer adrenaline through the use of an EpiPen/autoinjector.

2.7.103   However, if there is a high probability that an autoinjector will have to be used, staff should receive training in this procedure, especially if they work with individuals who carry these with them at all times in case of anaphylaxis.

2.7.104   As a generalised approach, a first aid provider could tailor their first aid courses to include slides and demonstrations on autoinjector use so all staff have baseline knowledge of this procedure. This will typically need to be discussed with the first aid training provider prior to the course delivery.

2.7.105   Where staff volunteer, they should fully understand what is required of them and how to use EpiPens as a result of the training provided. If they do not volunteer, they need to know the school policy as to what their limitations are, to contribute to a quick and effective response.

Sporting and off-site activities

2.7.106   Whenever a severely allergic student goes out of the school building, even for sports in the school grounds, their emergency kit must go too. A staff member trained to treat allergic symptoms must accompany the student. Having the emergency kit nearby at all times is a habit the student needs to learn early, and it is important the school reinforces this.

2.7.107   Where a child has a food allergy, if it is not certain that the food will be safe during an off-site activity, think about alternatives that will mean the child is not excluded from trips. For example, for a day trip, a student can take a lunch prepared at home, and for longer visits, some children can take their meals in frozen form to be reheated individually at mealtimes. In any event, the allergic child should always take plenty of safe snacks, and parents could be asked to provide and maintain a selection of safe snacks for these occasions.

2.7.108   Insect sting allergies can cause a lot of anxiety and will need careful management. Special care is required when outdoors. The student should wear shoes at all times, and all food and drink should be covered until it is needed. Staff supervising activities must ensure that suitable medication is always on hand.

The Use of Entonox in Schools

2.7.109   Entonox is a medical analgesic gas that is a mixture of **50% nitrous oxide and 50% oxygen**. Its pain-relieving effect is strong, and it is very fast acting. However, it wears off very quickly. It is most commonly used in pre-hospital care, childbirth and emergency medicine by medical professionals such as doctors, nurses, midwives and paramedics. **Entonox** is known colloquially as "**gas and air**".

2.7.110   Schools that wish to make Entonox available for use by staff who have medical, nursing or first aid responsibilities should seek suitable training from the local ambulance trust, hospital anaesthetic department or resuscitation training officer, as well as from the manufacturer. However, most common uses of Entonox in school situations (eg moving injured casualties to an ambulance and changing large, painful dressings) are more suited to trained medical or nursing staff, and generally outside the capabilities, knowledge and duties of a trained first-aider.

2.7.111   Entonox should not be used for individuals with a range of conditions (eg bowel obstruction, pneumothorax [collapsed lung], middle ear or sinus disease) and those with reduced levels of consciousness, such as in sporting injuries.

2.7.112   The final decision about whether or not to administer Entonox in schools needs to be made by the employer. A risk assessment considering the benefits and risks of administering pain management in the scope of the school's typical PESSPA injuries would be an appropriate process in making this decision.

HIV and AIDS

2.7.113   The human immunodeficiency virus (HIV) is a non-notifiable disease, which means that parents of students affected or infected, or the students themselves, may choose not to inform their school. This is because the infected students present no risk of onward transmission in everyday contact.

2.7.114   There are no known reports of HIV transmission occurring in a UK school either from a student or a member of staff.

2.7.115   Students may take part in PESSPA providing they do not have any other medical condition that prevents them from participating.

2.7.116   No cases have been recorded of HIV transmission from student to student by biting, fighting, playing or any other childhood interactions. Small cuts or grazes do not pose any concern.

2.7.117   Bleeding resulting from accidents should be dealt with immediately. First-aiders should wear disposable waterproof gloves following normal first aid procedures and standard hygiene practices. This will be effective in preventing transmission of all blood-borne infections, including HIV.

2.7.118   The Children's HIV Association (CHIVA) has produced clear guidance for schools, explaining how students known to have a diagnosis of HIV should be supported. This can be used to raise staff awareness of HIV, and to inform them about the procedures to take should a student disclose their condition. This information may already be contained in existing school policies. Where it is not, it can be accessed on the CHIVA website.

 For more information, visit the CHIVA website: https://www.chiva.org.uk

Concussion

2.7.119   Concussion is a minor traumatic brain injury that involves a sudden but short-lived loss of mental function. Concussion can occur after a blow or other injury to the head that involves the brain being shaken against the inside of the skull. Symptoms are often immediate but can be delayed for up to 48 hours. Concussion is known to have potential dangers both at the time of injury and in later life.

2.7.120   **All concussions need to be taken seriously** to safeguard the health and welfare of children and young people. Failing to do so can have serious consequences including, in extremely rare cases, death.

 To download the Sport and Recreation Alliance (2015) "Concussion guidelines for the education sector", visit http://goo.gl/07Grlo

2.7.121   All staff should be aware that concussion could affect **anyone, anywhere, at any time**. Play and PESSPA activities, and travelling to or from school, may be occasions when staff may be more aware of such incidents.

2.7.122   Special attention should be paid to children who may have:

- experienced a fall in the playground
- fallen from heights on to hard surfaces or while cycling
- been involved in road traffic collisions either recently or in the past
- been or are involved in contact sports.

Second impact syndrome

2.7.123   Second impact syndrome (SIS) is a very rare condition in which a second concussion occurs before the first concussion has properly healed. SIS can result from even a very mild concussion that occurs minutes, hours, days or weeks after the initial concussion. SIS can cause rapid and severe brain swelling and is often fatal, even if the second injury was far less intense. Survivors of SIS are frequently left with disabling conditions.

2.7.124   Most cases of SIS have occurred in young people, who are thought to be particularly vulnerable. In order to prevent SIS, guidelines have been written (see references listed on page 118) to ensure that all young people who have sustained a concussion, either in PESSPA activities or other contexts, make a full recovery before returning to any activities in which a second concussion is likely to occur.

 See **Case Law 40** in **Chapter 4**.

Recognising, treating and managing concussion

2.7.125   Guidelines highlight the importance of **removing** the individual with suspected concussion from participation and ensuring that they **recover** fully and appropriately (eg over a period of weeks) and **return** to academic studies before taking part in PESSPA activities again. (See **Table 9** below.)

Table 9: A summary of guidance on recognising, managing and treating concussion in PESSPA

Where any of the indicators in **bold type** are observed or reported:

- obtain immediate qualified professional medical opinion (where available)

or

- transport by ambulance for urgent medical attention.

Signs to Look for	Symptoms to Ask about, and Older Students to Self-express Feelings about
<ul><li>**Knocked out/loss of consciousness**</li><li>**Seizure or convulsion**</li><li>General confusion/**increasing confusion or irritability**</li><li>Vomiting/**repeated vomiting**</li><li>**Strange or inappropriate behaviour** (laughing, crying, getting angry easily)</li><li>**Deteriorating level of consciousness**</li><li>Slow to get up/lying motionless</li><li>Poor coordination or balance/unsteady on feet</li><li>Grabbing or clutching head</li><li>Does not know time, date, place, period of game, score, what the lesson is</li><li>Cannot remember things that happened before or after the injury</li><li>Blank stare or glassy-eyed</li><li>Slurred speech</li><li>Slow to answer questions or follow direction</li><li>Easily distracted</li><li>Poor concentration</li><li>Not playing or participating as well as before the incident.</li></ul>	<ul><li>Headache/**severe or increasing headache**</li><li>**Neck pain**</li><li>**Double vision or blurred vision**</li><li>**Weakness or tingling/burning in arms or legs**</li><li>Dizziness</li><li>Feels dazed/slowed down</li><li>Feels "dinged", "stung", "having my bell rung", "in a fog"</li><li>Sees stars or flashing lights</li><li>Feels pressure in head</li><li>Ringing in ears</li><li>Sleepiness</li><li>Loss of vision</li><li>Sensitivity to light</li><li>Sensitivity to noise</li><li>Difficulty concentrating</li><li>Stomach ache or stomach pain</li><li>Nausea or sickness</li><li>Fatigue or low energy.</li></ul>

Protocols to be Followed in the Case of Concussion	Additional School Procedures

• **Recognise** the signs, symptoms and danger signs of potentially more serious brain injury
• **Remove** immediately from further participation in the lesson, activity or match
• Do not leave alone
• Have them seen by a doctor/medical professional as soon as possible
• If knocked out, immediately call an ambulance to take them to hospital
• **Recover** – give time – avoid sports activity, running, cycling, swimming, fitness; minimum of 14 days' rest is advised unless cleared to return earlier by a doctor (parental responsibility to obtain this)
• **Return** – student should return to academic studies before returning to physical activity; sometimes, symptoms may be prolonged
• **Gradual return to participation** – if symptom-free following the recommended 14-day recovery phase, a gradual return to activity should be implemented; for example:
  – short session of light walking or stationary cycling
  – activity-specific, non-contact (including no heading in football) work
  – contact activities (once cleared by a doctor)
  – full activity/game participation
 	
Each phase should take a minimum of one day; if symptoms recur, then stop all activity for 1–2 days, recommencing at previous phase according to individual needs of student
 	
• **"When in doubt, sit them out"**.
	• Review and include in school policy/procedures
	• All staff to be aware of signs and symptoms
	• Consider school procedures for dealing with possible concussion in lessons, club activities and matches where a medical professional is not likely to be present
	• Keep parents informed of:
	  – policy and procedures
	  – any occurrences with their child
	• It is a parental responsibility to obtain confirmation from a medical source that a student is fit to return to physical activity – verbal confirmation will suffice if a fee for a medical letter is involved
	• Teach students about the symptoms of concussion, and action to follow if feeling concussed or dazed
	• Make all relevant staff in other subjects or classes aware when a student has concussion so that this is taken into consideration in lessons, and any impact on studies noted and referred if necessary.

Adapted from a collation produced by Peter Whitlam (2014) for use on afPE risk management courses. Sources:

- Concussion in Sport Group (2013) "Pocket concussion recognition tool", http://goo.gl/U51yKm
- Department of Education Northern Ireland (DENI) (2014) "Concussion", https://goo.gl/pL9Er8
- Forum on Concussion in Sport (England) (2014) "Concussion guidelines for schools"
- McCrory, P. et al (2013) "Consensus statement on concussion in sport", *British Journal of Sports Medicine*, 47: 250–258
- Parachute Canada (2014) "Concussion toolkit", http://goo.gl/lRF1CJ
- Rugby Football Union (2013) "Concussion – headcase", www.englandrugby.com

More guidance on concussion is available online for each home country:

England
Sport and Recreation Alliance (2015) "Concussion guidelines for the education sector", http://goo.gl/07Grlo

Northern Ireland
DENI (2015) "Concussion – Informing the school: Advice for parents", http://goo.gl/radn0o

Scotland
Scottish Government (2014) "Sports concussion: If in doubt, sit them out", https://www2.gov.scot/Resource/0044/00441743.pdf

Wales
Welsh Government (2014) "Concussion is dangerous: Welsh Government guidance on concussion for school and community sport up to age 19", https://gov.wales/sites/default/files/publications/2018-11/concussion-is-dangerous-welsh-government-guidance-on-concussion-for-school-and-community-sport-up-to-age-19.pdf

Students learning about concussion

2.7.126   Helping students to learn about the potential dangers of concussion, how to recognise the signs and how to take immediate and appropriate action if they suspect concussion is highly important.

 For more information on promoting student learning about concussion, see **Chapter 3, Section 11**.

Professional learning about concussion

2.7.127   Training is available through afPE (cpd@afpe.org.uk). **Table 9** is an integral part of this learning and collates information from a range of existing publications on the topic with additional information specific to school policy.

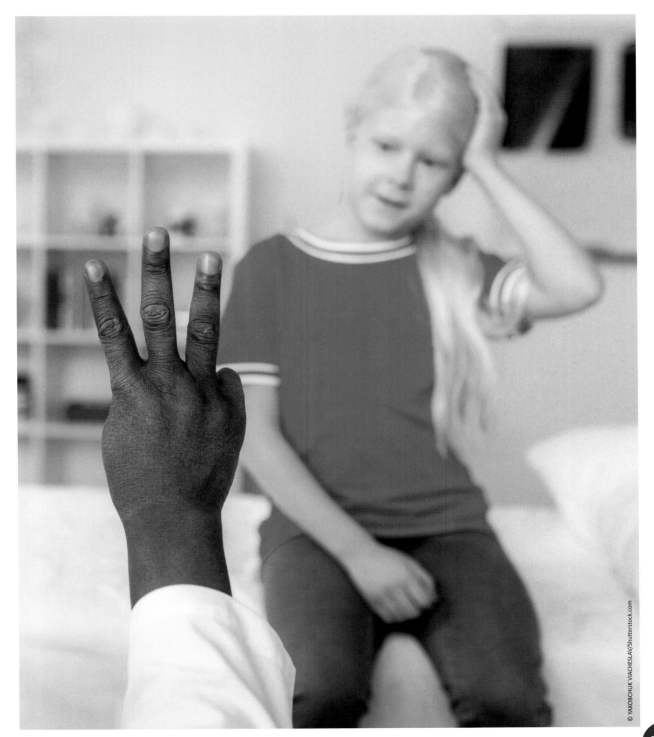

© YAKOBCHUK VIACHESLAV/Shutterstock.com

Section 8: Facilities

Work Spaces

2.8.1   Whatever physical education, school sport and physical activity (PESSPA) facilities are available for use, risk assessments will need to be specific to those, and to the particular school's use of the facilities, including the type of activity taught in them.

2.8.2   Adaptable facilities require a risk assessment that considers the variable use of the facility, the implications of converting the facility (particularly where students may be involved), the particular usage the school intends and any guidelines manufacturers provide.

2.8.3   Where schools **share facilities** with other groups within a network, it is good practice to establish an understanding that the host school will decide **normal operating procedures (NOPs)** and **emergency action plans (EAPs)**. These should be made available to other user groups, who should accommodate them within their risk assessments for travelling to and using a shared facility.

2.8.4   It is important that when utilising a facility owned by any other provider (eg a leisure centre) that the day-to-day working processes of that facility meet the needs of students. This should be checked because operating procedures have often been designed with an adult target group in mind.

2.8.5   Wherever a facility is used by a **new group** for the first time, the work area needs to be checked **before and during all lessons** to ensure that:

- the **floor**, **poolside** or **outdoor** work surface provides secure footing to prevent tripping, slipping or other injury
- **obstructions** are identified and removed, where possible, or the students made aware of any immovable obstructions, and the member of staff takes these into account throughout the session
- there is sufficient space for the planned activity; activities that involve freedom of movement (eg dance and games) require more space than those that involve restricted movement (eg performing exercises/movements on a personal mat); where insufficient space is available, activities should be adapted to suit the restricted space
- there is **safe and appropriate access**, including for people with disabilities
- transport implications have been addressed, such as the provision of a safe embarkation/ disembarkation area
- the use of additional equipment and the level of noise do not impact on the safety of others using the facility
- safe and appropriate storage and management of the movement of equipment in and around **storage areas** have been carefully considered
- there are **sources of liquid** to maintain hydration, where necessary.

2.8.6   **Fixed equipment** within a facility, such as **dance barres** or **folding gymnastics frames**, should be:

- stable
- substantial in design
- able to accommodate participants of different ages and abilities.

2.8.7   Where mirrors are installed, they need to be of strengthened glass.

2.8.8   **Basketball** goals can be wall-hinged, wall-mounted fixed, ceiling drop down, socketed or portable, and may be used for match play or recreational practice. Schools need to consider the use of the court and basketball goal systems available in order to make suitable choices. Where boards are freestanding or socketed in playground or court areas, padding can be used around the post to reduce the impact of collisions.

2.8.9   Indoor and outdoor courts should provide non-slip playing areas and be well maintained. Indoor courts, particularly in attacking areas, can hold perspiration from players making contact with the ground, which may constitute a hazard, so they should be regularly checked and wiped dry. Outdoor areas should be kept free of moss and leaves.

2.8.10   The court perimeter should be free from hazards with a safety zone surrounding the playing court. This may vary depending on the type of facility and governing body of sport guidelines should be checked regularly for guidance. Protruding obstacles should be removed or made safe behind the lines of the court.

2.8.11   Schools should be aware of governing body of sport specifications for reasons of safety and quality, and where these cannot be met, specific safety conditions be established.

Goalposts (fixed or portable) should be made **secure** at all times in such a manner that they cannot fall forwards or backwards for any reason. Both goalposts and corner flags should be checked regularly for safety.

2.8.12   **Netball** courts should be level and flat, with no loose objects, such as grit or wet leaves, on the court or surrounding area. Where netball is played on the same area as tennis, check that holes used for net posts have covers in place and that they are flush with the surface.

2.8.13   Portable goalposts should be placed on the centre point of each goal line with none of the base protruding on to the court. The use of post protectors is encouraged.

2.8.14   For **rugby football** (league and union) a suitable playing surface is essential and should be soft enough to safely accommodate falls during tackles.

2.8.15   Broken wire in surround **fencing** is particularly hazardous, and students should be reminded regularly to maintain a safe distance (indicated by the use of barriers or cones) until it has been repaired.

2.8.16   There should be sufficient space for the safe use of equipment, and **adequate electrical points and Internet connections** so that trailing wires or ill-placed or unstable items do not present a hazard.

Floors, Courts, Playing Surfaces and Pitches

2.8.17   **Indoor floors** should be kept clean and swept regularly. Any cleaning and/or polishing of floors should not leave a slippery finish. Loose boards, splintering, cracking and lifting edges sometimes occur with heavy use, and floor sockets and screws can become proud, creating an irregular surface that can affect the likelihood of harm and the security of footing. Dampness caused by condensation or residual wet mopping after school meals should be dried thoroughly before activity begins.

 See **Case Law 13** in **Chapter 4**.

2.8.18   **Sprung or semi-sprung floors** are most beneficial to certain activities within PESSPA programmes, such as dance, gymnastics and some health and fitness type activities, in that they offer bones and joints protection from damage that can arise from the absorption of impact energy. Where floors are not sprung, care should be taken with high-impact landings during such activities.

2.8.19   Where a facility is used for other purposes, such as dining, examinations and assemblies, safe use of the floor in PESSPA lessons may become compromised, and schools should seek to avoid this wherever possible by:

- raising this concern with the employer, who may not appreciate the detrimental effects the practice of using the facility for other purposes has on PESSPA situations
- investigating the use of alternative areas to accommodate these other activities
- developing strategies and procedures for dealing with hazards posed by alternative use.

2.8.20   Where such dual use cannot be avoided (eg following breakfast and lunchtimes), these areas will need cleaning before being handed back for use as physical activity spaces.

2.8.21   Whenever possible, school staff should be involved in decisions about cleaning schedules, highlighting concerns that affect PESSPA situations that may not otherwise have been considered. Staff will be able to understand the potential issues and offer useful ideas for establishing regular and effective cleaning schedules that also ensure safe working areas.

2.8.22   **All outdoor playing surfaces** need to be suitable for activity and in sound condition. They should be checked routinely to ensure security of footing, and where concerns exist, an effective reporting system needs to be in place.

2.8.23   School routines should be developed that account for the time of year and time of school day. For example, leaves may cause slipping injuries and therefore need to be cleared regularly.

2.8.24   Safety on **playing fields, sports pitches and athletics areas** can be adversely affected by the aftermath of trespass. For example, broken glass, cans and other rubbish create serious risks to students.

2.8.25   Deposits of dog faeces infected by toxocara (roundworm) can cause toxocariasis in humans, with symptoms that include blindness, asthma, epilepsy and general aches and pains. All practical measures should be taken to keep animals off the playing surfaces and encourage owners to remove any offending deposits immediately. In some schools, this poses a significant problem, and staff need to be guided by the leadership team and governors as to what is a safe standard for participation and how this safe standard is to be maintained.

2.8.26   **Remote pitches, courts and fields** require additional consideration. Staff who are working away from the main building on fields, courts or other play areas should be equipped with mobile phones/ smartphones, radios or alternative reliable communication devices in order to make immediate contact with colleagues if necessary. Some emergencies necessitate immediate support, often including access to first aid, including a defibrillator where installed.

 For more information, see **Chapter 2, Section 7**.

2.8.27   **Pitches** should be **marked out** safely in order that playing surfaces are and remain level. Corrosive marking substances should not be used. Regular maintenance is essential. Holes (including rabbit scrapes) should be filled as soon as possible after identification.

2.8.28   Under the rules of The Football Association (FA), any **3G artificial pitch** that is used for affiliated football is required to be tested, following which it will appear on the 3G Football Turf Pitch Register. Schools' league match football is affiliated so pitches used for this purpose will need a test to be performed.

To see the list of registered artificial 3G pitches, visit http://3g.thefa.me.uk

2.8.29   Where such pitches are only used for lessons and friendly matches, the inspection requirement would not necessarily be applied. However, for regular and correct maintenance of what is a costly investment, it would be seen to be good practice to follow this procedure. Schools should check the FA website to find a list of companies recommended by The FA to carry out this work.

2.8.30   Guidance on the design and specifications for artificial surfaces can be sought through the Sport England facilities department.

To access the Sport England guidance on artificial surfaces, go to www.sportengland.org

2.8.31   Where playing fields are used as **multipurpose play areas**, litter may be a problem that needs to be controlled. Gang mowers can shred plastic and metal containers into sharp shards that create significant risk.

2.8.32   Where **basketball** match or game play takes place on marked courts, the court perimeter should be free from hazard with a safe zone of at least 1.05 metres around the edge. Protruding **obstacles** should be removed or made safe behind and in line with the backboards. The overhang (measured from the front of the post to the front of the backboard) should be 1.2 metres and to the centre of the ring 1.575 metres. Where such space is not available, careful officiating and management of the situation are essential. Where wall-mounted boards are used for cross-court games, participants should be warned to avoid collisions with the end walls, and to refrain from using their feet against the end wall to help achieve height.

2.8.33   **Ultimate frisbee** is played both indoors and outdoors. When played outdoors, a field similar in size to a football pitch is used. The last 18 metres at either end of the field are the "end zones". When played indoors, the rules vary. The indoor playing area is ideally 35–40 metres long and 15–20 metres wide. In school, the distance from the end zone to the end wall should be at least one metre to reduce the likelihood of collision with the end wall.

See **Case Law 15–19** in **Chapter 4**.

Floor Areas and Pitch/Court Sizes

2.8.34   Staff need to consider how a specific PESSPA activity can be presented in order to allow safe movement for all students in the working area.

2.8.35   There should be a suitable distance between the playing area and the perimeter of the working space in which it is located, particularly if other students are working in adjacent areas. The distance between the playing surface and features such as boundary fences, roads and windows must be sufficient to avoid accident or injury, and the directions of play should account for this. Proximity to hazardous fixtures and fittings should be avoided. Reference should be made to Sport England: https://www.sportengland.org/how-we-can-help/facilities-and-planning/design-and-cost-guidance/outdoor-surfaces

2.8.36   The amount of **floor area** required for safe practical work indoors depends on the number of participants taking part, their age and mobility, and the type of activity planned. One Dance UK recommends a minimum of three square metres per student for primary **dance** and five square metres per student for secondary dance. Some styles/types of dance require limited movement, while others require significant freedom to move. Without sufficient space, variation in choreography or style may be necessary.

For advice and information from One Dance UK, go to https://www.onedanceuk.org/

2.8.37 **Gymnastics** generally requires more space per student than dance in order to allow for safe movement and the use of apparatus. Historically, approximately eight square metres per student was the standard for a then-typical class size of 30 in a typical secondary school gymnasium where a range of activities would be taught. Gymnastics activities and apparatus arrangements will need to be planned and adapted carefully if less space is available.

2.8.38 In **sports halls**, the space required for games depends on the standard of play – the higher the standard, the larger the space needed due to greater run-off areas and clearance heights. Where halls are divided into sections using partitions or netting, thought needs to be given to appropriate shared use. Netting should not foul footing at any time. Further specific guidance appears later in this section.

2.8.39 Pitches and courts should be suitable in size **for the ages and abilities** of those using them.

2.8.40 When using courts **for net games**, there should be sufficient space on court to accommodate group practice and to avoid students playing over post bases.

2.8.41 On occasions, it might be necessary to "condition" the rules or organisation of games activities to make safe use of restricted space or the space available.

 See **Case Law 20** in **Chapter 4**.

Playground Areas for Recreational Use

2.8.42 Playground activity occurring at break and lunchtime, preschool or at the end of the school day is varied and involves students of all ages. Playground activity may be student-regulated, with minimum levels of adult supervision, or directly controlled and supervised by a member of staff, depending on behaviour, skill, space etc. It may consist of highly creative activity or be based on traditional sports and games.

2.8.43 **Zoned play areas** should be defined and respected, and activities restricted to their particular designation. "Quiet areas" should not be intruded on.

2.8.44 Sufficient safe space should be allocated for specific activities. Careful planning of playground areas should help with this by:

- avoiding car park areas, and areas where there is any likelihood of traffic entering or leaving the school premises
- assigning activities involving rapid movement, the use of balls and sudden changes of direction to areas that are away from sloping ground or areas with sudden drops
- assigning individual activities such as skipping and circus skills to areas with appropriate vegetation or shrubs (that will not affect the activity)
- avoiding areas with poor drainage known to frequently retain lying water.

2.8.45 Schools should have procedures in place to ensure that the items in **Table 10** are regularly monitored, and strategies implemented to minimise the risk of injury.

Table 10: Potential hazards relating to playground areas

Play-area Surface	Surrounding Vegetation
• Uneven or cracked • Loose grit • Slippery in wet weather • Vegetation growing on or through surface • Litter, including broken glass • Patches of silt from poor drainage • Covers missing from post sockets.	• Possibility of students overrunning into plants/shrubs • Type of plants/shrubs (eg shrubs with large thorns, stinging nettles) • Possibility of poisonous berries adjacent to play area • Seasonal coverage of wet fallen leaves.
Play-area Drainage	**Access to Play Area**
• Standing water after rain • Drain grids below or above surface level • Drain grids with oversized spaces • Drain grids broken or missing.	• Possibility of unauthorised student access • Possibility of vehicular access • Vehicular deposits on play area if used as a car park outside school hours • Use as public right of way • Possibility of access by unauthorised adults.
Play Area Built on Sloping Ground	**Fixed Climbing Equipment**
• Steep steps • Lack of secure handrail • Condition of steps • Presence of rubbish or vegetation on steps • Possibility of students overrunning play area • Possibility of stones, gravel or dirt rolling on to play area.	• Lack of inspection and repair schedule • Peeling paint and rust • Inappropriate or lack of safety surfaces • Proximity to other hazards (eg windows or projections) • Excessive fall height.
Buildings Around Play Area	
• Exposed external corners adjacent to play areas • Projections below head height (adult) • Outward-opening windows • Outward-opening doors • Non-toughened glass.	

Safety Surfaces for Playground Climbing Areas

2.8.46　Safety surfaces should be provided indoors or outside wherever the fall height is greater than 600mm (BS EN 1177). However, a **school-specific risk assessment** may deem it safe practice to install a safety surface at fall heights below this requirement.

2.8.47　Appropriate impact-absorbing surfaces, such as rubber-based materials, have been shown to reduce injuries. Suitable safety surfaces, such as rubber combinations or natural bark, should be sourced for outdoor use, where required, to a depth of 300–400mm depending on the critical fall height. It should be free of entrapments, sharp edges or projections that could cause injury.

2.8.48   Recommended sizes of impact-absorbing surfaces increase in line with the critical fall height, typically:

Critical Fall Height	Free Fall Space Needed
1.5m	1.5m diameter
2.0m	1.85m diameter
2.5m	2.15m diameter
3.0m	2.5m diameter

For information regarding safe supervision of outdoor play and activity areas, see **Chapter 2, Section 12**.

Climbing, Traverse and Bouldering Walls

2.8.49   The construction of bouldering and climbing walls should meet the requirements of the standards EN 12572:1 and 2.

2.8.50   Two-metre-high wall matting is available to purchase, which can be used when climbing walls built within sports halls or gymnasiums are not in use. It prevents access to the wall, and provides protection against the uneven surface of the wall. Access to climbing walls inside and outside needs to be carefully managed and supervised. Procedures might include:

- educating students about rules regarding use of the facilities
- roping off the area, and using appropriate signage to clearly indicate when the area is out of bounds
- removing or tying up and securing all ropes and other equipment
- keeping facilities that house indoor climbing walls locked when they are not being supervised.

2.8.51   Many websites offer guidance on the design and maintenance of climbing walls. Schools considering installing climbing walls will find the guidance offered in the British Mountaineering Council (BMC) *Climbing Wall Manual* useful.

For more information on the BMC *Climbing Wall Manual*, see https://goo.gl/uxjXTi.

Safety surfaces for climbing and bouldering walls

2.8.52   Injury from falls is increased where inadequate safety surfaces are installed, or technique is poor. Both rubber crumb and dense foam products are available to help reduce the severity of injury from such falls.

2.8.53   For low traverse walls outside, where the fall height is less than 600mm, a safety surface may not be required. However, some schools identify a need for such a surface in their risk assessment even where the fall height is below this level.

2.8.54   For bouldering walls, a minimum depth of 300mm of matting should be installed where a maximum climbing height of 4.5 metres is possible.

2.8.55 For climbing and bouldering walls located outdoors, consideration needs to be given to providing slip-resistant flooring, and a surface that is frost-proof and water-permeable to prevent surface water presenting a hazard.

2.8.56 All walls built to the specification of standards EN 12572:1 and 2 should have appropriate impact flooring that is fit for purpose, but beyond this, set depths are not specified.

 See **Case Law 21** in **Chapter 4**.

Changing Areas

2.8.57 **Dignity, decency and privacy** should underpin all decisions on changing areas in order to meet student needs.

2.8.58 Any changing space should be **checked** regularly, before and during use, to ensure that:
- pegs, where installed, are not broken or exposing sharp edges
- additional accessible space is provided, where required, for students with special educational needs and disabilities (SEND) (eg wheelchairs users and those requiring help with changing)
- benching and other furniture is fixed to prevent it toppling over during use
- there are no sharp edges to tiling or heaters that could cause injury
- floor surfaces are not slippery when wet
- personal items and clothing do not litter the floor and cause potential tripping hazards
- where showers are provided, water mixer valves are regulated by one control key, positioned **out of reach** of students to reduce any risk of scalding.

2.8.59 Where **safety standards** are compromised, alternative arrangements need to be made and faults reported to the school leadership team.

2.8.60 Many **primary schools** lack purpose-built changing rooms but find spaces where the sexes, individuals or small groups can change separately. Students as young as the start of Key Stage 2 regularly express preferences for separate sex changing areas. Schools should begin to consider how they can accommodate this safely by:
- using screens in a classroom to separate the room into sections
- allowing one sex to change during a break time, if this occurs directly before the lesson
- using two different areas, such as a cloakroom and a classroom, if supervision is available
- considering how appropriate changing areas might be provided in their long-term planning.

Heating, Lighting and Structural Considerations

2.8.61 **Walls** should be smooth to avoid friction injury if body contact occurs, with rounded corners where the possibility of impact is likely, and to facilitate safe ball-rebound activities. Background colours and the need for the safe sighting of accelerating projectiles (such as balls) should be considered. Essential features other than physical education apparatus should be positioned, wherever possible, well above working height, or recessed if this requirement cannot be met.

2.8.62 **Ceiling height** needs to be sufficient so as not to restrict movements such as lifts in dance, vaults in gymnastics, throws in combat sports and clearance for trampolining at school or higher competitive levels.

2.8.63   **Doors and door frames** should be flush, wherever possible. Main access doors should open outwards and have some system of closure control. This is especially important on exposed or windy sites, to minimise the risk of doors opening or slamming unexpectedly.

2.8.64   **Glass doors** can be hazardous. Where they are necessary, the glass should be smoked or coloured for visibility, reinforced and resistant to impact fracture. If a pane is cracked, it should be replaced as soon as possible. Door glazing should be at a height that accommodates wheelchair users. Where doors are glazed around hand-pushing height, there should be push battens across the door on both sides. While recommended, it should not be assumed that all glass in a school is toughened in case someone falls into it or seeks to push off from it. **This needs to be confirmed**, and systems put in place to minimise the likelihood of injury occurring.

2.8.65   **Lighting** should be uniform wherever possible, and adequate for safe participation.

2.8.66   In indoor environments, the effectiveness of artificial lighting needs to be taken into account. It would be hazardous to ask students to undertake any activity where their safety was compromised due to inadequate or overly bright lighting. Artificial lighting should be made from unbreakable materials or set in protective cages. Strip lighting that produces a flickering or stroboscopic effect should be avoided as this could impair visual focus, induce disorientation and trigger seizures. Lighting should provide clear visibility for any activity being undertaken.

2.8.67   Any risk of being dazzled by sunlight coming through windows or directly into students' eyes, or glare reflected from water needs to be managed by the considered placement of apparatus, direction of play or movement, frequent changing of teaching position or a more permanent resolution, such as tinting the glass or the use of blinds.

2.8.68   **Heating systems** should provide an adequate working temperature, adjustable to accommodate varying conditions, and be designed so that there is no danger of any student being adversely affected by burns, fumes or other hazards to health.

2.8.69   Where old models of radiators are still in place, exposed spindles with caps removed or lost can present a danger to students if they fall on to them. A regular inspection and maintenance programme for all heating systems should be established.

2.8.70   The **temperature** needs to be adequate for safe activity, and maintained evenly throughout the facility. The minimum temperature for **indoor** PESSPA activities is technically 15°C. Where this temperature is not met, warm-up and preparation might be extended, and the pace increased, if the lesson can continue reasonably safely. Alternatively, the lesson may be shortened or abandoned completely.

2.8.71   There is **no upper limit** to temperature for activity and no statutory maximum working temperature. Staff will need to be sensitive to the impact of significantly high temperatures on active sessions and plan accordingly. If outside, sun protection and regular hydration should be encouraged.

 For more information about weather conditions, see **2.10.58**.

Fire Safety and Emergency Evacuation

2.8.72   Schools are responsible for determining their own assessment of fire safety. It is the responsibility of the leadership team to ensure specific fire safety regulations are applied in the school. This should form part of a school's risk assessment or be a separate risk assessment.

2.8.73 Fire precaution procedures should be known and applied by all school staff. In the **PESSPA context**, this would typically involve staff visually checking:

- emergency evacuation signs are in place and illuminated where required
- emergency exits are operative
- emergency exits are not locked or blocked when a facility is in use, such as where trampolines or other equipment are placed across them
- fire safety equipment is in place and not misused.

2.8.74 It must be possible for both staff and students to open fire doors from the inside of the facility.

2.8.75 Where possible, fire exit doors should have flush-mounted push pads to minimise the likelihood of injury.

2.8.76 Mats should be stored in a specific mat store, where provided, or stored away from electrical circuits to minimise the possibility of fire causing toxic fumes.

2.8.77 Staff must know how many and which students they are responsible for, be familiar with the emergency evacuation procedures, and know the quickest routes to safety.

2.8.78 Staff should plan for the possibility of **emergency evacuation** taking place in cold or inclement weather, and any implications for potential hypothermia when students may need to leave an indoor facility for an extended period of time while wearing minimal clothing or in bare feet. These procedures should enable evacuation without students needing to delay in order to put on clothing and footwear. Schools might consider providing a set of emergency (foil) blankets that are taken out by one of the appointed fire officers during every evacuation.

2.8.79 The implications for the evacuation of students and staff with reduced mobility, and wheelchair users, need to be considered and planned for. Discussion with students will inform them of their role in an emergency evacuation.

2.8.80 The **head teacher** is the "senior manager on site" directly responsible for fire safety in law. If they are not on site, then the next most senior person on site temporarily becomes the responsible person.

Security

2.8.81 Security of working areas is essential. Facilities that offer unauthorised access to high-risk environments (such as a pool or climbing wall) or equipment (such as trampolines) need to be made secure when not in use.

Activity-specific Facility Information

> Alongside the generic advice outlined above there now follows some activity related information which is context specific.

Athletic facilities

Throwing areas

2.8.82 Most schools will not have access to safety nets and cages that meet UK Athletics standards. These facilities are needed when any student is deploying a turn/rotational technique. Anything beyond a side-on standing technique should not be practised without safety nets and cages. This applies to both discus and hammer activities in lessons and extracurricular competition.

Landing areas

2.8.83   Landing areas need to be sufficiently large to accommodate all abilities of performer.

2.8.84   **Sand areas** in **high jump** are only suitable for horizontal and low-level jumping for height, involving feet-to-feet landing. In these cases, wooden or concrete surrounds should not present a danger. Where a sand area is not available, schools should consider using a **standing jump** technique.

2.8.85   In **long jump**, multiple take-off boards (ie set at different distances from the sand) are helpful to ensure that jumpers of different abilities can land safely in the sand area.

2.8.86   Sand levels should reach the top of the long-jump pit and be level with the runway. They need to be regularly checked for fouling and dangerous objects.

2.8.87   Non-caking sharp sand should be used and should be **at least 30cm deep** to prevent jarring on landing. A sand landing area should be **regularly dug and raked during practical sessions** to avoid compacted sections.

2.8.88   Digging and raking implements should be stored at least three metres from the landing pit, with prongs and sharp edges into the ground.

2.8.89   Students should be taught how to rake pits effectively, and to do so before the sand becomes compacted, which might cause impact injuries.

2.8.90   Approach and take-off areas for jumping events should be checked to see that they are stable, level, smooth and non-slip, with sufficient space between participants to avoid collisions.

2.8.91   Primary schools wishing to introduce jumping activities should only consider doing so if they have a sand area that meets the requirements set out above.

Running areas (can be applied to other activities involving running)

2.8.92   Work areas for all running activities should be checked to see that they are level, free of potholes and litter, and non-slip, with sufficient space between participants to avoid collisions.

2.8.93   Running areas should include sufficient space to allow for "run-off" at the end of a practice or race, which means that walls and netting should not present obstacles. If necessary, the teacher should adjust the working space to ensure sufficient run-off distance is available.

2.8.94   Risk assessments should consider whether running activities should be adapted, limited or abandoned if the **grass surface** of a work area is wet.

Combat arenas

2.8.95   Combat arenas should:

- be sited in a clear area away from walls and other obstacles
- be large enough to accommodate the group and allow safe activity, ie sufficient floor area and ceiling height
- be level, even and clean, with a non-slip surface
- provide secure footing.

2.8.96   **Fencing pistes** (playing areas) for both competition and practice need to be well **spaced out**, at least 1.5 metres apart. There should be a clear **run-off** at each end for the safety of participants and spectators.

Dance areas

2.8.97 Different dance styles can require **varying amounts of space**. Some South Asian and African styles, for example, may require limited space, while "creative dance" or contemporary dance may require larger areas, especially if lots of travelling is involved.

2.8.98 One Dance UK recommends a minimum of three square metres for each primary student and five square metres for each secondary student in order to enable them to move safely and freely when engaged in dance sessions as part of the PESSPA programme.

2.8.99 Any **mirrors** in dance studios need to be made of toughened, shatterproof glass.

Fitness rooms

2.8.100 Care should be taken when planning the layout of fitness rooms. Staff should check that:

- sufficient space is available between and behind items of equipment to enable a group of students working on one machine to position themselves correctly
- the layout allows clear visual supervision across the room
- working surfaces are firm and stable
- emergency exits are accessible and clear of equipment
- regular inspection and repair programmes are organised and that these are carried out by recognised specialists
- floor areas are protected with mats in areas where free weights are used – these should not cause a tripping hazard
- the room is of a consistent temperature (Sport England recommends an air temperature of 12–18°C with adequate ventilation where heat gains are likely).

2.8.101 Fitness rooms should always be locked when not in use, to **prevent unauthorised access** to potentially dangerous equipment.

2.8.102 All cardiovascular (CV) machines, fixed resistance machines and other specialist equipment should be checked regularly by a company competent in working with such apparatus.

2.8.103 Many fitness rooms do not provide equipment appropriate for school use. In situations where facilities are shared with the community (ie dual use), schools often make compromises in using adult equipment with young people. Equipment "donated" by any leisure provider should be checked thoroughly to establish whether it is appropriate for use with students.

2.8.104 In cases where adult-oriented machines cannot be adjusted sufficiently to accommodate the needs of specific students, the adult equipment should not be used. Instead, alternative exercises (eg using resistance bands or light dumb-bells) should be provided.

2.8.105 Too much equipment packed into a fitness room can be a potential safety hazard and also result in the space being ineffective as a learning environment.

2.8.106 Where possible, a school fitness room should have some floor space available for:

- mats to be placed for floor exercises (eg stretches or abdominal curls)
- mats, dumb-bells, exercise balls and resistance bands/tubing to be used
- students to sit while being addressed as a whole group.

Swimming pools

2.8.107 Schools will often use swimming pools or special needs school pools on **premises other than their own**. By law, the pool operator of any facility must ensure that it is safe and presents no unreasonable risk to health for visiting persons or groups. This applies equally when schools use pools belonging to other schools.

2.8.108   A swimming pool on a school site is regarded in law as part of a place of work and, as such, is the responsibility of the host school. However, visiting staff with duty of care for aquatic sessions should always ensure that, before allowing students to use the facility at another school, they make whatever operational safety checks they can, both prior to setting up the programme and as part of each visit.

2.8.109   As with all facilities, where the user hires a swimming pool, they do so under a **contract for hire**, which they and the pool owner/operator are required to adhere to. Responsibility for the facility is not handed over but always remains with the pool owner/operator. The contract for hire may not be in writing, but it is nevertheless implied. The responsibility of the pool owner/operator is to ensure that the pool is provided in a safe condition and is fit for purpose. It is the pool owner/operator's responsibility to ensure that the pool hirer acts in a safe and responsible manner. It is not unusual for the contract for hire to specify that the hirer is responsible for the safe operation of the activity the pool has been hired for. The pool operator may even request the hirer's risk assessment of their activities with the additional pool safety operating procedure (PSOP) for the activity.

2.8.110   Every pool owner/operator is responsible for the health and safety of their employees, pool users and other people on the premises. The Health and Safety at Work etc Act 1974 and the subsequent Safety at Work Regulations place general obligations on pool operators.

2.8.111   In addition to the legislation, the Health and Safety Executive (HSE) and the industry lead bodies have combined to produce a specific health and safety guidance document for swimming pools entitled **"Health and Safety in Swimming Pools"**.

   "Health and Safety in Swimming Pools" (HSG179) is available as a free download from the HSE website at https://www.hse.gov.uk/pubns/priced/hsg179.pdf

2.8.112   The health and safety regulations require that all facilities and managed operations produce a written risk assessment and, based on that risk assessment, a written PSOP and written EAP.

2.8.113   Swimming pools are high-risk environments. School staff accompanying students, together with specialist swimming staff, should ensure that they know and implement the PSOP and EAP for the facility being used.

2.8.114   The PSOP will identify potential hazards and associated risks at the particular swimming pool in question and detail how to manage these.

2.8.115   The EAP will detail the methods for dealing with a variety of emergency situations and include evacuation arrangements.

2.8.116   It is essential that any school hiring another school's swimming pool understand their role in the emergency evacuation procedure.

2.8.117   The risk assessment applied to a swimming pool environment frequently highlights common hazardous design features that should then be identified in the PSOP together with methods for managing and reducing the risks they pose.

Common design hazards in swimming pools

2.8.118   **Water clarity** is essential in swimming so that lifesavers can see the bottom of the pool at all times. Lifesavers and teachers should frequently **scan** the bottom of the pool during lessons to ensure that no student has inadvertently slipped below the surface of the water. Pools should not be used if the water clarity is such that the bottom of the pool cannot be seen at all depths.

2.8.119   **Glare** and spectral reflection across the water's surface, from natural or artificial lighting, may restrict the ability to see beneath the pool surface across large areas. In such circumstances, frequent movement by staff (both supervisory and teaching) is necessary to maintain maximum visual awareness. Glare may also trigger an adverse reaction in students with identified special needs or medical conditions.

2.8.120   The **depth** and extent of shallow- or deep-water areas should be clearly marked and noted by those responsible for safety. A pool divider, usually a rope, should normally be positioned to delineate shallow from deep water whenever non-swimmers are present. However, this is not always feasible during mixed sessions. It is particularly important that any sudden changes in pool depth via a slope are highlighted. This can be achieved using brightly coloured painted lines down the sides and along the floor of the pool.

2.8.121   **Signs** should identify potential risks and be positioned in order that pool users can see them clearly and interpret them easily. Staff should explain their significance, especially to beginners. All signs should conform to the appropriate British Standards/British Standard European Norm, and the Health and Safety (Safety Signs and Signals) Regulations 1996, where they apply.

 For more information on regulations about signs and signals, see http://goo.gl/Rp2ahg and http://goo.gl/XB67qz

2.8.122   **Access** from the changing rooms on to the poolside is safest where the water is shallow. Where pool design precludes this precaution, students should be made aware of the hazard, both verbally and by the use of signs and barriers or cones. Care should be taken when entering on to the poolside, and strict behaviour standards applied.

2.8.123   **Steps and rails** should be of a design that prevents any part of the body becoming trapped. Where this risk exists, warning signs and regular verbal reminders to pool users should be provided.

2.8.124   The swimming pool should be designed to have at least two connected bottom **outlet pipes** that are securely fastened to avoid vacuum entrapment. Holes in grilles should not be large enough for fingers to become trapped.

2.8.125   Leisure pools, many with special water features and irregular shapes, may cause potential supervisory **blind spots** that need to be checked regularly.

2.8.126   Pool surround, pool depth, the implications of any protruding ladders or steps, and the use of electrical equipment are key considerations when determining whether the facility is suitable for other aquatic sporting activities, such as competitive swimming, water polo or synchronised swimming.

Common operational management hazards in swimming pools

2.8.127   The most significant operational hazard is the provision of **inadequate poolside supervision**.

2.8.128   Most public swimming pools provide lifeguards especially for un-programmed general swimming. The term "lifeguard" indicates a person who holds a qualification and has competency to safely supervise swimmers and provide rescue assistance and first aid. In the case of programmed and managed activities, such as school swimming lessons, a pool lifeguard is not always necessary, although it may be a requirement of the pool operator's hire agreement. Where a lifeguard is not deemed essential, an alternative method of supervision is to require the competent swimming teacher or teacher from the school to hold an additional relevant lifesaving qualification so that they can act as a lifeguard for their own classes. Children should not be unsupervised, and some form of lifesaving presence is required.

2.8.129   Swim England recommends that the **temperature of the water** should be about 29°C to enable young people to be comfortable and not become unduly cold during the period of time allocated to swimming. Water temperatures for disabled swimmers may be set much higher (as high as 32°C for learner pools and special needs school pools). The ambient air temperature should be the same or slightly above that of the water, to avoid condensation.

2.8.130   All swimming pools need to operate **pool cleaning systems** that meet acceptable hygiene standards.

2.8.131   **Chemical levels** should be monitored at the beginning of the day and at regular times throughout the day. At no time should chemicals be added to the water when swimmers are present. The water standards should conform to the Pool Water Technical Advisory Group recommendations in their publication "Swimming Pool Water – Treatment and Quality Standards for Pools and Spas".

 For more information visit https://www.pwtag.org/

2.8.132   Swimming **pool surrounds** should be kept clear at all times. Pool equipment (eg floatation aids, emergency equipment and lane markers) should be stored appropriately, taking into account the need for safe access to and from the pool. Particular care should be taken on poolside surrounds where **wet surfaces** may contribute to slipping injuries.

2.8.133   Adequate, well maintained **lifesaving equipment** must be readily available in known locations and staff (and students, as appropriate) must be trained in its use.

Pool safety operating procedures

2.8.134   **PSOPs**, consisting of NOPs and an EAP, should be known, applied and practised, as relevant, by all staff (school and pool) working in the lesson.

Table 11: Pool safety operating procedures

NOPs (Normal operating procedures)	EAP (Emergency action plan)
These are the day-to-day organisational systems based on risk assessment, and would typically include information relating to:	This should establish who assumes leadership in managing emergencies and the action to be taken in relation to such issues as:
<ul><li>pool design and depth</li><li>potential areas of risk</li><li>arrangements for lessons</li><li>responsibility for safety</li><li>staffing levels and qualifications</li><li>supervision and student conduct</li><li>arrangements for students with particular needs (eg very young children, or those with SEND or medical conditions)</li><li>pool safety and equipment</li><li>clothing and personal equipment</li><li>maximum numbers</li><li>first aid provision</li><li>water quality.</li></ul>	<ul><li>serious injury to a bather</li><li>dealing with casualties in the water</li><li>sudden overcrowding in a public pool</li><li>sudden lack of water clarity</li><li>disorderly behaviour or physical violence</li><li>faecal/blood/vomit contamination</li><li>emergency evacuation due to:<ul><li>– fire and fire alarm</li><li>– bomb threat</li><li>– power and lighting failure</li><li>– structural failure</li><li>– uncontrolled toxic-gas emission.</li></ul></li></ul>

2.8.135   **Safety notices** should be highly visible and located in positions relevant to the issue. For example, signs indicating "shallow water, no diving" should be placed at the sides of the pool where they are clearly visible from the shallow end, and not behind the person entering the shallow water. Safety signs should be brought to the attention of all students, and should be clear and understandable, including for those who are visually impaired or have difficulties with reading, or for those for whom English is not their first language.

2.8.136   Consideration needs to be given to the fact that, during an **emergency evacuation**, students will have bare feet, be wearing little clothing and may be outside for an extended period of time. Pool operators should make provision for these factors in their EAPs. Some pool management systems provide, for example, space (foil) blankets and, in some instances, rubberoid surfaces near the emergency exits.

2.8.137 Access to a **telephone** giving direct contact from the pool to the emergency services is essential. The system for providing this access should be guaranteed during all hours when the pool is in use.

Further information can be found in HSE (2003) *Managing Health and Safety in Swimming Pools*. London: HSE. ISBN: 978-0-717626-86-1. (Available from https://www.hse.gov.uk/)

The revision of this guidance by a number of industry stakeholders with HSE support has recently been completed. Following HSE agreement, the six documents that make up the revised publication will be available online. See www.hse.gov.uk for details of updates.

Special needs school pools

2.8.138 Special needs school pools are located in special needs schools, provide opportunities for students to exercise in warmer water and with additional auditory and sensory equipment. This is of particular benefit to students with complex physical difficulties.

2.8.139 The teacher:student ratio should not be determined in accordance with any specific swimming lesson written guidelines that may exist. A safe ratio can only be determined by carefully examining individual students' medical profiles and education, health and care plans (EHCPs) in conjunction with relevant medical staff as part of the risk assessment process.

For information regarding managing warm water swimming sessions, see **Chapter 2, Section 3: Special Educational Needs and Disabilities.**

For more information about working with students with SEND in special needs school pools and swimming pools, see:

National Co-ordinating Committee – Swimming for People with Disabilities (no date) *Let's All Swim*. Billericay: National Co-ordinating Committee – Swimming for People with Disabilities.

National Co-ordinating Committee – Swimming for People with Disabilities (no date) *Safe at the Pool*. Billericay: National Co-ordinating Committee – Swimming for People with Disabilities.

Further guidance about facility design

2.8.140   Technical guidance about the design and use of all sports facilities is available from governing bodies of sport, commercial companies, such as Continental Sports (www.continentalsports.co.uk) and national sport associations, particularly the Sport England website: www.sportengland.org

Swim England: http://goo.gl/wPU5rH

Swim England school swimming and water safety: http://goo.gl/G4fuz3

Chartered Institute for the Management of Sport and Physical Activity (CIMSPA): www.cimspa.co.uk

Government safety advice on water sports and coastal activities: https://www.bing.com/search?q=Government+safety+advice+on+water+sports+and+coastal+activities&FORM=ANNTA1&PC=LCTS

Marine and Coastguard Agency (MCA): https://www.gov.uk/government/organisations/maritime-and-coastguard-agency

National guidance document 7x swimming pools (swimming on visits): http://goo.gl/JOFVqu

Royal Life Saving Society (RLSS) UK: https://www.rlss.org.uk/

Sport England advice and guidance on swimming pool design: www.sportengland.org

Scottish Swimming: www.scottishswimming.com/

Swim Ireland: www.swimireland.ie/

Swim Wales: www.swimwales.org/

Swimming Teachers' Association (STA): www.sta.co.uk/

Basketball Northern Ireland: www.basketballni.com/

Basketball Scotland: www.basketball-scotland.com/

Basketball Wales: www.basketballwales.com/

England Basketball: https://www.basketballengland.co.uk/

British Handball Association: www.britishhandball.com/

England Handball: www.englandhandball.com/

Scottish Handball: www.scottishhandball.com/

England Netball: www.england-netball.co.uk

Netball Northern Ireland: www.netballni.org

Netball Scotland: www.netballscotland.com/

Welsh Netball: http://welshnetball.com/

Irish Rugby: http://goo.gl/CEfiQl

RFL: www.rugby-league.com

RFU: www.englandrugby.com

Scottish Rugby: www.scottishrugby.org

Welsh Rugby Union: www.wru.co.uk/

Ultimate frisbee: www.ukultimate.com

Badminton England: www.badmintonengland.co.uk/

Badminton Ireland: www.badmintonireland.com/

Badminton Scotland: www.badmintonscotland.org.uk/

Badminton Wales: https://www.badminton.wales/

England Squash and Racketball: www.englandsquashandracketball.com

Irish Squash: www.irishsquash.com/

Scottish Squash: www.scottishsquash.org.uk/

Squash Wales: www.squashwales.co.uk/

Lawn Tennis Association: https://www.lta.org.uk/

Tennis Ireland: www.tennisireland.ie/

Tennis Scotland: http://goo.gl/IX0eo2

Tennis Wales: http://goo.gl/HROmis

One Dance UK: www.onedanceuk.org

Section 9: Equipment

Managing Equipment

2.9.1   Equipment should **be used for the purpose for which it is designed. Improvisation** is rarely necessary due to the range, quality and quantity of equipment available to schools. Where a decision is made to use an item for a purpose for which it is not actually designed, the member of staff would need to have a very strong justification for deciding to improvise. Modification can cause safety features to be undermined. It is generally recommended that equipment is not adapted without manufacturer guidance. One common example is benches being turned on their side for use in indoor games of five-a-side football. Benches are not designed for this purpose so should not be used in this way due to the increased risk of tripping.

2.9.2   Staff need to be confident that the physical education, school sport and physical activity (PESSPA) equipment they plan to use is of **acceptable quality** in terms of its design, manufacture and durability. A British and European Standards Kitemark (BS and BS EN respectively) on equipment provides such assurance. PESSPA equipment is best purchased from a reputable and reliable company that guarantees to supply products that meet this quality standard. Not all equipment has provision for a BS EN standard, and if this is the case, staff should seek alternative confirmation that the products they intend to purchase and use with students are safe and well made. This could be achieved through discussion with other users and research of product reviews.

2.9.3   The awarding of a particular BS or BS EN standard ensures the consistency and fitness for purpose of certain products and procedures. However, compliance with a British Standard does not in itself confer legal immunity, although it will strengthen any defence against accusations of negligence in activities that use this equipment.

2.9.4   On occasion, it may be appropriate to adapt the use of equipment, such as the use of cones to create mini goals, but this requires careful risk assessment. Some adaptations may be required when modifying a PESSPA activity for a particular playing surface or space (eg using lighter-weight balls for hockey on a hard court surface).

2.9.5   Staff discussion about the use of particular items in any activity not directly related to their design and purpose will be of benefit in eliminating extraordinary use, and establishing consistent practice and safety standards throughout the school. Such processes can be decided, for example, through subject and departmental meetings.

2.9.6   Whatever the function of equipment, staff should ensure that:

- only equipment that has been officially provided, approved and/or Kitemarked is used
- improvisation beyond the design specification of the equipment is avoided
- equipment is assembled and dismantled systematically and that students are taught to do this, wherever possible (see **Chapter 3** for further information on learning about safe practice)
- equipment is checked by staff to ensure correct assembly before activity commences, and that students are encouraged to remain alert to, and report, any unintended adjustment to equipment as work proceeds
- sufficient space is left between pieces of equipment to allow safe movement around them
- dismount points and planned landing areas are free from obstruction and always well away from walls – mats may be used to designate intended direction of dismount
- equipment is returned to its designated storage space and left in a stable position after use
- equipment is regularly inspected and repaired, where necessary, by qualified maintenance engineers on at least an annual basis
- between inspections, the condition of equipment is constantly monitored by staff, on a day-to-day and lesson-by-lesson basis, and students are encouraged and equipped to do the same
- equipment deemed unsafe but reparable is moved well away from the working area and clearly labelled as unsafe until it is made good
- equipment "condemned" following an inspection is completely removed from the facility and disposed of
- staff familiarise themselves with key safety points to check on gymnastic equipment
- equipment is age-appropriate so that students are able to manage **lifting**, **carrying** and placing it in a safe manner
- students learn how to lift, carry and place equipment safely:
  - keep back straight
  - keep load close to the body
  - keep feet apart with one foot in front of the other
  - lift with knees bent, using the legs as the lifting power
  - have a good grip on the load before lifting
  - do not change grip when carrying a load
  - do not allow the load to obstruct fields of view
  - face the intended direction of travel without excessive twisting
  - set the load down gently with a straight back and knees bent.

2.9.7   Students should be taught how to **lift and carry** equipment safely from an early age. They should learn how many people are needed to lift, carry and place specific items of equipment safely, how to carry items correctly and about the importance of remaining focused on the task to avoid any trips, falls or collisions that may be caused by lack of concentration. Teaching **correct lifting technique** should be an important part of a PESSPA curriculum and can encompass health messages about lifelong back care. Learning should start in the early years and progress to Key Stage 4/5.

 For more information about students learning to lift, move and place equipment safely, see **Chapter 3**.

Checking PESSPA Equipment Prior to Use

2.9.8   A minimum requirement is that equipment used in a physical education session should be **visually checked** prior to students using it, to ensure it is safe to use, assembled correctly and not damaged or faulty. While staff should make this practice part of their preparation, **students** should also become involved, reporting any faulty equipment at a level that is compatible with their age, ability and previous experience. In addition to annual contractor inspections (see **Chapter 2, Section 9**), all schools should have a system for staff to report faulty equipment, and for ensuring that staff are in turn made aware of any **faulty** equipment. Where students take out equipment for use, such as wall bars and beams, a member of staff should check that this has been done correctly so that the equipment is ready to use.

2.9.9   Where students take part in **centrally organised sports events** away from the school site and using equipment provided for them, staff and students should carry out their own checks prior to commencing, reporting any faults to the organisers.

2.9.10 Where organisers of off-site sports events have requested that schools bring equipment to be used at an event, this equipment should be checked by staff from the school providing the equipment and the event organiser together, to confirm agreement that all items are safe for use.

Mats

2.9.11 It is essential that both staff and students understand the structure, function, capabilities and limitations of mats when using them within the PESSPA programme.

2.9.12 Mats are primarily designed to **absorb impact** when someone lands on the mat on their feet. The construction of mats allows them to dissipate force, thereby reducing the reaction of the person landing on what would otherwise constitute a hard and unyielding surface.

2.9.13 Over the years, considerable improvements have been made to the design and specification of mats to enhance safety. However, it is important to recognise that mats, whatever their construction and size, should **never be seen as fail-safe protection** systems that supersede effective technique. Students need to be aware that a correctly performed landing contributes significantly to preventing injury. **Correct landing technique**, whatever the activity or skill being practised, needs to be taught and re-emphasised regularly.

2.9.14 Care should be taken when **buying new mats** to ensure that they meet any current standard, where available, and that they fully comply with **fire regulations**. Assurance should be sought from manufacturers about both of these requirements.

2.9.15 The following guidance relates to the **maintenance of mats**. In order to promote safe practice, mats should be:

- covered with material that is **easy to clean**; in order to minimise slippage, the underside will need to be cleaned from time to time, and the top surface periodically, according to the extent of use; they should be checked regularly for any embedded objects, such as stones or pins
- **stable and lie flat** to the floor; wherever practical, mats should be **stored in a horizontal** position to prevent warping of closed-cell polyethylene foam and disintegration of foam padding; the manner of storage should ensure that safety features do not become compromised
- free from holes and tears, and display no rucking in the cover or foam infill
- **light enough for students to handle easily**, preferably in pairs if the mats are lightweight; four students may need to carry mats according to their size and strength in relation to the size and weight of the mat
- subject to regular inspection; damaged mats should immediately be taken out of service until repaired by a specialist maintenance firm, or replaced.

2.9.16 **In gymnastics**, mats should never be **indiscriminately placed** around the working area. Each mat should be placed with a **specific purpose** in mind.

2.9.17 **Examples of safe use of mats would be where they are used to:**

- provide a comfortable, cushioned area for aspects of floor work (eg developing rolling activities)
- identify suitable landing areas to students as they work around equipment
- promote students' confidence in feet-first landings from apparatus such as beams and equipment used for vaulting and balancing (though it is the efficiency of technique in landing from a height that minimises injury, not dependence on a mat absorbing the momentum; for example, placing mats under wall bars will not prevent injury and is no substitute for the teaching of correct and safe dismounts)
- extend sequence work by providing choices for changes of direction, level and mode of travel.

2.9.18   General-purpose mats (approximately 25mm thick) are generally suitable for curriculum work in gymnastics. Thinner mats are often so lightweight that they slide around when in use. Thicker mats (eg 200mm) may be necessary for more specialised, advanced gymnastic activities in which the performer generates high levels of momentum. Staff need to exercise **caution** when using thick weight-absorbing mattresses ("crash mats" or "safety mats") as landing areas. Too much absorption may compromise safe dismounts on to feet by creating rotation on landing. Using such mattresses can lead to over-reliance on them for safe landings and can be detrimental to the development of correct landing technique. Where such mattresses are used in this way, it is advised that the landing surface is "firmed up" by overlaying the mattress with general gymnastic mats where necessary. Staff should ensure that the mattress is being used because it meets the needs of the activity, not just because it is in the vicinity.

2.9.19   If more than one weight-absorbing safety mat is used to create a longer area (eg for landing from a vaulting horse), the mats should be secured together by placing a longer agility mat roll on the surface of the safety mats. This will lessen the risks associated with a student landing on the line where two mats meet, and offers protection from the safety mat "bottoming out".

2.9.20   Where mats for landing areas are placed together or overlaid in this way (most commonly in secondary schools), regular checks should be made to ensure that no gaps appear. The use of a coverall is useful in this context. Procedures to ensure these checks are carried out should be introduced. The practice of using mats together like this is not recommended in primary schools and should be carefully planned and monitored when used in a secondary school setting.

2.9.21   **Mats should never be used to protect against the foreseeable outcomes of poorly developed skills,** such as anticipating that students will fall while suspended from a horizontal ladder or similar apparatus. In such situations, it is better to modify the equipment and task to reflect student needs and capabilities accurately, thereby **minimising the risks of falling** and poorly controlled dismounts.

2.9.22   **Athletics landing modules** are necessary for the safe performance of high-jump technique in which the transference of weight moves from the feet to some other body part (eg as in the "Fosbury flop" technique and its related progressions). It is strongly recommended that staff using specialised high-jump facilities have undergone **appropriate training** through the governing body of sport (UK Athletics) or as part of a specialist physical education training programme.

2.9.23   When using landing modules, staff should ensure that:

- multiple modules, where used, are firmly locked together, and a coverall pad used to prevent slippage
- the landing area is sufficiently large and deep to accommodate the abilities of the students involved and probable variations in landing position, extending beyond both uprights
- the density of the landing module is sufficient to avoid any "bottoming out".

2.9.24   Mats used in **martial arts** activities need to be specific to the activity to minimise the risk of injury from high-impact falls and throws. Mats should comply with BS EN 12503-3 in order to provide adequate shock-absorbing properties, and have a strong base to prevent sliding during activities. General-purpose gymnastic mats should not be used as their density is inadequate for martial arts activities.

2.9.25   Canvas covers should not be used to cover or secure martial arts arenas. Frames can be constructed to secure mat areas permanently. Frames are usually purchased upholstered and cushioned with fabric or carpet to prevent injury or hazard. Where frames are not available, particular attention needs to be paid to ensuring there is no mat "creep".

Gymnastic Equipment

2.9.26   **Primary school gymnastic equipment** includes fixed and portable apparatus, such as climbing frames, ropes, benches, movement platforms, nesting tables, boxes, low-level beams, planks, trestles, springboards and mats.

2.9.27 **Secondary school gymnastic equipment** includes fixed and portable apparatus, such as wall bars, ropes, benches, movement platforms, nesting tables, boxes, planks and trestles, and might also include equipment associated with competitive gymnastics (including apparatus for vaulting and agility activities such as trampettes).

 For information about students learning about safe exercise practice, see **Chapter 3**.

Play Equipment

2.9.28 Soft play shapes should offer firm and predictable support, and should be replaced as wear and tear becomes evident. The surfaces of soft play equipment should be cleaned periodically.

2.9.29 **Wheeled equipment**, such as tricycles, should be confined to designated areas.

2.9.30 The use of **bats and balls** can prove hazardous in confined areas whether indoor or outdoor. Careful planning using **zoned areas** of the playground can help reduce any risk of injury.

2.9.31 Where lunchtime supervisory staff are involved in setting up activities or distributing equipment, they should be trained to do so. Care should be taken to ensure that equipment appropriate for different age groups is **not mixed up**. This avoids students inadvertently using equipment not designed for them in subsequent sessions.

2.9.32 Any "young leaders" leading activities using play equipment should be supervised at all times.

2.9.33 Accepting **used play items** from parents and other charitable sources, or purchasing them from Internet sites, should be done only after careful consideration of the quality and condition of the items.

2.9.34 Recycled **tyres** are used in some playgrounds to add fun and interest. Where this is considered, ensure the following:

- Choose tyres that are intact, with no exposed wires.
- Check the tyre source to ensure there is no petrochemical contamination.
- Test, using a white cloth, that the surface will not mark clothing too much.
- Check fixings regularly if tyres are bolted together.
- Supervise students carefully, particularly while they are developing the appropriate skills and awareness to use the tyres safely.

Playground Climbing Equipment

2.9.35 All climbing equipment should be appropriate for the age and developmental needs of the students who use it. It is advisable to provide separate use of climbing frames for younger and older students, and for more timid students and more adventurous individuals.

2.9.36 Professional judgement should be used to decide whether to restrict the use of outdoor climbing frames in inclement weather. Considerations would include the type of footwear worn by students, the age and experience of the users, and the materials used in the climbing frames' construction.

Storage of PESSPA Equipment

2.9.37   Staff should discuss the storage of equipment so they are all aware of what equipment is stored where and why.

2.9.38   All storage areas should be **kept tidy** in order to minimise the potential for tripping, and to allow safe accessibility for students to pick up, transport and place the equipment they are using.

2.9.39   Storage areas need to be of **sufficient size** so as not to create hazards. Access should be as **wide** as possible to prevent "bottlenecks". Where a separate fire-rated mat store is available, it should be used. Most schools store mats with other equipment, and in this situation, the mats should be stored well away from heating sources and electrical circuits to minimise the possibility of fire causing toxic fumes.

2.9.40   Where equipment is stored around the perimeter of an indoor facility, it should be positioned in a safe manner to minimise encroachment on the work area, and placed, if possible, close to where it is generally used, to minimise carrying distances.

2.9.41   The Work at Height Regulations 2005 address situations where anyone could fall a distance likely to cause personal injury. Where equipment is stored above reach height, appropriate steps, ladders or platforms should be used in order to comply with the regulations. Heavy items are best **stored at waist height** to minimise the likelihood of back injury through lifting a heavy weight from the floor or dropping the heavy item on to feet if over-reaching above.

 For more information on the Work at Height Regulations 2005, see http://goo.gl/cbJMRl

2.9.42   Storage areas located outdoors should be secured, to **prevent unauthorised access** to potentially dangerous items. Outdoor storage areas should be located in an easily accessible area and have wide enough access to allow large groups of students to take out and return equipment. The location of the storage area should take into account the best placement to prevent mildew, which could make surfaces slippery underfoot.

PESSPA Equipment Inspection and Maintenance

2.9.43   Correctly maintaining PESSPA equipment prolongs its life and use, and helps to ensure that safety standards are met.

2.9.44   The Health and Safety at Work etc Act 1974 (http://goo.gl/JjdaTM) requires employers to provide safe plant and equipment for employees and other visitors (eg students, community use and lettings), and the Provision and Use of Work Equipment Regulations 1998 (PUWER) (http://goo.gl/Oy1nmL) require that all equipment should be subject to **systematic and regular inspection** to identify any signs of damage or wear and tear that may cause injury.

2.9.45   The British Standards Institute (BSI) (https://www.bsigroup.com/) states that "it is important that all physical education apparatus is maintained in a first class, fully safe condition. An inspection should be carried out at **least once a year**." **BSI 1892 Part 1:1986**

The frequency of inspection may vary, depending on the environmental conditions/level of use and quality and durability of the equipment. For example, equipment that is subject to harsh outdoor conditions is likely to need more frequent inspections than that used in an indoor environment.

2.9.46 Regular maintenance by external contractors of sports hall, gymnastic, fixed play, fitness and sports equipment is essential for safety. **"Regular"** is not defined with a specific frequency by the BSI. However, **it is typically interpreted as annually**, with more frequent inspections recommended if use is higher than normal for a school (such as where community use adds significantly to equipment usage levels). If a school chooses not to undertake annual inspections, presentation of a clear rationale for this is strongly advised. Daily/weekly inspections can be completed by anyone who has sufficient knowledge and experience of the equipment to enable them to identify issues such as wear and tear. However, full technical safety checks should be carried out by a reputable supplier who knows:

- what to look at
- what to look for
- what to do if they find a problem.

2.9.47 The necessary level of competence to carry out inspections will vary according to the type of equipment and how/where it is used. The nature of these inspections does not have to be determined by the same person who undertakes them, provided the person determining them is competent.

2.9.48 **BS EN 1176** suggests a more rigorous approach to the inspection of outdoor fixed play equipment, recommending recorded visual, periodic and annual engineering inspections by a competent person.

2.9.49 **BS EN 1177** concerns safety surfaces around fixed play equipment that should be checked as part of an inspection of the equipment itself.

2.9.50 An annual inspection of school PESSPA equipment should include, as appropriate:

- gymnastic equipment
- trampolines and trampettes
- fitness equipment – multi-gyms and free weights
- indoor and outdoor adventure play equipment
- indoor and outdoor sports posts, nets, goals and tables
- indoor and outdoor cricket nets
- high-jump landing modules
- parkour equipment
- adventure activities facilities – climbing towers and climbing walls
- fixed play equipment and safety surfaces
- ball courts.

2.9.51 In an **"inspection"**, contractors check the equipment and produce a report indicating all the minor and major work they have identified as being necessary.

2.9.52 In a **"maintenance inspection"**, contractors check the equipment and carry out any minor repairs at the same time, plus provide a report on more extensive and expensive repairs that are advised. "Same day" minor work to bring slightly faulty equipment up to an acceptable standard may be negotiated as part of the basic contract or costed separately.

2.9.53 Many schools combine inspection arrangements and maintenance provision into one contract for convenience. Others may require separate inspection and maintenance provision as part of quality assurance.

Planning a PESSPA equipment inspection

2.9.54 Academies, free schools and other non-local-authority (LA) schools are responsible for making their own contractual arrangements for PESSPA equipment inspections. They are advised to put in place procedures to ensure that inspections are carried out annually, or in accordance with the arrangements specified by their employers and insurers. Where the LA is the employer, it generally makes central contractual arrangements for its schools' annual PESSPA equipment inspections. However, there are several LA contexts where the authority devolves the funding so individual schools have the task of organising their inspections. The responsibility for external maintenance effectively remains with the LA as the employer under health and safety law so it needs to have some form of monitoring system in place. Employers and the school leadership should check their own position.

2.9.55   Any action in response to an inspection report is the responsibility and decision of the head teacher (HT) and governing body. Accurate records should be kept that include quality assurance of any provider used and details of any maintenance undertaken.

2.9.56   In order to achieve appropriate safe-practice standards for PESSPA equipment and facility maintenance, inspection contracts should include reference to the scope of the work, the quality and standards of work, the identification of hazards and risks to be managed, and the maintenance tasks to be carried out. The school leadership team has a responsibility to ensure agreed maintenance requirements are met.

2.9.57   The inspection schedule should include all necessary timber repairs, cleaning and re-covering of plastic and leather surfaces, checking metal items for wear, lubrication of moving parts, inspection of wall and roof fittings, and replacement of worn parts and items including those on trampolines, multi-gyms, and sports and play equipment.

2.9.58   The content of the contract needs to be sufficiently detailed to ensure that all PESSPA equipment is checked and repaired/reported on. It should not be assumed that any equipment outside the agreement will be checked without incurring extra costs.

2.9.59   The "employer" should read thoroughly the contract and any promotional information provided by an equipment inspection company, and clarify any uncertainties before committing to the contract.

2.9.60   Employers should check that the work will be carried out in compliance with BSI 1892 (1986) with some period of guarantee.

2.9.61   In addition, employers should check the following:

- The equipment inspection company has a known **reputation** for competent inspection and maintenance using fully trained personnel, and this can be checked through references. Any company should be audited to the ISO 9001:2008 level of quality assurance.
- Appropriate **insurance** is held by the contractor and made available for scrutiny if necessary – typically, public and product liability insurance and employer's liability insurance for £10million for each.
- The company has sufficient workers, tools and materials to fulfil the agreed schedule of work (eg there might need to be at least two operatives where heavy trampolines have to be erected for inspection; appropriate access equipment might need to be used if the contract requires that high-level apparatus, such as ropes, is inspected at the installation points rather than visually from the floor).
- All company personnel should be vetted to ensure they are safe to work on the premises. Further information on the need for Disclosure and Barring Service (DBS) checks can be found in **2.2.22**.

2.9.62   The Association for Physical Education (afPE) liaises with a range of reputable suppliers and may provide general information, without prejudice, where sought.

2.9.63   The maintenance and inspection work should seek to disrupt teaching as little as possible but be open to observation and monitoring.

2.9.64   Agreeing the time and date for an inspection will ensure the contractors have access to all facilities and items involved in the inspection, which, in turn, should prevent complicated arrangements and wasted time caused by inspection team visits outside school hours. In some areas, LAs have arranged for these inspections to take place during school holiday periods. This is not good practice as it reduces the possibility of staff being present during the inspection, and the benefits related to this.

2.9.65   An appropriate school representative should be involved in the overall inspection process. In addition, school staff should have an opportunity to highlight any concerns about equipment or apparatus prior to the inspection/maintenance work commencing, and where feasible, a member of the physical education department should be present during the PESSPA equipment inspection.

After the inspection

2.9.66   The PESSPA equipment inspection company should provide a dated, written report describing the condition of all equipment checked, separate costings for all recommended repairs and any recommendations for prioritising repairs.

2.9.67   Signed authorisation should be given and a receipt obtained for any equipment needing to be removed to a workshop for repair before being returned to school. A return time for such equipment should be agreed, and checks made that the cost of return is included in the overall repair cost.

2.9.68   Any item judged to be unsafe and beyond economic repair needs to be clearly identified as **condemned** and **must be taken out of service immediately.** It is unlikely the inspecting company will physically remove condemned items. The system for completing this needs to be clear and to guarantee the removal or decommissioning of items from use.

2.9.69   Condemned items should not continue to be used even for limited (eg "only sitting on") or non-PESSPA purposes. All condemned items need to be removed so that they cannot come back into use "inadvertently". Condemned equipment needs to be made readily identifiable by the inspecting company in order that teachers do not continue to use it in ignorance of the fact that it is unsafe.

2.9.70   Commonly condemned items include benches and matting, both of which should be removed from the storage area. It is not sufficient for condemned mats to be placed at the bottom of the pile, or benches to be written on to say that they should not be used. Removal is the only safe option in these scenarios.

2.9.71   The employer and the inspecting company need to agree that any PESSPA equipment requiring repair is shown to a nominated member of the school staff so the situation can be explained. Whether or not such equipment can continue in use until it can be repaired needs to be confirmed before the inspection concludes.

2.9.72   Any equipment inspection report is like an "MOT" in that it comments on the state of the equipment at the time of the inspection and does not guarantee its condition and safe use at a later date.

2.9.73   A specialist PESSPA equipment inspection does not negate the obligation on teachers to inspect all equipment visually prior to each use.

More information on the inspection of fixed play equipment can be found at http://goo.gl/L3c2MM

Electrical Equipment

2.9.74   **Portable appliance testing (PAT) helps** to protect staff and students from the increased likelihood of harm caused by electrical equipment in a variety of PESSPA environments and during the movement of such items. In addition, PAT testing assists in the identification of safe and tested electrical equipment, eases the tracing of such equipment and provides an audit trail.

2.9.75   Someone in school should have the responsibility for ensuring that regular PAT tests are carried out by an authorised person who is usually external to school.

2.9.76   All portable electrical appliances, such as computer equipment, music systems, timers, score boards, whiteboards or kettles, must be inspected for safety at regular, appropriate intervals, and a small PAT sticker attached to each individual item, identifying the date of their last test. The frequency of testing varies depending on the item.

Information regarding this issue can be found on the Health and Safety Executive (HSE) website: http://goo.gl/mU9S7x

2.9.77   Staff providing their **own items** of electrical equipment need to have them PAT certified by the school before using them in their work.

2.9.78   PAT testing is a whole-school responsibility, and it is important that the leadership team is kept informed of all portable appliances that need to be PAT registered for use in PESSPA.

2.9.79   Any portable electrical appliance lacking a current PAT certificate should not be used.

Principles Applied to Specific Contexts

Athletic activities

2.9.80   **Storage** – Ensure hazardous equipment (any equipment that, if left out, could cause injury if misused) is stored in lockable units. These could include cages within storage areas or storage containers.

Transporting, handling and storing throwing equipment

2.9.81   Staff should supervise the carrying of throwing implements **in transit** to the lesson as well as during the lesson. All throwing implements should be carried and retrieved singly using two hands to prevent students attempting "mock" throwing actions. Javelins should be carried upright, and the ends protected if possible. Multiple shots, discuses and hammers may be carried in baskets provided the overall weight is not excessive.

2.9.82   All throwing implements should be carried and retrieved at **walking pace**. They should always be **carried** back to the throwing line (never thrown), and placed on the ground (**never** dropped).

2.9.83   Javelins, when not in use, should be placed vertically in a storage rack or, when a rack is not available, laid flat on the ground.

Running equipment

2.9.84 **Spiked shoes** should be stored and placed with the spikes facing down.

2.9.85 **Finishing tapes**, historically used to indicate winners, should be avoided wherever possible.

2.9.86 **Hurdles** for lessons and extracurricular competition need to conform to UK Athletics standards and be positioned appropriately so as to **topple over** if struck. Hurdles should never be jumped in the wrong direction, ie with the struts on the far side of the hurdle.

2.9.87 **Relay batons** should be smooth and easy to grip.

Health-related physical activities (HRPAs) and dance activities

2.9.88 **Mats** should be available for any exercises that require kneeling, sitting or lying on the floor (eg resistance exercises working against body weight, or cool-down stretches). Lightweight, portable, individual exercise mats are ideal for this purpose. However, **exercise mats should never be used in other activity areas as substitutes for proper gymnastics mats**.

2.9.89 **Music** is often used as an accompaniment for specific HRPAs (eg aerobics and circuits). Staff should ensure that:

- the volume of the music allows their students to hear staff instructions and peer conversations relevant to safe practice, procedures and learning
- the use of music does not adversely affect the ability of students to access learning (eg those with hearing impairments or autism/autistic spectrum disorder [ASD]/Asperger's syndrome).

2.9.90 When positioning equipment, staff should ensure that:

- items of equipment are located at a safe distance away from any obstructions such as doors, windows and other equipment, to enable safe access, circulation and use of each piece
- free weights, weight stations and multi-gyms are positioned appropriately, preferably in separate areas so that they can be clearly signed as "not for use" in some lessons
- free weights are stored on purpose-built stands, with heavier weights near the top for ease of lifting
- locking collars are utilised on free weights whenever they are in use.

Weightlifting

2.9.91 Weights should be 450mm in diameter to ensure the barbell has a safe minimum height from the floor, to allow for weightlifting activities. Exposed metal weights are to be avoided, and the use of rubber or plastic-covered weights is suggested.

2.9.92 Barbells should be available that are appropriate for use by young people. A variety of bars are available (eg technique bars weighing around 5–12kg and lighter bars from 15kg – known as the women's bar – with a bar shaft diameter of 25mm).

 Standards for bars can be found on the International Body for Weightlifting website: www.iwf.net/

Scooting

2.9.93 It is recommended that any scooter a child uses is appropriate for their age and ability.

2.9.94 Children under five years old are recommended to use a three-wheeled scooter to help them develop balance and stability.

2.9.95 Children aged five and over who have developed their core skills of balance and stability are recommended to transfer to a two-wheeled scooter.

2.9.96   Children aged 5–8 years are recommended to use a scooter with a spring brake.

2.9.97   Children aged eight years and over can transfer to a stunt scooter with a flex brake when they are strong enough to push the brake on to the wheel.

2.9.98   Some secondary schools have introduced scooting into their PESSPA programme to meet students' needs. In such cases, equipment should match the size and physique of participants.

Combat activities

2.9.99   It is recommended that weapons are not used in martial arts in the school context and are preferably only introduced in the club situation. Where hazardous equipment such as fencing foils are permitted, they should be made secure and stored in a safe place that prevents unauthorised access.

2.9.100   Mats should be inspected regularly and comply with BS EN requirements for the specific activity. Gymnastic mats are inappropriate and should not be used as they are likely to separate during activity.

Trampolining (including use of trampettes and rebound activity)

2.9.101   Trampolines suitable for use in schools vary in size, and in the thickness of the bed webbing. The potential for higher performance is increased the larger the trampoline, and the narrower the bed webbing. The bed webbing options are 6mm (higher performance), 13mm or 25mm (standard performance). It is the combination of the two aspects that determines the suitability of the trampoline for the level of performance required. Based on this, a high-performance trampoline for competition purposes is likely to be a 101 series with a 6mm by 6mm or 6mm by 4mm bed.

2.9.102   When choosing a trampoline, schools need to consider all the potential users. If a trampoline has shared use with a community club, it makes sense to address the needs of both. While a 77 series trampoline with a 25mm or 13mm bed may be suitable for school use, this may not be adequate for the needs of a club. It is recommended that schools always consider the highest performance level of potential use as it is possible for students in a physical education lesson to safely work on a higher performance trampoline, but not advisable for a higher performer to work on one with a lower specification.

2.9.103   For the reasons outlined above, the 99 series trampoline with a 13mm bed is a popular choice in schools. It is suitable for secondary age students who may achieve a high performance level. Where shared use is not a concern, or where storage space is limited, the 77 series with a 13mm bed may be more suitable as its frame is smaller, but it is still adequate for secondary students.

2.9.104   Where the trampoline is used with younger students or for rebound therapy (see **2.3.26**), the 77 series with a 25mm bed is a type commonly used.

Positioning and assembling trampolines

2.9.105   It is important that trampolines are assembled, positioned and folded under the supervision of a person who has received training from a qualified tutor. Manufacturer's guidelines must always be adhered to.

2.9.106   In schools, this could mean that older students, sufficiently mature and strong enough, may fold and unfold trampolines, with training, under the **close supervision of qualified staff** who are ready to give immediate hands-on assistance if needed.

2.9.107   There have been several accidents where younger students, lacking the necessary strength and physique, have been left to fold or unfold trampolines without direct staff involvement. It is important that, in circumstances with such students, qualified staff are directly physically involved as part of the process.

2.9.108   Clear communication, awareness and a responsible attitude are essential, particularly in the phase where the end of the trampoline has been opened, to ensure it is held with sufficient force to counter the tension of the springs. Injury most commonly occurs when elbows and forearms become trapped in the trampoline, and for this reason, they should be kept clear of the gap between the folding ends and frame while lowering under control.

2.9.109 Trampolines need to be **positioned** well away from any overhead obstruction such as hanging beams or lights. Governing body of sport recommendations state that an overhead clearance of at least **five metres** from the floor to the lowest hanging object is required for non-somersault trampolining, ie low-level shaped jumps and body landings, and **eight metres** where somersaults or other rotational skills are being taught.

  For guidance from British Gymnastics, see https://goo.gl/Mxculx

2.9.110 Hydraulically assisted trampoline wheeling devices are available to assist with setting up and putting away trampolines. Where these and fixed-height roller stands are used, they should be safely stored away from the working area when not in use. Care must be taken when operating the hydraulic system depending on the mechanism it uses. Contact the manufacturer for any additional guidance or instruction.

2.9.111 When **unfolding** a trampoline, staff should ensure that:

- training shoes are worn, and feet kept well away from the wheels
- the trampoline is angled and lowered carefully, and that the lower leg section is held firmly so it does not crash to the floor
- the frame sections are opened with a firm, continuous movement, and with steady force applied and maintained to prevent them from springing back
- fingers, forearms and wrists are kept clear of all hinges.

2.9.112 The space under and around trampolines should be clear and free from obstructions.

2.9.113 **Before** allowing a trampoline or trampette to be used, staff should check that:

- all leg braces have been properly fitted, and hinge units securely housed
- all adjustments are tight
- the hooks of the springs/rubber cables are properly attached, with the hooks pointing down
- the springs/cables are all in good condition
- the safety pads are fitted and entirely cover the springs/cables
- Allen screws are tight (if present)
- the bed is clean and free from damage of any kind
- all coverall pads are in good condition and in place to cover the frame surround.

2.9.114 For trampolines, also check that:

- the wheeling devices are operating smoothly, and the pivotal housing on the frame holds the hub of the wheeling mechanism at right angles without any movement of the hub and the housing
- the floor surround has a minimum of 20-25mm non-slip **matting one metre wide along the sides of the trampoline**
- each end of the trampoline has safety mats, supported where possible at trampoline level, of a sufficient size and weight absorbency to meet the requirements of body impact in the event of unwanted travel forwards or backwards; to achieve this, "spotting deck platforms" or **"end deck platforms"** may be purchased, either with or separately from the mattress
- safety matting is placed on the floor behind the end mats
- where trampolines are positioned in a line, weight-absorbing mattresses are placed on the frame and springs between each trampoline; specific "middle mats" can be purchased for this purpose or standard large safety mats used.

2.9.115 When **folding** a trampoline, staff should ensure that:

- training shoes are worn
- the wheeling mechanism is securely housed
- adults are directly at hand to provide support and supervision, and step in if needed
- the frame sections are closed using a firm, continuous movement, and with steady force applied and maintained to resist the tension of the springs or cables
- fingers, forearms and wrists are kept clear of all hinges
- feet are kept well away from the wheels
- the lower frame and leg sections are positioned inside the upper frame and leg sections as the trampoline is rotated from the horizontal to the vertical.

2.9.116   **Once folded**, trampolines should be **locked** to prevent unauthorised use. This can be achieved by locking together two links of one of the leg chains.

2.9.117   **Trampettes** should be disabled in some way when not in use or kept in secure storage. Once this has been done, staff should be satisfied that the trampette cannot be easily re-assembled. Locking trampettes would be seen as good practice.

2.9.118   Damaged trampolines and trampettes should never be used until repaired or replaced.

2.9.119   Any overhead support rigs provided should be supplied and fitted by recognised specialist manufacturers and engineers. On no account should improvised rigs be used. An overhead support rig may be used to help students to learn movements involving rotations or twists on the trampoline. The supporter (usually an adult) needs to be competent in the use of the rig, and capable of holding the weight to control the descent of the student. The positioning of the trampoline and rig needs to be checked to ensure the centre of the rig is vertically aligned to the centre of the trampoline.

2.9.120   Training for staff in the correct use of rigs is essential. British Gymnastics offers specific training for the use of an overhead rig within the Teachers' Trampoline Awards or as an add-on module.

 For more information on the Teachers' Trampoline Awards, see www.british-gymnastics.org/courses/search/school-teacher

Trampoline and trampette activities in primary schools

2.9.121   It is not common practice for trampolining to be taught within the curriculum in primary schools. The use of trampettes as pieces of gymnastic equipment is not recommended within primary curriculum lessons. Both trampolines and trampettes require very specialised knowledge, and **staff are expected to be appropriately qualified** to teach trampolining (ie hold a Teachers' Trampoline Award, and to have received training in the use of trampettes, before using them with students).

2.9.122   Where coaches or specialist staff are brought in to deliver these activities in after-school clubs, care should be taken to secure the equipment during the day, to prevent it being accessed by students, or used by staff who are not sufficiently trained.

2.9.123   Mini trampettes for rebounding classes (on the spot, low-level bouncing) have been introduced into some schools as a fun activity with beneficial health outcomes, but safe storage of sufficient numbers of rebounders for a class prevents many schools from pursuing this. Staff leading this activity need to be suitably trained. Similarly, springboards will introduce rotation in flight so any member of staff using this piece of equipment should be appropriately trained.

2.9.124   The use of trampolining as a **therapeutic activity** is considered to be beneficial for some students with special educational needs and disabilities (SEND), at both primary and secondary levels.

Short tennis (short court or Mini Tennis)

2.9.125   Shorter rackets, light or slower balls and lower nets (approximately 80cm in the middle) should be used.

Table 12: Safety checklist for PESSPA equipment in specific contexts

Gymnastics Equipment	Check that:
Wooden rebound/ springboards	• the board is stable on impact • the surface is non-slip and free from splinters • rubber feet are stable and are not worn through to the wood
Benches and planks	• the construction is not warped, and is free from splinters • rubber buffers on the supporting feet are secure and the bench is stable • the surface is clean and smooth • fixing hooks are intact and covered with leather or plastic • rubber pads on the top surface are in place if the bench is intended for use in an inverted position
Ropes and suspended apparatus	• ropes are not frayed or damaged • pull-out lines are not worn, and their securing wall cleats are secure and not broken or with sharp edges • the runway operates smoothly • ropes are knot-free, and the leather end caps are intact • rope ladder floor fixings are intact
Hinged apparatus fixed to a wall	• bracing wires are taut with no visible fraying at any point • castors run smoothly • floor sockets are clean and free from obstruction • securing bolts are firmly fixed, and engage properly with their floor and wall sockets • wooden components are free from cracks or splinters • painted components are well maintained, with no evidence of flaking • consideration is given to replacing traditional bare metal tension clamps with padded, boxed in versions
Single and double beams	• hauling cables are free running • trackways are well maintained, enabling smooth movement of the upright • there are sufficient pins and wedges • beam surfaces are clean and smooth • beams run smoothly when lowered and raised • floor sockets are clean
Vaulting equipment and movement platforms	• all wooden components are splinter-free • all covers – vinyl, material or hide – are free from tears, clean and, in the case of hide, suitably textured • construction is stable and solid with no weakness allowing dangerous movement on impact • wheeling mechanisms work efficiently.
Games Equipment	**Check that:**
Outdoor socket-type goalposts	• they are correctly located • they are securely cemented into the ground, or wedged in to prevent unauthorised lifting out of the ground • they have protective padding in line with governing body of sport guidelines • they are regularly checked to ensure that bolts are in place, and that metal is not corroded • they meet British and European Standards (BS EN 748 and 8462), dependent on size
Goal netting	• it is stored and carried in a way that avoids it becoming a trip hazard • it is attached and dismantled using a stepladder, and never by jumping up to the crossbar • it is attached to both top corners before hooking along the crossbar • it is well fitting and does not extend beyond the area covered by the base of the posts • it is secured with plastic hooks or tape (metal cup hooks are banned, and should no longer be used) • it is secured firmly using metal pegs fully pushed into the ground

Portable or free-standing goalposts (used for football or hockey)	• they are obtained from a reputable manufacturer and comply with British and European Standard BS EN 8462 • they have a lightweight construction and integral wheels, where appropriate, in order to limit the lifting required • they are assembled in accordance with the manufacturer's instructions • they are smooth in construction, with no sharp edges • they are equipped with an integral safe stabilising device that presents no hazard to players or spectators, or they are secured using chains or anchor weights, when in use or stored, outside or inside • the anchor systems are appropriate to the ground conditions, and do not present any tripping hazard • they are regularly checked for wear and tear and, where practical, any damage made good by a suitably qualified person • they are not "home-made" or altered from their original specification – such equipment should not be used • staff or students with responsibility for moving and positioning the posts apply safe lifting and carrying techniques; use an appropriate number of people who are strong enough and trained in manual handling techniques, and pull or push the posts backwards according to the design • **staff and students are fully aware of the danger of serious injury or death resulting from unstable goalposts falling on to them; climbing or swinging on the uprights and crossbars should be strictly forbidden** (for additional information, see "Harrod UK Goalpost Safety Information Pack", www.harrodsport.com)
Unfixed posts (eg netball posts)	• posts are slotted into holes in the ground; where this is not possible, free-standing posts need to be safely weighted • posts are padded along the entire length of post where required by the governing body of sport, in accordance with specifications, particularly at competitive level • posts are adjustable for different age groups, if applicable • when not in use, unfixed posts that cannot be stored inside a building are secured at all times to prevent unauthorised use • unfixed posts are carried from the work area to storage by staff or students who have been shown safe lifting techniques • students are supervised if they are moving unfixed posts • metal posts are free from corrosion and sharp edges
Playing area markers	• cricket stumps or sharp-ended items are not used as markers or posts – a fall on to a sharp point could cause serious injury • corner flags are flexible and sufficiently high so as not to constitute a hazard to falling players • throw-down discs and lines, cones and skittles are not used in fast-moving activities, where a fall is foreseeable • beanbags and hoops are not used as markers for indoor work if the floor surface is shiny as they can present a slipping hazard when stepped on.
Athletics Equipment	**Check that:**
	• items are carried correctly • all staff and students are familiar with the required procedures for carrying and retrieving discuses, shots and javelins • all staff and students are familiar with the correct use and purpose of rakes and spades in sand jumping pits • hurdles are positioned correctly with stabilisers facing the approach and not the other way round • all staff and students know about storage of equipment that is appropriate for safe retrieval (eg javelins should be stored horizontally on a rack or, where one is not available, on the floor).

Section 10: Programme Management

Planning and Preparation

2.10.1   **Well prepared, structured lessons contribute to safe learning situations**. There is clear evidence that there are more injuries in unstructured situations than structured ones. **Planning** is therefore essential to safe practice, using whatever method the individual teacher needs, prefers or is required to use.

2.10.2   **Throughout the planning stage**, staff should think through the following process:

- This is what I want students to learn. This is how I plan for the learning to take place. **Is this learning experience safe?**
- If something happened to make the learning experience unsafe, what could I do to maintain the safety of the students?
- If I cannot introduce a safe alternative, I will have no option but to abandon or further adjust the learning experience.

2.10.3   Staff should assess students' **learning needs** against well structured **schemes of work (SoW)** that set out progressive learning targets, essential techniques and skills, and relevant safe-practice information. SoW should make reference to relevant aspects of the risk assessment for physical education, school sport and physical activity (PESSPA), which should include guidance on the organisation and teaching of safety so that safe practice is embedded in the learning process, and addressed and implemented in every lesson.

2.10.4   It is important for all schools to have **SoW** that inform lesson planning, fulfil the statutory requirements of any curriculum being followed (eg national curriculum – NC) and meet local circumstances and needs.

2.10.5   In cases involving negligence (see **Chapter 1, Section 4**), the issue of whether students have experienced the appropriate **stages of development** through a particular physical task is frequently raised.

2.10.6   Reference to a planned and progressive SoW that has been methodically followed helps to respond to such investigation.

2.10.7   Planning should take account of, and accommodate, all levels of competence and confidence to ensure effective, meaningful, relevant and inclusive content. The importance of meeting the needs of students with special educational needs and disabilities (SEND) is exemplified by the particular focus in the Education Inspection Framework (2019) and any other appropriate national frameworks.

 For more information on the Education Inspection Framework, visit www.gov.uk/government/publications/education-inspection-framework

---

2.10.8   **Matching student capability** to an appropriately challenging task is enhanced when founded on progressive and structured learning experiences. Engaged students are more likely to stay on task, thus decreasing the potential for poor behaviour that could undermine a safe learning environment.

2.10.9   "Doubling up" of classes to provide some form of activity should be planned and managed with care, with particular thought being given to relevant aspects of safety such as space, student ability and teacher experience.

Contingency Planning

2.10.10   Despite careful pre-planning, there are occasions when the planned PESSPA task, activity or session cannot proceed for reasons of safety. Alternative plans need to be considered and applied where possible, or when unavoidable, the session may need to be abandoned (see **Chapter 2, Section 11**).

2.10.11   Contingency plans should be developed by asking "what if" questions throughout the planning process. This will ensure a more rapid and appropriate response to incidents such as sudden inclement weather, injury or mismatch between student ability and the demand of an activity.

 For an illustration of the importance of contingency planning, see **Case Law 29** in **Chapter 4**.

Learning Objectives and Outcomes

2.10.12   Planning clear learning objectives/intentions and outcomes/success criteria contributes to safe experiences, as well as to learning about safety. **Chapter 3** provides detailed guidance on how safe-practice learning can be embedded in lessons.

2.10.13   Learning objectives/intentions are a key aspect of structured lessons, and these should be planned and made clear to students. Students should know what they are learning, how this will build on their prior learning, and why this learning is relevant and important to them.

2.10.14   In addition, learning outcomes and/or success criteria need to be planned and/or negotiated with students so that these are appropriate for their stage of learning, and students are clear about what will indicate learning progress. Well planned learning outcomes/success criteria will help students and teachers to judge when and how it is appropriate and advisable to make further progress, which is a key element of ensuring a safe learning environment.

2.10.15   It is important that teachers:

- include explicit learning about safety in appropriate lessons (see **Chapter 3**)
- monitor students' understanding of, and ability to effectively apply, principles of safe practice.

2.10.16   This is key to students becoming progressively more independent in relation to keeping themselves safe when engaged in independent physical activity.

Appropriate Preparation/Recovery

2.10.17   Preparation for physical activity can reduce the likelihood of injury, and ensure that the activity experience feels more comfortable. Helping the body to recover gradually after intense physical activity is also important and can combat problems such as muscle stiffness and soreness, and dizziness, fainting and nausea, which may occur if a gradual easing-off process is not followed.

2.10.18   An appropriate **warm-up** and cool-down should be included in every lesson, and should be relevant to the activity and appropriate for the learning environment/weather conditions. Students should learn about the purpose of the components and about how to perform warm-up and cool-down exercises, paying attention to the principles of **safe exercise practice**. Although it may not be possible to use warm-ups and cool-downs of ideal duration in every PESSPA session, ensuring they are included models good practice and what is expected of students when they work independently.

2.10.19   Progressively, students should take responsibility for planning and carrying out their own warm-ups and cool-downs as a step towards independent activity in later life. However, the content should be closely **monitored** by the teacher, to ensure that it is safe, effective and appropriate.

 For more information on safe exercise practice, see **Chapter 2, Section 11**.

Progression

2.10.20   Progression is about the **staged development** of knowledge, skills and understanding in accordance with confidence, ability and successful prior experience. Carefully planned and graduated progression is fundamental to enabling students to improve their skill and understanding in PESSPA in a manner that is safe.

2.10.21   Progressive practices enable students to develop or proceed competently and confidently to more complex movement and skills applications over time.

2.10.22   Staff intervention in students' practical work leads on from sound planning. Appropriate **adjustment, modification or conditioning** of PESSPA activities should attempt to accommodate the relevant ability range, previous experience, confidence or group size in lessons, thus improving the overall safety of the experience for all.

2.10.23   Applying the **"STEP"** framework can help to achieve such modifications by making appropriate changes to the:

- **s**pace – where the activity is happening
- **t**ask – what is happening
- **e**quipment – what is being used
- **p**eople – who is involved.

2.10.24   Using this approach can enable all students to achieve success in an environment that safely meets their needs.

2.10.25   Staff should check that students have competently and confidently achieved each stage of learning before moving on to more complex or demanding tasks. Well planned learning outcomes/success criteria should support these judgements and enable students to become increasingly involved in making appropriate decisions about their own progress. Careful management of the lesson should prevent peer pressure resulting in students progressing on to tasks beyond their capability until they are sufficiently prepared to do so. The Ofsted Education Inspection Framework (2019) emphasises the importance of curriculum coherence and appropriate scaffolding in its Quality of Education judgement, and this principle can be applied by all those planning physical education programmes of study.

2.10.26   In addition, it is an essential element of safe provision for staff to be knowledgeable about, and able to organise, PESSPA activities that are developmentally appropriate. They should understand how to apply "overload" (working the body beyond its normal everyday level) appropriately in physical activity programmes, and take account of developmental needs when "staging" and organising specific sport events (eg in terms of pitch size, duration and equipment used). This contributes to safe teaching and the setting of physical challenges at an appropriate level.

2.10.27   Safe and appropriate progression within a PESSPA session may be developed through various **strategies**, including progressing from:

- single to combined tasks
- non-contact to contact situations
- simple to more complex tasks

- copying to practising and then to refining, adapting and varying movements, skills and tasks
- identifying and describing to comparing, to analysing and evaluating performance
- familiar to unfamiliar situations
- set to negotiated tasks and possibly to self-determined tasks
- individual to pair and small-group activities
- large spaces to more restricted spaces (or vice versa depending on the specific nature of the activity)
- cooperative to competitive tasks
- closely supervised to remotely supervised activities.

2.10.28   Staff should assess an individual's **mental and physical readiness** before introducing a new skill or progressing to greater complexity. Staff should also be confident that they are themselves competent to progress the teaching safely. Where this is not the case, they should seek further professional learning.

 For demonstrations of the importance of ensuring students have been readied and well prepared for the task and activities they are asked to undertake, see **Case Law 30–33** in **Chapter 4**.

Personalised Learning

2.10.29   Individual students have variable levels of prior experience, ability and confidence. They need provision to make safe progress at individual or small-group rates. No class has a uniform level of ability or need to progress at the same rate, even if grouped or "streamed" according to ability.

2.10.30   All students can learn if they are provided with appropriate learning conditions. Differentiated work, or **personalised learning**, involves matching tasks to students to enable progress at an appropriate pace within lessons, over a series of lessons and throughout a programme of study.

2.10.31   In addition, the range, quality and availability of age- and ability-related equipment for most activities should enable schools to meet the specific needs of students without risking injury through the use of items of inappropriate size, weight or design.

2.10.32   Staff should understand that individuals may need to work differently and the implications of this for safe practice, and should respond by **adjusting the demand of the activity**, making it easier or more difficult according to the specific requirements of the individual.

2.10.33   Safety may be compromised if a student or group of students cannot match the demand or pitch of a task or activity. Equally, work that is **not sufficiently challenging** may lead to boredom and casual application by a student, compromising safe practice.

2.10.34   To provide **personalised learning**, staff should know:

- what is to be achieved
- students' ability levels and prior experience
- students' stage of development
- how students prefer to learn within each context
- how to extend students' responses in an appropriate and safe manner
- how to manage groups so that individuals can function individually as and when necessary.

2.10.35 Personalised learning can be addressed through:

- enabling or extension activities, such as modifying the general task
- setting different tasks for different students
- providing different levels of information, support and intervention
- providing more teacher time for some students than others
- allowing more or less time to complete a task
- using modified equipment and resources to promote success
- modifying the playing area or work space for some students
- modifying the task
- modifying the language used
- responding to an individual's ability, such as in challenging some for more creative or complex responses.

2.10.36 The STEP framework (see **2.10.23**) is commonly used to support effective planning of personalised learning in PESSPA.

Regular and Approved Practice

2.10.37 Regular and approved practice is that which is **common and widely practised** as safe, as opposed to an idiosyncratic practice adopted by individuals or organisations.

2.10.38 Following regular and approved practice is good practice and provides a strong defence against a charge of alleged negligence as this practice is **typical** of what the profession would utilise across the country in delivering aspects of the PESSPA programme.

2.10.39 When choosing not to follow practice that is generally accepted as regular and approved, organisations should be able to **justify** clearly their reasons for this decision.

2.10.40 **Typical sources** of widely used, established practice include guidelines provided by local authorities (LAs), governing bodies of sport, government agencies, professional associations (eg afPE, BASES) or respected and acknowledged experts in a particular field.

2.10.41 **Improvisation** of equipment, or improvised use of equipment for purposes other than those it was designed for, is not widely held to be good practice and should be considered only with great care and forethought.

2.10.42 It is recognised within law, however, that there is no one set response to situations, but that acceptable practice can be achieved within a number of appropriate choices, ie there are a **"range of reasonable options"**.

 The importance of adhering to regular and approved practice and/or one of a range of reasonable options is illustrated in **Case Law 34–36, Chapter 4**.

Introducing New Activities

2.10.43   Where staff plan to introduce a new activity into the PESSPA programme, they should: (please tick)

• consult with the head teacher and employer	
• check insurance arrangements in relation to the activity	
• where the sport or activity has a recognised governing body or national association, make use of any information and guidance it offers, either through its website or by contacting it directly, to inform your own policies	
• during a visit to a local club, check that all necessary policies are in place	
• meet with any development officers available for the new activity	
• consider staff expertise and any professional learning requirements	
• talk to other schools that have introduced the activity and learn from their experiences	
• carry out a risk-benefit analysis.	

Keeping Registers and Records

2.10.44   It is a legal requirement that a school records the presence or absence of students.

2.10.45   It is important to maintain evidence of students' **participation** by recording their presence at or absence from physical education lessons and the extent of their participation.

2.10.46   Where a student has been absent from physical education lessons for a period of time, staff need to **reintegrate** that student with care. Extra observation is important to ensure that the student can cope with the pitch and pace required to catch up with the progression made during their absence. The same principle applies where a student joins a group part way through a lesson.

2.10.47   For the same reasons, schools should consider extending their policy of keeping registers to include extracurricular activity sessions run either by school staff or external coaches and volunteers. This practice is recommended.

2.10.48   Records of achievement and attainment also provide hard evidence of what individual students do or do not know or understand, or are able to do. They indicate the extent to which individual students have achieved the intended learning outcomes. These records enable the teacher to pitch the **demand of activity** at a level appropriate to the confidence, prior experience and ability of individual students and to take account of any work missed.

 For an illustration of the importance of ensuring students are ready for the activity in which they are expected to engage, see **Case Law 37** in **Chapter 4**.

Practical Demonstrations

2.10.49   Students' perceptual preferences differ in terms of the extent to which they favour **visual, auditory and kinaesthetic** experiences in movement-related learning (ie learning through seeing a movement, hearing information about how it should be performed, or placing the body or relevant part into the desired position[s]). Practical demonstrations provide one or more of these experiences. Where students are asked to perform demonstrations in front of other class members, the teacher should ask them and ensure that they are comfortable to show their work in this way.

2.10.50   During practical demonstrations and when this is necessary, students might need to be agreeable to the use of appropriate physical contact to enable a staff member to demonstrate correct positioning. In the case of students with SEND, appropriate communication and response methods will need to be developed between staff and the student over time. Staff should be aware of **safeguarding procedures** with regard to appropriately positioning parts of a student's body correctly. Staff should adhere to their own school policy when working in this way.

For more information about physical contact from adults in student activities, see **2.15.32**.

Rules

2.10.51   All sports have rules. These have evolved to make competition **fair and safe**. Anyone involved with officiating games has a duty of care and a duty of control. They need to **know the rules** relevant to the specific PESSPA activity and must **apply** the rules stringently in order to avoid unnecessary, foreseeable injury.

2.10.52   Where activities have a governing body of sport to administer the way they operate, the rules of those activities are set by that body. School PESSPA, in many aspects, acknowledges and reflects these rules. However, in an educational setting, it is not always practical or possible to apply the rules of the governing body of sport, and schools need to consider adjustments that they can make to enable maximum participation while retaining the safety of the activity (eg in relation to the wearing of personal protective equipment [PPE]).

For more information, see **Chapter 10, Section 13**.

Fatigue, Injury and Exhaustion

2.10.53   **Fatigue, injury and exhaustion** may occur when students are required to use equipment or attempt a task:

- that is inappropriate to their age, stage of development or ability
- where they are required to play on pitches and courts that are inappropriate for their level of fitness or disability
- where they are required to carry out events over longer distances than those recommended for their age or stage of development.

2.10.54   Age-appropriate sized pitches/courts should be made available, either in a permanent or temporary form (such as by using marker discs). Information regarding recommended pitch and court sizes is available on governing body of sport websites and home country sport agency technical websites and publications; for example, Sport England (2015) "Comparative sizes of sports pitches and courts":

- outdoors – https://goo.gl/vN8jYk
- indoors – https://goo.gl/vkzJXA

2.10.55   Staff should constantly **monitor** students to check that the demand of a PESSPA activity does not create an unacceptable level of physical or emotional stress on any individual. Increased demand should be progressive and at a rate and level of challenge appropriate for the individual.

2.10.56   **Physical signs** are evident in students as fatigue and exhaustion occur. These may vary, but a flushed face, rapid shallow breathing, wide eyes, frantic or disjointed movements and loss of performance are frequent indicators.

2.10.57   PESSPA staff should familiarise themselves with any additional "elite" or community sports club training that students may be undertaking outside school that may increase the likelihood of fatigue. In cases where possible fatigue is identified, discussions should take place with the student to consider reducing the level of exertion from school PESSPA sessions to accommodate external training expectations that may put additional physical demands on them.

 See also fatigue through fasting in **2.10.63**.

Weather Conditions

2.10.58   Before PESSPA sessions commence, forethought should be given to the **weather conditions** (for sessions on or off site). There is always the potential for **adverse** weather to affect lessons. Careful and thoughtful planning of safe indoor alternatives is important, where these can be accommodated.

2.10.59   The physical demands of athletics, games and adventure activities are such that the body is often moving quickly so it is essential that the weather conditions do not impede safety. On damp or frosty mornings, the risk of slipping on a **grass or painted court surface** is increased and needs to be carefully assessed.

2.10.60   The position and brightness of the sun in relation to the students and types of activities they undertake can also impact on safe performance. The risks associated with overexposure to the two bands of ultraviolet light (from the sun) are well documented.

2.10.61   It is unreasonable to try to base decisions about carrying out PESSPA activities on specific **maximum temperatures** as there are no specific recommendations about this. However, during periods of unusually hot weather, teachers should monitor students for signs of heat exhaustion (eg headaches, dizziness, nausea, cramps, muscle weakness or pale skin).

2.10.62   Staff should be particularly mindful of a range of precautions for ensuring the well-being of students when working outside in hot/sunny conditions. Staff should ensure that:

- lengthy periods in direct sunlight, particularly around midday when the sun is at its hottest, are avoided whenever possible; this may occur when students have a physical education lesson outside followed or preceded by an outdoor lunchtime practice
- there is a system for providing access to drinking water in a way that is manageable for staff (eg students might provide their own water bottles when outside)
- they handle body image issues sensitively with students (eg with overweight or obese students wearing unnecessary layers of clothing in hot temperatures)
- students are taught how to screen themselves from the harmful effects of the sun through wearing light clothing and using sunscreen products; parents should be reminded about the need for students to use sunscreen products, and asked to provide these (for further information on the application of sun cream, see **FAQ 13** in **Chapter 4**)
- students are permitted to wear hats as long as they pose no danger to the wearer or other participants in terms of the quality of the items and the nature of the activity; some primary schools purchase sun hats for students, which are then kept in school
- additional shaded areas are provided during sports days, or when attending tournaments, festivals and other events where students may be exposed to the sun for long periods of time (eg by using gazebos or tents)
- students showing early symptoms of heat exhaustion are moved into a cool area and rehydrated.

Additional guidance is provided by the National Institute for Health and Care Excellence (NICE) at https://goo.gl/Hiko4G

Also see information provided by the Outdoor Kids organisation at www.oksunsafetycode.com

Considering Religious and Cultural Issues when Managing a Programme

2.10.63 The broad religious and cultural demographics in schools present a range of health and safety issues that need to be managed within PESSPA programmes to enable all students to take part safely. The most frequent health and safety **questions** arise in relation to:

- the wearing of certain items of clothing and/or religious artefacts (see **Chapter 2, Section 13**)
- the impact of religious/cultural festivals (eg Ramadan – Muslim month of fasting, which changes from year to year)
- cultural expectations relating to PESSPA activities and procedures
- participation in single- or mixed-gender groups (see **2.12.44**)
- language issues, which may put newly arrived students for whom English is an additional language (EAL) at risk due to difficulties in understanding the requirements of the task, safety procedures and expectations relating to conduct, and may affect their ability to stop work immediately in the event of danger or emergency.

2.10.64 Staff should be aware that religious and cultural **festivals** (eg Ramadan, which involves fasting from dawn to dusk over the period of a month) may require some students to engage in specified dietary regimes. As a result, energy levels may be low and the risk of dehydration increased. In such situations, staff expectations relating to participation in physical activity (eg sustained running) may need to be reviewed and levels of physical demand adjusted to accommodate individual needs.

2.10.65 Younger students, particularly, may be prone to a lowering of concentration levels if **fasting**. This has clear implications for the supervision and management of physical activity, and care needs to be taken in maintaining a safe working environment. For example, work on apparatus in gymnastics may require modification, and intensity levels in other activities may need to be reduced to a point where fasting students may continue to participate safely.

2.10.66 Staff need to remain responsive to student needs at all times. However, particular care needs to be taken when Ramadan or similar festivals fall in the summer months, which may exacerbate the risks of dehydration and fatigue.

2.10.67 Religious and cultural customs and beliefs fundamental to certain faiths may initially be seen to conflict with the demands made by some PESSPA activities within a prescribed curriculum. **Swimming**, for instance, presents particular issues for some communities (possibly from the Hindu and Muslim faiths), associated with unacceptable exposure of the body, mixed-gender settings or the wearing of adornments.

2.10.68 As well as being a statutory requirement in some contexts (eg the primary national curriculum in England and Wales), swimming is a potentially lifesaving skill that all children have an entitlement to access. In securing this access, school staff should apply all practical means to respect any religious or cultural sensitivities, while providing a swimming programme that at least meets the requirements of the curriculum being followed. To enable this, staff should try to:

- establish ongoing discussion with local faith leaders and parents so that policies concerning swimming provision are effectively communicated and understood
- accommodate adjustments in swimming attire to satisfy religious and cultural sensitivities while maintaining safe practice
- ensure that changing arrangements take into account any mixed-gender issues and provide acceptable levels of privacy
- operate a swimming programme that builds in single-sex teaching, whenever practical and wherever this preference is feasible.

2.10.69   EAL students may not fully understand the requirements of, or how to set about, a particular physical activity. This could potentially pose a risk to themselves and the rest of the group. It cannot be assumed that the complexity of the language used in PESSPA activities is any less demanding than elsewhere in the curriculum, and the speed of response often required puts further pressure on the ability of such students to comprehend. PESSPA staff should ensure that:

- where learning support staff are available, they should be effectively briefed about the learning outcomes of the lesson and alerted to any safety features
- time should be taken, initially, to ensure individual EAL students clearly understand the command "Stop!" and know that an immediate response to cease activity is required, should this command be necessary; over time, other key phrases, identified through risk assessment procedures, can be introduced into EAL students' vocabulary
- all staff are familiar with the names of EAL students in order that they can quickly attract and maintain their attention
- focused demonstrations are used, when appropriate, to attempt to overcome linguistic difficulty – linked to an acknowledgement by the students that they have understood what is required
- a "buddy" system is used, where necessary, in which an EAL student is paired with another student known to have a responsible and mature disposition; this reflects good practice.

Programme Management Principles within Specific Contexts

Combat and martial arts activities

2.10.70   **Combat activities** are competitive contact sports that are characterised by one-on-one combat in which a winner is determined against a set of rules. In many combat sports, a contestant wins by scoring more points than their opponent (eg boxing, fencing, self-defence and wrestling). Some combat activities are regulated by **recognised governing bodies of sport**, and others are not. This does not necessarily imply unsafe practice.

2.10.71   **Martial arts** are traditions of combat techniques practised for a variety of reasons, such as self-defence, competition, physical health and fitness, and entertainment, as well as mental, physical and spiritual development. Martial arts include the activities aikido, judo, karate, kendo, ju-jitsu, kung fu and taekwondo. The activity known as **"mixed martial arts"** (MMA) takes place within a caged arena for safety. This is currently not an activity that afPE condones in schools.

2.10.72   Lessons of **mixed combat activities** are becoming common, providing a "taster" of several different sports. Where schools offer more than one combat activity in any one session, staff should be appropriately qualified in **each of the activities involved**. The term "mixed combat activities" should not be confused with the activity of MMA as detailed above. Before taking a decision to introduce any such activities, employer and insurance requirements need to be checked and adhered to.

Guidance on specific combat activities

Boxing

2.10.73   Boxing involves two participants of similar weight fighting each other with gloved fists in a series of rounds that last 1–3 minutes. Technical points are scored according to the accuracy, frequency and direction of blows landed on the opponent. If there is no stoppage before an agreed number of rounds, a winner is determined through a points accumulation. If the opponent is knocked down and unable to get up before the referee counts to 10, or if the opponent is deemed too injured to continue, the result is a knockout.

2.10.74   The British Medical Association (BMA), as a body of medical experts, does not support the teaching or coaching of boxing, or any participation in the sport, due to evidence indicating detrimental effects on health.

2.10.75   Schools may wish to consider non-contact versions of boxing only. Wherever non-contact boxing is introduced to the curriculum, schools should ensure that all parents and students involved are aware of, and accept, the inherent and obvious risks. Parents can then make the decision as to whether their child progresses to contact boxing within a club situation.

2.10.76   England Boxing's development pathway is designed to ensure that the correct safety standards are upheld and applied in all settings. It has developed "Standards for coaching Olympic-style non-contact boxing in schools" (https://www.englandboxing.org/).

2.10.77   England Boxing has introduced non-contact versions of boxing for primary and secondary students (eg for primary level at some School Games events).

2.10.78   Also at primary level, simple, fun, non-contact activities concentrating on stance and movement are introduced. Participants wear no gloves or additional equipment.

2.10.79   Schools engaging **boxing coaches** to work with them should be clear about the qualifications they are looking for. (See **Chapter 2, Section 1**.)

Useful websites

Amateur Boxing Scotland: https://www.boxingscotland.org/
England Boxing: www.englandboxing.org
Irish Amateur Boxing Association: www.iaba.ie
Welsh Amateur Boxing Association: http://welshboxingassociation.org/

Fencing

2.10.80   The rules and safety requirements of British Fencing, the relevant governing body of sport, need to be strictly observed.

2.10.81   The three common forms of fencing are **epee, foil and sabre**. Safety measures need to be thoroughly addressed in order to minimise the risks involved in these potentially dangerous activities.

2.10.82   Students should be taught the basic safety requirements. They should **never**:

- run in the salle (fencing hall) (unless under the direction of a teacher or coach and then never holding a weapon)
- point a weapon at anyone not wearing a mask and correct clothing
- mishandle equipment
- use a blade that shows signs of "softness" or is badly bent or kinked
- fence against anyone whose blade shows signs of "softness"
- carry a weapon other than by the pommel with the point towards the floor or by gripping the point with the weapon hanging down vertically, other than when practising or fencing
- remove masks until told to do so by the coach.

2.10.83   Students under the age of 10 should fence with weapon blades of size 0, and those under 14 should normally fence with weapon blades of size 3 or smaller, corresponding to the competition requirements for their age. Adult-sized blades (size 5) are to be used by all fencers of 13 years and older.

2.10.84   Any **electrical equipment** used for scoring should be stored safely and observed carefully while in use.

GO/FENCE

2.10.85   This is the soft form of fencing using foam or plastic swords and a simple plastic face mask.

2.10.86   Guidelines for GO/FENCE are as follows:

- Check plastic foils have a large rubber button firmly affixed at the tip, that the plastic guard and blade have no cracks, and the guard is fitted securely.
- Check there is no excessive bend in the blade and that any slight curvature is in the correct direction, ie downwards (see inside guard for the word "Thumb" and an arrow indicating where to place the thumb – the blade should be straight, but if not, a slight downward curve is allowable).
- Check the integrity of the plastic mask by ensuring all rivets are in place, especially around the visor, and that the elasticated back strap is properly fixed to the plastic and that the Velcro fastenings are intact and secure.

Useful websites

British Disabled Fencing Association: www.bdfa.org.uk
British Fencing: www.britishfencing.com
England Fencing: www.englandfencing.org.uk
GO/FENCE: www.britishfencing.com/new-go-fence-website-goes-live/
Welsh Fencing: www.welshfencing.org

Self-defence

2.10.87   There are a number of different self-defence styles and activities, some of which include weapons. In many cases, a range of combat and martial arts moves are combined to achieve successful control, restraint and self-protection.

2.10.88   Self-defence training for students will usually cover aspects of personal safety awareness skills, as well as physical self-defence techniques. Schools should check that any self-defence or self-protection training they offer is suitable for the age group in question.

Wrestling

2.10.89   The rules and philosophy of the internationally agreed freestyle form of wrestling (ie Olympic-style wrestling) are formulated to enable two wrestlers to engage in hard physical combat without pain and/or injury.

2.10.90   Schools that provide wrestling as an activity for students list the many benefits it offers as including improvements in strength, stamina, flexibility and coordination, as well as development of confidence, discipline and respect for others.

2.10.91   A trained and experienced mat chairperson should be positioned at the edge of the mat during competitions. They should intervene immediately if any move or hold performed is likely to cause pain. School staff/coaches should adopt the role of mat chairperson during practice sessions.

2.10.92   Moves that put pressure on, or twist, the neck are **extremely hazardous** and should not be taught.

2.10.93   Wrestlers aged under 17 are not allowed to execute any form of **full nelson**. A scissor lock with the feet crossed on the head, neck or body is forbidden. Students under the age of 11 are not allowed to use any form of nelson or bridging. The nelson is not allowed to be used in female wrestling.

2.10.94   Clothing should be close-fitting without being too restrictive. Swimming costumes are ideal for training, but shorts are unsuitable and should not be worn. Specifically designed wrestling singlets are recommended for competition.

2.10.95   **Footwear** for beginners should be free of metal lace tags or eyelets, and have smooth soles.

2.10.96   The wrestling **area** normally covers 12 metres by 12 metres (depending on the level), with smooth mats, in good condition, firmly secured together and meeting the United World Wrestling standards.

2.10.97   No outside footwear should be worn on the mats. Disinfecting mats before or after every session can prevent the spread of germs and disease.

2.10.98   The minimum ceiling height should be as for judo, at 3.5 metres high, with no objects hanging below this height. Any potentially hazardous walls should be padded.

Useful website

British Wrestling Association: www.britishwrestling.org

Guidance on specific martial arts activities

Aikido

2.10.99 Aikido is a martial art that involves neutralising an attack by using holds and locks that are usually taught by modern/practical or classical/ceremonial methods.

2.10.100 Dangerous locks, holds or movements are **not** appropriate to be taught or practised in school programmes.

2.10.101 Students should wear a loose tunic and loose-fitting trousers such as tracksuit trousers. The traditional Japanese Gi (loose white trousers and belted jacket) is also suitable.

2.10.102 Requirements for mats, mat space per person and ceiling height are the same as for judo.

 For more information about mat space and ceiling height, see **2.8.62**.

2.10.103 Mat space per person increases and additional ceiling clearance is required if weapons are used. This should only be in a club situation.

2.10.104 Aikido has no recognised governing body of sport in England.

Useful website

British Aikido Board: www.bab.org.uk

Disability martial arts

Useful websites

Adaptive Martial Arts Association: http://adaptivemartialarts.org
Disability Martial Arts Association: www.dmaa.org.uk

Judo

2.10.105 Judo involves two participants in a contest where the object is to throw the opponent largely on to their back with considerable force and speed. This scores "ippon" (one point or 10 scores) and ends the contest. It is also possible to score ippon by pinning the opponent to the mat for a period of 25 seconds. In addition to the sought-after ippon, smaller scores are given for less successful throws and hold-downs broken before the 25-second limit.

2.10.106 It is essential that students are taught the various **ways to submit** and that they understand how important it is to accept submission and to stop applying technique immediately.

2.10.107 Students should not practise throwing techniques while others are practising groundwork skills.

2.10.108 Strangle and arm locks are **not** appropriate to be taught as part of a school programme of tuition.

2.10.109 Whenever possible, judogi **(judo suits)** should be worn in practice. These are mandatory in competition.

2.10.110 Only **bare feet** are permitted on the tatami (judo mat).

2.10.111 A minimum **ceiling height** of 3.5 metres is needed, with no objects hanging below this level.

2.10.112 The recommended **mat area** is one metre by one metre for young children, increasing to two metres by one metre for adults. More space may be required, depending on the type of activity and intensity of practice or "randori".

2.10.113 The edge of the mat area should be at least two metres away from any walls, projections or open doors.

2.10.114 GCSE syllabuses provide useful guidance for the organisation of judo activities.

Useful website

British Judo Association: www.britishjudo.org.uk

Karate

2.10.115 Karate is a Japanese, weapon-free martial art based on scientific principles that encompass physical culture, character development, self-defence and sport.

2.10.116 There are many different karate organisations in the UK. It is essential that only coaches from approved organisations are appointed to lead karate sessions in schools. Details of **approved organisations** can be obtained from national sports councils or Active Partnerships.

2.10.117 One hour is the **maximum time** recommended for curriculum karate sessions, and 90 minutes is the maximum time recommended for extracurricular sessions. Sessions should emphasise technical competence and comprise:

- a safe, effective and relevant warm-up and cool-down (see **Chapter 3**)
- fundamental techniques (kihon)
- formal exercise (kata)
- sparring (kumite).

2.10.118 **Non-contact sparring** should be introduced initially, with careful progression to touch contact. Reckless fighting should never be allowed.

2.10.119 Face masks and body armour should be worn at competition level.

2.10.120 An area of three square metres per student is required when practising fundamental techniques (kihon) and four square metres per student when practising formal exercises (kata).

2.10.121 GCSE and A Level syllabuses can provide useful guidance for the organisation of karate activities.

Useful websites

Disability Karate Federation: www.disabilitykarate.co.uk
English Karate Federation: www.englishkaratefederation.com
Scottish Karate Association: www.scottishkarateassociation.co.uk
Welsh Karate: www.welshkarate.org.uk

Ju-jitsu, kendo, kung fu and tang soo do

2.10.122 As the potential for harm in these activities is high, school staff are recommended to discuss with the employer their inclusion in a school programme.

Useful websites

British Council of Chinese Martial Arts: https://bccma.com/
British Ju Jitsu Association: www.bjjagb.com/
British Kendo Association: www.britishkendoassociation.com/
UK Tang Soo Do Federation: www.uktsdf.org.uk/

WTF taekwondo

2.10.123 Taekwondo is described as a Korean martial art and a full contact combat sport. It appeals to young people as it is characterised by fast, high, spinning kicks and energetic movements, often in sequence. In addition, participants learn to apply powerful hand and joint-locking techniques.

2.10.124 Holds and locks should be taught safely, with students made aware of the potential for injury.

2.10.125 Students need to be matched according to gender, size, weight, age, experience and ability when sparring.

 For more information about matching students in groups, and mixed-gender and mixed-age sport, see **2.10.34**.

2.10.126 Mats should be joined together securely so they do not move apart.

Useful websites

British Taekwondo: https://www.britishtaekwondo.org.uk/
British Taekwondo Council: https://www.tkdcouncil.com/

Games

Alternative versions of specific games

2.10.127 It is possible to provide alternative versions of many games activities played in school or club settings. This is particularly useful when:

- introducing a game to younger or less able students
- making a game more inclusive and accessible to a wider range of participants
- less space is available for learning
- fewer participants are available.

2.10.128 Where applicable, information regarding alternative versions of games is included in the guidance on specific games activities that follows.

2.10.129 Where "outdoor" games are played indoors (as a result of poor weather or limited facilities), it is important that adjustments are made to ensure the safety of those involved. Consider:

- clearly marking the reduced playing area, and making players aware of this
- ensuring adequate run-off areas are available
- reducing team numbers
- considering any necessary changes to the rules of the activity.

 Information regarding playing areas can be found in **2.8.9**.

2.10.130 Whichever version of a game is used, it is essential for the safety of all involved that PESSPA staff know and apply the rules of the activity they are supervising, teaching or officiating, whether in an educational or club context. Similarly, students should be taught to manage any risks within the different types of games activity, and be encouraged to always play within the spirit and rules of the game, to reduce levels of risk to themselves and others.

Association football/soccer

2.10.131 Since the start of the 2015–2016 football season, The Football Association (FA) has allowed boys and girls to play in the same teams up to the under-18 age limit. This can also apply in competitive situations, but individual league or competition organisers should be consulted directly for confirmation.

2.10.132 Schools can make their own decision regarding this issue, applying matching principles such as size, ability, confidence and previous experience.

For more information about mixed groupings, see **2.12.34**.

2.10.133   Studded and bladed boots should be maintained to an appropriate safety standard.

 For more information about footwear, see **Chapter 2, Section 13**.

2.10.134   The wearing of shin pads at all times is recommended. Where students do not have shin pads, staff should manage the situation to ensure the safety of all participants.

 For more information about PPE, see **Chapter 2, Section 13**.

2.10.135   The FA permits the wearing of glasses (spectacles) up to the under-14 age level, at the discretion of the official.

 See **2.13.50** for guidance on eyewear that can support schools in developing their own policy in relation to this aspect.

2.10.136   Goalposts, netting and corner flags should be checked regularly for safety.

 For more information about checking equipment prior to use, see **Chapter 2, Section 9**.

Useful websites

English Schools Football Association: www.esfa.co.uk
The Football Association: www.thefa.com
Football Association of Wales: https://www.faw.cymru/en/
Irish Football Association: www.irishfa.com
Northern Ireland Schools Football Association: www.nisfa.co.uk
Scottish Football Association: www.scottishfa.co.uk
Scottish Schools Football Association: www.scottishfa.co.uk/ssfa/
Welsh Schools Football Association: www.welshschoolsfa.co.uk

Futsal and five-a-side football

2.10.137   These games are normally played indoors on a flat, smooth, non-abrasive surface. Five-a-side may also be played outdoors within a restricted, enclosed area. Where futsal is played outside, it would usually be on artificial grass. The main difference in futsal is the absence of rebound boards, which are more common in five-a-side games.

2.10.138   The rules of futsal regarding accumulated fouls contribute to safety by discouraging teams from being overly physical or disputing the decisions of the two referees.

Useful website

Futsal and five-a-side: http://goo.gl/RWBEN7

Trampoline parks and inflatable arenas

2.10.139   Trampoline parks are large warehouse units, similar to soft play centres, with a number of trampoline beds linked together in a "patchwork" arrangement both on the floor and the walls. Many incorporate additional facilities into or around the trampoline area, such as climbing walls, basketball courts and trampettes, with large inflatable landing areas that encourage participants to try somersaults. Such facilities have become very popular for young people and provide opportunities for high energy activity. However, given sessions are generally open to large and diverse groups, from the very young to adults, they can be chaotic environments. It may be appropriate for staff to seek a private session where possible.

2.10.140   As outlined in **Chapter 2, Section 1**, staff teaching trampolining to students at school are recommended to have a formal qualification, and to develop the skills students require progressively and safely. While centres provide staff to monitor activity, many do not have formal qualifications, nor do they engage in developing students' skills in a controlled manner.

2.10.141   Most centres require participants to sign waiver forms to absolve the centre of liability in the event of an accident. The extent to which such waivers would be effective is debatable. However, staff are not able to sign such a form on behalf of students, nor can students under 18 years of age sign their own waiver. Also, the waiver will not act to absolve the school of liability in the event of an accident.

2.10.142   Bearing in mind the nature of such parks, staff must consider the educational objectives of any visit. In private, controlled sessions, parks can offer opportunities for younger students or those with additional needs to develop balance and coordination skills in line with curricular requirements.

2.10.143   Given the particular issues that trampoline parks present, some employers have taken the view that they are inappropriate for the purposes of educational visits. Staff must therefore be aware of and follow their employer's policy on the matter.

Aquatics

2.10.144   **Programmed aquatic activities** are those with formal structure, supervision, control and continuous monitoring from the poolside. School swimming lessons are programmed sessions where the risk is reduced due to the nature of the activity and degree of control exercised.

2.10.145   **Unprogrammed aquatic activities** are sessions without a formal structure but with supervision and continuous monitoring, in most cases from the poolside. "Free swimming" time at the end of a school swimming lesson, or a public session in a community pool are examples of unprogrammed aquatic activities.

2.10.146   The Health and Safety Executive (HSE) has clearly identified a reduced level of risk to the safety of swimmers when participating in programmed aquatic activities, compared to **unprogrammed** public sessions. It is therefore recommended that school swimming lessons avoid any periods of **"free swimming"** and maintain a structured, programmed approach.

Management of aquatic sessions

2.10.147   A nominated school staff member should be responsible for ensuring risk assessments are carried out, and for monitoring:

- student progress
- the confidence and competence of accompanying staff
- the application of policies and procedures
- that other staff have been informed of procedures and standards.

2.10.148   Whoever is responsible for the water safety of the group should be told the **number in the group** by school staff so that regular scanning and accurate head counts can be carried out during the session.

2.10.149   Where an adult has responsibility for teaching more than two students, the recommended **teaching position** is from the side of the pool as this provides the best position to oversee the whole group and respond quickly to any teaching or emergency situation.

2.10.150   All school staff and specialist aquatic staff should be able to see all students throughout the lesson. The bottom of the pool should be **clearly visible**, and any problems of **glare**, light reflected from the water surface, or shadow caused by hoists or similar apparatus should be satisfactorily overcome. Where this cannot be achieved, staff should regularly change their teaching position and/or request additional help in monitoring "blind spots" from accompanying adults available on the poolside.

2.10.151   **It is imperative that staff count the students out of the pool and off the poolside. Staff should walk around the pool at the end of each aquatic lesson to ensure that all areas are clear of students.**

2.10.152   **Additional adults** may be in the water to assist individual students or small groups according to their age, ability and confidence. Where manual support is provided, care needs to be taken to:

- avoid embarrassment to the student or adult
- ensure support is provided in an appropriate form
- promote student learning about feeling safe in relation to the use of manual support in PESSPA activities.

2.10.153   Students with **medical problems** may need clearance provided in the form of written permission from parents before they are allowed to participate in school aquatic programmes. Additional advice may also be necessary from relevant organisations with regard to specific risk factors relating to aquatic activity that may affect individual students.

2.10.154   The requirements of students with **epilepsy** may vary depending on whether an effective medication regime is in place. They may need to:

- be observed from the poolside by a staff member assigned specifically to that role
- work alongside a responsible person in the water when out of their depth
- if appropriate, work within a "buddy" system with a student or helper in the water to provide **unobtrusive** paired supervision that avoids embarrassment.

2.10.155   The extent of their participation will need to be informed by the effectiveness of their medication in controlling the onset of epilepsy, and whether the student has a history of episodes while swimming.

 For further information about education, health and care plans (EHCPs), see **2.3.7** and about epilepsy, see **2.3.5**.

2.10.156   Pool lifeguarding staff should be trained in the use of **spinal boards/special recovery stretchers**, where these are available at pools. Spinal boards more effectively meet the needs of recovering patients, especially where they may have suffered head and neck injuries. School staff and those on poolside duty should know how to assemble and use such equipment, where it is available and where their role may include responsibility for water rescues.

2.10.157   All students should be made aware of the necessary procedures, and learn the importance of taking increasing responsibility, for personal **safety routines**, including:

- removing, or making safe, all jewellery
- not chewing sweets or gum
- carrying out appropriate hygiene procedures
- reporting any illness
- walking (not running) on the poolside
- remaining away from the pool edge until told to approach the water
- knowing and responding appropriately to the emergency procedures for stopping activity and evacuating the pool
- reporting unseemly or unacceptable behaviour that may compromise safety
- responding immediately to all instructions.

 Swim England provides guidance and resources to support the management of aquatic programmes: http://goo.gl/DjYqwU

The Swimming Teachers' Association (STA) "Swimming Teaching Code of Conduct" is available from
https://www.sta.co.uk/wp-content/uploads/2016/04/STA-Swimming-Teaching-Code-of-Practice-v16.1.pdf

Health-related exercise

Age-related issues about student use of fitness suite

2.10.158 Many LAs or private providers set age restrictions for use of their fitness suite facilities. Reasons given for this are often linked to insurance barriers. Staff should check their own employer guidance and insurance arrangements.

2.10.159 Current guidelines indicate that it is not only safe for adolescents to take part in well supervised, developmentally appropriate resistance exercise programmes, but that there are many health benefits to be gained from doing so. The British Association of Sports and Exercise Sciences (BASES) recommends that:

> facilities and equipment should be designed to suit the needs of individuals; be well supervised and led by suitably qualified staff; young people should be helped to understand the place of resistance exercise in a balanced programme of health-enhancing activity.
>
> Stratton, G., Jones, M., Fox, K.R., Tolfrey, K., Harris, J., Maffulli, N., Lee, M. and Frostick, S.P. (2004) "BASES position statement on guidelines for resistance exercise in young people", *Journal of Sports Sciences*, 22 (4): 383–90.

2.10.160 For this reason, schools should not hesitate to seek to use fitness suites with students aged 11–18 providing that the above guidance can be met.

Section 11: Safe Exercise Practice

Safe and Effective Practice Principles

2.11.1   In order to make decisions about the safety of specific physical education, school sport and physical activity (PESSPA) exercises or movements, staff need to address the following questions relating to each of the four principles of safe exercise practice:

Principle of Safe Exercise Practice	Risk Assessment Question
Control	Can the exercise/activity be performed in a controlled manner?
Impact	Have any risks associated with high impact been minimised?
Alignment	Can the exercise/activity be performed with correct joint alignment?
Developmental appropriateness	Is the exercise/activity appropriate for the physical maturation of the student?

2.11.2   Staff should incorporate these principles of safe practice into their planning, and implement them in their teaching.

 For further explanation of key terminology, refer to the Glossary of Terms.

Table 13: Making judgements about the developmental appropriateness of physical activities/exercises for safe exercise practice

Developmental Appropriateness		
Is the activity/exercise appropriate for the physical maturation of the student?		
What is developmental appropriateness?		
This refers to how appropriate the exercise/activity is for the physical maturation of the child or young person. For the purposes of this table, children are 4–10 years and young people 11–18 years.		
Fact	**Risk Implication**	**Recommendations for Minimising Risk**
Children's body proportions differ from adults (ie they are bottom-heavy with a weak upper body and big head).	Children's weak torso can struggle to support their weight, especially during actions that involve supporting long levers.	Use "child-friendly" exercises. Avoid asking children to perform adult versions of exercises that incorporate long levers (eg side bends with arms stretched overhead, curl-ups with hands by ears).
Children have a lower rate of sweat production and a higher rate of heat production than adults. They also have a larger ratio of body surface area to weight.	Children cannot regulate their body temperature as efficiently as adults (ie they heat up rapidly, overheat easily and lose heat rapidly).	Ask children frequently how they are feeling, and monitor their response to activity and how they look. Implement the following measures to reduce overexposure to sun/heat: • Establish policies for wearing hats/caps and loose, light clothing. • Advise parents to provide sun cream protection for their children to apply. • Reduce exercise intensity. • Provide frequent rest periods. • Have plenty of fluids available. • Continually monitor for signs of overheating.
		Implement the following measures to reduce overexposure in cold conditions: • Allow children to wear appropriate additional clothing, and keep them as active as possible. • Continually monitor for signs of the onset of hypothermia. Help children and young people learn to monitor and respond appropriately to how they feel when taking part in PESSPA activities. Help children and young people learn how to conduct their own risk assessments in relation to taking part in PESSPA activities in extreme temperatures. For more information, see **Chapter 3**.
Children have less carbohydrate stored in their muscles than adults and a reduced ability to use it for energy production.	Children are less efficient at performing short burst, high intensity (anaerobic) activities than adults.	Ensure high intensity activities (eg fast running, jumping) are short and intermittent with adequate periods of active recovery.

In both children and young people, growth plates at the ends of bones are weak and soft.	Children and young people's bones are more susceptible to injury than adults', especially the ends of the bone where the growth plate is situated.	Encourage children and young people to place and move joints in correct alignment. Avoid exposing children and young people to physical activities that put bones and joints under excessive stress (eg falling on to hands, working against maximal resistance). Ensure high impact activities are performed with protective footwear, with safe and effective technique, and intermittently.
Young people of the same age and sex may be at very different stages of growth. Growth rates are not linear during adolescence.	Staff may assume one version of a physical activity/exercise: • is appropriate for all young people of the same age • can be performed at the same intensity and level for the same duration by all young people.	Include different versions of each exercise that fulfil the same purpose. Enable young people to decide the most appropriate level/intensity for themselves. Adapt physical activities/exercises to accommodate the needs of individual children and young people. Help children and young people learn to adapt physical activities/exercises to accommodate their own individual needs.
Following a growth spurt, young people's muscles might be relatively thin, weak and tight.	Young people may have: • a restricted range of movement around some joints • an imbalance between flexibility and strength that may result in poor joint alignment. An exaggerated pull on the tendon-bone insertion may cause damage to a growth plate.	Ensure that during a growth spurt, young people are encouraged and helped to: • reduce muscle tightness, avoid muscle imbalance and maintain range of movement about joints by performing mobility exercises, resistance exercises and stretches as part of a regular exercise programme • perform exercises with correct alignment of joints • vary participation. Do not allow young people to take part in PESSPA activities when they are in pain.

2.11.3   Students should learn about the principles of safe exercise practice so that they are able to take part in PESSPA activities both at school and in the community with increasing independence and confidence, and without personal physical injury either in the short or long term. **Chapter 3** covers this in detail.

Warming Up and Cooling Down

2.11.4   The use of warm-ups and cool-downs is standard practice in all sessions. Although the activities themselves may provide only minimum physiological benefits due to the need to shorten them to meet the requirements of curricular and extracurricular time, their regular use helps to normalise such behaviours in any PESSPA context. Staff should be able to embed effective warming up and cooling down into their sessions, and students should be encouraged to learn about this. (See **Chapter 3, Section 3**.)

2.11.5   The appropriate length of a warm-up depends on:
   • the intensity and duration of the activity to follow (a more vigorous/very energetic activity may require a longer warm-up)
   • the physical and psychological condition of the participants (eg children and young people who are sedentary may need a more gradual, longer warm-up)
   • environmental factors such as temperature and humidity (a longer pulse-raising section may be required in colder temperatures and a shorter pulse-raising section in higher temperatures).

2.11.6   The appropriate length of a cool-down depends on the:
   • intensity and duration of the preceding activity (a more vigorous/very energetic activity may require a longer cool-down)
   • physical and psychological condition of the participants (eg children and young people who are active on a regular basis will recover more quickly).

2.11.7   **All exercises and activities included in warm-ups and cool-downs should comply with the principles of safe exercise practice.**

2.11.8   Students need to acquire practical knowledge and understanding of warming up and cooling down. This process starts with them following consistent good practice, and culminates in them designing their own relevant and appropriate procedures. Students should be progressively involved in designing, conducting and evaluating their own warm-ups and cool-downs.

 For more information on how students can learn about the development of such good practice, see **Chapter 3**.

2.11.9   Staff should closely monitor student-led warm-ups and cool-downs to ensure that both choice of exercises/activities and performance are safe, effective and appropriate.

Supervision

Please also refer to **Group Management, Chapter 2, Section 12**.

2.11.10   Effective supervision of activity areas during playtimes is essential, particularly where hazards are unavoidable (eg windows opening outwards, the exposed corners of buildings).

2.11.11   When changing, there is no statutory requirement for students to be **supervised** at all times. However, case law provides a clear indication that the incidence of injury is much higher when students are not supervised than when they are.

2.11.12   The degree and method of supervision will vary according to the particular circumstances, but age, behaviour, potential bullying, and safety aspects of the space itself will contribute to deciding whether constant direct supervision is necessary or intermittent direct supervision is safe. The location of the staff responsible for the group is of particular importance. Consideration must be given to whether they can provide the level of supervision required while they are fulfilling their usual pre-lesson organisational tasks. Some schools use changing time as a positive part of the learning experience.

Safe and Effective Practice within Specific Contexts

2.11.13   When teaching in any PESSPA context, the safety of students must come first. Many principles and safe teaching behaviours have been developed over time and become accepted as best practice. These are outlined in the text that follows. As always, each practitioner should check with their employer to ensure that these principles and behaviours are what would be expected in their own teaching environment. Many employers accept Association for Physical Education (afPE) best practice as their own benchmark. However, where practice differs from that outlined here, the employer's requirements take priority. Some principles are generic, but where they apply to specific contexts, they have been highlighted as such. Where activities are higher risk, this may require staff to undertake additional professional learning. (See **Chapter 2, Section 1**.)

Athletic activities

2.11.14   It is recommended that any multi-event athletic session within a PESSPA programme should comprise a maximum of four activities at any one time, with only one of these to be a throwing event, which should be closely supervised.

2.11.15   Staff should use auditory and visual **"ready and response signals"** to indicate when students are to start and stop, for example, throwing and retrieving implements, and wait for areas to be clear. Staff should check that these signals are clearly understood by all students and that they know how to respond appropriately. These procedures should be introduced in the very first session.

2.11.16   Staff should ensure that each new activity and each stage of a new activity is carefully introduced so that students are made aware of the potential dangers involved, the necessary safety procedures to be observed and the rules that must be obeyed. Staff have a specific obligation to see that these precautions are followed during sessions. It is unwise to hurry these preliminary stages. Sufficient time should be given to the early stages of learning so that safe habits are established from the outset.

Throwing activities

It is important that all throwing activities are properly managed and supervised. Safety **must** come first. Impact or contact from an "in-flight" hammer, discus, javelin or shot will almost certainly result in a serious or fatal injury.

2.11.17   Staff should be clear about which throwing activities/events are developmentally appropriate for their students.

2.11.18   Basic standing throws should be taught before adding turns or run-ups.

2.11.19   Competitive throwing events (eg javelin, shot, discus, hammer) are **higher risk activities**. **Higher risk activities** are those that would require understanding of clear safe practice principles and procedures that may be unique to the activity being taught. Staff and officials teaching, supervising and/or officiating competitive throwing events need to be competent to do so.

2.11.20   Equipment should be kept in good repair and stored in a safe place.

2.11.21   Throwing implements should be treated with respect at all times. They should not be played about with or mishandled, especially when being carried from the school to the playing field or track.

2.11.22   There should be adequate supervision of distribution, and the apparatus should be transported in a safe manner. Nets or baskets can be of help when apparatus is being carried in bulk. Helpers should be advised of the correct way to lift heavy items, and care should be taken to ensure that no person attempts to carry more weight or bulk than is appropriate for their size.

2.11.23   Initial training in throwing activities should be undertaken under the control of the member of staff. Through experience and good judgement, they will decide if and when students are capable of assuming responsibility for themselves and can be permitted to undertake practices on their own.

Transporting, carrying and storing throwing equipment

2.11.24   In secondary schools, staff should supervise the carrying of throwing implements **in transit** to the lesson as well as during the lesson. All throwing implements should be carried and retrieved singly using two hands to prevent students attempting "mock" throwing actions. Javelins should be carried upright, and the ends protected if possible. Multiple shots, discuses and hammers may be carried in baskets, provided the overall weight is not excessive. In primary schools, the use of lighter foam and rubber equipment is common practice. Although this equipment does not present the same risks as heavier/ sharper equipment, it is good practice to teach students the same routines that they will be expected to follow as their school career progresses.

2.11.25   All throwing implements should be carried and retrieved at **walking pace**. They should always be **carried** back to the throwing line (**never** thrown), and placed on the ground (**never** dropped).

2.11.26   Javelins, when not in use, should be placed vertically in a storage rack or, when a rack is not available, laid flat on the ground.

Managing the throwing area

2.11.27   All throwers should stand well behind the appropriate circle or scratch line and remain there until the appropriate time to make a throw. Normally, this distance would be around ten metres. The scratch line or circle and the safety area can be marked using cones or an appropriate similar method.

2.11.28   Throwers should themselves make sure that there is no one **in** the landing area, **approaching** the landing area, or in the **possible** line of flight of the implement before making their throw. **It is very important that this should be the responsibility of the individual thrower as well as the staff member.**

2.11.29   After throwing, throwers should move back to the safety area and must not immediately retrieve the implement. It should be retrieved only on instruction after all members of the group have thrown. Under no circumstances should a shot, javelin, discus or hammer be thrown back to the scratch line or circle. Students should never run towards implements they have just thrown.

2.11.30   Wet implements increase the risk of accidents, and extra vigilance should be exercised in such conditions, with particular care taken to allow for implements sliding after landing.

2.11.31   In wet conditions, grass and some artificial surfaces can prove slippery and dangerous.

2.11.32   Particular care should be exercised to ensure that runways and take-off areas are suitable for use.

2.11.33   Throwers in group situations should throw **sequentially** and in a predetermined order. Students waiting to perform need to **stand well behind** the throwing line or circle, and focus on the thrower until told by staff to move forward. To ensure a safe waiting distance is maintained, staff may use cones or mark a line.

2.11.34   Staff and/or officials should always be **appropriately positioned** before and during throwing activities/ events, and should regularly remind students of required safety procedures and correct technical points, and encourage them to contribute to checking safety and demonstrating safe practice.

Javelin

2.11.35   Both ends of javelins are dangerous. Special care should therefore be taken in controlling their use.

2.11.36   They should never be permitted to remain stuck in the ground at an angle.

2.11.37   Special care should be taken to establish a safe and controlled procedure for retrieving javelins. Retrievers should never be permitted to run towards them, particularly in wet conditions.

Discus/hammer/shot

2.11.38   If employing any kind of turn (other than when using adaptive equipment), a cage should be used. The basic discus and shot standing throw can be taught without a cage (eg on a dry school field). Even with a standing throw, there is some rotation so spacing between participants must be carefully considered in any group or class practice prior to throws taking place. The areas of greatest danger are to the right of a right-handed thrower and to the left of a left-handed thrower.

2.11.39   For this reason, always start the throwing order at the right-hand end of the row of right-hand throwers, followed by starting from the left-hand end of the row of left-hand throwers. The safety area should always be behind throwers and on the side not being thrown from.

2.11.40   All students awaiting their turn should:
- be behind the throwers – the distance depends on the risk assessment but 10 metres minimum is strongly recommended
- pay attention at all times, watching the release and landing of the thrown implement
- only collect the thrown implement when instructed
- walk out to collect the thrown implement.

2.11.41   Staff should also stand behind throwers.

2.11.42   As throwers advance to being able to turn into their throws, a cage should be used. **Safety cages should always be used when teaching hammer** because the direction of flight is so unpredictable.

Jumping activities

2.11.43   Staff and/or officials should always be **appropriately positioned** before and during jumping activities/ events, and should regularly remind students of required safety procedures and correct technical points, and encourage them to contribute to checking safety and demonstrating safe practice.

2.11.44   Staff should be clear about which jumping activities/events and equipment are developmentally appropriate for their students.

2.11.45   Competitive jumping events such as pole vault and high jump using Fosbury-flop technique are **higher risk activities**. Staff and officials teaching, supervising and officiating competitive jumping events need to be competent to do so. This may require them to undertake additional professional learning.

2.11.46   Wood or concrete edges to pits should be flush with the surrounding ground.

2.11.47   Any hard surfaces should be protected to ensure soft landings.

2.11.48   The sand used in all pits should be sharp sand and deep enough to prevent jarring on landing.

2.11.49   Pits should be dug before use and also at frequent intervals during use.

2.11.50   Pits should be carefully examined for hidden sharp objects, broken glass etc before use.

2.11.51   It is important to ensure that all run-up areas are well maintained, especially at take-off points.

2.11.52   Students, teachers, coaches and officials should take particular care to ensure that no jump is made while the pit is being dug or raked, and that spades, forks and rakes are not left where they can cause injury.

Vertical jumps

2.11.53   For younger students, beginners and preliminary practices, well dug sand pit landing areas for high jumpers can be used quite safely for training purposes at low heights. In those styles of jumping in which the jumper normally lands on their feet (eg scissors), well dug sand provides a safe and acceptable landing medium.

Students should understand and be competent in basic **feet-to-feet** jumping before progressing to more advanced techniques.

2.11.54   For those styles of jumping in which it is normal for the jumper to land on their back (Fosbury flop, and straddle style of high jumping and pole vaulting), appropriate manufactured landing areas need to be used (foam sections).

2.11.55   Minimum recommended sizes of landing areas for competition are:
- pole vault – five metres by five metres and 0.8 metres deep, excluding front protection pads
- high jump – five metres by four metres and 0.7 metres deep (in schools' competition, a suitable minimum size is five metres by three metres).

2.11.56   Larger landing areas provide safer conditions for vertical jumps.

2.11.57   Smaller landing areas for high jump are acceptable for training purposes where the take-off point can be established with reasonable certainty and the member of staff is qualified and experienced in the event.

2.11.58   Individual landing units should be fastened together to reduce the risk of athletes going through joins between two sections.

2.11.59   All foam landing areas should be capable of preventing the athlete from "bottoming out". Good manufacturers will give guarantees in this respect.

2.11.60   Soft landing areas deteriorate. They should be regularly inspected and maintained.

High jump

2.11.61   Take-off markers or zones should be used to indicate take-off positions in the early stages of learning **high jump** to ensure that the bar is negotiated at the midpoint and that landing occurs in the centre of the sand pit or landing module.

2.11.62   Round bars are recommended for feet-to-body high-jump styles (eg Fosbury flop). Triangular bars should no longer be used. Only bars of circular cross-section should be used when jumping on to a mat of any kind.

2.11.63   The uprights for flexi-bars need to be secured so that they do not collapse on jumpers.

2.11.64   Unless spikes are worn, grass and some artificial surfaces are not suitable for take-off areas.

Long jump

2.11.65   Brightly coloured boards placed on a long-jump runway can help to indicate when jumping is not allowed. Take-off boards should be flush with the runway to prevent tripping injuries.

2.11.66   Take-off boards should be firmly fixed flush with the surface of the runway and positioned so that there is no chance of a jumper landing on the pit surrounds.

2.11.67   Where possible, it is desirable to provide separate facilities for long jump and triple jump.

2.11.68   Where it is possible to provide only a single landing area, it is better to make this wider than usual so that adjacent runways can be provided.

Pole vault

2.11.69   Fibre-glass vaulting poles need to be checked regularly for damage and:
- discarded if cracked or spiked
- stored suitably to prevent bending
- be used only in planting boxes with a sloping back plate (not vertical).

2.11.70   Only suitably qualified staff should teach students how to bend a vaulting pole.

Running activities

2.11.71   Staff should be clear about which running events and distances are developmentally appropriate for their students.

2.11.72   Staff and/or officials should always be **appropriately positioned** before and during running activities/ events, and should regularly remind students of required safety procedures and correct technical points, and encourage them to contribute to checking safety and demonstrating safe practice.

Track activities

2.11.73   Careful instructions should be given at the earliest opportunity to prevent accidents from spiked running shoes.

2.11.74   In events of more than one lap, in which all or part of the race is not run in lanes, due consideration should be given to the number of students who are permitted to enter each run in order to avoid accidents arising from jostling for position.

2.11.75   Hurdles should be well maintained.

2.11.76   Hurdles must only be used in the correct direction. They are designed to fall when students make contact with them so they should be placed properly to allow this to happen. Students should not jump "against" the hurdle as this would negate this design feature.

2.11.77   In wet conditions, grass and some artificial surfaces are not suitable for hurdling unless suitable footwear is worn.

2.11.78   Steeplechase barriers should be stable, well maintained and conform to UK Athletics specifications. This is particularly the case for the water jump and landing areas.

Cross-country

2.11.79 The safety of students should be of paramount importance when planning a course.

2.11.80 The start should be sufficiently wide to eliminate any danger of spiking. There should be a clear, wide and lengthy run before any narrowing of the course occurs to prevent students bunching up and queuing.

2.11.81 Basic provision should include first aid and casualty transport, washing facilities and drinks to counter the effects of adverse weather conditions.

2.11.82 Courses should be planned in order to ensure:

- ease of supervision
- maximum visibility of students by staff
- suitability for the age and capability of the students participating
- the slowest students can be easily tracked
- a wide start and long clear approach before any constrictions (eg narrow gateways)
- ease of counting students out and in.

For some students with specific mobility issues a smooth surface is essential.

Combat activities

Demonstrations involving students

2.11.83 Careful consideration and forethought should be given to whether adults should perform dynamic **demonstrations using students**, and to ensure that technical guidance is provided without placing any student in an unsafe situation. Static demonstrations are acceptable.

2.11.84 Students should be carefully matched for demonstrations. Staff should not compete with students.

Technique

2.11.85 Correct instruction is important where strike pads are used to practise punching and kicking, both in the way the pads are held and the impact allowed.

2.11.86 Students should be taught how to land safely (eg to break falls) before take-downs and throws are practised, and mats need to be used.

Mixed-gender practice

2.11.87 This is allowed in some combat and martial arts activities (eg fencing, taekwondo and judo), but mixed-gender competition is not allowed.

Games activities

Hockey

2.11.88 Players should seek to develop and exercise good stick and ball control at all times. Controlled pushing should be well established before the introduction of hitting.

2.11.89 Goalkeepers should try to remain on their feet whenever possible.

Netball

2.11.90 Players should keep fingernails short and well trimmed.

2.11.91 During competitive matches, **gloves** may only be worn at the discretion of the umpire.

2.11.92 High 5 netball can be played with **mixed-gender** teams so care needs to be taken with matching opponents.

Rugby football – league and union

2.11.93   **Contact** versions of the game should only be introduced and managed by suitably experienced staff and coaches following recognised teaching progressions and guidelines, and the regulations of the governing bodies of sport for rugby union and rugby league. Teachers should not teach or officiate contact rugby until they are competent to do so. Where they are not competent, additional professional learning should be completed.

School teams

2.11.94   Schools are advised to follow governing body of sport regulations that permit players to play in teams one school year group above their own. This might result in teams including players of three different ages. For example, a year six team could incorporate players from year five, resulting in players' ages spanning 9–11 years old. In special circumstances, where skill level, size and experience are appropriate, players can be permitted to play in a team two school year groups above their own. Age bandings (eg under-9s, under-11s) are determined by a player's date of birth in relation to the playing season. In all cases of students playing above their age group, appropriate assessment should be carried out, and parents should be informed and their consent gained.

For further information relating to England Rugby's Age Grade Rugby, see
https://www.englandrugby.com/participation/coaching/age-grade-rugby

For Ireland, see http://goo.gl/SKjXru

For Scotland, see http://goo.gl/glOR00

2.11.95   A player should not participate in mixed-gender teams once they have reached the age of 15.

Touch rugby

2.11.96   This is a version of rugby where tackling is replaced by touching or tapping the opponent.

2.11.97   Teams can be mixed so matching needs to be carefully managed.

Tag rugby

2.11.98   It is important that the **non-contact** element is enforced throughout the game. The ball carrier is not allowed to run directly into defenders, and defenders are not allowed to block the progress of the ball carrier.

2.11.99   Hand-offs, or use of hand, elbow or ball to block or shield a "tag" are not allowed.

2.11.100   As a mixed-gender game, matching needs to be carefully managed.

Association football

Heading the football

2.11.101 Following detailed analysis and consolation, the National Governing Bodies of the home nations have **all now issued guidance on heading** to provide support for parents, coaches and teachers. The guidance covers all aspects of how to coach heading the ball, including the correct size of ball to use, the best techniques and how often the ball should be headed. The focus is on quality of heading training, rather than quantity. The guidance also reinforces the important information relating to NGB concussion guidance. For more detailed advice in relation to age groups and the guidance, please visit the appropriate website listed below. A key message to come from the recommendations is:

No heading in training in the foundation phase (primary school children).

It is believed that offering this best practice guidance to the game is a balanced and measured step to take. The English FA, alongside the Irish FA and Scottish FA, and in consultation with UEFA, have come together to implement steps to reduce and remove repetitive and unnecessary heading from youth football, with the intention of not impacting on how the game is played.
www.thefa.com
www.irishfa.com
www.faw.cymru
www.scottishfa.co.uk

Ultimate frisbee

2.11.102 As this is a self-refereed sport, delays can occur in fouls being called, leaving a period of time of potentially unsafe situations. When teaching students in schools, this should be considered so that participants are aware of the implications in their own play.

Tennis

2.11.103 Courts should be arranged in the same **direction** of play in order to avoid the possibility of a player being hit by a ball from another game.

Short tennis (short court or Mini Tennis)

2.11.104 This version is played in a more restricted space than the full game, usually half a tennis court or a badminton size court, so players need to be aware of others in their area.

Dance activities

2.11.105 Staff should be well informed about, and able to apply effectively, the principles of safe exercise practice when completing risk assessments of specific dance exercises and movements, especially in relation to:

- developing and monitoring safe, effective and correct dance technique (eg knees in line with toes when bending, correct spinal alignment in different moves, avoiding moves/exercises that put stress on the neck, lower back or knees)
- developing safe technique for lifting or supporting others' weight (when appropriate)
- helping students to develop flexibility, muscular strength and endurance, and cardiovascular fitness for dance
- meeting the basic psychological needs of the students, and providing effective and appropriate feedback in a safe and healthy psychological environment
- providing adaptations for students with additional needs
- providing opportunities for rest and recovery based on the demands of the dance activity.

Health-related exercise activities

Fitness monitoring

2.11.106 Fitness testing/monitoring is common practice in the majority of secondary schools and an increasing number of primary schools, and involves the administration of a range of simple tests that measure the components of health-related fitness (eg cardiovascular fitness, strength, endurance, flexibility) and performance-related fitness (eg agility, balance, power, reaction time).

2.11.107   It is recommended that any form of fitness testing carried out with students in curriculum time should be **positive**, meaningful, relevant, **developmentally appropriate**, and part of a planned, progressive programme of study, the primary aim of which is to promote healthy, active lifestyles.

 To access the afPE (2020) "Health position statement", see https://www.afpe.org.uk/physical-education/wp-content/uploads/afPE_Health_Position_Paper_Web_Version.pdf

2.11.108   afPE advocates that fitness testing is **not good use** of the limited curriculum physical education time in primary schools. Any use of fitness testing and monitoring should be for the purpose of supporting learning rather than comparing fitness scores of groups or individuals over time. This is to ensure that students do not become demotivated and that they understand the limitations of fitness testing in field-based situations.

2.11.109   For fitness testing to be seen as part of a PESSPA programme that promotes the health, safety and well-being of all young people, staff would be wise to consider:

- the appropriateness of the fitness tests chosen
- the implementation methods used
- over-use of fitness testing as a means for promoting and enhancing students' participation in physical activity.

2.11.110   Maximal tests, such as the Multistage Fitness Test ("beep test") and abdominal curl conditioning test, were designed **for elite adult performers**. The appropriateness of these tests for safe use with young people and children is questionable.

2.11.111   Maximal tests are problematic for use with mixed ability groups of students because:

- they can impose inappropriate physiological demands
- self-imposed and peer pressure can encourage exercise beyond safe limits
- screening is required prior to such tests
- close and continuous monitoring is essential.

2.11.112   Fitness tests that are individualised and developmentally appropriate are recommended for curriculum use. Such tests might include:

- maximal tests that allow students to pace themselves during the time or distance allowed (eg **time/ distance runs** and timed/paced muscular or endurance tests)
- **sub-maximal tests** (eg taking a pulse rate after 2–3 mins of paced step-ups), which make more appropriate demands on developing systems and provide more information for learning about fitness components.

Fitness suites

2.11.113   A fitness suite is a high risk environment. Depending on the size of the facility, staff may need to consider how the lesson can be organised to manage the learning safely. Where lack of space presents a hazard, staff may decide to discuss with the leadership team ways to reduce the group size.

2.11.114   Fitness suite activities should always be **supervised appropriately**. Students should be provided with an adequate introduction to all fitness room exercises. This should include:

- information concerning how to adjust cardiovascular (CV) or resistance machines to ensure joints can work in correct alignment
- a practical demonstration showing safe and correct technique
- teaching points explaining correct joint alignment (eg knee, wrists, spine, elbows)
- information about how to start and stop exercising safely
- essential safety points (eg only the person using the CV machine is to adjust the controls; keep hands away from pulleys and weight stacks; place free weights equipment safely and in readiness for the next person).

2.11.115   Some exercises using a barbell or heavy dumb-bells require **spotters**. It is recommended that only teachers with specific training/qualifications in "spotting" technique (eg UK Coaching Certificate [UKCC] Level 2 Gym Instructor or 1st4sport Level 2 Certificate in Coaching Weight Lifting or 1st4sport Level 2 Award in Instructing Weight Lifting) or significant personal experience of spotting should attempt to teach exercises that require the use of spotting skills.

2.11.116   Where schools are considering allowing older students (year 12 or 13) to use the fitness suite with remote supervision but with regular staff visual oversight, this should in the first instance be discussed and agreed with the employer. Parents should be informed that the opportunity is being offered to their child. Procedures should be put in place to manage this arrangement appropriately. These may include students:

- having experience of, and being deemed competent by a staff member to use, the equipment in the facility
- signing in and out of the facility
- not using the facility alone
- being restricted in the equipment they use (eg free weights may not be used)
- agreeing and signing up to a code of conduct for use of the facility
- understanding the emergency procedures, should assistance be required
- being intermittently supervised by staff.

Staff personal use of school fitness suite

2.11.117   Schools that have their own fitness suites may decide to allow staff to use the room in their own time. Where this is an option, staff need to be aware that they use the facility at their own risk, but regardless of this fact, they will still be expected to observe the safety requirements and code of conduct.

2.11.118   Staff should:

- be inducted on how to use the machines, even if they have attended fitness suite inductions elsewhere; ideally, a trained member of the physical education staff or a qualified fitness instructor (UKCC Level 2 or above) should deliver this induction
- complete a participatory agreement, declaring that they have no known medical conditions for which fitness suite activities could be harmful, and confirming that they have been advised of the code of conduct and emergency procedures
- be advised not to exercise alone, although they do not need to be directly supervised; this is important because, however skilled a member of staff is in this environment, any accident when alone would mean they could be alone for some period of time and unable to ask for help
- understand that if exercising unsupervised, they are only covered by occupier's liability (ie that the facility and equipment are safe for the purpose they are being used for, as long as they are being used correctly)
- understand that if exercising with supervision, they may also be covered for third-party liability arising from negligence on the part of the supervisory staff.

2.11.119   The school should inform its employer that staff are using the facility in this way.

High intensity training

2.11.120   High intensity training (HIT) is a form of resistance training that focuses on performing high quality resistance exercise repetitions to the point of muscular failure. This is not recommended for use with students in PESSPA.

High intensity interval training

2.11.121   High intensity interval training (HIIT) is a version of CV interval training that involves short intervals of extremely intense CV exercise, followed by short, sometimes active, recovery periods.

2.11.122   While HIIT is a suitable training method for some young people, it is not recommended in mixed ability PESSPA sessions. Peer pressure could lead to students overexerting themselves when they have already reached their safe exercise limit.

Resistance exercise

2.11.123   Resistance exercise involves contracting muscles against a resistance. It has benefits for students of all ages as it develops muscular strength and endurance, and promotes healthy bone growth and development. Resistance exercise includes weight-bearing activities (eg climbing, throwing, pushing, pulling and travelling on different body parts), body-weight activities (resistance exercises working against the resistance of personal body weight as in push-ups and squats), resistance training or weight training (using external resistance provided by equipment such as elastics, tubing, fixed resistance machines, dumb-bells and kettlebells) and weightlifting (which uses external resistance usually provided by barbells and free weights).

2.11.124   Common causes of accidents in resistance exercise include:

- using inappropriate equipment in an unsafe environment
- excessive loadings
- programmes not being developmentally appropriate
- lack of supervision by appropriately qualified and competent professionals.

2.11.125   It is recommended that:

- resistance exercise programmes are individualised to meet the needs of each student
- well supervised resistance exercise is led by suitably qualified staff to reduce the risks of physical injury and psychological harm.

Isometric resistance exercises

2.11.126   These are static strength exercises in which muscles contract or "tense" but without movement about joints (eg "the plank" or "wall sit"). These exercises are commonly used in circuits and, with secondary students, can be effective in developing strength and endurance in muscles in the position in which the exercise is performed.

2.11.127   If staff are using isometric exercises in their programmes with students, it is wise to:

- complete accurate **risk assessments** for all exercises
- check that students are able **to perform "isotonic" (dynamic/moving) resistance exercises (eg squats, abdominal curls, push-ups) for the same muscle groups with safe and correct technique, and showing a good level of core stability**
- avoid challenging students to perform these exercises to the point of extreme fatigue or "failure" – this can prove extremely uncomfortable, distressing and demeaning for some individuals, is at variance with the principles of safeguarding and is not necessary in order to gain physical health benefits from performing such exercises.

Kettlebells

2.11.128   A kettlebell is a cast-iron weighted ball with a handle attached to the top of it. Kettlebell "workouts" comprise a range of explosive exercises that challenge all of the major muscles, strengthen the core, burn fat and build power.

2.11.129   It is wise for physical education staff who are teaching kettlebell exercises within the school programme to:

- have appropriate personal experience of performing kettlebell workouts (eg in community classes)
- carry out thorough risk assessments of all exercises to ensure safe exercise practice and developmental appropriateness.

2.11.130   Some organisations offer professional development for teaching kettlebell exercise. These courses are sometimes restricted to qualified UKCC Level 2 fitness instructors or those with appropriate practical experience of working with kettlebells. In many cases, qualified specialist physical education teachers can access them.

Weightlifting

2.11.131 Weightlifting is associated with the sport of Olympic weightlifting, which involves the performer working against resistance using techniques such as the "snatch" and "clean and jerk". Weightlifting, as a form of resistance training, can be beneficial to older secondary students' health when delivery is planned, programmed and monitored by appropriately qualified and competent professionals.

2.11.132 All staff teaching weightlifting in schools should have a **relevant qualification**. The 1st4sport Level 2 Award in Instructing Weight Lifting can be accessed by:

- specialist qualified physical education teachers
- physical education trainee teachers.

2.11.133 All staff teaching weightlifting who are not qualified teachers should have at least a 1st4sport Level 2 Certificate in Coaching Weight Lifting.

2.11.134 Holders of the 1st4sport Level 2 Award in Instructing Weight Lifting are **not automatically eligible** to coach weightlifting in a non-school setting such as a community club.

2.11.135 Mats for lifting weights are for the purpose of protecting the equipment and facilities from unnecessary damage. A **platform** is a specific piece of flooring apparatus/matting used for the sport of weightlifting that provides a hard surface to stand on (for stability) while performing the exercise, and soft surfaces either side for dropping the weights in a manner that is safe and protective for the facility and equipment.

2.11.136 British Weight Lifting recommends that there should be an emphasis on skill mastery and technique development, rather than just weight lifted, until the age of 13 years.

2.11.137 The British Association of Sport and Exercise Sciences (BASES) recommends that:

- high intensity resistance exercise is avoided during periods of rapid growth
- rest and resistance exercise are alternated where the training stimulus involves considerable overload
- a 48-hour recovery period follows heavier resistance exercise programmes.

Other exercise and fitness activities

Exercise to music

2.11.138 An increasing number of exercise to music genres are currently used in school PESSPA programmes, including aerobics, body pump, step and Zumba.

2.11.139 It is wise for physical education staff who are teaching exercise to music within the school programme to:

- have appropriate personal experience of taking part in these activities (eg in community classes)
- carry out thorough risk assessments of all exercises to ensure safe exercise practice and developmental appropriateness.

2.11.140 Exercise to music has no recognised governing body of sport in England.

Indoor rowing

2.11.141   It is wise for staff leading indoor rowing within a school programme to:

- provide adequate supervision
- organise safe and secure storage of ergos (ergometers – the rowing machine equipment)
- teach safe lifting and transport techniques if moving ergos
- check that ergos are correctly assembled and in appropriate working order before use
- check that ergos are positioned appropriately (eg to allow sufficient space for the rower to work safely, to avoid obstructing fire exits)
- check that students are wearing appropriate clothing (eg no loose, long baggy tops that might get caught in the mechanism, no jewellery)
- check that students are wearing training shoes
- be sufficiently competent and knowledgeable to ensure that high quality technique is developed and maintained
- make well informed decisions concerning when it is appropriate for students to progress to competitive challenges.

2.11.142   The following recommendations are made in British Rowing (2016) "Guidance: On-water and indoor rowing by school children", https://www.britishrowing.org/about-us/policies-guidance/br-guidance-document-on-water-and-indoor-rowing-by-school-children-final-2016/:

- Appropriate, correct, suitable coaching and learning of "The British Rowing technique" provide the basis for performance and enjoyment of the sport, and allow the rower to be safe, providing their spine and other injury risk areas with proper protection.
- The drag factor should be kept low for all rowers but especially for beginners and younger participants.
- The session length and content must be suitable for the ability and training age of the rower.

Skipping

2.11.143   Skipping is a high impact exercise activity that is commonly included in PESSPA programmes in many primary schools and some secondary schools. It also remains a very popular playground activity. Skipping can develop CV fitness, muscular endurance and bone health, as well as agility, balance, coordination and creativity.

2.11.144   The floor should be smooth, flat, dry and clear of any articles that might cause tripping. Wooden sprung floors or rubberised surfaces offer more resilience than tarmac or concrete and are therefore safer if skipping is to be performed regularly. Skipping on mats should be avoided.

2.11.145   Skippers should have sufficient space around them to avoid hitting others with the rope as it turns. There should also be sufficient space overhead, if working indoors, to avoid bringing down light fitments and other objects from the ceiling.

2.11.146   Skippers should be encouraged to check that the space around and above them is clear before they start to skip.

2.11.147   Good landing technique should be taught, monitored and encouraged to ensure that impact is minimised by keeping the height of the jump to a minimum, bending the knees and landing on the ball of the foot followed by touching the heels gently on the ground.

2.11.148   Staff should avoid exposing students to long durations or excessive amounts of jumping as this may cause unnecessary stress to bones and joints. During a skipping session, it is wise to intersperse jumping activities with non-jumping activities.

2.11.149   Skipping is not appropriate, safe or comfortable for all students, and care should be taken when working with young people who are obese or very sedentary, or who have special educational needs and disabilities (SEND) to ensure they are integrated safely and appropriately.

Yoga and Pilates

2.11.150 **Yoga** is an ancient form of exercise that focuses on strength, flexibility and breathing to boost physical and mental well-being.

2.11.151 **Pilates** is similar to yoga, but focuses on using both the mind and body to achieve optimum performance. The stabilising or "core" muscles of the body are conditioned and strengthened through sequences of movements that use gravity and body weight as forms of resistance.

2.11.152 It is wise for physical education staff who are teaching yoga or Pilates exercises within the school programme to:

- carry out thorough risk assessments of all exercises to ensure safe exercise practice and developmental appropriateness (for further information, see **Table 13**)
- undertake additional training in children and young people's yoga or Pilates
- work alongside a fully qualified yoga/Pilates teacher, trained in working with children or young people as appropriate.

2.11.153 It can also be helpful if the member of staff has personal experience of taking part in these activities.

Aquatic activities

Diving into swimming pools

2.11.154 The definitive guidance document for diving into swimming pools is Chartered Institute for the Management of Sport and Physical Activity (CIMSPA) **"Diving and jumping into swimming pools and open water areas"**.

2.11.155 Other documents that provide specific detail on diving for competition are available from the International Swimming Federation/Fédération Internationale de Natation (FINA) but only apply to diving from boards.

2.11.156 Prior to any standing dives from the poolside being taught, students should have developed an appropriate level of confidence and competence in aquatic practices in the water and from a sitting or kneeling position on the poolside. These activities are not necessarily constrained by the water depths outlined in the text that follows as the students may well be very young and small enough to effect these practices safely in shallower water. A relevant risk assessment process should be applied. Typical progression from this is for students to learn to perform the jumps and simple plunge dives from standing on the poolside. As well as being taught technique, the students should also learn when it is appropriate to use the dive.

2.11.157 **Where diving forms part or all of a swimming lesson**, the pool **freeboard** (the distance from the poolside to the water surface) should be less than 0.3 metres with a sufficient **forward clearance** (the horizontal distance at which the minimum depth of water is maintained) typically in excess of 7.5 metres.

2.11.158 The depth of a dive is affected by:

- the height from which the dive is made – more height can lead to a deeper dive
- the angle of entry – a steeper entry can lead to a deeper dive
- flight distance – a short flight can lead to a deeper dive
- the strength and drive from the diver's legs – a strong drive can result in a deeper dive.

2.11.159 The minimum water depth for the teaching of diving from the poolside should be 1.8 metres. However, staff should ensure dives are executed into the deeper end of the swimming pool as a matter of routine safety.

2.11.160 Where fitted, diving blocks should always be placed at the deepest end of the swimming pool.

2.11.161 Where diving provision is made in a main pool rather than a diving pit, the designated diving area should be **clearly defined**, and other swimmers discouraged or prohibited from entering that area. Students should check the diving area is clear before commencing any dive.

2.11.162 Good class organisation and discipline are paramount in diving activities. To ensure safe practice, staff and students need to be fully aware of the additional safety implications for diving, over and above those for general aquatic activities. These include the following:

- Divers should not wear goggles.
- Toes should be curled over the pool edge for each dive.
- Dives should be performed from a stationary position.
- Arms should be extended beyond the head, with the hands clasped for a safe entry.
- Prolonged underwater swimming after a dive should be discouraged.

2.11.163 Students should be thoroughly familiar with the water space and environment in which they learn to dive. Diving should never take place in **unknown waters**.

2.11.164 To avoid the risk of collisions during simultaneous dives, there should be:

- sufficient pool space
- sufficient forward clearance
- no underwater obstructions
- clearly understood exit routes from the entry area on resurfacing from a dive.

2.11.165 Care should be taken with a feet-first entry from a jump as this can cause damage to the ankles, arches of the feet or lower spine if the pool bottom is struck with force when water is shallow. Safe feet-first entry can be achieved by considering the:

- extent of knee bend
- water depth
- freeboard height
- size and weight of the student.

2.11.166 Competitive shallow-entry dives should be taught in water of no less than 1.8 metres in depth. When students have achieved the standard of the Swim England Competitive Start Awards and can execute a competitive shallow dive consistently, they may progress to performing such a dive in water of no less than 0.9 metres in depth.

 For more information on the Swim England Competitive Start Awards, see http://goo.gl/BgyE51

2.11.167 Any student commencing a swimming race with a plunge-dive entry should be checked for their competence to do so safely, especially when the entry is from a starting block. It is not recommended that raised blocks are used for school swimming instruction, unless the school has a very highly developed programme taught by suitably qualified instructors.

2.11.168 **Vertical poolside dives and diving from a board should not form part of mainstream school swimming unless delivered by a qualified diving teacher in an environment where the following safety factors have been applied:**

- Diving boards and springboards should conform to FINA standards, and diving boards should be checked before use to ensure that security of footing will not be affected by damage or slipperiness.
- Only one student should be allowed on any part of the board at any time.
- Both the student and the teacher should check that the water is clear of other swimmers or obstructions before each dive is performed.
- Progression should be achieved gradually and appropriately from low level to greater heights.
- Dives of three metres or more require the water surface to be disturbed by a specialist facility or hosepipe with a spray nozzle played across the surface. This helps the diver to identify the water level, and avoids them mistiming their entry, which might possibly cause injury.

Water safety sessions

2.11.169 It is important that students are taught personal survival and water safety skills. Students should have knowledge and understanding of the **effects and dangers of cold water**, their ability to assess a water safety situation and the application of the principles of personal survival.

2.11.170 **Swimming in clothes** is common practice in water safety sessions as it helps to simulate real situations. These sessions should teach students how to conserve energy and body heat while staying afloat, through the use of gentle swimming movements and holding specific body positions. Swimming teachers should take account of the fact that wearing clothes presents different challenges for swimmers in that clothes offer more resistance, which can result in swimmers tiring more easily and swimming more slowly.

Lifesaving sessions

2.11.171 When being taught lifesaving, children below eight years of age should only learn to reach with a pole or similar item, and to perform throwing rescues.

2.11.172 **Contact rescues** should not be taught to children under 13 years of age.

2.11.173 Information about teaching resources and lifesaving awards for primary and secondary students are available from the Royal Lifesaving Society (RLSS), Swimming Teachers' Association (STA) and Swim England.

Open-water swimming

2.11.174 Where open-water swimming opportunities are offered to students, either as part of a residential experience during curriculum time or outside of normal school hours, parents should be fully informed.

Guidance documents on open-water swimming are available from Swim England and the RLSS:

- Swim England (2016) "The management of open water swimming events", https://www.swimming.org/library/213

2.11.175 A thorough **risk assessment** in consultation with agencies that have local knowledge of the venue should be undertaken and reliable weather information included. Plans should be continually reviewed, to inform decisions regarding whether to continue at any given time.

2.11.176 Swimming in open water needs to be closely supervised by **competent staff** who are able to effect rescue and resuscitation procedures. Depending on the nature of the event, this may involve the need for lifeguards with an **open-water endorsement**. Consideration should also be given to the benefit of safety boats, rescue equipment, provision of facilities to treat hypothermia, the presence of emergency services and changing accommodation.

2.11.177 Before allowing anyone to enter the water, precautions should be taken to check:

- for easy entry and exit points
- for underwater obstructions
- the depth of the water
- the extent of weed
- the composition of the bottom
- the likelihood of hazardous rubbish
- for any possible effects of currents, tidal flow, wave height or wind-chill factor
- that water traffic is not impinging on safety.

2.11.178 While the extent of pollution is difficult to establish, a professional judgement may need to be made on the **quality of water** and its suitability for recreational or competitive swimming.

2.11.179   One of the most prevalent diseases found in urban rivers and canals as well as lakes is **leptospirosis**, more commonly referred to as **Weil's disease**. This is a bacterial infection spread by animal urine, especially rat urine, that can be caught either through swallowing water or by it getting into the bloodstream through a cut or graze.

2.11.180   Symptoms of the disease can develop between two and 30 days after exposure, and include:

- a high temperature
- chills
- headaches
- loss of appetite
- muscle pain
- irritation of the eyes
- a rash.

2.11.181   If untreated, the symptoms of a severe infection can develop 1–3 days after the milder symptoms have passed. The disease can become life-threatening, through organ failure.

2.11.182   Any cuts or grazes should be covered with a waterproof plaster before swimming, and swallowing water should be avoided. Swimming in urban canals is not recommended.

 For more information about leptospirosis, see: www.nhs.uk/Conditions/Leptospirosis/Pages/Introduction.aspx

2.11.183   Appropriate **footwear** is advisable when swimming in open water in order to avoid the likelihood of foot injuries.

2.11.184   Swimmers are recommended to wear **wetsuits** when swimming or diving in open water, to reduce any risk of hypothermia. **Adequate clothing** needs to be available for swimmers to change into when they leave the water.

2.11.185   **Students should be briefed** thoroughly and made aware:

- that the temperature of open water is often lower than temperatures in swimming pools
- that they should proceed with caution when entering the water
- of set boundaries that should be clearly visible and over a manageably contained area
- that they should not venture outside the set boundaries
- that weaker swimmers should keep to areas where it is easier to stand up.

2.11.186   Supervising staff positioned around the boundaries should make regular **head counts**, and **monitor** swimmers for:

- their ability to cope with the conditions
- signs that they are cold
- signs of fatigue
- signs of discomfort
- signs of fear
- staying within the set boundaries
- signs of adverse effects caused by sun, wind, tide, sea state, current or weather.

Supervision

2.11.187 **Adults accompanying students to aquatic lessons** should:

- be given a clear role
- understand the limits of their role
- be confident on the poolside
- communicate effectively and appropriately with the other adults on safety issues
- have the necessary discipline and control standards
- regularly carry out head counts during, as well as at the beginning and end of, sessions
- know, understand and be able to apply the pool normal operating procedures (NOPs) and emergency action plan (EAP)
- be suitably dressed for the role they are to play in the lesson.

2.11.188 Staff should not be deployed in a poolside role if they:

- **lack confidence** in carrying out such a role
- cannot swim
- are reticent about being on the poolside.

2.11.189 Staff should have the opportunity to express a lack of confidence or ability before being deployed in a poolside role.

2.11.190 Whenever students are in water, and for all aquatic activities, a **suitably qualified adult** should be present at the poolside who is able to effect a rescue from the water and carry out cardiopulmonary resuscitation (CPR). The total number of adults required in relation to student numbers should be decided through risk assessment.

 For more information about risk assessment, see **Chapter 1, Section 7**.

2.11.191 A minimum of **two** people on the poolside is common, and good practice to cover eventualities in the teaching and safety aspects of aquatic activities. Where only one adult is present, the risk assessment needs to indicate clearly why this ratio is acceptable and should highlight alternative emergency arrangements.

2.11.192 Where specialist aquatic teachers are employed to lead a lesson, it is strongly recommended that **school staff remain on the poolside** to act in an assisting role.

2.11.193 Specialist aquatic staff may also provide essential **lifesaving cover**. Another responsible adult should be available to supervise the students in any situation where the specialist aquatic teacher has to enter the water to carry out a rescue.

2.11.194 Ratios of adults to students will be different for each class. A risk assessment to decide an appropriate ratio should consider:

- numbers of "qualified" staff
- numbers of "non-qualified" adult helpers who are on the poolside in a supervisory role
- student ability
- the facility, including water depth and unprogrammed activities taking place at the same time
- student behaviour
- students with SEND.

2.11.195 While a minimum number of staff may satisfy ratio requirements, schools should consider whether the safety of the session and quality of teaching would be enhanced by assigning additional staff, to teach smaller groups or carry out monitoring roles such as head counts or watching for signs of student fatigue.

2.11.196 In some cases, employers will set **local requirements**, and these must be followed. Ratios should allow for all students to be managed safely.

2.11.197 Some governing bodies of sport and other professional bodies may also set maximum generic adult:participant ratios. While these should be considered, they may not take into account the specific or varied circumstances that need to be addressed by staff leading school swimming sessions.

2.11.198 **Unprogrammed** sessions, such as leisure and play sessions, or sessions where the pool space is shared between unprogrammed and programmed activities may require **higher levels of supervision** and lifeguard expertise because of their less controlled nature.

2.11.199 The supervision of activities such as canoeing or scuba diving in pools requires **specialist knowledge** in both teaching and lifesaving, which needs to be identified in an appropriate risk assessment.

2.11.200 **Direct supervision** of students enables the member of staff to intervene at any time. Decisions to supervise less directly should not be taken lightly.

2.11.201 At **swimming pools**, separate school **changing areas** should be made available. Where this is not possible, and "village style" changing areas are used, attendance at the pool at different times to the public may be requested. Failing this, schools should request that students are provided with a section of the changing area specifically for their use, away from areas being used by the public.

 For information on swimming pool changing rooms and supervision, see **2.12.11**.

Gymnastic activities

2.11.202 Staff should be well informed about the principles of safe exercise practice, and able to incorporate them into their gymnastic activity sessions in relation to:

- developing and monitoring safe, effective and correct joint alignment (eg knees over toes when bending, correct spinal alignment in different moves, avoiding moves/exercises that put stress on joints, especially the neck, lower back or knees)
- developing and monitoring safe, effective and correct technique to minimise the risks associated with high impact (eg safe jumping and landing technique) and appropriate use of control (eg ensuring that all movements are "stoppable")
- developing safe technique for supporting others' weight (when appropriate).

Trampolining

2.11.203 On no account should students ever be left **unsupervised**. It is recommended that teachers attend the British Gymnastics Teachers' Trampoline Award (Part 1 and/or Part 2) to gain the confidence to deliver safe and effective trampoline lessons and/or after-school sessions to their pupils.

2.11.204 Only one student at a time should normally be allowed on the trampoline. Work should only begin when everyone is appropriately positioned and ready.

2.11.205 Rebounding should take place as near to the **centre** of the bed as possible and at a height that enables the maintenance of full control.

2.11.206 Should **loss of control** occur, the student should be taught to flex at the knee and hip joints on the very next contact of the feet with the bed to deaden the bounce.

2.11.207 Teaching should emphasise basic skills, correct techniques and quality of movement, with **graduated progression** according to the ability, confidence and responsible attitude of the individual student, avoiding unnecessary risks and over-rapid progress. Skills should be learnt and consolidated in isolation before being combined into routines.

2.11.208 Basic straight jumps should be mastered before any student progresses to rotational movements.

2.11.209 Typically, **beginners** should work for about 30 seconds, gradually increasing to about a minute, but should stop if they are tired or losing concentration.

2.11.210 With experience, staff can safely **supervise a number of trampolines** at once. In such instances, the importance of appropriate positioning in order to maximise observation and allow frequent scanning of the whole activity area cannot be overemphasised. Appropriate positioning enables prompt intervention and advice to be provided where necessary.

2.11.211 It is recommended that trampolining activities are carried out with smaller groups, dependent on the number of trampolines and qualified teachers available. In some instances, where staff are very experienced and students at a level where they can work independently, it may be acceptable for half the class to be doing trampoline-related practices on the floor while the teacher is supervising the other half of the students on the trampoline.

2.11.212 Safe practice is compromised where one teacher supervises half the class working on the trampolines as well as the other half doing a different activity, even when this is in the same space.

2.11.213 Any competition or display routine should consist only of movements successfully **practised and consolidated** as a result of learning and practice. It is not acceptable to place students at risk by changing their routines in a bid for higher marks during a competition.

2.11.214 **Tag-on-type games**, in which students in turn add a movement to the routine, are not recommended as they may encourage students to jump beyond their ability or endurance.

Table 14: Self-evaluation for trampolining practice

Trampolining Safe Practice Teaching Principle	This is our practice. Tick once confirmed.
Students are never left **unsupervised**.	
Suitable **clothing** is similar to that used in gymnastics, with a long-sleeved top worn to prevent friction burns when performing a front drop.	
Non-slip trampoline **slippers** are used to prevent toes entering the gaps in the webbed bed. Alternatively, cotton or wool socks are allowed. Nylon socks on a webbed nylon bed are not permitted as they may not provide adequate traction.	
Only one student at a time is normally allowed on the trampoline. Work begins only when everyone is appropriately positioned and ready.	
Rebounding takes place as near to the **centre** of the bed as possible and at a height that enables the maintenance of full control.	
Should **loss of control** occur, the student is taught to flex at the knee and hip joints on the very next contact of the feet with the bed to deaden the bounce.	
Teaching emphasises the basic skills, correct techniques and quality of movement, with **graduated progression** according to the ability, confidence and responsible attitude of the individual student, avoiding unnecessary risks and over-rapid progress. Skills are learnt and consolidated in isolation before being combined into routines.	
Basic straight jumps are mastered before any student progresses to rotational movements.	
Typically, **beginners** work for about 30 seconds, gradually increasing to about a minute, but know to stop if they are tired or losing concentration.	
Tag-on-type games, in which students in turn add a movement to the routine, are not used as they may encourage students to jump beyond their ability or endurance.	

The Daily Mile

2.11.215 The Daily Mile is designed to develop student fitness levels and inspire students to be active, with the aim of improving their physical, emotional and social health and well-being. It has a simple approach – to help students get fit by running/walking or a combination of both for 15 minutes a day in school. (This 15 minutes includes all time from leaving the classroom until returning.)

2.11.216 Training shoes are recommended by the Daily Mile website as ideal for the activity, along with the use of a firm, mud-free surface. Schools are advised to cancel the Daily Mile on days when there is heavy rain or it is icy underfoot. A further suggestion for schools is that if a student has unsuitable footwear for running, they should take part and walk the route, as if they were walking to school. The website also recommends appropriate clothing for the weather, particularly wearing coats if it is wet or cold. As with any activity, footwear and clothing must be considered and be deemed appropriate. **All** participants (including staff) should wear clothing and footwear that are fit for purpose. The wearing of blazers, suits and ties, and slippery and toeless school shoes is not conducive to safe practice.

2.11.217 Whatever route is used for the Daily Mile, a risk assessment process should be applied. The website – www.thedailymile.co.uk – provides a generic risk assessment that schools may find useful as a starting point.

Useful Websites

afPE Health Position Statement: https://www.afpe.org.uk/physical-education/wp-content/uploads/afPE_Health_Position_Paper_Web_Version.pdf
British Rowing: www.britishrowing.org/
British Weight Lifting: www.britishweightlifting.org
British Wheel of Yoga: www.bwy.org.uk/
Daily Mile: www.thedailymile.co.uk
Indoor Rowing for Young People: https://goo.gl/RkXFRw
Pilates Teacher Association: http://www.pilatesteacherassociation.org/
Register of Exercise Professionals: www.exerciseregister.org
YMCA Fitness Industry Training: www.ymcafit.org.uk

© dotshock/Shutterstock.com

Section 12: Group Management

Ratios and Supervising Groups

2.12.1   Across the UK, class numbers vary, depending on legislation. **Table 15** lists the current legislation:

Table 15: Legislation for class sizes for practical subjects in the UK

Scotland	All secondary practical classes must not exceed 20 students. (http://goo.gl/G0Yf2C)
Northern Ireland	Post-primary – practical group sizes must not exceed 20 students (statutory rule 2004). (https://goo.gl/Hy2Bb0)
England	There is currently no legislation regarding sizes of classes for practical subjects: *There is no legal limit to class size for health and safety reasons. To help raise education standards in maintained schools, children between five and seven have a maximum class size of 30.* (https://goo.gl/SGa71F)
Wales	There is currently no legislation regarding sizes of classes for practical subjects.

2.12.2   In England and Wales, the school leadership team has responsibility for deciding what group sizes and adequate workspaces are safe, including the responsibility not to create situations that are overcrowded and thus unsafe. Dependent on the school authority, and their specific insurers, there may be additional factors regarding class sizes that would need to be adhered to. Where the Health and Safety Executive (HSE) becomes involved and determines that overcrowding is sufficient to cause injury, an improvement or prohibition notice could be served on the school. Information concerning such notices issued since 2006 is available on the HSE website (www.hse.gov.uk). An example provided on the site highlights the inability of a school to keep a practical work area in a classroom free from materials and tools, presenting the possibility of potential slips, trips and falls. Space should be sufficient to allow appropriate levels of movement for students, and equipment to be used safely.

2.12.3   A class may be divided into smaller groups for reasons of safety, opportunity to progress, optimising activity levels or effective management of the available space. Group sizes and make-up will also vary according to age, experience, knowledge of the group and behavioural issues.

2.12.4   Teacher:student ratios may be determined on the basis of various different factors, including:

- staff competence and specific expertise
- student age
- student behaviour
- student ability levels
- previous experience of students and staff in particular circumstances
- a higher risk environment (such as aquatics, adventure activities, trampolining)
- the nature of the activity
- the size and layout of the work area
- the condition of the facility
- the quantity of safety equipment available
- the type, location and amount of equipment in the work area
- the way the activity is most effectively organised
- any history of accidents and/or incidents occurring.

2.12.5   It is **not advisable to define teacher:student ratios** generically for school-organised physical education, school sport and physical activity (PESSPA) because of their highly contextual nature. For example, the same activity would merit more generous staffing levels if it were known that the teaching group involved presented challenging behaviour, had very limited experience or lacked confidence. Ratios should be determined in each context by the teacher, based on a thorough risk assessment (RA) of the activity and group being taught.

2.12.6   A rigorous RA of the **particular circumstances** in question, culminating in a professional judgement by the head teacher (HT) and teacher involved (on the HT's agreed behalf), should indicate suitable staffing arrangements in terms of competence, number, type of activity and available space.

2.12.7   In order to maintain a safe learning environment, teachers need to consider how they will work with the **group numbers** assigned to them in the activity space provided. For example, when working in a restricted space, such as a small fitness room, the teacher needs to plan how students can be grouped to work on the equipment available, and how they can move safely around the space. "Wet weather" lessons need particular thought because the number in the space may be significantly increased from what was originally planned.

2.12.8   Where a teacher or subject leader believes group size may compromise safety in the work environment, they should consider whether the **organisation of the lesson** can be amended to establish a safe learning situation before approaching the leadership team to seek a reduction in the group size.

    See **Case Law 41** in **Chapter 4**.

2.12.9   Visiting **coaches** working in schools may question the size of the group with which they are asked to work. This could be because their insurance, if organised through a governing body of sport, may restrict their cover to a maximum group size. Some governing bodies of sport recommend or impose teacher/coach:participant ratios, particularly in potentially higher risk activities, such as adventure activities, aquatic activities and some contact sports, because of the type of environment. These ratios can require groups considerably smaller than the "normal" school class size. Subject leaders and teachers responsible for liaising with coaching staff should be aware of these differences, and bring them to the attention of those planning the staffing.

2.12.10   Greater flexibility is possible where the coach works under the school or local authority (LA) insurance cover, ie in the same way as a member of the school staff. Subject leaders need to clarify with their employer whether a visiting coach operates under the employer's insurance or the coach's own insurance and, where the latter is the case, ensure that sizes of groups comply with any restrictions imposed by the coach's individual insurance.

See **Case Law 42** in **Chapter 4.**

Supervision

2.12.11   There is **no legal requirement** to supervise students all of the time, but schools should have a clearly stated position about supervision, both in changing areas and lessons. Teachers need to be aware of the school's requirements and follow them.

2.12.12   The level of supervision will be determined by the students' age, behaviour, ability, previous experience, work environment, identified risk and other contextual factors. However, analysis of case law provides a clear indication that the incidence of **injury** is much higher during **unsupervised** activities than supervised ones.

 See **Case Law 43** in **Chapter 4.**

2.12.13   **Direct supervision** of students enables the teacher to intervene at any time. Their teaching **position** should enable them to observe clearly and intervene should it be necessary. This does not mean always being close enough to touch an individual, but rather to be able to attract attention and a response from individuals even at a distance.

2.12.14   Decisions to supervise less directly should not be taken lightly.

 See **Case Law 44** and **45 in Chapter 4.**

2.12.15   Groups undertaking higher risk situations, such as adventurous activities, aquatic activities, combat sports, contact sports, athletic throwing events, gymnastics, trampolining and free weights sessions, require closer supervision, and where possible, smaller groups should be considered.

2.12.16   The nature of the supervision needs to be clear. For example, it is recommended that trampolining activities are carried out with smaller groups, dependent on the number of trampolines and qualified teachers available. Safe practice is compromised where one teacher supervises half the class working on the trampolines as well as the other half doing a different activity, even when this is in the same space. Where this has to occur, staff should be very experienced, students should be at a level where they can work independently, and the alternative activity assigned should not distract the teacher from safe supervision of the trampoline.

 See **Case Law 46** in **Chapter 4.**

2.12.17   Older students may be given less supervision, but should not be totally independent as the teacher remains legally responsible for their well-being. Remote supervision may take different forms (eg during trips and tours), and should be progressively achieved and very carefully managed. The school's own policy should be clearly understood and applied during trips and tours.

2.12.18   Remote supervision refers to a situation in which a member of staff responsible for a group of students is not directly present. This type of supervision may be implemented in appropriate circumstances where only one member of staff is available for changing-room supervision (eg in situations such as teaching mixed-gender groups). Remote supervision might involve tasking a reliable student with reporting any concerns in the changing area to the member of staff, who is outside the changing area.

2.12.19 The suitability of remote supervision would be dependent on the location of the changing areas, student behaviour, age and ability. This method is only satisfactory when the member of staff remains on hand in the immediate vicinity outside the changing area to respond to any alert.

2.12.20 If these arrangements are not to the school's satisfaction, it may be necessary to combine classes and take single-gender groups, where appropriate staffing allows this. Adults supervising students need to be familiar with, and adhere to, the relevant safeguarding policies.

Supervising Mixed-gender Student Groups when Changing

2.12.21 Whatever the circumstances, changing rooms should be adequately supervised. Ideally, a male and female member of staff should accompany each mixed-gender class in order to fully supervise the changing areas. Staffing pressures may mean a known adult volunteer of the opposite gender is used. If this adult is unsupervised, disclosure and barring clearance would be required for this role with children in this situation. Where this level of staffing is not available, for example, at a swimming pool, it may be possible to enlist the cooperation of pool staff to supervise the other changing room. This arrangement with the pool management needs to be assured and consistent. If only one suitable adult is available, they would need to establish procedures to deal with any emergency in the other changing room.

2.12.22 Where circumstances prevent full supervision, such as where a single staff member is responsible for a mixed-gender group changing in separate changing areas, a clear, safe management procedure needs to be devised and communicated to the students. Methods can include appointing one or more responsible students to inform the member of staff should any disruptive or dangerous activity arise in the changing area. Where this and similar methods of supervision are relied on, the member of staff should be available at all times in the immediate vicinity of the changing rooms.

2.12.23 Using members of the opposite gender to supervise mixed-gender groups in separate changing rooms is acceptable unless there are significant elements of relatively intimate contact that may affect the dignity, comfort and confidence of either students or staff.

 See **2.8.57** for more information about changing areas.

Supervision of Outdoor Play and Activity Areas

2.12.24 Those responsible for supervising outdoor activity areas within a school setting should be suitably trained and competent to do so. Clarification is required about exactly which aspects of supervision form part of their role, and how this should be carried out. This may involve break-time supervisory staff completing additional training in the supervision of playground activities, for example. Staff should be competent in setting out equipment if they are required to do so.

2.12.25 The level and type of supervision to be undertaken should be clear and not exceeded. For example, it is highly recommended that younger primary-aged students on climbing equipment have dedicated supervision by at least one member of staff, or more if an RA identifies this as necessary. However, older, well behaved and trustworthy students may be considered to need less supervision on simple low-level traverse walls. Where the need for a dedicated member of staff assigned to this role is identified, they should not be required to supervise other areas of the playground at the same time. It is recommended that clear rules are put in place and understood for such activity.

2.12.26 Students should be **grouped** for practical activities according to age and developmental stage. Zoning areas of the playground for specific types of activity also acts as a useful supervisory strategy.

2.12.27   The maximum number of students who can use different items of equipment, particularly in a climbing area at any one time, should be determined by an RA, and communicated to staff and students.

2.12.28   Any student given **leadership responsibility** for practical activities must work under the direct supervision of a member of staff, who should be present. The staff member should be clear about the extent and function of this supervisory role. This is particularly important when utilising students as play leaders, which sometimes results in school certification to reward their efforts.

2.12.29   All supervisory adults should be fully aware of emergency procedures and how to rapidly access first aid in the event of an accident.

2.12.30   Students need to comply with behavioural expectations and any playground **code of conduct**. Where possible, they should be included in the design of such a code.

 See **Case Law 47–49** in **Chapter 4**.

Matching Students in Groups

2.12.31   Students' individual levels of confidence, strength, prior experience, size and ability need to be accommodated in teaching contexts and at the earliest stages of competition. Grouping and pairing students according to any of these individual characteristics need to be considered in order to establish a safe learning environment.

2.12.32   Such group management is essential where the following form part of the learning experience:
   - **weight bearing** (such as counterbalancing in gymnastics)
   - **physical contact** (such as tackling in contact sports)
   - **"accelerating projectiles"** (such as when a hard ball is thrown or bowled at an opponent).

2.12.33   **Mixed-ability** pairing or grouping, as in peer teaching and learning, is acceptable where the outcome is clearly understood to be assisting and supporting cooperatively, rather than competing.

Mixed-gender Group Activities

2.12.34   Mixed-gender teaching and participation in activities have increased over the years. Potential advantages for safety include improved attitudes to learning, improved behaviour, and effective use of specific staffing expertise.

2.12.35   It is recommended that strength, confidence, previous experience, ability and attitude are key considerations in matching students in learning activities, whatever the gender involved. Age alone is not relevant to safe groupings unless it affects attitude and behaviour.

2.12.36   **Physical contact and strength** translated into power are fundamental considerations for safe groupings as students mature. In instances where bodily contact, support and power applied to actions such as tackling or hitting a ball form part of the context, separating the genders for practical experience does become a key consideration. This also applies to same-gender pairs/groups where skill, confidence and understanding are relevant.

Facilities for transgender students

2.12.37   It is always best to ask the student involved what changing space will work best for them. This may be male changing, female changing or the unisex/accessible toilet. Teachers also need to be prepared for the possibility that where they choose to change may vary from lesson to lesson or week to week. Schools are advised to consider each situation uniquely and sensitively. Staff should speak openly and honestly about participation in PESSPA and how potentially difficult situations can be overcome.

2.12.38   Participating in physical education is important to the physical and mental well-being of students. A young trans person has the same right to access physical education as their peers and also to take part in competitive sports.

2.12.39   Toilets and changing facilities are often deemed the most sensitive of all the issues for transgender students, and there is much debate around the inclusion of trans young people in gender-segregated facilities. Concerns usually stem from a worry that young trans people may find themselves in a vulnerable position and may be subject to transphobic bullying or unwanted attention that has the potential to escalate to something more serious such as physical or emotional harm. Equally, young trans people want to be able to "pass" as their true gender and want to be seen and treated as such.

2.12.40   Trans students should be able to use the facilities of their preferred gender. This is often seen as a way of "passing". If a child or young person is not comfortable with using these facilities, then an accessible toilet/changing area should be provided.

2.12.41   It is sensible to rename these facilities so that there is less stigma attached for any student who may need to use these toilets. Recommended names for these toilets include unisex accessible toilet, larger toilet, and toilet and changing facility. This ensures that the school respects the dignity and privacy of trans students and others using the toilet while ensuring their safety.

2.12.42   Changing facilities need to be managed safely and sensitively. In general, schools can apply the same guidelines as they do for toilets. It is advisable to conduct an RA and, where appropriate, provide facilities that ensure privacy and safety.

See **FAQ 15** in **Chapter 4**.

Schools that have students dealing with **transgender or gender dysphoria** concerns that affect how they will participate in PESSPA will find information on the Gender Identity Research and Education Society (GIRES) website: http://goo.gl/EjwQ7v

Mixed-age Sport

2.12.43   Some governing bodies of sport stipulate team selection restrictions to **narrow age bands** for reasons of safety, particularly in contact sports, such as rugby, and martial arts activities, such as judo. This is intended to address possible differences in size, ability and confidence. Where any competitive situation occurs under the aegis of that governing body of sport, the requirement must be met.

2.12.44   While the principle of promoting safe practice through **matching student size and experience can be** generally sound, it is not necessarily appropriate to make decisions solely on chronological age due to variations in rates of physical development, confidence, skill and gender.

2.12.45   On occasions, the principle of competing within the age group recommended by the governing body of sport might be considered in an RA but not applied as strictly as the governing body of sport sets out. This is acceptable if the safety and welfare of the students are maintained. For example, where a slightly younger but experienced, skilful and well-developed player would benefit from playing in an age band slightly outside their chronological age, an RA should determine that the selection is safe.

See **Case Law 50** in **Chapter 4**.

Physical Contact from Adults in Student Activities

2.12.46   Physical contact, as defined in a safeguarding context, is intentional bodily contact initiated by an adult with a child.

2.12.47   Staff should be aware of the limits within which such contact should properly take place, and ensure decency, dignity and respect are never compromised. Contact should remain impersonal and be made in a manner that cannot be misconstrued by a student, parent or observer, and only for the duration necessary for safe practice.

2.12.48   Any physical contact should be for the purpose of **meeting a student's needs** in order to:

- develop techniques and skills safely
- treat injury
- prevent injury occurring
- respond to any special educational needs and disabilities (SEND)
- prevent harm to the student or others.

2.12.49   All schools should have a clearly stated policy and **code of practice** about physical contact with students as part of their safeguarding policy. Aspects of this will apply to PESSPA contexts.

2.12.50   It is very likely that most students will need some form of manual support or physical contact from staff during their PESSPA experiences, and it is a school's responsibility to inform parents of this, and not that of the individual staff member.

2.12.51   Physical contact for reasons of safety, support, providing confidence or demonstration is typical within PESSPA situations (eg supporting a balance in gymnastics). It is important that the student is made aware beforehand of the purpose of such provision, what form it will take, and that they confirm that this is acceptable to them.

2.12.52   Staff should only ever deploy the degree of contact or physical force they genuinely believe to be necessary in order to safeguard a student against a hazard and/or for the purpose of avoiding injury.

2.12.53   Where any **complaint** is made about a member of staff's physical contact with a student, the situation should be reported immediately to the staff member responsible for safeguarding in school, to explain the circumstances and obtain guidance and support.

2.12.54   Children with SEND may require a greater degree of support and proximity. Manual support should always take place in an open environment with no intimate touching at all, other than for specific care needs.

 For information regarding manual handling of children with disabilities in swimming, see "The inclusion of swimmers with a disability", www.swimming.org

Staff Participation in Student Activities

2.12.55   Staff should be aware of the risks associated with **personal participation** while teaching or coaching PESSPA activities, particularly those involving physical contact or in which hard projectiles (eg cricket/rounders balls) are used.

2.12.56   Staff should **avoid** playing a full part as a participant in a game with students. Their involvement should be restricted to providing practical demonstrations in a controlled, essentially static way, or to bring increased fluency into a game situation; for example, if bowling to allow students to hit the ball in the right place with the correct technique.

2.12.57   It can be good practice for staff to take a limited role in a game periodically to set up situations that enhance the students' learning. This would exclude full practical involvement in activities such as tackling (other than static demonstrations), shooting with power and bowling or pitching with pace. Staff's involvement should not compromise their ability to retain acceptable control of the whole group so due consideration should be given to teacher position during this part of the activity.

2.12.58   **Staff versus student matches are not advised**, whether in lesson time or extracurricular, competitive contexts, because of the likelihood that differences in size, strength, weight, ability and previous experience, plus the element of competition, could lead to injury.

    See **FAQ 16** in **Chapter 4** and **Case Law 50** in **Chapter 4**.

Staff Teaching Physical Education School Sport and Physical Activity while Pregnant

2.12.59   As soon as a member of staff knows that she is pregnant, it is best practice to let the HT know. At that point, it is the duty of the school to undertake an RA to consider how the pregnancy will affect the person's role.

2.12.60   Within PESSPA, there are obviously things to be careful about from the outset, but each pregnancy is different and will affect the member of staff differently. For this reason, the RA will need to be revised as things change at different stages of the pregnancy.

2.12.61   In assessing what action may be appropriate, the following points should be considered:

- Lifting and carrying may become difficult. In some cases, students can be asked to assist under supervision.
- Certain activities are not advisable: teaching trampolining (from the bed or the floor); teaching activities in which a hard ball is involved (eg rounders, cricket, softball); high intensity demonstrations; or a sequence of moves.
- Officiating from the sides should be acceptable, particularly in the early stages, as long as the member of staff remains vigilant to projectiles.
- In the early stages of pregnancy, while physical size may not cause any issues, feeling nauseous during a lesson, and/or having to exit the lesson, may require certain procedures to be put in place (eg appointing a student to alert another member of staff, ensuring students know to stop all activity if the member of staff needs to leave the lesson urgently).
- It is sensible to share the news with students so that they also take some responsibility for safety in the lesson.

Section 13: Personal Protective Equipment (PPE)

Introduction

2.13.1   The term PPE is now more widely used in physical education, school sport and physical activity (PESSPA) than personal protective equipment.

2.13.2   PPE refers to any device worn or held by an individual for protection against one or more health and safety hazards or medical considerations. Mouth guards, shin pads, helmets, padding and swimming goggles are the most frequently used PPE in schools.

2.13.3   Injury in PESSPA sessions most commonly occurs through physical contact with another individual, or contact of part of the body with:

* a hard ball
* an implement
* a rough surface or chemically affected environment.

2.13.4   Most PPE works by dissipating direct force relative to both time and impact, thereby offering a measure of protection to parts of the body. However, swimming goggles, for example, are worn more for comfort.

2.13.5   Wearing PPE will not guarantee protection from injury. It can though, in many cases, **mitigate** the severity of injury by reducing a high-risk situation to one of reasonable or acceptable risk.

2.13.6   PPE should be **fit for purpose**. Manufacturers are encouraged to ensure that their products conform to specified standards, where these exist. British Standards Institute (BSI) and European (EN) standards are advisory standards and not regulatory, but where any equipment is involved in an injury, these standards are considered to be a benchmark.

2.13.7   It is a **parental responsibility** to provide PPE where the school has suggested it. However, where the amount and cost of kit is extensive, such as that for a hockey goalkeeper, or for reasons of convenience, such as cricket helmets and batting pads/gloves, then schools often provide equipment for communal use.

2.13.8   It is insufficient for schools simply to tell students to bring mouth guards or shin pads, for example, into school or expect them to inform their parents. For this reason, it is recommended that well communicated PESSPA policy and procedures should **strongly advise** the provision of particular PPE items, and outline the process for informing parents about providing them.

2.13.9   Communications to parents should include information about the range and quality of PPE relevant to the PESSPA programme and about how staff will determine whether it is safe to continue or necessary to amend a planned session where students lack the required PPE.

2.13.10   Where the use of PPE in physical-contact situations is made mandatory by schools, it is part of their duty of care to ensure **all participants** have access to the PPE required. If such a policy exists, the member of staff in charge of an activity is not absolved of responsibility for any injury that occurs to a student as a result of them not using the PPE stipulated.

2.13.11   Staff cannot exclude students from taking part on the basis that they do not have the correct PPE. The member of staff in charge must establish a **safe playing environment**, and adaptations will need to be made in terms of how students without the required PPE take part in the practical aspects of the lesson.

Managing the Use of PPE

2.13.12   When PESSPA staff believe that PPE for a specific activity is important but their students do not have the necessary item(s), staff should **modify** how the activity is carried out in order to enable safe participation without the required item.

2.13.13   This may mean:

- providing PPE items, where possible and practical, for those who cannot provide them or have not provided them
- grouping together students who do not have the required PPE, and assigning them tasks that can be safely carried out without this equipment
- rotating groups to take part in different activities or tasks, some requiring PPE and some not requiring PPE
- changing the task for all students so that those without PPE are not put at risk
- if only one or two students do not have the required PPE, allowing them to take part in as much of the learning as possible, and assigning them a different role during any parts of the lesson where lack of PPE would put them at risk.

2.13.14   Staff should not proceed with the planned format of the PESSPA activity if their planning has identified, based on school policy, that PPE is required by all students, but that this requirement is not being met.

2.13.15   School fixtures, team practices and intra-school matches are generally situations where students have a choice and have opted to take part. These are also competitive situations in which it would be appropriate to insist that the recommended PPE is worn.

2.13.16   Within curricular lessons, staff could consider providing spare PPE, where possible, for any students who cannot supply the stipulated PPE themselves, and who might otherwise be excluded from taking part.

2.13.17   As with all accidents and injuries, those relating to the use or lack of PPE should be recorded, and used to inform and add gravitas to future recommendations regarding the school's PPE policy.

Specific PPE Principles

2.13.18   PESSPA staff should **inform students** about the purpose, function and **limitations** of PPE in order to counteract any false sense of security that may arise as a consequence of wearing protective gear. In all PESSPA activities, it is the application of good technique and skill, and rigorous adherence to the rules that remain the most important features of safe participation.

Helmets

2.13.19   When wearing helmets, users should be aware of any potential reduction in hearing and, in some cases, vision. A badly fitting helmet or one that is too large may reduce the level of protection provided, and may even add to the hazard or contribute to injury. Additionally, a helmet should be properly looked after. Dropping a helmet on a hard surface can significantly reduce the level of protection it would provide in the event of a fall.

2.13.20   Soft **rugby** headgear is considered to provide protection for the head against blood injuries and fractures, which are most likely to be sustained when taking the ball into contact situations. Helmets need to fit comfortably and can provide a sense of protection, with the contoured soft padding usually made of impact-resistant foam. However, head guards and helmets offer little added protection against concussion where the brain is shaken within the skull.

2.13.21   **Head protectors for cricket** are helmets with a face guard or grille. The design and manufacture of cricket head protectors is governed by British Standard BS 7928:2013.

2.13.22　The England and Wales Cricket Board (ECB) has issued guidance on head protectors in order to increase understanding so that informed decisions can be made about which head protectors to purchase and use.

 For further information on the ECB guidance, see https://www.ecb.co.uk/news/79227

2.13.23　Head protectors that have been tested against and comply with the relevant BSI specification will be clearly labelled "BS 7928:2013" and will set out whether the head protector has been tested against a men's standard ball size of 5½ ounces, a junior standard ball size of 4¾ ounces or both men's and junior size balls.

2.13.24　Only helmets displaying a European Conformity (CE) quality mark should be used.

2.13.25　Since 2000, the ECB has published safety guidance regarding the wearing of head protectors by all cricketers under the age of 18. The ECB's current guidance is that **all cricketers under the age of 18 should wear a head protector** that has been tested against the junior-sized ball if they are batting in matches or practice sessions. The ECB also strongly recommends that wicketkeepers under the age of 18 should wear a head protector with a face guard at all times when standing up to the stumps. Any individual taking responsibility for players under the age of 18 should take reasonable steps to ensure this guidance is followed at all times.

2.13.26　Helmets for pedal **cyclists, skateboarders, roller skaters and scooter** users should comply with BS EN 1078, which states that a helmet is designed to withstand an impact similar to an average rider travelling at 12mph falling on to a stationary kerb-shaped object from a height of 1.5 metres. Despite the protection that a cycle helmet can offer, there is currently no legislation in the UK that places any requirement on a cyclist to wear a helmet. However, it is recommended by Transport for London and the Highway Code that "you should wear a cycle helmet that conforms to current regulation, is the correct size and securely fastened".

 For further information on the Highway Code, see www.gov.uk/guidance/the-highway-code/rules-for-cyclists

2.13.27　A standard has also been established for younger children's helmets, known as EN 1080. The difference between this and the EN 1078 standard is that the chin strap is attached differently to an EN 1080 standard helmet. With these helmets, the chin strap is designed to snap off during a collision to prevent the child from choking or being strangled if the helmet snags.

 For further information on cycle helmets, see https://www.rospa.com/rospaweb/docs/advice-services/road-safety/cyclists/cycle-helmets-factsheet.pdf

2.13.28　**Ski helmets** are becoming mandatory in several countries. Where the wearing of helmets is still a personal option, schools are advised to build provision for them into the required kit list, whether through hire or purchase, so that all students wear them. The employer's requirements and/or school or tour company insurance arrangements may also dictate this practice. Helmets (including those for snowboarders and snowbladers) should comply with the standard BS/EN 1077.

2.13.29　The decision to wear helmets for **climbing** varies depending on the setting. The British Mountaineering Council does not provide prescriptive policy or guidelines but suggests that staff should assess the requirements of the surface and whether helmet use is appropriate or not. Where staff feel unable to make this assessment, they should seek additional guidance from appropriately qualified practitioners.

Other specialist PPE

2.13.30   **Padding, or body armour**, has developed from traditional shoulder pads. It provides the shoulders, chest and back with some protection from physical impact when tackling or being tackled in rugby.

2.13.31   **Hockey** goalkeeper equipment may often be provided by the school, unless the student elects to participate to a high level in that position, in which case they may choose to obtain their own.

2.13.32   **Mouth guards** protect the teeth and gums, and can reduce lacerations inside the mouth of the wearer, and injury to an opponent, caused by teeth, in the event of unforeseen collision. There is also some evidence that mouth guards might reduce incidences of concussion, but this is less certain, and possibly only in situations where a bespoke, personally fitted mouth guard is worn.

2.13.33   A mouth guard crafted and properly fitted by a dentist or dental technician offers the most effective protection. However, for some students, cost may be prohibitive. Relatively cheap, but less effective "boil-and-bite" versions of mouth guards are now available. These should carry a CE marking, which indicates that the product has been subject to some quality assurance in assessing its fitness for purpose. There is currently no British Standard available.

2.13.34   The safety benefits of wearing mouth guards for match play and competitive practices have been widely recognised for a considerable time. Schools are strongly advised to consider introducing mouth guards as part of their PESSPA kit requirements both at primary and secondary levels. For hygiene reasons, mouth guards cannot be shared, but schools may consider purchasing them, and consider how their use is best managed.

2.13.35   **Shin pads** offer protection to the lower leg, and should be worn for competitive matches and whenever there is a risk of injury. It is recommended that students are encouraged to wear shin pads during lessons that involve game or match play. Better protection is provided where the pad covers much of the length of the leg between the knee and the ankle. However, the pad should not hinder performance. Some shin pads provide protection for the ankles as well as the shins, which can be particularly useful in hockey. Unlike mouth guards, shin pads can be "shared" so while schools can include shin pads on their PESSPA kit list, they might also keep additional sets for students who "forget" them or are unable to provide them.

2.13.36   **Swimming goggles** may be worn by students when swimming at competition level and for extended, regular training sessions. They can help to maintain the required body position and improve vision through the water. In contrast, within short curriculum swimming lessons (typically 20–25 minutes' water time) for beginners, or for single, short races in school galas, goggles are **not** considered to be necessary unless there is some justified medical reason.

2.13.37   In cases of extreme short-sightedness or in rare instances where individuals have particularly sensitive eyes or wear contact lenses, schools should require a parental letter stating that the student has particular needs to warrant the use of goggles. Such a letter would have the status of simply being informative and **would not constitute any form of indemnity** should injury arise later through the misuse of the goggles. Additional medical certification about such particular needs is costly to obtain and should **not be sought** as this information is likely to have been previously set down in the student's records.

2.13.38   Students learning to swim or improving their swimming ability often do not swim in straight lines, and as a result, they might get close to, or come into contact with, other swimmers. If goggles are worn, any contact with others (eg the flailing arm of a beginner learning a new stroke) might result in injury to both the swimmer wearing the goggles and those who are not. Feeling confident and safe in the water, and swimming underwater, should not be dependent on wearing goggles; neither are goggles designed for such activity, as the eye pressure cannot be relieved.

2.13.39   When swimming goggles are used, they should be made of unbreakable plastic or rubber materials. The British Standard for the manufacture of goggles (BS 5883:1996) includes the requirement that the packaging should contain instructions for putting them on and removing them. Students should be taught to remove goggles by slipping them off the head and not by stretching the retaining band away from the face as wet plastic is slippery and may cause injury to the eye area. Goggles that are not properly fitted may mist up and adversely affect visibility.

2.13.40   Given the potential for injury in curriculum lessons, the teacher responsible for the group should have the prerogative to require any student to remove their goggles for reasons of safety if they are constantly adjusting, removing and replacing them. The teacher is not responsible for fitting or adjusting students' goggles. Where a student does wear goggles, they need to be able to fit them independently.

2.13.41   As with the management of any risk in PESSPA, all aspects of the situation should be taken into consideration before the school, along with the provider (if lessons are taken externally), makes a decision about policy regarding the wearing of swimming goggles. Where the employer sets a water safety policy, this should be adhered to, and schools should inform parents of the contents of this policy.

2.13.42   In some cases, according to the stage and ability of the student, the use of goggles may be permitted. The reasons for a decision either way should be fully explained in the risk assessment for the particular activity.

2.13.43   In a swimming pool environment, students who are very short-sighted may not be able to see the teacher's gestures or read any signage unless they are in extremely close proximity. Not being able to see the teacher clearly can also affect how students receive verbal instructions, which might impact significantly on safety. In cases of extreme short-sightedness (myopia), prescription goggles, which are now more widely available and reasonably priced, may result in a safer swimming experience for the student.

2.13.44   When students complain of eye irritation during swimming sessions, the cause, in almost all cases, is an incorrect chemical balance in the water. If several students are reporting eye irritation as a result of swimming, the pool provider should be informed. This imbalance can be eradicated. In other situations, hospital records show that irritation might result from a reaction to the chemicals used to clean the lenses of the goggles at home.

2.13.45   Swimmers who are training daily usually wear goggles because they are exposing their eyes to the effects of the chemicals in the water for long periods. In some cases, the tissue around the eyes does not dry out between training sessions and thus becomes more susceptible to infection. Goggles offer regular swimmers some protection against this happening.

2.13.46   Goggles should never be worn when diving.

2.13.47   The use of **sports goggles for other sports and activities** has become increasingly common, with high profile sports players demonstrating their use in a wide range of sports, including squash, basketball, football, skiing, combat activities and tennis.

2.13.48   Sports goggles may be used solely for protection, such as in squash where the likelihood of the ball hitting a player in the eye at speed is fairly high, but also for necessity, with prescription goggles providing a welcome improvement in the experience of sport for participants with different eye conditions.

2.13.49   Hard plastic resin (CR39), or even more durable polycarbonate or Trivex, is used to produce lenses that are far safer than glass and offer the necessary protection.

2.13.50   The European standard EN 166:2002 covers all protective eyewear, and Association of British Dispensing Opticians (ABDO) (2014) "Protective eyewear" provides general information about sports goggles, as well as details about those best suited to different sports.

  For more information on the ABDO guidance, see https://www.abdo.org.uk/
information-for-the-public/eyecare-faq/sports-eyewear/

2.13.51   Local dispensing opticians can give advice on the most appropriate type of sports goggles, whether for protection or with prescription lenses.

2.13.52 **Exposure to the sun** is an aspect of personal protection that is increasingly important. The risks associated with overexposure to the two bands of ultraviolet light from the sun are well documented, and staff need to implement a range of necessary precautions.

 For more information about weather conditions, see **Chapter 2, Section 10**.

Governing Bodies of Sport and PPE

2.13.53 In some circumstances, governing body of sport requirements relating to the wearing of PPE may be directly adopted within educational settings. For example, during inter-school competitions or fixtures, the wearing of PPE may be mandatory.

2.13.54 However, a physical education risk assessment of a specific activity may result in some **flexibility in interpreting governing body of sport requirements** in order to achieve optimum levels of participation and involvement within the curriculum, such as modification of equipment, organisation of different groups, and non-contact versions of physical-contact games in order to remove the need for PPE.

2.13.55 A number of governing bodies of sport have introduced their own regulations, which impose the **mandatory** use of certain items of PPE. Students who are involved in competitions and events organised and regulated by a governing body of sport must comply with the governing body of sport's ruling in relation to use of PPE. Where such activities are **organised by schools, the governing body of sport** mandatory requirement can be regarded as good-practice guidance that needs to be given careful consideration.

2.13.56 Governing body of sport regulations for the use of PPE apply to both boys and girls participating in the respective sport. **Table 16** summarises a selection of these sports. Details are available on governing body of sport websites regarding any additional recommended items or different recommendations between sexes.

Table 16: Governing body of sport recommendations and mandatory requirements relating to PPE

Similar requirements and recommendations are provided by governing bodies of sport in England, Northern Ireland, Scotland and Wales.

Governing Body of Sport	PPE Requirements
England and Wales Cricket Board	• Helmets with a face guard, pads, gloves and, for boys, an abdominal protector (box) are mandatory when batting against a hard ball.
England Hockey	• Mouth guards and shin/ankle pads are recommended at all levels of participation. • Specialist protection for goalkeepers is mandatory.
England Lacrosse	• Mouth guards are mandatory for representative matches. • Specialist protection for goalkeepers is mandatory.
Football Association (England)	• Shin pads are mandatory in practice and training at all levels of participation.
Rugby Football League	• Mouth guards are recommended. • Shoulder pads are permitted at all levels of participation. • Padded helmets are permitted. • Glasses should not be worn beyond the under-eight age band.
England Rugby (RFU)	• Mouth guards are mandatory for representative matches above school level. Otherwise, they are recommended. • Head guards or scrum caps are permitted. • Soft shoulder padding is permitted.
British Cycling	• British Cycling recommends that cyclists wear a correctly fitted helmet while cycling. • In a sanctioned race or Sportive, the use of a helmet is mandatory.
Scoot GB	• It is recommended that children moving at speed in a playground setting riding a scooter should have a helmet, elbow pads, knee pads and gloves. There should be no exposed skin.
Archery GB	• It is best practice and highly recommended that arm guards are worn by students to reduce the chance of bruising if the bow string catches.
GB Boxing	• If taking part in contact versions, a mouth guard, protective hand bandages, gloves, cup protectors, force-absorbent headgear and a shirt are required. • Women boxers are also required to wear breast protectors.
British Fencing	• Adequate body protection is essential and should be worn at all times for practice and competition.
British Wrestling Association	• Suitable support protection, in line with wrestling rules, should be worn, including protective arm and knee pads. Ear guards should also be encouraged.
British Taekwondo	• Headgear and shin protectors should be worn. At competitive levels, mouth guards, body protectors, groin guards and shin protectors are compulsory.
Wheelchair Football Association (WFA)	• For power chair users, The FA promotes the use of lap seat belts. Leg, feet and chest straps should be used if normally worn. Other safety equipment may include helmets, headrests and other assistive or protective technology.
Futsal (The FA)	• All players, including the goalkeeper, are recommended to wear shin pads.

2.13.57 **Readers should continue to refer to the appropriate governing body of sport websites to keep up to date with ongoing changes in relation to the use of PPE.**

Section 14: Personal Effects, Clothing and Footwear

Establishing Policy Regarding Personal Effects, Clothing and Footwear

2.14.1   A clear, unambiguous policy should be established and made available to all staff so they can put into practice what the school policy requires.

2.14.2   There should be clear expectations throughout the school, and with parents, about the management of personal effects, clothing, footwear and personal adornments.

2.14.3   Such a policy sets out the standards expected by the school for PESSPA, and should be provided to new parents on their child's entry to the school, as well as being easily available on the school's website or through school newsletters.

2.14.4   Any **changes to such a policy** need to be communicated to parents through the channels described above, with notice of the forthcoming changes and the reasons for them. Having well communicated policies in place can help to support schools in their attempts to maintain high standards of safety in these areas.

 For more information about policy and procedures, see **Chapter 1, Section 6**.

2.14.5   **Disclaimers** from parents alleging the removal of responsibility from teachers in the event of an injury occurring while their child takes part in PESSPA while wearing jewellery, personal effects, or non-policy clothing or footwear should be declined.

2.14.6   Such indemnities have no legal status, and the duty of care remains firmly with the school on such matters. As the student may make a claim for compensation in relation to any injury suffered when they become an adult, this nullifies any agreement made in good faith. Schools should work with parents to achieve a solution that does not compromise the safety of the student and others, nor the employer's duty of care.

 For more information about disclaimers and parental consent, see **2.4.11**.

Personal Effects, Including Jewellery and Cultural or Religious Adornments – Students

2.14.7　Schools have a duty of care to ensure students are able to participate actively without unnecessarily endangering themselves or those working around them.

2.14.8　A clear and consistently applied policy for the removal of personal effects should be in place. The Association for Physical Education (afPE) strongly recommends the practice of removing all personal effects at the commencement of every lesson to establish a safe working environment. This applies to **all** ear and body piercings, including retainer and expander earrings.

2.14.9　If a school/employer adopts a policy where taping is utilised to enable participation then appropriate action needs to be taken at the start of the lesson. Staff are not required to remove or tape up earrings for students. Students should come ready for the lesson, preferably with earrings removed or adequately taped. Taping over ear and body piercings may offer a measure of protection in some physical activity situations, where individuals are required to work within their own personal space. However the amount of tape used needs to be sufficient to prevent the piercing penetrating, for example, the bone behind the ear should an unintentional blow be received from someone or some item of equipment, such as a ball. (See also sports goggles – 2.13.36.)

2.14.10　Where the school accepts taping, the teacher supervising the group has the legal responsibility to ensure the taping is fit for purpose. If the teacher considers the taping to be unsatisfactory to permit safe participation, they will need to make adaptations in terms of how the student takes part in the practical aspects of the lesson. The student can contribute to group planning, designing and tactical discussions, but can have different tasks assigned to them during the practical elements of the lesson (for example, individual skills practices, peer coaching, observation and feedback tasks, videoing others to analyse at a later stage, or officiating in a games context).

2.14.11　Exclusion from a lesson should be avoided at all times if a student is unable to remove personal effects or the taping is deemed unsatisfactory.

2.14.12　Staff should always give a verbal reminder to students and, where necessary, visually monitor the group and/or individuals. Particular vigilance may be required when dealing with body jewellery.

2.14.13　**Body jewellery** should be removed or taped to a safe standard. Where staff observe body jewellery being worn during any PESSPA activity, they should stop the activity and initiate procedures to make the situation safe.

2.14.14　**Medical bracelets:** Recent developments in the manufacture of **medical-aid wristbands** have resulted in products with an acceptably low risk factor (ie soft materials, Velcro fastenings). Such items should be acceptable for most PESSPA activities without the need for removal. However, these bracelets need to be regularly checked by the owner to make sure there are no hard or sharp edges that may cause injury. Where there is any concern, the bracelet can be covered with tape, padding or a soft, sports-style wristband.

2.14.15　**Fitness watches** and wristbands monitoring activity should be removed for PESSPA sessions, clubs and activities.

2.14.16　**Religious artefacts** need to be removed or made safe. Health and safety law would usually take precedence over equality law because of the implication of the "safety of others" and the specific duty set out in the Health and Safety at Work etc Act 1974. Case law relating to human rights legislation has established that a student does not have the right to manifest their belief at any time and place they choose at school, and this includes the wearing of jewellery. Generally, to attempt to succeed in making a claim on the grounds of human rights, there would be a commonly acknowledged religious obligation on a follower to wear the jewellery. However, where the safety of others is compromised through the wearing of such an item, the claim is unlikely to be successful.

2.14.17   In seeking, wherever possible, to respect religious or cultural sensitivities, it is recommended that schools enter into discussion with local faith leaders and parents to establish and maintain constructive communication with them and the local community, and to establish an inclusive school policy.

2.14.18   Where removal of religious artefacts proves to be extremely contentious and agreement for removal in PESSPA sessions cannot be achieved, the activity and involvement of the wearer needs to be suitably modified to mitigate undue risk.

2.14.19   **Sensory aids:** The decision as to whether it is safe or possible to wear **glasses** or **hearing aids** will usually be determined by the nature of the activity. Activities involving physical contact and full game situations may not be appropriate. For example, England Rugby (RFU) allows the wearing of glasses (in non-contact games) up to the under-8 age group, while The Football Association (FA) leaves this to the referee's discretion up to the age of 14. (See also sports goggles – **Chapter 2, Section 13.**) Where sensory aids need to be worn, the activity can be amended, for example, by providing more space and time or using a soft ball instead of a harder one.

2.14.20   **Long hair** should always be tied back with a suitably soft item to prevent entanglement in apparatus and to prevent vision being obscured.

2.14.21   **Nails** need to be sufficiently short to prevent injury to self and others.

Clothing or "Kit" – Students

General principles

2.14.22   Students should wear clothing that is **fit for purpose** according to the PESSPA activity, environment and weather conditions. From the earliest ages, they should change into suitable PESSPA clothing (or "kit") in order that they may participate safely and securely.

2.14.23   Clothing for PESSPA should be well suited to its function. For indoor sessions, it should be light and allow good freedom of movement, without being baggy or loose. **Loose clothing** in gymnastics, for example, may catch on equipment and cause injury. Any items of clothing for PESSPA, including those of cultural significance, need to be relatively close-fitting, made safe or removed for reasons of individual safety.

2.14.24   Although vest and pants were, in the past, an acceptable, easy and time-saving option for the youngest children, contemporary views on safeguarding, personal development and hygiene mean this is no longer advisable practice.

2.14.25   For classroom-based movement in a limited space (eg "active" maths activities), it can be acceptable for students to remain in their everyday clothes or school uniform. During this type of activity, participants normally work within a small area or on the spot, and safety concerns linked with slips, trips and falls are reduced.

2.14.26   Students should wear sufficient and appropriate clothing for the **weather conditions** in order to minimise the likelihood of injury or hypothermia in cold conditions, and illness or heatstroke in very hot conditions.

2.14.27   When participating in hot weather, sun protection is advisable. Many schools have established policies for wearing hats and light, loose clothing, as well as advising parents to provide sun-cream protection for their children.

2.14.28   Clothing for outdoor lessons and activities should allow good freedom of movement, but will also need to offer some insulation from **cold weather** in the winter months, when additional layers for warmth are advisable. Students who are insufficiently warm and experience discomfort will not be appropriately focused, and may lack concentration, leading to injury.

2.14.29   The **Daily Mile** aims to increase students' physical activity levels by running/walking or a combination of both for 15 minutes a day in school. The Daily Mile website advises that school footwear should be suitable for active play and that "many schools have chosen to make black trainers part of the school uniform". afPE recommends that appropriate and relevant footwear should be worn, and if a student has unsuitable footwear for running, they should take part and walk the route with care.

2.14.30   An increasing number of schools offer kit displaying their school logo for students to buy. Hooded sweatshirts are popular, but care needs to be taken with these items. While useful for group trips, as team "travelling" kit or wearing in warm-ups, staff should consider safe practice and recommend that students remove hooded sweatshirts during contact or non-contact invasion games or similar activities to ensure they have adequate peripheral vision.

2.14.31   If students arrive at a PESSPA session with clothing deemed to be inappropriate, strategies need to be applied to make their inclusion safe, or to limit the extent of the activity element of their participation.

Some activity-specific clothing considerations

2.14.32   Risk assessing specific activities may mean adjustments are made to clothing; for example, wearing a long-sleeved top to prevent friction burns to the forearms when performing front drops in **trampolining** or deciding whether a fabric that reduces friction on **gymnastic apparatus** may be inappropriate as it could cause slipping, particularly if working at height or in inverted positions.

2.14.33   Loose clothing for **swimming** is not advised (other than during personal survival skills tests in controlled situations) due to the drag created, which may adversely affect the confidence and buoyancy of weaker swimmers.

2.14.34   It is strongly recommended that wetsuits and appropriate footwear are worn for activities where students are in **open water** for a long period of time.

Religious and Cultural Clothing – Students

2.14.35   To maximise safe and meaningful participation, staff should use sensitive management when dealing with any concerns arising from the wearing of certain items of clothing specific to religious requirements. (See **Chapter 2, Section 10**.) Students should be able to experience a broad PESSPA programme whatever their cultural background, while schools must continue to have regard to health and safety, equality legislation and delivering the statutory requirements of a specified curriculum.

2.14.36   Staff should ensure the following:

- Any clothing worn to comply with a faith commitment should be appropriate for the PESSPA activity. Clothing should be comfortable and allow for freedom of movement, while not being so loose as to become a hazard. A tracksuit is perfectly acceptable clothing for Muslim students and is not seen as offending the principles enshrined in Haya relating to modesty and decency.
- **Headscarves** (such as the **hijab**), where worn, should be tight, secured in a safe manner, particularly at the side of the face, and unlikely to obscure vision or catch on anything that may put the wearer at risk. Students can also consider obtaining a sports version of the hijab, for improved suitability. These are available from high street stores and on the Internet.
- In **swimming** lessons, unacceptable exposure of the body should be managed through adjustments in swimming attire to accommodate religious and cultural sensitivities while not compromising the safety of the students concerned. Leotards and tights are advised or other suitable tight clothing to support the buoyancy of the swimmer.

Footwear – Students

General principles

2.14.37 Footwear that is **fit for purpose** is essential for student safety. **Security of footing** is crucial in all situations. All students need to change into footwear that is appropriate for the lesson location and for the PESSPA activity being taught. Students need footwear that is capable of transmitting feel for the movement and the surface they are working on.

2.14.38 **Outdoor footwear** should give **effective grip and support** and reasonable protection for outdoor PESSPA activities.

2.14.39 Outdoor footwear may vary according to the playing surface, and according to the availability of particular footwear to some students. Studded, bladed or ribbed soles are beneficial in sports where the surface is soft or slippery and in conditions in which smooth soles would not provide secure footing. Security of footing is an essential requirement, along with consideration as to whether outdoor footwear presents any foreseeable risk to other participants, such as a group presenting a variety of footwear for outdoor activities. In such cases, staff must determine how to proceed; for example, conditions may need to be applied to maximise safety (eg splitting the group according to footwear and assigning different tasks as appropriate).

2.14.40 Procedures need to be applied to ensure students avoid, wherever possible, walking over hard surfaces to access the playing area. This can result in studs and other traction devices becoming unacceptably rough and sharp, which might prove hazardous to opponents in competitive games and practices. It is likely that all PESSPA footwear will need some form of maintenance so as not to cause a hazard to anyone.

2.14.41 Footwear is advisable for **indoor games** activities due to the higher frequency of sudden stopping and changing direction quickly where toes can be stubbed, and also for games that require the ball to be kicked (eg football) or involve a hard, fast-moving ball at ground level (eg indoor hockey). **Training shoes**, which provide good traction, will often prove effective for a range of indoor games and will also support the feet when carrying out activities that are largely high impact.

2.14.42 Students should never participate in **socks** on polished wooden or tiled surfaces as the level of grip provided is poor. Well-fitting socks may be acceptable on a carpet surface if traction is not affected, and transfer between carpeted and wooden surfaces, such as benches, is not required.

2.14.43 Students should never be excluded from taking part in a lesson due to not having the correct footwear. Every effort should be made to involve the student in as much of the physical part of the lesson as possible, and to provide alternative activity-related tasks when this is not possible.

2.14.44 **Students should be taught to take responsibility** for preparing and checking that all of their kit (clothing and footwear) is fit for purpose for the lesson being undertaken, and that it is safe.

2.14.45 Systems need to be in place to ensure students regularly **check the safety** of their footwear.

2.14.46 All footwear should be of the correct **size** and correctly **fastened** in the manner of its design to ensure appropriate support for the ankles. As fashion evolves, there are items of casual or leisure footwear on the market that have the appearance of trainers. It is important that footwear meets the required specification and provides the necessary support for safe participation.

2.14.47 Footwear that does not provide **effective grip and support** for the activity being undertaken should not be worn for PESSPA sessions, clubs and activities.

Some activity-specific footwear considerations

2.14.48   In **gymnastics and dance**, barefoot work is safest, whether on the floor or apparatus, because the toes can grip. Barefoot work in both gymnastics and dance can improve aesthetics by allowing the foot and toes to move through a full range of flexion and extension, which in turn strengthens the muscles, bones and joints.

2.14.49   Decisions about the appropriateness of bare feet for dance should consider the type of contact between the floor and feet, which is closely associated with the style of dance or nature of the movements being explored.

2.14.50   Where the condition of the floor makes it unsuitable for barefoot work in gymnastics and dance, students should be permitted to wear clean, soft footwear.

2.14.51   Situations where a **wet-weather indoor alternative activity** means that some students are wearing training shoes and others have bare feet should be avoided where possible. This situation needs to be managed correctly (eg all students in bare feet or all students in trainers, or students being set different tasks that are appropriate for their footwear).

2.14.52   For **trampolining**, non-slip socks or trampolining slippers are necessary to prevent toes entering the gaps in the webbing. Cotton and wool socks are suitable, but nylon socks on a webbed nylon bed are unlikely to provide adequate traction.

Clothing, Footwear and Personal Effects – Staff

2.14.53   Clothing and **correct attire** for particular PESSPA activities represent important features of safe practice that apply in equal measure to both staff and students.

2.14.54   **Staff** should always endeavour to **change** into appropriate clothing for teaching PESSPA sessions or leading PESSPA clubs and activities. On the rare occasions that this proves difficult or impractical, a change of footwear and removal of jewellery, at the very least, should always be undertaken.

2.14.55   All staff need to change into **footwear** that is appropriate for the session location and, ideally, for the PESSPA activity being taught. This is very important to allow safe supervision by staff as they may need to respond quickly to prevent a potential injury to a student, making effective mobility essential.

2.14.56   Staff should never teach in socks or tights on polished wooden or tiled surfaces as the level of grip provided is poor.

2.14.57   **Staff** need to be mindful of their own adornments and remove them prior to teaching PESSPA sessions. The wearing of rings and large hooped or drop earrings, for instance, has been responsible for unnecessary injury in the past and represents a hazard to both staff and students involved in the lesson. It is also advised that lanyards should be removed before the lesson commences.

Section 15: Sports Fixtures, Festivals, Tours and Club Links

2.15.1   When schools include fixtures, attendance at school tournaments and festivals, and sports tours in their programme, planning should be methodical and precise. The planning process should consider:

- pre-event planning
- assembly
- outward and return journeys
- the venue and event
- post-event evaluation.

Sports Fixtures

2.15.2   Sports fixtures held at and away from the school site are common practice. Procedures for such events should be routine, and all staff and students who participate in them should be familiar with these. The head teacher (HT), on behalf of the employer, must be aware of, and **approve**, all activities that students undertake within a school sport programme.

2.15.3   Safety issues relating to **home fixtures** should be addressed within the risk assessment for physical education, school sport and physical activity (PESSPA) as normal procedures should apply.

2.15.4   Normal school procedures for informing parents, and requirements for consent forms should be followed.

 For more information about parental consent, see **Chapter 2, Section 4**.

Stage of Planning	Away Fixtures	Tick
Pre-event	Is the HT aware of the fixtures programme?	
	Are school policies and procedures known and applied?	
	Are consent forms required, and if so, have they been obtained? What is the procedure for non-returned consent forms?	
	Are parents aware of the itinerary, programme, particular needs and conditions, insurance provision, emergency contact system and venue address?	
	Have roles and responsibilities, ratios, competency, group management and knowledge of the group been discussed with the staff involved? Has this included, if relevant, discussion about equality in size, experience and confidence of participants?	
	Is a group register available to take to the fixture?	
	Are medical backgrounds known by staff involved?	
	Have first aid arrangements been made and agreed, including knowledge of dealing with incidents of concussion?	
	Have general school and PESSPA risk assessments been completed and requirements followed?	
	Are the school's crisis-management plan requirements built in to risk assessment and planning?	
	Are reciprocal arrangements with the host school clarified/known?	
	Have all other "what ifs" and contingency planning been considered?	
Assembly	When does the school duty of care begin and end? When does this take over from, and revert back to, the parents?	
	Has a register been taken and a corresponding register left at school?	
	Has kit/footwear been checked?	
	Do relevant students have their required medication with them, and understand their own responsibility to administer this?	
	Is emergency contact information to hand during the trip?	
	Do students know, and are they following, the code of conduct?	
	Are mobile phones/smartphones available to use in an emergency?	
Outward and return journeys	Does the form of transport chosen meet legal, employer and local requirements, including volunteers' cars?	
	Has it been decided whether the driver will supervise and drive, or drive only, with additional staff to supervise?	
	Has the driver carried out a vehicle check?	
	Is a first aid kit available, and are arrangements for administering first aid known?	

	Have safe embarkation and disembarkation points been decided?	
	Are the register and head count before leaving consistent?	
	Are the emergency action plan and critical incident arrangements known?	
	Are arrangements and communication plans in place to alert parents of any delay?	
	Have strategies for dealing with illness or incident on the journey been decided?	
Venue and event	Has a venue risk assessment been supplied to visitors by the host team? (If not, carry out a visual check on arrival.)	
	Have any reciprocal arrangements agreed been reconfirmed (eg in relation to first aid, supervision, taking students to hospital, staff sickness)?	
	Have any group or activity management and supervision issues been established (eg one staff with two teams/officiating and supervising)?	
	Are officials competent and/or qualified? Are any young sports leaders supervised by competent staff?	
	What is the procedure for assuring acceptable behaviour?	
	Are periodic head counts being carried out?	
	Is equality in size/experience/confidence being monitored?	
	Are kit and footwear appropriate to the weather/playing surface, and requirements consistently applied by all teams?	
	Has responsibility for managing personal effects been established?	
	Have personal protective equipment (PPE) requirements been agreed (eg pads/helmets/mouth guards)?	
	Has the facility/equipment been checked before use as part of a host school risk assessment? Has this risk assessment been agreed by the visitors?	
	Have weather issues been considered and managed appropriately (eg sun/heat protection/rehydration/storms/other seasonal considerations)?	
Post-event evaluation	Are there any near misses/incidents to review?	
	Have injuries been recorded and outcomes followed up?	
	Have improvements for the next event been identified?	
	Has any feedback been provided to HT/subject leader (SL)/staff/activity leaders/students/parents?	
	Have any adjustments to the risk assessment been formally recorded to inform future planning?	

Sports Festival and Tournament Risk Assessment Process

2.15.5   Sports festivals and tournaments are centrally organised events in which individual schools are invited to participate. Schools will need to plan and risk assess considering the three areas outlined below.

The venue risk assessment

2.15.6   The venue manager/owner/host needs to have completed a risk assessment that identifies hazards, evaluates risks and establishes appropriate controls to make the venue safe for the purpose for which it is being offered or hired out to the user group. This may be known as a risk assessment or normal operating procedures (NOPs) and emergency action plan (EAP). Swimming pools, leisure centres and independent arenas are usually thorough in completing risk assessments, but school venues can vary widely. Where the venue risk assessment is lacking or not available, the event organiser needs to complete a venue assessment prior to the event.

2.15.7   Single-use venues (ie swimming pools) will have a risk assessment. However, multi-use venues, such as schools, may be specifically hired out on the basis that they are not guaranteed to be suitable for the purposes of the group who wish to use them.

The organiser's event risk assessment

2.15.8   When an event organiser hires a facility to use for an event, they in effect become the legal occupier for the duration of that event. The event organiser needs to complete an event risk assessment that covers venue issues and the organisation of the planned event. The venue provider's **contract** should clarify matters such as the responsibilities of each party, and **public liability insurance requirements**. The relevant issues from this assessment need to be clearly communicated to the staff who are managing groups attending the event, and should form part of the **pre-event guidance and information** provided to the schools, along with the event programming, procedures and any other essential information.

2.15.9   Organisers should also establish a **contingency date** that is acceptable to all to cover any situation where an event may need to be postponed (eg due to poor weather or exceedingly high temperatures).

School risk assessment

2.15.10   Taking account of the information received from the event organiser about the venue and organisation of the event, school staff need to carry out a **risk assessment for their group**. This risk assessment should consider preparations for the event, outward and return journeys, managing and supervising the group at the event, and returning them to their parents' care safely.

Stage of Planning	Festivals and Tournaments	Tick
Pre-event	Is approval needed from the governors?	
	Is additional staffing needed (eg to cover supervision/officiating)?	
	Have group issues been clarified (eg age, ability, behaviour, selection)?	
	Has a "telephone tree" (cascading communication system to convey messages/delays back to parents) been organised?	
	Has a pre-event visit been made to venue?	
	Has the risk assessment been received from the venue host or completed during a pre-event visit?	
	What is the first aid order of responsibility (eg school, then host or private company)?	

Assembly	If outside of the school day, do students and parents know what time to meet and what to do, for example, if they miss the coach?	
	Have large groups been subdivided into smaller groups for ease of management, with an adult designated to manage each subgroup?	
Outward and return journeys	Are additional drivers needed?	
	How are breaks in the journey to be managed (eg motorway service areas)?	
	Has a head count been completed after any break in journey?	
Venue and event	Does the programme allow sufficient rest/recovery periods?	
	Is supervision appropriate where changing is involved?	
	Is total playing time within the capability of those students involved?	
	Has it been decided who provides refreshments and rehydration? Are additional supplies available?	
	Is there a contingency plan in case of early completion/abandonment of the programme (eg telephone tree)?	
	Is there a system for granting consent if necessary for any photography that may be involved?	
	Is sunshade/rain cover available, or is additional portable cover required (eg gazebos or tents)?	
	Do participants need a change of clothes?	

Sports Tours

2.15.11   The planning and management of sports tours in the UK and abroad is complex, whether they are arranged through a commercial company or by the school staff themselves.

For more information, see https://www.gov.uk/government/publications/health-and-safety-on-educational-visits/health-and-safety-on-educational-visits

2.15.12   The **employer's requirements** for events that take place at a considerable distance from the school base and/or are residential in nature should be part of an off-site and educational visits policy, and made known to, and applied by, all involved in the organisation of sports tours.

2.15.13   Many overseas sports tour companies are accredited by the School Travel Forum, which is the awarding body for the Learning Outside the Classroom Quality Badge issued in this sector.

For more information on the School Travel Forum, see www.schooltravelforum.com

Stage of Planning	Sports Tours	Tick
Pre-event	Is employing authority approval needed? If so, have all requirements been met?	
	Have all paperwork and/or online approval forms been completed and submitted?	
	Has a pre-visit been made to the area/venue where possible?	
	Have expiry dates of passports been checked to allow for sufficient time before expiry as set by the country to be visited?	
	Has any additional insurance been obtained if needed?	
	Have any injections/medications that are required prior to, and during, the tour been confirmed?	
	Has a student code of conduct been developed from basic school visit requirements (eg communication/mountain code/country code/safety on water)?	
	Do parents have a copy of the itinerary, contact details and other relevant information?	
	Do accompanying staff and adults demonstrate appropriate leadership skills?	
	Have additional "expert" staffing requirements been identified and met (eg for students with special educational needs and disabilities [SEND], residential/adventure activities/city tours/swimming)?	
	Have the implications of taking non-school staff been considered?	
	Have safeguarding issues been checked (eg non-school staff, centre staff, host families)?	
	Are students adequately prepared for the tour – physically, emotionally and behaviourally?	
Assembly	Have methods for supervising groups at airport, ferry or train terminals been decided?	
Outward and return journeys	What are the package tour conditions? Will the Package Travel and Linked Travel Arrangements Regulations 2018 apply?	
	Have the implications of foreign law, standards, health and language been considered?	
	Have the international driving requirements been considered?	
	What information will be carried by students, in case of separation from the main group?	
Venue and event	Is the itinerary decided and agreed as appropriate?	
	Is security sufficient and appropriate at the accommodation?	
	Are home care abroad standards, including safeguarding requirements, being met?	
	Is the student code of conduct being applied?	

	Is additional insurance needed?	
	Have down/free-time issues been considered?	
	Has a policy on student use of mobile phones/smartphones been decided?	
	Do students have an accessible point of contact in the host country?	
	Have reciprocal arrangements been clarified if hosted by another school/group?	

2.15.14   **All advice in this section will complement any additional documentation** and requirements set out by the school employing authority in respect of off-site and educational visits. It is important that all staff are aware of their employer's current policy and guidelines for off-site and educational visits, as these may include requirements for timescales around approvals, and staff qualifications.

Information for Travel Abroad

2.15.15   For many visits abroad, additional insurance cover is usually worth considering, such as:

- employer's liability insurance
- public liability insurance
- personal accident insurance
- comprehensive travel insurance
- tour operator insurance packages.

2.15.16   For specific support and guidance on insurance matters, staff should contact whoever provides insurance advice to their school.

2.15.17   When organising a tour abroad, consideration should be given to whether the Package Travel and Linked Travel Arrangements Regulations 2018 will apply.

2.15.18   The Package Travel and Linked Travel Arrangements Regulations 2018 place certain legal obligations on organisers of package travel arrangements. It is unlikely that the regulations will apply to most establishment-organised visits, but there are some circumstances where they might.

Useful resources from the Outdoor Education Advisers' Panel (OEAP) National Guidance website – https://oeapng.info/ – include:

- good practice basics
- a visit leader checklist
- information on provider-led study and sports tours
- guidance on overseas visits.

Club and Community Links Outside of the Curriculum

2.15.19   All schools should have in place arrangements for ensuring that their functions are exercised with a view to safeguarding and promoting the welfare of children. It follows that it is essential that schools ensure that **safeguarding** is addressed in all school-club/community sport links in order to provide the best possible protection and fulfil their duty of care towards children and young people.

2.15.20   Clubs and community sport providers are likely to develop their protocols for safeguarding children according to guidelines set out by organisations such as governing bodies of sport, the Child Protection in Sport Unit (CPSU) and the Sport and Recreation Alliance. Consequently, they should have policies, processes and clear guidance in place to safeguard children. In addition, clubs and community sport providers can access specific safeguarding training courses that should be undertaken by coaches and volunteers working with children.

    CPSU: https://www.thecpsu.org.uk/
Sport and Recreation Alliance: www.sportandrecreation.org.uk

2.15.21   Using such information, the **link club or community sport provider** should have a regularly reviewed, openly accessible safeguarding policy that outlines how it will ensure children are kept safe when taking part in their sport/activity. It should also have delegated officers to monitor this, and coaches and volunteers who are appropriately qualified and trained in child safeguarding. The policy should include clear procedures for dealing with welfare and safeguarding issues, and specify a named person, with contact details, who any child or adult can contact should they have a concern.

2.15.22   When linking with a school, a club or community provider should understand the requirements set out in the safeguarding policy of the school or organisation with which it is working.

2.15.23   The **school should** ensure that safeguarding protocols are in place that clarify the shared roles and responsibilities prior to any session delivery.

2.15.24   The school safeguarding policy should be fit for purpose and reflect the school context.

2.15.25   A **school induction** needs to take place for **each coach or volunteer**. The school safeguarding policy, which should make reference to out of curriculum hours work, should be shared with each volunteer or coach as part of their induction process.

    Further information around safe recruitment can be found in **Table 2 in Chapter 1, Section 5: Competence**.

2.15.26   The school should provide information on reporting procedures, including the names of the emergency contact and designated safeguarding lead (DSL) for the school, with contact details, and information on specific group needs, medical needs and SEND.

2.15.27   The staff:student ratio required in a school may differ from that specified by the provider's governing body of sport or insurance requirements. This will need to be addressed prior to the sessions commencing to ensure there are sufficient qualified adults present to deliver the session.

2.15.28   The "**Partnership Check and Challenge Tool**", available from the **CPSU** is a useful online resource that provides templates and guidance to support schools in keeping children safe in PESSPA.

    To access the "Partnership Check and Challenge Tool", see: https://thecpsu.org.uk/resource-library/tools/partnership-check-and-challenge-tool/

2.15.29   It should not be presumed that a school's safeguarding policy is sufficient to cover activities outside school hours. For example, it may be more likely that, at the end of a club session, a child may be left alone with a coach while waiting to be collected by a parent. In school, the likelihood of a number of adults being in the building is higher. In such a situation, the coach needs to be clear about what policy to adopt.

2.15.30   All coaches working in school clubs should be monitored and supported on an ongoing basis. They should be informed and aware of all relevant school procedures. Where schools feel that established coaches are regularly meeting the standards expected of them, the school may take the decision to allow the coach to work remotely from supervising staff.

2.15.31   The link club/community sport provider should:

- promote the jointly agreed policy and procedures to all club members and parents in order to demonstrate the club's commitment to a safe, friendly and supportive environment
- have guidance in place covering a range of practices and procedures relevant to the sport or activity
- provide appropriately qualified, trained and Disclosure and Barring Service (DBS)-checked coaches to work with children and young people
- ensure appropriate training is available for coaches and others working with children and young people
- consider the use of agreed codes of conduct that individuals can sign up to, and understand the sanctions imposed when failing to adhere to these; such codes of conduct may be aimed at:
  - parents
  - volunteers
  - coaches
  - students.

2.15.32   All of the above requirements, where relevant, apply to individual coaches and volunteers working with students. In addition, the adults who are responsible for **managing activities should be alert** for any of the following signs:

- activities where other adults are discouraged from staying to watch
- any individual who appears to ignore organisational guidelines
- staff who appear to show favouritism or personally reward specific students
- any engagement in inappropriate physical contact, such as taking part in physical activities other than demonstrations, or physically supporting students where little or no support is necessary
- poor communication from the adults and negative responses to the students
- a "win at all costs" attitude towards the sport or activity
- use of extreme additional activity as a "punishment"
- students who drop out of an activity for no apparent reason (registers are important for curriculum, school sport and off-site activities)
- invitations offered to specific students to spend time alone with the adult, such as on the pretext of individual coaching.

2.15.33   Many sports have developed **club accreditation schemes**, and included within these are minimum standards for safeguarding that provide assurance for schools and others commissioning links. For more information on sport-specific accreditations, visit the relevant governing body of sport website.

2.15.34   At a more local level, some Active Partnerships (formerly county sports partnerships) and local authorities (LAs) have developed their own club or coaching accreditation standards, and work with clubs in the area to help them reach this level.

2.15.35   Club accreditation, either through a governing body of sport, LA or Active Partnership, is an **indication of quality**, and schools should seek to build links with clubs that have achieved, or are working towards, achievement of club accreditation, wherever possible.

2.15.36   When establishing a satellite club, guidance can be sought from Active Partnerships to help schools put in place safe club links.

For more information, see the Active Partnerships website: www.activepartnerships.org

2.15.37   For martial arts, which do not have a recognised governing body of sport to coordinate and administer a club accreditation scheme, there is the "Safeguarding Code in Martial Arts". The code recognises clubs or providers in England that have demonstrated that they have reached and are maintaining good safeguarding standards. The "Safeguarding Code in Martial Arts mark" has been created so that parents and schools can clearly identify clubs that have successfully signed up to the code.

 For more information on the code, see www.safeguardingcode.com/

Section 16: Transport

Preparations when Considering Transporting Students

2.16.1 The Health and Safety Executive (HSE) has urged schools across the country to review traffic management and wherever possible to divide children from traffic. Planning and parking should take into account "desire lines", which are the routes most people will choose to take. Children may not be risk aware, there will be a rush of children all leaving school at once, and they will race for the back seat. This predictable behaviour makes it all the more important that transport risk is properly managed, and regularly reviewed.

2.16.2 Staff taking groups off site should be **competent** in discipline, control, organisation and dealing with any crisis that may arise. They should ensure there is an effective **emergency contact system**, such as via mobile phone/smartphone or an alternative arrangement if a mobile phone/smartphone is not available.

2.16.3 **Effective management** and control, particularly with younger students, are more easily achieved where large groups are subdivided into smaller groups with a designated adult responsible for each subgroup.

2.16.4 In readiness for transporting students, staff need to have considered plans for:

- deciding safe embarkation points
- deciding where staff will sit in the mode of transport in order to maintain adequate supervision and control
- deciding where students will sit, leaving the rearmost seats empty if possible in case a vehicle runs into the back of the bus, coach or minibus
- knowing the number of students on the vehicle and for counting them out of, and back on to, the vehicle after any break in the journey
- taking the emergency contact information of all students in the transport, and ensuring access at any time to information held back at school
- organising dismissal and dispersal of the group after the event, ie students should be dropped at the location the teacher has informed the parents of prior to the event; parents need to be made aware of arrangements for any additional drop-off points that may be requested and agreed
- the number of staff required for the journey – this is determined by the type of transport, group-management implications at the event, behaviour, discipline, disability, length of journey or driving requirements.

2.16.5 A **risk assessment** including transport arrangements to cover all regular activities (such as away fixtures, swimming lessons at external pools) should be carried out, as well as additional specific assessments for each special event involving travel.

2.16.6 Consideration of the school's **crisis management plan** (sometimes referred to as a critical incident plan or disaster plan) should be built into the risk assessment. In the very unlikely event of the transport in question being involved in a major road traffic accident, this will support individual members of staff who are unable to deal with the situation alone.

For further information on parental consent in relation to transport, see Parental consent – **2.4.15**.

Supervision

2.16.7 A driver cannot drive and supervise at the same time. It is **not a legal requirement that more than one adult accompanies a group on a minibus**, but the driver should not be distracted except on safety grounds. Where a risk assessment identifies that student needs or behaviour warrant additional supervision, a second adult (or more if required) should be present to fulfil the supervisory duty. A risk assessment should be undertaken for each journey to help determine the adult:student ratio for that specific context. All drivers should be equipped with a mobile phone/smartphone for emergency contact, and be familiar with any emergency plans and procedures.

2.16.8 **Safe embarkation and disembarkation** are important. The location should be away from the roadside where possible. It is advisable for passenger loading to be allowed only by the side doors, and not the back doors where passenger safety may be compromised by passing traffic.

Walking Routes

2.16.9 Wherever possible, if movement off site involves walking, staff should check the route personally before embarking on the excursion so that it is **familiar** to them. Potentially hazardous points should be identified, and precautionary strategies known by all staff and shared in an appropriate way with the students.

2.16.10 **Ratios** of accompanying adults need to be calculated according to the students' age, safety awareness, behaviour, and familiarity with the route, and staff competence in relation to group management, knowledge of the group, familiarity with the route, and the distance and safety demands of the route.

2.16.11 Immediate **communication** with the school base should form part of the planning and organisation of the trip. Schools will also need to check with their employing authority in respect of any further requirements that would need to be adhered to.

2.16.12 If at any time staff judge that the route is unsafe for any reason, or has become unsafe over time (eg through shrub growth, weather conditions or increase in vehicles parking), they should consult the leadership team.

Pushing Wheelchairs

2.16.13 There is no **legal age limit** for pushing a wheelchair. Employees who are trained in manual handling would cover pushing/pulling wheelchairs within this training. When transporting students in wheelchairs within and beyond the school, a risk assessment would need to be undertaken, taking individual circumstances into account.

See **FAQ 7** in **Chapter 4**.

Seat Belts and Child Restraints

2.16.14   On school trips, staff should consider their duty of care in taking all measures necessary to ensure that students are transported safely, that transport is in good condition, and that selected outside transport companies use fit and competent drivers. Where a **school arranges the transport**, it remains responsible for ensuring that the correct child restraints and seat belts are available.

2.16.15   While some vehicles may still not have seat belts fitted, schools have a responsibility, when sourcing transport for student use, to use reputable companies whose vehicles are fitted with seat belts.

2.16.16   By law, a **seat belt must be worn** in all vehicles where one is fitted. There are very few exceptions to this. The driver is legally responsible if a passenger under the age of 14 does not use a seat belt provided. Anyone aged 14 or over must wear a seat belt, but is responsible for doing so themselves. It is, however, expected that in accordance with their duty of care, staff will remind all students (including those over 14) of this requirement.

2.16.17   Children aged up to three years old must use a **"child restraint"** when travelling in the front or back seat of any **car** or van. At this age, it should take the form of a child seat. This also applies in a licensed **taxi or private hire vehicle** where child restraints are available. Where they are not available in a taxi, the child may travel in the rear seat unrestrained. Care should be taken to ensure that diagonal fitting seat belts, when used, do not present a danger to the head or neck of a small child.

2.16.18   Children aged 3–11 years and under 135cm tall must use an appropriate child restraint if available, and if not available, wear a seat belt. On reaching 135cm tall or their 12th birthday (whichever comes first), the student must wear a seat belt where one is fitted.

2.16.19   Schools using **staff and parents' cars** to transport students to matches and events will need to apply these requirements on the use of child restraints. It is the school's responsibility, on behalf of parents, to check that booster seats are provided and used. Seat belts must be worn.

2.16.20   Students must use an adult seat belt if the correct child restraint is not available:

- in a licensed taxi or private hire vehicle
- in a minibus
- for a short distance in an unexpected emergency
- where two occupied child restraints prevent the fitting of a third.

2.16.21   **Minibuses and coaches** used to carry three or more students on an organised school trip where the transport of children is central to the journey must have seat belts fitted.

2.16.22   The minimum requirement is for all children and young people between the ages of three and 16 years (but not including 16-year-olds) to be provided with a forward-facing seat with seat belt in minibuses or coaches used to take them on organised trips, including journeys to and from school or college.

2.16.23   **Buses** are not required to have seat belts.

Additional information about seat belts can be found on these websites:
- Royal Society for the Prevention of Accidents (RoSPA): http://goo.gl/DCSX3i
- Outdoor Education Advisers' Panel (OEAP) National Guidance: http://goo.gl/YxOMzw

Using Private Cars to Transport Students

2.16.24   **The employer's policy** on the use of private cars to transport students should be checked. Local requirements vary considerably. Some employers do not allow it.

2.16.25   If using private cars to transport students, drivers are usually expected to have a clean driving licence. Definitions of a **clean licence** may vary from one employer to another. Having some penalty points may be accepted as a clean licence, and staff need to check with their employer.

2.16.26   The car must be **roadworthy** and have a valid MOT certificate if relevant.

2.16.27   Enquiries should be made about the **insurance procedures** required to use private cars for school business. School staff are advised to check whether the school's insurance covers the use of their personal car for school business, within and beyond the school day. In addition, they should contact their own insurers to let them know what they intend to do. In most cases, staff will be advised to add **business use** cover to their policies.

2.16.28   Staff working at academies, free schools and other eligible schools that are signed up to the government's risk protection arrangement (see **Chapter 2, Section 5: Insurance**) will find that this scheme does not cover staff intending to use their own or others' private cars for occasional "business use". Parents and volunteers must have fully comprehensive insurance and may add a business use clause in line with their insurer's requirements.

2.16.29   Section 19 of the Transport Act 1985 allows non-profit-making organisations, such as schools, to make a charge to passengers for providing transport. Without this permit, the school would need to have a public service vehicle (PSV) operator's licence, and drivers would need a passenger-carrying vehicle (PCV) entitlement on their driving licence (a full category D addition).

2.16.30   **Charging** is not allowed when using a private car to transport students. Optional general donations are permissible where this is for the purpose of ensuring the activity is sufficiently funded to go ahead.

2.16.31   Agreed procedures should ensure **no adult is ever alone** in a car with any child, other than where parents provide transport for school activities. Where a "responsible adult" transports a student in an emergency, it is advised that, where possible, a second adult is in the car. This may not always be possible in emergency situations. (See **2.16.7.**) Appropriate **disclosure certification** should be obtained if applicable. This would usually arise if the driver is in **regulated activity**, ie is used to transport children on four or more days in any period of 30 days.

 For more information about vetting and barring, see **Chapter 2, Section 2.**

2.16.32   The driver of the car **cannot drive and supervise** student passengers at the same time. For this reason, the behaviour of the students being transported should be taken into account. Where this is a concern, an adult in a supervisory role, wherever possible, should also be in the car.

2.16.33   Staff, parents and volunteer drivers are legally responsible for themselves and their passengers complying with all seat belt and car child restraint legislation. (See **2.16.16.**)

2.16.34   Travelling **in convoy** is not recommended as it can divert a driver's attention. Drivers should know the route to their destination and not rely on following others.

2.16.35   It is recommended that parents give consent for their child to travel in **another adult's car**.

2.16.36   Local requirements will apply in relation to whether **senior students** may use their own cars to transport their peers.

Using Taxis to Transport Students

2.16.37   Taxis are increasingly used as a more cost-effective means to transport small groups than hiring coaches.

2.16.38   Staff should check the **employer's policy** to ensure that the use of taxis is allowed.

2.16.39   Checks to establish whether or not the taxi firm is **accredited** by the employer should be carried out. Some local authorities (LAs) maintain lists of approved firms that employ Disclosure and Barring Service (DBS) checked drivers. If using a firm not on an approved list, schools will need to make their own arrangements with the firm in relation to DBS clearance.

2.16.40   Discussions with the taxi firm with regard to timings of taxi arrivals and departures will help to inform decisions about how staff will supervise disembarkation and check student numbers.

2.16.41   A **risk assessment** should determine whether each taxi should have an adult supervisor or whether a student may be designated to carry a list of names, base contact details and details of procedures to be implemented in case of an accident or emergency during the journey.

2.16.42   **Seat belts**, where provided, must be worn. Taxi firms used regularly for transporting students may also provide child restraints. These should be used where required.

2.16.43   Parents should be informed and their **consent obtained** prior to children being transported by taxi.

Using Minibuses to Transport Students

The minimum statutory requirements for operating minibuses

2.16.44   School minibuses are usually operated with what is called a **Section 19 or "Standard" Permit** (a section 10b permit in Northern Ireland).

2.16.45   It is the school governors' responsibility, as the **operator** of the minibus, to apply for a Section 19 Standard Permit. To obtain such a permit, the minibus cannot be run with a view to making a profit. In other words, the minibus is used for voluntary purposes only, but a charge can be made to cover running costs and so forth, directly as a fare or indirectly as a general contribution to school.

2.16.46   If **no charge** is made for the use of the bus at all, then no permit is required. However, any payment that gives a person a right to be carried on a vehicle (the legal term for this is "for hire or reward") would require the operator to hold either a Section 19 Standard Permit or PSV operator's licence.

2.16.47   Maintained schools, free schools and academies are considered non-commercial bodies, as are independent schools that hold charitable status. They are considered to be using the minibus for social purposes, ie non-commercial activities. This includes school trips and travel to sporting fixtures within the school day or as an extracurricular activity.

2.16.48   Fee-paying schools that do not have charitable status may not be viewed as non-commercial bodies with automatic exemption from the need to hold a PSV operator's licence. They should take legal advice about their status regarding hire or reward and eligibility for permits.

2.16.49   The Section 19 Standard Permit must be **displayed** in the windscreen of the minibus.

Who can drive a minibus?

2.16.50 Drivers who passed their car test **before 1 January 1997** were automatically granted additional entitlement to drive minibuses with 9–16 passenger seats (**category D1**) not used for hire or reward. For as long as they hold a D1 (not for hire or reward) entitlement, these drivers may drive a 9–16-seater minibus of any weight used under a permit and may receive remuneration for this. Drivers with a D1 + E (not for hire or reward) entitlement can also tow a trailer over 750kg (0.75 tonnes).

2.16.51 Drivers who passed their test on or after 1 January 1997 are no longer granted a D1 (not for hire or reward) entitlement. However, they may still drive a 9–16-seat minibus under a standard permit, provided the conditions set out below are met.

2.16.52 **Drivers** of a minibus with a Section 19 Standard Permit must:

- be aged 21 or over
- have held a category B licence for at least two years
- be driving the minibus for a non-commercial body for social purposes
- receive no payment or consideration for driving the vehicle, other than out-of-pocket expenses.

2.16.53 For a driver without a **D1 licence**, the minibus weight **must not exceed 3500kg (3.5 tonnes)** or 4250kg (4.25) tonnes when including any specialised equipment for the carriage of disabled passengers. A trailer cannot be towed.

2.16.54 Thus, where the school offers the minibus to students for a charge, but on a non-profit basis under a Section 19 Standard Permit, the driver is exempt from the D1 requirement. This is because the Section 19 Standard Permit exempts the employer from holding a PSV operator's licence and exempts the driver from the D1 requirement, providing they receive no payment for driving the minibus, and they meet the criteria listed.

Additional Conditions for Driving a Minibus

2.16.55 There is no national standard other than that set out in the Transport Act 1985. However, employers are entitled to apply whatever additional conditions they wish as to who may drive a minibus. Some employers choose to demand a D1 addition. Others do not, but, as recommended by the Driver and Vehicle Standards Agency (DVSA), they may require some additional training. This might be the Minibus Driver Awareness Scheme (MiDAS), or Royal Society for the Prevention of Accidents (RoSPA) or local driving course/test (hence schools having their own minibus driving tests) for what is a "small bus".

2.16.56 Anyone who has obtained a **driving licence abroad** is not usually entitled to drive a vehicle with more than eight seats.

2.16.57 **For drivers applying for their first licence or to renew their licence on or after 19 January 2013**, where it includes category D1 (minibus) or D1E (minibus with a trailer), the licence issued will be valid for a **maximum of five years**.

2.16.58 Such a five-year licence must be renewed when it expires. For people who have already passed a driving test in one of the above categories, these rules will apply when they next renew their driving licence.

Driving a minibus abroad

2.16.59 Driving a minibus under a Section 19 Standard Permit is acceptable **only within the UK**.

2.16.60 The governing body, as the operator of the minibus, should ensure that staff driving a minibus abroad meet the requirements set out in the latest **European Directive** (EU3D) (2006/126/EC), which came into force on 19 January 2013.

2.16.61   The requirements of this regulation include the following:

- A specific **PCV licence** is required. Section 19 Standard Permits are not recognised abroad. The PCV licence will provide a D1 category on a licence obtained since 1 January 1997.
- Higher **medical criteria** are applied. For example, insulin-dependent diabetics cannot drive a minibus.
- The **tachograph** is to be completed and used. This is not a requirement in the UK. However, when the journey starts in the UK, the tachograph must be initiated in the UK – see **Table 17, page 236**.
- Familiarity with the driving requirements and regulations in the countries to be visited is required, including carrying the **safety equipment** specified by the countries to be visited (eg French law requires drivers to be able to produce an unused and in date approved breathalyser kit).
- Maximum **driving hours** and minimum rest requirements are imposed, which are more stringent than in the UK – see **Table 18, page 236**.
- Vehicle **documentation** must be carried at all times. For example, passenger lists are to be carried with the vehicle.

Management of the minibus

2.16.62   The Public Passenger Vehicles Act 1981 identifies **the operator** as the person for whom the driver drives the vehicle. If the driver is driving the minibus on authorised school business, then the operator who is responsible for the lawful use of the vehicle is the governing body, trustee, proprietor or LA, according to the type of school.

2.16.63   Best practice is for someone on the school staff to be responsible for effectively organising maintenance, confirmation of roadworthiness, scheduling, record-keeping and driver management.

2.16.64   The responsible person must ensure that regulations and responsibilities regarding positioning of seats, seat belts and child restraints are understood and applied by staff and students. (See **2.16.14**.)

2.16.65   Adequate **wheelchair passenger restraints** must be provided to enable wheelchair users to take advantage of, and travel safely on, minibuses. An occupied wheelchair must itself be held securely in position using a recognised wheelchair-securing system.

2.16.66   **Trailers** should not be used unless unobstructed access is provided at all times to at least two doors – one on the nearside and one on the offside. This is in case any incident causes the trailer load to slide forward and block the rear exit.

2.16.67   The yellow and black **"school bus" sign**, compulsory for home to school transport, is not a requirement for minibus use on other types of journey, but many schools choose to have it on display in the rear window as a warning notice to other traffic.

Minibus driver responsibilities

2.16.68   The driver is responsible for:

- the roadworthiness of the vehicle when it is on the road
- ensuring that the minibus is not overloaded and not carrying more passengers than allowed
- doing a risk assessment for the journey
- ensuring that all seat belts and child restraint regulations are adhered to (see **2.16.14**)
- knowing how to adjust seat belts
- ensuring all passengers have their own seat – three children sharing two seats is not allowed, neither are standing passengers
- satisfying him/herself that passenger supervision is adequate
- ensuring luggage is securely stored with no obstructions on the floor between the seats or in front of any exit
- notifying the employer of any changes in their driving circumstances
- observing speed limits and other traffic controls – buses carrying eight passengers or more are now restricted to a maximum stabilised speed of 100kph (62mph), with lower speeds according to the type of road being travelled
- knowing the locations and use of the fire extinguisher and first aid kit
- driving with the doors unlocked and good visibility through all windows.

Safe Driving Hours

2.16.69   Driving is defined as being at the controls of a vehicle for the purposes of controlling its movement, whether it is moving or stationary with the engine running, even for a short period of time. Vehicle operators and drivers must assess the likely risk of suffering from fatigue, particularly on long journeys or **working days extended by additional activities**.

2.16.70   When driving a minibus or a private for-profit vehicle, if a driver is going to drive for more than four hours in any one day, then they must comply with British domestic **rules for driver hours** if operating solely within the UK, and with EU rules if operating in any other EU country. In light of the UK leaving the EU it is important to keep up to date with any subsequent implications.

2.16.71   If they drive for more than **four hours** for up to **two days in any week**, they are exempt from the British domestic rules, **but** on these two days:

- all working duties must start and finish within a 24-hour period
- a 10-hour period of rest must be taken immediately before the first duty and immediately after the last duty
- rules on driving times and length of working day must be obeyed.

2.16.72   If any working day overlaps into a week in which drivers are not exempt from the rules, the limits on driving time and length of working day must be obeyed on that day.

2.16.73   An exemption from the rules on driving time and rest applies during any time spent dealing with an emergency.

    For more information, see **Table 17: Domestic driving limits – buses and coaches.**

European travel and tachographs

2.16.74   In the EU as a whole, the requirement to fit a tachograph applies to all vehicles with 10 or more seats, including the driver. However, the UK has made use of a national derogation from these regulations so that minibuses with 17 seats and under (including the driver) are exempt from the requirement to fit and use a tachograph within the UK.

2.16.75   When taking a minibus with 10 or more seats abroad, the EU driver hours and tachograph rules will apply from the start of the journey in the UK until the final destination.

2.16.76   Under EU rules, any tour that starts or finishes in an EU member state is subject to EU regulations. Other tours between UK and non-EU countries are subject to EU or European Agreement Concerning the Work of Crews of Vehicles Engaged in International Road Transport (AETR) rules. If travelling to a non-EU country, staff should check which rules apply. A record of hours driven must be kept, and all vehicles with nine or more seats (excluding the driver) must have a tachograph, as explained in DVSA (2015) "Drivers' hours and tachograph rules: buses and coaches (PSV375)", https://goo.gl/bs8ySS

    See **Table 18: EU drivers' hours.**

    Further information regarding operating a minibus:
HM Government (2015) "Driving a minibus", https://goo.gl/eAf94Q
OEAP (2014) "Transport in minibuses", http://goo.gl/iTZrJJ
Minibus website: http://goo.gl/rzGYXX

Using Buses and Coaches to Transport Students

2.16.77   Where schools use buses or coaches, it is good practice to use a **reputable transport company.** Many schools and LAs maintain an approved list of companies.

2.16.78   As outlined previously in this section, buses are not required to have seat belts, and staff should therefore seriously consider whether buses should be used to transport students involved in physical education, school sport and physical activity (PESSPA) activities.

2.16.79   **Supervision levels** need to be considered according to the students involved, the journey, and any breaks in the journey. The adults should be positioned through the coach so that they can observe all students.

2.16.80   **Evacuation procedures** need to be known by all before departure. When disembarking, it is good practice for the adults to disembark first to direct students to an assembly point away from the roadside or in the car-park area.

 See **Case Law 22** in **Chapter 4**.

Using Public Transport to Transport Students

2.16.81   Schools should establish a **code of conduct** for students who use public transport for PESSPA events, to ensure group interaction with the public is of an acceptable standard.

 See **Codes of conduct** in **2.4.17**.

2.16.82   Some schools choose not to provide transport to off-site events, and leave students' transport arrangements to parents. Where the event is within school time, the school, under its duty of care, may still be seen as responsible for any accident that occurs if the parent claims that the school failed to provide transport, and as a result, the parent had to make alternative arrangements to allow the student to take part.

2.16.83   This position could also be taken where parents are asked to arrange transport to an event outside school time, when it is felt that the student had little option but to attend. These scenarios have not yet been contested in law, but schools should be mindful of their position, and maintain clear and informative communication with parents regarding their ability to transport students, and about when responsibility is understood and agreed to have been transferred.

Table 17: Domestic driving limits – buses and coaches

Daily driving	10 hours on any working day.
Cumulative or continuous driving	5½ hours – after this, a break of at least 30 minutes must be taken in which the driver is able to obtain rest and refreshment; or 8.5 hours' driving, as long as breaks from driving totalling at least 45 minutes are taken during the driving period so that the driver does not drive for more than seven hours and 45 minutes. In addition, the driver must have a break of at least 30 minutes to obtain rest and refreshment.
Length of working day	No more than 16 hours between the time of work starting and finishing work (including work other than driving and off-duty periods during the working day).
Daily rest periods	10 hours continuously must be taken between two working days; this can be reduced to 8½ hours up to three times a week.
Fortnightly rest periods	In any two weeks in a row (Monday–Sunday), there must be at least one period of 24 hours off.

Table 18: EU drivers' hours

Maximum daily driving	Nine hours, extendable to 10 hours on two days in the driving week.
Maximum weekly driving	Maximum of 56 hours.
Maximum fortnightly driving	90 hours.
Maximum driving before a break	4½ hours.
Minimum breaks after driving	45 minutes or other breaks of at least 15 minutes each.
Minimum daily rest	11 hours, reducible to nine hours three times a week; compensation must be given before the end of the following week; alternatively, 12 hours if split into two or three periods (one of which must provide at least nine hours of continuous rest).

Adapted from DVSA (2015) "Drivers' hours and tachograph rules: buses and coaches (PSV375)", https://goo.gl/bs8ySS

Section 17: Outdoor and Adventure Activities

The Outdoor and Adventure Activities Context

2.17.1   Outdoor and adventure activities (OAA) recognise the benefits of environmental education and adventure, which encourage students to take responsibility for their own actions in appropriately challenging situations. OAA include:

- **local/low-level outdoor activities** such as problem-solving activities, introductory orienteering, low-level climbing, excursions in normal lowland countryside, and team-building activities, which can develop trust, communication and leadership skills using simple equipment in safe, controlled environments
- **outdoor adventurous activities (often conducted off site)** such as rock climbing, sailing, caving, canoeing and abseiling, in which the spirit of adventure needs to be balanced against responsibility for the well-being and safety of those participating.

Provision of Local/Low-level Outdoor Activities

2.17.2   Most schools are able to deliver outdoor activities both within the school site and the immediate locality. The level of demand and risk in such activities can be relatively low.

2.17.3   In such circumstances, the technical demand on teachers is such that experience is often a key component of competence, along with knowledge of the locality and the school's system for managing groups off site.

2.17.4   Where the activity makes **basic demands** on students and staff, such as using the school and its immediate local environment (eg problem solving, orienteering using the school grounds or walking in local lowland countryside), competence through experience and relevant training is often the only requirement of the employer, combined with a plan that meets the needs of the group and identifies significant issues.

2.17.5   The organisation, planning and risk management of these types of activities can be covered both within a school's policy and as part of normal lesson planning. The Department for Education (DfE), in its health and safety advice for schools, points out that schools are not required to complete a risk assessment every time they undertake an activity in the locality during the school day. Visits that require risk assessments and greater planning are shared in https://www.gov.uk/government/publications/ health-and-safety-on-educational-visits/health-and-safety-on-educational-visits

2.17.6   The **Outdoor Education Advisers' Panel (OEAP)** provides advice and support on high quality outdoor learning and adventurous activities through training, hot topics and downloadable resources. National guidance resources can be accessed by visiting https://oeapng.info/

2.17.7   Where an initial risk assessment is carried out, it should stipulate the required levels of competence for staff to lead and manage an activity.

2.17.8   Employers need to set out their requirements for staff competence and arrange periodic monitoring to ensure good practice. Planning and monitoring will be supported by the Educational Visit Co-ordinator (EVC) function in each school. Evaluating visits is outlined in https://www.gov.uk/ government/publications/health-and-safety-on-educational-visits/health-and-safety-on-educational-visits

Key Information for Specific Outdoor and Adventure Activities (Often Off Site)

2.17.9   School staff leading **higher risk activities** must follow their employers' requirements for competence, qualifications, experience and management. It is recommended that teachers planning to provide challenging adventure activities for students should regularly check the latest guidance provided by the relevant OAA governing bodies, and ensure that staff who are leading students are qualified to the appropriate level of challenge and/or specialist experts are used.

2.17.10 Where activities are led by an external provider, the provider assumes responsibility for risk assessing its services and provision. School staff should understand, and be satisfied with, these as part of their overall assessment of the provider, and take responsibility for risk assessing those elements of the visit falling directly under their supervision. Overall duty of care remains the responsibility of the school (employer) and cannot be delegated to the service provider. School staff competency is essential in this situation. The school staff deployed must be confident and competent to make the correct decisions and intervene where appropriate. Schools using an outside organisation to provide an activity must check they have appropriate safety standards and liability insurance. The Council for Learning Outside the Classroom (LOtC) awards the Learning Outside the Classroom Quality Badge to organisations who meet nationally recognised standards.

2.17.11 The websites of governing bodies of sport for specific activities will provide up-to-date guidance and information on relevant coaching, leading and personal performance awards, recommended supervision levels, current best practice and risk assessment considerations. Where an employer sets specific requirements, these must be adhered to.

2.17.12   The latest DfE guidance 'Health and Safety on Educational Visits' (November 2018) outlines:

> **Adventure activities, caving, climbing, trekking and watersports**
>
> *These kind of activities should be identified and risk assessed as part of the visit beforehand. Staff managing or leading visits must not decide to add such activities during the trip.*
>
> DfE (2018) "Health and safety on educational visits", https://www.gov.uk/government/publications/
> health-and-safety-on-educational-visits/health-and-safety-on-educational-visits

2.17.13   The **Adventure Activities Licensing Authority (AALA) regulations** ensure that, for licensable activities (those identified within the categories of trekking, climbing, caving and water sports), activity providers follow good safety management practices, which should allow young people to experience exciting and stimulating activities outdoors without being exposed to avoidable risks of death or disabling injury.

2.17.14   Further information and a list of providers holding an Adventurous Activities Licence can be checked on the Health and Safety Executive (HSE)/AALA website.

2.17.15   A statement issued in January 2016 by the HSE confirmed that the licensing arrangements for adventure activity providers in England, Wales and Scotland were to remain as they currently stand – providers of activities in the scope of the current arrangements must still hold a valid licence.

2.17.16   Competent leadership and appropriate safety management are essential in delivering safe, high quality outdoor and adventure activities.

2.17.17   Before leading such an activity, an individual needs to ensure that they **meet their employer's criteria for competence and planning requirements for the activity**. Assessing competence can take into account a number of factors. In the case of specific OAA, competence may include:

- holding a governing body of sport leadership/coaching award at an appropriate level – governing bodies of sport regularly update and develop their awards, resources and best practice relating to safe organisation, leadership and risk assessment
- being approved by a suitably competent technical adviser, where available, who is appointed by an employer and recognised as suitably qualified by the relevant governing body of sport.

2.17.18   The qualifications matrices produced by the AALA provide further information about qualifications to lead or advise on specific OAA, including qualifications appropriate for technical advisers: http://goo.gl/KXBolp

2.17.19   Schools seeking competent leaders to deliver OAA may also require them to have:

- relevant recommended qualifications and skills related to particular environments required by their employer (and the relevant governing body of sport if applicable) including basic first aid and training in how to manage an emergency or remote incident that has the potential to develop into an emergency
- recent experience or knowledge of the intended location, taking into account weather conditions/ forecasts and other variables
- clear educational objectives for the activities planned
- a good knowledge of the students for whom they will be responsible
- knowledge of the fitness and experience of students to help match the proposed activity to these appropriately
- proven qualities of leadership and responsibility that are evident from other aspects of their work
- a flexible approach to altering a plan appropriately if conditions dictate
- the capacity to react effectively if things do not go to plan
- the ability to say "no", despite student protestations, if circumstances make the original plan unworkable
- the necessary mental and physical fitness to undertake the proposed activity
- the ability to establish safe supervision levels, taking into account all relevant variables

- a positive track record in active supervision
- the ability to recognise, and remain within, the extent of their competence
- communicated with parents about expectations of leaders and students (eg appropriate behaviour).

Organisation and Planning

Supervision and staff responsibilities

2.17.20   A suitable risk assessment that meets the employer's requirements should be carried out, covering all aspects of the trip. This is the responsibility of the member of staff leading the visit.

2.17.21   The school leader and other staff, where appropriate, should have recent knowledge and experience of off-site venues or locations, and it is highly recommended that some staff make a preliminary visit to the location prior to the commencement of the activity.

2.17.22   Where a preliminary visit is not possible, it is advisable that local knowledge is sought and a risk assessment is carried out on arrival to determine whether a planned activity can proceed.

2.17.23   Where off-site visits require transport, please refer to **Chapter 2, Section 16: Transport**.

2.17.24   In anticipating the possibility of changed circumstances, the school leader should make sure that supervision is always sufficient to ensure safety by having realistic **contingency plans/a Plan B**. This necessitates a further risk assessment (eg for an alternative venue) even if the activity remains the same.

2.17.25   It is recommended that at least two responsible adults accompany a group off site to allow for unanticipated events to be dealt with. An **assistant leader**, capable of fulfilling the leader's role or managing the group until help arrives, should be identified where there is more than one member of staff with the group. Employers' requirements and the risk assessment will have a bearing on the decisions made.

2.17.26   Mixed groups benefit from having staff of each gender, particularly for overnight stays. The needs of the students should be assessed to determine whether same-gender staff are required. Where mixed-gender staff provision is not possible, parents should be informed so they can decide whether to consent to their child's participation.

2.17.27   If students are to use their own clothing and equipment (eg for camping), this should be checked to ensure it is appropriate before the group leaves the school, and before the activity commences.

Emergency planning

2.17.28   All members of the school leadership team should be aware of the specific plans for a visit, and trained to manage an emergency or incidents that have the potential to become an emergency situation. Schools should have an emergency plan that covers what to do if there is an incident off site. Further guidance can be found at https://www.gov.uk/government/publications/health-and-safety-on-educational-visits/health-and-safety-on-educational-visits and www.oeapng.info

2.17.29   Where a leader operates alone for an off-site visit, effective communication with the school is essential, and the group should be trained in what action to take in the event of the leader being absent, and be deemed able to take this action if required.

2.17.30   Relevant information should be accessible at the school or base to enable effective emergency action if required. This should include:

- contact information (eg school and parent emergency communication)
- activity location
- expected time of arrival and return (and action to take if the group fails to return on time)
- equipment carried
- names and number of students and staff
- agreed procedures to be followed in the event of an accident or emergency.

2.17.31   **An effective communication system** with the school should be in place while the group is away. Where communications are limited (eg by a lack of phone signal), alternative strategies should be considered and put in place.

2.17.32   Discipline must be maintained at all times, and staff must be prepared to intervene if students take potentially unsafe action.

2.17.33   It is accepted practice, and an integral part of high quality provision, for students participating in activities such as the Duke of Edinburgh's Award scheme to undertake carefully planned expeditions under progressively more **remote supervision**, providing they have been trained to do so. Before taking part in more independent activities, students should first demonstrate sufficient skill, experience and maturity under the supervision of a competent leader.

2.17.34   Once the leader is satisfied that the students have acquired the necessary skills and have the necessary confidence, physical ability and judgement, the withdrawal of direct supervision should be a gradual **four-stage process**, evolving through:

- accompanying the group
- shadowing the group
- checking regularly at agreed locations
- checking occasionally at agreed locations.

This reflects the direct, close, remote supervision model.

2.17.35   Adequate safeguards and progressive steps should be put in place by relevantly qualified and experienced staff before proceeding with activities under remote supervision. Staff should always consider apprehensions and the level of ability of individual students, and avoid putting undue pressure on individuals to progress when they do not feel ready.

2.17.36   Where remote supervision is considered, students need to:

- be clearly briefed
- be informed of potential hazards
- be left in no doubt about actions to take in the event of emergencies
- carry suitable emergency equipment to deal with foreseeable incidents
- be able to contact the leader if required.

2.17.37   If **external providers** contribute, with school staff, to the activity programme, roles and responsibilities should be identified and understood. Where schools engage a third party to deliver an activity, the duty of care is not delegated to that third party, but remains with the school. School staff have a duty to intervene where unsafe practice is observed or felt likely to occur. The employer remains liable for any negligent act by that third party in the delivery of their service or programme. Schools using an outside organisation to provide an activity must check they have appropriate safety standards and liability insurance. The Council for Learning Outside the Classroom (LOtC) awards the Learning Outside the Classroom Quality Badge to organisations who meet nationally recognised standards. Further guidance can be found at https://www.gov.uk/government/publications/health-and-safety-on-educational-visits/health-and-safety-on-educational-visits and information on the Quality Badge at www.lotc.org.uk

2.17.38   When external agents or **tour operators** are used, schools should follow their employers' requirements for engaging their services. Systems should be in place to ensure that tour operators:

- are reputable
- meet relevant statutory requirements, including financial bonding arrangements
- are able to fully satisfy the school's duty of care expectations.

Planning Checklist for Off-site Outdoor and Adventure Activities

Table 19: Planning checklist for off-site OAA

Long-term Planning Does It:	Medium-term Planning Does It:	Short-term Planning: Does It:

• meet employer's requirements with regard to OAA
• include consultation with the educational visits coordinator (EVC) where one exists
• allow sufficient time for necessary planning and coordination and, where appropriate, visit approval
• clarify necessary staff competence, availability (eg enforced staff-substitution arrangements) and staff:student ratios
• identify timescales covering important aspects of the itinerary, which might include:
  – a preliminary visit to the intended location
  – EVC clearance and submission of any necessary paperwork (eg risk assessment), as required by the employer
  – a detailed plan for the proposed trip, with timescales
  – written information to parents if it is an optional activity, including outline plan, consent forms, educational aims and a proposed programme of activities
  – expectations and codes of behaviour
  – times of meetings and information evenings if these are relevant to the event
  – any finance details and student costs
  – travel arrangements, including the management of breaks in the journey
  – any accommodation details with arrangements for mixed-gender groups
  – information concerning personal insurance and the limit of the school's liability
  – appropriate equipment lists
  – Disclosure and Barring Service (DBS) checks
  – designation of approved-adult status, where relevant
  – responsibilities and supervision arrangements for the duration of the trip
  – meal arrangements
	• establish a schedule for the supervision of students
	• provide for contingency arrangements in the event of accident, illness or inability to participate in the proposed programme
	• establish the necessary equipment requirements and ensure equipment is:
	  – in good condition
	  – fit for purpose
	  – correctly sized to fit the students involved
	• ensure students are emotionally prepared and physically fit for the proposed activity
	• take account of the weather forecast, and include contingency arrangements for any effects of this
	• identify workable accident-reporting procedures?
		• provide for flexibility on the day, taking into account variables such as weather, the presence of other groups and the disposition of the group in question
		• include ongoing consideration of:
		  – the educational aims of the event
		  – staff:student ratios and appropriate supervision arrangements for the group
		  – the capabilities, individual needs and physical state of students and staff
		  – the development of weather systems as the day progresses
		  – site-specific issues relating to the proposed venue
		  – transport logistics and travelling times
		• enable the adult in charge of the activity to:
		  – follow accepted current good practice in the conduct of the activity
		  – provide an appropriate level of challenge for the range of individuals involved
		  – ensure the group is adequately clothed and equipped
		  – ensure the group is adequately briefed on the plan for the day
		  – take into account the medical background of students and staff, and ensure prescribed medication, such as asthma inhalers, is accessible
		  – ensure accessories such as watches and jewellery are removed if they pose a danger or are liable to be damaged; long hair is tied back and spectacles secured if necessary
		  – check any equipment used is fit for purpose

– individual needs, such as diet, educational and medical information – an accurate register of participants and appropriate adult:student ratios – contingency arrangements for when adverse circumstances prevent the planned programme from taking place – anticipation of staff changes and their effects on continuity – agreed and workable emergency procedures – an effective communication system with the school – ensuring an appropriate level of challenge for participants with a progressive approach to skill acquisition • allow sufficient time for the submission of plans to the leadership team and, where appropriate, school governing body for approval?		– monitor and take account of changes in the physical and mental state of students during activities – carry out the plan, unless unforeseen circumstances dictate otherwise, so the group can be located in the event of an emergency – ensure emergency equipment is adequate and readily accessible – consider the experience and abilities of other members of staff, clearly define roles and responsibilities, and delegate only appropriate levels of supervision – consider communications systems and emergency procedures in the event of an accident – modify the activity as necessary to ensure safe participation?

Land-based Outdoor and Adventure Activities

Team building and problem solving

2.17.39   Problem-solving and team-building activities can develop trust, communication and leadership skills using simple equipment in safe, controlled environments.

2.17.40   Students are encouraged to think both logically and critically, as well as creatively, when problem solving. Staff experience and a dynamic approach to risk management during the activity are important to safety. Sensible precautions can reduce risk without stifling initiative, enterprise and excitement.

2.17.41   Some problem-solving activities can appear relatively hazard-free (eg "crossing an imaginary swamp using mats"), and students may not fully appreciate the real risks involved. Despite this, **participants should always be required to act in a safe manner and take responsibility for their own and others' well-being**.

2.17.42   Where activities may require working some distance above the ground, students may need personal protective equipment (PPE), such as helmets. This should be **supported by a systematic inspection regime**. Students' clothing and equipment for such activities should provide an acceptable level of protection by being fit for purpose.

2.17.43   Consideration should also be given to the nature and size of the equipment relative to the capabilities of the group and individual students concerned.

2.17.44   Students should be adequately **briefed** on the potential hazards of the activity, and the parameters within which they may act independently should be carefully defined. The hazards and consequences of overtly competitive activities should be fully considered.

2.17.45   If the activity involves **independent** work, staff should supervise from the "position of most usefulness" (eg 'where can I place myself to be of most benefit to the group?') to manage potential identified hazards, such as busy roads, entrances, exits and deep water.

2.17.46   Activities that involve students physically supporting each other should be carefully managed in terms of groupings, safe and effective technique, and time given for familiarisation and practice.

Orienteering

2.17.47   Staff leading the activity should always consider their operating remit. (This refers to working parameters and staff should work within the scope of their training and qualifications.)

2.17.48   Many schools establish introductory orienteering activities and short courses on the school site, and some expand these into the immediate locality.

2.17.49   Holders of British Orienteering's qualification Teaching Orienteering Part 1 or 2 (depending on location and level of delivery) and **competent** adults with experience of orienteering are both **competent** to deliver a basic introduction to orienteering in the school grounds, local parks or small areas of woodland with clear boundaries and observable paths.

2.17.50   Whether the leader is **competent** through the governing body of sport qualification or experience, British Orienteering guidance (www.britishorienteering.org.uk) should be adhered to, unless employer requirements differ from this.

2.17.51   Safe and appropriate route planning is an essential part of the risk management process.

2.17.52   **Clothing** should be appropriate for the prevailing weather conditions and type of orienteering course. Complete coverage of the arms and legs is strongly advised for orienteering in thick vegetation and woodland.

2.17.53   **Footwear** should be suitable for the course terrain and weather conditions. The leader should advise students on this.

2.17.54   All students should carry a whistle or other means of calling for help if orienteering in areas where they will be out of sight of the leader.

2.17.55   Students should be briefed with clear ground rules. All foreseeable hazards should be identified and brought to their attention.

2.17.56   A **call-back signal** and prearranged cut-off time should be communicated, agreed and understood by all participants. Escape instructions may be issued to enable students to retreat safely to a prearranged point.

2.17.57   Inexperienced students should take part in pairs or small groups and remain together.

Remote Supervision/Unaccompanied Activities

Remote supervision (as opposed to direct or close supervision) usually occurs when, as part of planned activities, a group works away from the supervising staff. Even though not physically present, staff remain fully responsible for the safe management of the young people. This is a reasonable practice based on a rigorous assessment of risk.

All participants (both students and staff) should be sufficiently prepared for the task/activity being undertaken and their performance regularly monitored when using remote supervision as a group management strategy.

2.17.58   If groups are to be remotely supervised, consideration should be given to:

- educational aims
- first aid provision
- the potential hazards associated with proposed routes
- the potential threat from other people
- emergency procedures in the event of injury or getting lost
- a realistic cut-off time
- the boundaries of the course.

2.17.59   Only experienced and relevantly trained students should take part in **night-time orienteering**, except on the most straightforward sites (eg school grounds or fully enclosed areas of limited size).

2.17.60   Procedures for locating students who become lost should be handled by the leader.

2.17.61   First aid kits must be available when working off site.

Traverse walls and bouldering

2.17.62   Low-level traverse and bouldering walls are becoming more common, particularly in primary schools. Adjustable holds are attached to a wall, enabling students to manoeuvre along the wall at very low heights. Low-level traversing and bouldering do not involve the use of ropes, and require a minimum level of leadership expertise while offering challenging situations to the students involved.

2.17.63   Traverse walls for beginners should incorporate low **holds** to enable less confident students to complete very low-level traverses. Other than tightening loose holds, any adjustments should only be undertaken by competent persons with route-setting skills.

2.17.64   Sufficient space should be provided so that climbers have the opportunity to look at the location of holds. This allows effective spotting to take place if required, and enables safe landings to be executed.

2.17.65   Students should take part in the risk assessment process before the activity begins, as this allows them to contribute to the agreed safety rules.

2.17.66   Consideration needs to be given to the control and supervision of all group members.

2.17.67   A range of guidelines on the management and use of climbing walls are available from the Association of British Climbing Walls (ABC).

Useful websites

ABC: www.abcwalls.co.uk
Mountain Training (skills and awards): www.mountain-training.org

Walking in lowland country

2.17.68   Venues should offer levels of educational, environmental and/or activity challenge appropriate to the abilities, confidence and experience of the group. Lowland areas could include walking in urban streets or country parks and fields.

2.17.69   **Staff competent** in the activity should carefully choose appropriate venues, be able to offer appropriate advice to participants, and plan routes, taking into account all variables, including their own level of competency and operating remit of the award held.

 For more information about the Mountain Training Lowland Leader Award, see http://goo.gl/CGHG56

2.17.70   **Planning** should include:

- weather conditions and appropriate responses
- suitable stops for rests
- an estimated time for completing the journey
- consideration of equipment needs
- a level of demand appropriate to the abilities and experience of the group
- possible hazards (eg road crossings) and how they might be managed
- emergency procedures that might need to be implemented.

2.17.71   To ensure their comfort, each **group member** should wear suitable clothing and carry suitable equipment. This will typically include:

- waterproof and windproof clothing
- food and drink
- appropriate spare clothing
- appropriate footwear.

2.17.72   In addition, the **group** should carry equipment to allow them to deal with emergencies. This will typically include:

- a first aid kit, which must be carried when off site
- a map and compass, where appropriate
- an emergency procedures aide-memoire
- a means of summoning external assistance.

2.17.73   The level of supervision should be appropriate for the group, as determined through the risk assessment process.

2.17.74   Low-level walking may be an appropriate context where groups can be **remotely supervised**.

Useful website

Mountain Training (skills and awards): www.mountain-training.org

Camping

2.17.75   There are various forms of camping, ranging from "standing camps", which involve the use of some permanent on-site facilities, to remote lightweight camping and backpacking expeditions, which demand greater levels of skill and knowledge. It is essential that potential hazards relating to camping sites and associated activities are identified at the planning stage.

2.17.76   When leading camping, whether in the school locality or hills, staff should be competent, with appropriate experience and training that qualifies them for the particular context.

2.17.77   All sites should be thoroughly **risk assessed** by an appropriately experienced person and any necessary control measures put in place.

2.17.78   If the party is to camp **near water**, group leaders should be familiar with issues relating to water safety.

2.17.79   Sufficient space should be left between tents to allow free movement and prevent the spread of fire.

2.17.80   A first camp should be held under controlled conditions, located near permanent shelter and close to vehicle access.

2.17.81   **Contingency plans** for alternative routes, venues or activities, in the event of bad weather, should be agreed at the planning stage.

2.17.82   Group leaders should ensure that students receive appropriate training in key aspects of camp craft, including effective pitching of tents for anticipated weather, the importance of hygiene, the safe packing and carrying of loads and a "minimum impact" approach to the environment.

2.17.83   Careful thought needs to be given to the training and supervision required for safe use of stoves, including:

- the type(s) of **stove** used
- safe placement of stoves
- consideration of the venue
- fuel storage
- safe refuelling, ie:
  - after the stove has cooled
  - in a ventilated area
  - when other nearby sources of ignition have been extinguished.

2.17.84   Students should be taught how to prepare and store food safely, and to clean utensils with consideration for the environment and hygiene.

Useful websites

Mountain Training (skills and awards): www.mountain-training.org
OEAP: www.oeap.info

Bushcraft/Forest Schools

2.17.85   Activities should be adapted to students' ability levels and educational needs, the weather and the context. Activities linked to the prescribed curriculum and personal and social development include hide and seek, shelter building, tool skills, lighting fires, building dens and environmental art.

2.17.86   A Forest School Level 3 Leader Training award (or equivalent) is advised as the standard for leading Forest School sessions. However, competent adults with some experience of Forest Schools may be able to deliver basic activities in the school grounds, local parks or small areas of woodland with clear boundaries and observable paths.

2.17.87   For all activities, consideration should be given to:

- educational aims
- the potential hazards associated with the environment and activities
- the potential threat from other people
- emergency procedures in the event of injury or getting lost.

2.17.88   Where Forest Schools take place outside school grounds, prior **permission** needs to be sought from the landowner, and the site must be risk assessed and prepared before use. Appropriate boundary setting is an essential part of the risk management process.

2.17.89   Clothing should be appropriate for the prevailing weather conditions and types of activities being undertaken. Complete coverage of the arms and legs is strongly advised for activities in thick vegetation and woodland.

2.17.90   Students should be briefed with clear ground rules. If the activities are planned to take place over a number of sessions, a progressive plan should be in place.

2.17.91   A briefing area is recommended as a focal point for starting and finishing activities.

2.17.92   Fire making and tool use are practised in Forest Schools in a traditional woodland manner and should be carefully introduced by demonstration and supervised throughout. Supervision and monitoring of tools and fires are essential.

2.17.93   Students should be encouraged to think about and assess their actions, and become aware of safety issues in order to manage risk.

2.17.94   First aid kits must be available for all off-site activities.

Useful websites

Bushcraft Specialist Interest Group: http://goo.gl/a035F6
Forest School Association: www.forestschoolassociation.org

Caving and mine exploration

2.17.95   Underground systems other than show caves and tourist mines present many of the challenges and adventure opportunities associated with climbing and water. These, along with darkness and confined spaces, make the underground experience uniquely challenging and exciting. Competent leaders should be used for all caving and mine activities.

Useful website

British Caving Association: www.british-caving.org.uk

Climbing and abseiling

Useful websites

British Mountaineering Council: www.thebmc.co.uk
Mountain Training: www.mountain-training.org
Mountaineering Council of Scotland: www.mcofs.org.uk
Mountaineering Ireland: www.mountaineering.ie
National Indoor Climbing Award Scheme: www.nicas.co.uk

Ropes courses

2.17.96   High- and low-level ropes courses have become very popular in recent years, both for recreational visits and as part of school adventure programmes.

2.17.97   New guidelines have been published to help providers to comply with EN 15567:2015 – the standard for the installation and operation of new and existing ropes courses. Staff should satisfy themselves that any centre visited complies with this standard.

2.17.98   Schools should comply with provider guidelines on groups' use of their facilities, while adhering to their own employer policy on higher risk activities.

2.17.99   It is very important that the guidance presented in HSE/AALA (2015) "UK Ropes Course Guide" (Guidance note 6.05), listed below, is understood by staff before visiting these centres.

Useful websites

HSE/AALA (2015) "UK Ropes Course Guide" (Guidance note 6.05): http://goo.gl/McJv3v
European Ropes Course Association: www.erca.uk

Cycling and mountain biking

2.17.100   Great care should be exercised when planning and organising cycling activities. Risk assessments should take into account the levels of technical difficulty, objective dangers, overall distance (including height gain and loss), escape routes and whether a leader with a mountain-biking qualification will be required (and available) to ensure acceptable margins of safety.

2.17.101   The competence of the group should be assessed before taking to the road or trail, and this assessment should take place in controlled conditions in a safe area. **Venues** should be chosen that take account of the fitness, ability and experience of the group.

2.17.102   A competent leader will cover basic techniques and hazard awareness as defined by the risk assessment. Additionally, they will normally include the following:

- weather effects
- fitness of bikes for purpose
- clothing and safety kit.

2.17.103   Cyclists should wear **clothing** and carry equipment suitable for the activity, venue and conditions. Suitable clothing will normally include:

- gloves
- properly fitted and sized helmet
- appropriate footwear – trainers are normally acceptable, but it should be remembered that riders can be susceptible to cold feet when wet
- long-sleeved top and full-length, close-fitting trousers
- waterproof/windproof top (in warm weather, it is usual to carry this in a rucksack; otherwise, riders may suffer from overheating).

2.17.104   It is wise to consider wearing some item of high-visibility clothing. During the day, fluorescent colours work best. The introduction of colour will make riders stand out on the road; bright green, yellow or orange colours are most effective.

2.17.105   Each **group** should carry equipment to deal with foreseeable emergencies, depending on the route and other variables.

2.17.106   The qualifications suggested for leaders of cycling sessions are outlined in the table below.

On/Off-road Cycling	
Suggested Qualifications Required	**Defined Areas**
British Cycling Ride Leader Award	On-road cycling
British Cycling Mountain Bike Leader Award at an appropriate level	Off-road Cycling

2.17.107   The British Cycling "Guidelines for Coaching Cycling" provide information on bike, helmet and clothing checks a British Cycling coach should perform prior to activities. This is a coaching-specific document as it is recommended that those delivering cycling activities should be appropriately trained.

2.17.108   British Cycling offers a "Cycling for Schools" workshop for people delivering sessions in a school environment, which covers these guidelines and gives delegates ideas on how to deliver fun, engaging and safe cycling activities.

Useful websites

British Cycling: www.britishcycling.org.uk
Cycling UK mountain-biking and cycling courses: http://goo.gl/3ihtlq
Scottish Cycling: https://goo.gl/xSJ14m

Horse riding and pony trekking

2.17.109 Horse riding and pony trekking are popular activities with many young people, and provide an excellent context, particularly for some students with special educational needs and disabilities (SEND). Schools should use only approved riding schools, trained horses and qualified staff when offering equestrian activities.

2.17.110 Horses and riders should be relevantly equipped in line with British Horse Society (BHS) standards and guidelines.

2.17.111 Staff **ratios** should reflect the:

- demands of the terrain
- needs of the group
- risk assessment requirements of the riding centre.

2.17.112 Clear, comprehensive and concise guidance from the centre's staff should be given to all responsible adults if they are to lead particular horses.

Useful websites

Association of British Riding Schools: www.abrs-info.org
BHS: www.bhs.org.uk
Riding for the Disabled: www.rda.org.uk

Skating

2.17.113 The advice in this section applies to ice, roller and in-line skating.

2.17.114 As part of preparation, a pre-visit inspection of the location by the leader is highly recommended. School staff should not assume that students have any prior experience of the activity.

2.17.115 At the planning stage, the focus should be on control measures to minimise the risk of injury:

- **New to skating – start with the basics:**
  - Learn to fall correctly and get up without assistance.
  - Learning to stop is as important as pushing and gliding. Never grab on to others to avoid falling. Understand that crashing into the surrounding barrier is unacceptable (specific to ice skating).
  - March before they glide – marching in place on the ice is widely used as a precursor to gain balance and feel comfortable standing still. This is an essential step before attempting to acquire the balance to glide on two feet (specific to ice skating).
- **Learning the basic skills:**
  - Someone new to ice skating will benefit from enrolling in a "Learn to Skate" series of group classes for beginners.
  - If the activity is an annual experience, rather than over a series of weeks, induction on arrival following boot allocation could be arranged with the centre staff. This will enable ice rink staff to go through the basics to encourage safe practice on the ice.

2.17.116 With regard to **appropriate clothing**, as long as students are in motion in the rink, they will stay warm. However, on stopping and being inactive for a few minutes, the body will get chilled. Layering is one way to help keep students' body temperature up.

2.17.117 The **skating surface** should be:

- even
- free from obstructions
- routinely maintained and regularly checked, including a pre-session inspection (consider making a preliminary visit to the venue to gather sufficient information to make an adequate assessment of the facilities in order to assist your planning).

2.17.118 For taught sessions, skating should be supervised by school staff, and a competent instructor should always be present. Leaders should have previous experience of skating at rinks and leading groups in similar environments. Where possible, it is advisable for beginners and advanced skaters to skate in separate groups.

2.17.119 For recreational skating, the terms and conditions of the particular commercial venue must be observed. The group should observe any local requirements for direction of skating. This is usually an anticlockwise direction, skating on the right and passing on the left.

2.17.120 Students should wear suitable **clothing** that provides adequate protection. Beginners should wear gloves. Helmets may be required in certain circumstances. Elbow and knee protection is advisable. Ice/roller boots should provide firm ankle support.

2.17.121 In-line skating is increasing in popularity, and guidance should be sought from the relevant local authority (LA) or employing organisation for its policies on skating in public areas and/or on highways.

Useful websites

British Artistic Roller Skating: www.british-roller-skating.org.uk
Federation of Artistic Roller Skating: www.fars.co.uk
National Ice Skating Association: www.iceskating.org.uk

Skiing and snowboarding

2.17.122 Skiing and snowboarding can encourage students to develop a wide range of physical skills and qualities, including general fitness, coordination, balance and strength. Foreign residential visits, as cultural experiences, also offer wide-ranging opportunities for personal and social development in challenging new environments.

2.17.123 The wearing of **ski helmets** has become compulsory in several countries. Employers may have their own policy regarding this. The Association for Physical Education (afPE) endorses the principle of wearing safety helmets when skiing.

Useful websites

British Association of Snowsport Instructors: www.basi.org.uk
OEAP guidance on overseas visits: http://goo.gl/E17oDV
OEAP Snowsport visits guidance: http://goo.gl/Y8gvZJ
Snowsport England: www.snowsportengland.org.uk
Snowsport Scotland: www.snowsportscotland.org
Snowsport Wales: www.snowsportwales.net

Triathlon

2.17.124 Triathlon (combining swimming, cycling and running) has grown in popularity in recent years. Students can be introduced to the activity through school events.

2.17.125 The British Triathlon website listed below provides clear rules and regulations to be followed during all three aspects of this event.

Useful websites

British Triathlon: www.britishtriathlon.org
HSE/AALA (2016) "Off-road Cycling Leader Qualifications" (Guidance note 6.12): http://goo.gl/Zfh2dm

Parkour and free running

2.17.126 Parkour, free running or art du deplacement is the primarily non-competitive physical discipline of training to move freely over and through any terrain using only the abilities of the body, principally through running, jumping, climbing and quadrupedal movement. All the terms are used interchangeably to ensure that an English-speaking audience understand the French term.

2.17.127 The sport aims to develop the functional strength and fitness, balance, spatial awareness, agility, coordination, precision, control and creative vision that are required to achieve the movement while at the same time aiming to build confidence, determination, self-discipline and self-reliance, and a responsibility for one's actions.

2.17.128 As a specialist, **higher risk activity**, teachers wishing to teach parkour during curriculum time or as an extracurricular activity are recommended to undertake the Parkour UK 1st4sport **Introductory** CPD Award in Teaching Parkour/Freerunning. This enables them to deliver the activity **indoors** using appropriate equipment and/or purpose-built equipment/facilities.

2.17.129 At the next level, the **Intermediate** CPD Award in Teaching Parkour/Freerunning includes information about delivering parkour indoors and **outdoors**, in curriculum and extracurricular time. This does not qualify teachers to teach or coach in an external or community setting.

2.17.130 Training awards are also available for teaching assistants and lunchtime supervisors to assist a teacher, and achieving and activator awards are available for students.

2.17.131 In cases where external coaches are used to deliver parkour as part of the school programme, schools should look for an individual to hold at least the Parkour UK 1st4sport Level 2 Parkour/Freerunning Coach qualification. In addition to this, they should be registered on Parkour UK's Parkour Professionals Register, which assures proof of occupational competence and insurances of £10million. It is also recommended that a DBS check and/or update service number is supplied.

2.17.132 In most cases where parkour is taught in schools, it may take place in school gyms or sports halls. It can be taught outdoors, dependent on the type of qualification that is held by the teacher/coach(es).

2.17.133 Existing indoor physical education equipment can be used, or purpose-built parkour equipment/facilities can be purchased from a number of suppliers. Equipment should comply with the relevant European Standard for parkour equipment, BS EN 16899:2016.

2.17.134 Students should wear suitable footwear and comfortable physical education kit.

2.17.135 In preparation for learning parkour movements, staff should ensure that students have been taught correct techniques for jumping and landing, rolling and some vaulting, and that they understand how these contribute to safe exercise practice.

Useful website

Parkour UK: www.parkour.uk

Useful websites

AALA: www.hse.gov.uk/aala
Adventuremark: www.adventuremark.co.uk
Association of Heads of Outdoor Education Centres: www.ahoec.org
British Activity Providers Association: www.thebapa.org.uk
British Mountaineering Council: www.thebmc.co.uk
Council for Learning Outside the Classroom: www.lotc.org.uk
eduFOCUS: www.edufocus.co.uk
(offers a managed online service called EVOLVE, which is specifically designed to enable the efficient processing of educational visit proposals)
Expedition Providers Association: www.expeditionprovidersassociation.co.uk
Foreign and Commonwealth Office: www.fco.gov.uk
Handsam: http://handsam.co.uk
(offers an online "School trip learning outside the curriculum organisation and management system" that aids the planning, administration and coordination of off-site visits)
HSE (2011) "School Trips and Outdoor Learning Activities – Tackling the health and safety myths": www.hse.gov.uk/services/education/school-trips.pdf
LOtC Quality Badge: www.lotcqualitybadge.org.uk
Mountain Training (skills and awards): www.mountain-training.org
OEAP: www.oeap.info

Outdoor and Residential Centres

2.17.136 Many schools use outdoor and residential centres to provide students with experience of the outdoors, and opportunities to work with specialist staff.

2.17.137 Centres offering activities that are subject to licensing under the **Adventure Activities Licensing Regulations 2004** must demonstrate to the licensing authority that they meet acceptable standards of safe practice in those activities. Accredited centres are issued with a unique licence number, which gives assurance that the provider is following sound safety management practice.

2.17.138 Centres that hold a current AALA licence are listed on the AALA website: www.hse.gov.uk/aala/index.htm

2.17.139 The AALA scheme does not cover OAA offered by voluntary associations to their members or by schools to their students, or provision for young people accompanied by their parents. However, its guidance on safety in the outdoors is appropriate to schools' provision.

2.17.140 While centres' specialist staff are responsible for technical aspects, school staff maintain overall duty of care for their students. Clarity of role and responsibility is essential.

2.17.141 Prior to booking at a centre, checks should be made by the school to confirm:

- the centre is appropriate for the students and planned learning outcomes
- the education credentials, staff competence and reputation of the centre are sound
- whether an AALA licence is held and, if so, what it covers
- fire and emergency procedures are satisfactory
- which facilities and services are offered
- whether sole use is possible or shared use with other groups will occur
- insurance arrangements are appropriate and acceptable
- who is responsible for what and when
- regular meetings with centre staff are scheduled to resolve issues and evaluate progress.

 KEY LEARNING: School staff maintain the duty of care – where school staff have concerns about any unreasonable or unnecessary risk, including the behaviour of the group affecting its safety, they should intervene, and measures should be taken to ensure the continued safety and well-being of the students.

Overseas outdoor and adventure activity expeditions

2.17.142 Challenging overseas expeditions are an area of growth in adventure activities, and present significant issues involving insurance, quality assurance of activities and providers, and communication with school.

2.17.143 When organising such educational visits, schools should establish good ongoing communication with providers, tour companies and the parents of those participating to ensure that all aspects of preparation and planning are understood, completed and understood by all. Visits abroad can have extra risks and require a higher level of risk assessment. See https://www.gov.uk/government/publications/health-and-safety-on-educational-visits/health-and-safety-on-educational-visits

Water-based Outdoor and Adventure Activities

2.17.144 Group leaders are strongly recommended to ensure at least one member of the party is trained in lifesaving and first aid. They should have practical experience of the waters in which the activity will take place.

2.17.145 An accurate weather forecast and knowledge of local water conditions (eg susceptibility of the venue to flooding, tide times, and the effects of wind on tide and sea states) should inform the risk assessment.

2.17.146   Students need to be adequately equipped and clothed for the prevailing weather conditions. Appropriate activity-specific footwear should be worn.

2.17.147   Where appropriate, students should be adequately dressed for immersion. In such cases, wetsuits, helmets and buoyancy aids should be worn, even in shallow water.

For information regarding the use of **wetsuits**, see the British Outdoor Swimming Association website: http://goo.gl/tsCG4y

For information regarding water safety, see the Royal Lifesaving Society website: http://goo.gl/OqI5Li

Angling

2.17.148   Angling is popular with many young people. It can provide opportunities to develop an awareness of environmental issues, address conservation matters and promote respect for other water users.

2.17.149   Angling can take place in many environments, including:

- fast-flowing rivers
- meandering streams
- ponds, lakes and reservoirs
- from the seashore
- on the open sea.

2.17.150   When fishing from a **boat**:

- it should be fit for purpose and appropriately licensed (see "Fishing vessel licence requirements": https://www.gov.uk/guidance/do-i-need-a-fishing-vessel-licence)
- it should not be overloaded, and there should be sufficient space
- there should be a method to retrieve anyone who falls overboard
- that is hired, the boat should conform to the requirements laid down by the Maritime and Coastguard Agency (MCA) and other relevant agencies
- staff members should be vigilant at all times.

2.17.151   Students need to be adequately equipped for the prevailing weather conditions. Appropriate footwear (usually wellingtons) should be worn.

Useful websites

Angling Trust – Angling Course for Schools and Teachers: www.anglingtrust.net
Environment Agency fishing information: https://goo.gl/SO9jsn
Marine Management Organisation (licenses, regulates and plans marine activities in the seas around England): https://www.gov.uk/government/organisations/marine-management-organisation
MCA: https://www.gov.uk/government/organisations/maritime-and-coastguard-agency

Canoeing, kayaking and paddle sports

2.17.152   Canoeing and kayaking take place in a wide variety of contexts and environments, from open boating to flat-water marathon racing and offshore sea kayaking.

2.17.153   Group leaders should hold a governing body of sport qualification that is appropriate and relevant for the specific craft and environment. Governing body of sport qualifications are divided into two areas – coaching/guiding/leading and personal skills.

2.17.154   Specialist information is available from the British Canoeing website.

Useful websites

British Canoeing: www.britishcanoeing.org.uk
Canoe Association of Northern Ireland: www.cani.org.uk
Canoe Wales: www.canoewales.com
Scottish Canoe Association: www.canoescotland.org

Combined water/rock activities

2.17.155 Combined water/rock activities are adventure activities where hazards associated with the rock environment may, at times, combine with those of the water environment. Some activities involve participants jumping into the sea from height, and seeing aspects of the coast that are not normally accessible. These include:

- gorge walking
- sea-level traversing and coasteering
- canyoning
- adventure swimming
- river running.

Useful websites

British Caving Association: www.british-caving.org.uk
British Mountaineering Council: www.thebmc.co.uk
HSE AALA (2015) "Coasteering" (Note 6.20): http://goo.gl/DbtboV
HSE/AALA (2016) "Combined Water Rock Activities – A Safety Checklist" (Guidance note 6.06): http://goo.gl/HSlozF
International Coasteering Federation: www.coasteering.org

Dinghy sailing

2.17.156 Sailing is a long-established adventure activity that has become a core component of outdoor education. It offers opportunities for developing physical skills, self-confidence and self-esteem, and is used frequently for team building, leadership and management development programmes.

Useful websites

National School Sailing Association: www.nssa.org.uk
Royal Yachting Association (RYA): www.rya.org.uk
RYA Northern Ireland: www.ryani.org.uk
RYA Scotland: www.ryascotland.org.uk
Welsh Yachting Association: www.welshsailing.org

Improvised rafting

2.17.157 Improvised rafting using barrels and planks as building materials is an outdoor activity that is often used for team building and management development programmes.

2.17.158 For improvised rafts, group leaders should be experienced in construction techniques. Rafts may distort when placed on the water, and care will be needed during design and construction to anticipate the effect of this.

2.17.159 Students should be made aware of the hazards involved in lifting and handling the construction materials, which should be fit for purpose. Clear **communications** will be necessary to ensure safe lifting and handling techniques are used. Construction and safety guidelines should form part of the initial briefing. At the construction stage, helmets may be useful.

2.17.160 A **capsize or break-up** of the improvised raft should be considered a real possibility, and an action plan established to rescue anyone in the water. On stretches of open water, an appropriately staffed **safety boat** may be required where individuals could have difficulty reaching the shore in the event of capsize. Where safety boats are to be used, competent and qualified staff following RYA guidelines should be deployed.

2.17.161 Students should be dressed adequately and safely for immersion – wetsuits, helmets and buoyancy aids should be worn, where possible, even in shallow water. The risk of entrapment needs to be anticipated and managed appropriately.

Useful website

OEAP: www.oeap.info
HSE/AALA (2015) "Improvised Raft Building" (Note 6.08): http://goo.gl/Lct70g
RYA: www.rya.org.uk

Rowing

2.17.162 Rowing has become very popular as an indoor activity at school. Schools need to carefully manage the transition between the indoor activity and outdoor activity, using appropriately qualified staff, or providers, and ensuring that students appreciate the additional safety aspects of the outdoor activity.

Useful website

British Rowing: www.britishrowing.org

Sub-aqua activities

2.17.163 Underwater exploration often begins with snorkelling, but the proficient use of scuba equipment significantly enhances levels of enjoyment and challenge, and opportunities for sub-aqua activities farther afield. Due to the specialist nature of sub-aqua activities, only recognised and fully **accredited teaching centres** should be used to deliver diving programmes.

Useful websites

British Sub-Aqua Club: www.bsac.org
Professional Association of Diving Instructors: www.padi.com

Surfing and windsurfing

2.17.164 Appropriate competent staff and accredited providers who adhere to activity standards should be used. Where instruction takes place in the sea, the instructors should ensure that students are taught about tidal activity, currents and staying safe in the surf.

Useful websites

Royal Life Saving Society UK: www.lifesavers.org.uk
RYA windsurfing: http://goo.gl/KE9b2n
Surf Life Saving Association of Great Britain: www.slsgb.org.uk
Surfing GB: www.surfgb.com

White-water rafting

2.17.165 White-water rafting involves paddling purpose-made inflatable rafts on white-water rivers or artificial courses. School staff should ensure that raft guides are appropriately qualified and are accredited providers adhering to the activity standards.

Useful website

British Canoeing: www.britishcanoeing.org.uk

Chapter 3:

Teaching and Learning about Safety in PESSPA

Promoting effective learning about safety through physical education, school sport and physical activity (PESSPA) is as important **as** the teacher creating and managing safe environments.

The Association for Physical Education (afPE) recognises good practice as "teaching safely" and "teaching safety", which can be achieved through effective teaching and management **and** effective student learning about safe practice.

This chapter focuses on the importance of learning about being safe and feeling safe, in and through the context of PESSPA.

Following the introduction, there are examples of objectives, outcomes and tasks provided to support students' learning in the areas listed below.

Introduction

The Importance of Learning about Safety

3.0.1   Learning about safety in PESSPA in a relevant, fun, progressive, inclusive and practical way is a key part of developing a healthy and active lifestyle.

3.0.2   Accidents account for a large number of preventable deaths and serious injuries in children and young people, and this may be partly due to their lack of knowledge and understanding of safe practice in PESSPA, particularly assessing and managing risk.

3.0.3   Promoting effective learning about safety will involve helping students not only to understand why this learning is important but also how it can directly and personally benefit their lives.

3.0.4   The Royal Society for the Prevention of Accidents (RoSPA); Personal, Social and Health Education (PSHE) Association; Institute of Health Promotion and Education (IHPE); and Ofsted are all in agreement about the importance of promoting effective learning about safety in schools.

National Guidance for Learning about Safety

3.0.5   Home country national curriculum statutory requirements and schools inspectorate documentation provide useful guidance to inform schools' planning for learning about safety.

3.0.6   In the **Northern Ireland Curriculum**, Personal Development and Mutual Understanding is a statutory curriculum component from Foundation Stage to Key Stage 4:

> *Personal Development and Mutual Understanding (PD&MU) focuses on encouraging each student to become personally, emotionally and socially effective. It also encourages them to lead healthy, safe and fulfilled lives and to become confident, independent and responsible citizens, making informed and responsible choices and decisions throughout their lives.*
>
> Council for the Curriculum, Examinations and Assessment (CCEA) (2019) "Key Stage 1 & 2 Personal Development and Mutual Understanding", https://ccea.org.uk/key-stages-1-2/curriculum/personal-development-mutual-understanding

3.0.7   In **Scotland**'s Curriculum for Excellence:

> *Health and well-being is organised into six areas: mental, emotional, social and physical well-being; planning for choices and changes; physical education, physical activity and sport; food and health; substance misuse; and relationships, sexual health and parenthood.*
>
> Education Scotland (2019) "Health and wellbeing in schools", https://www.gov.scot/policies/schools/wellbeing-in-schools/

3.0.8   In the **National Curriculum for Wales:**

> *Learners can be helped to maintain their emotional and physical health and well-being, sustain their growth and development, and know how to keep themselves safe.*
>
> Department for Children, Education and Lifelong Learning Skills (2008) "Personal and social education framework for 7 to 19-year-olds", https://hwb.gov.wales/curriculum-for-wales/health-and-well-being/

3.0.9   The **National Curriculum for England** (2014) refers to the importance of "water safety" and "using technology safely". However, the importance of learning about safety is implied in other parts of the statutory framework.

To access the National Curriculum for England, visit https://www.gov.uk/national-curriculum

3.0.10   Health and relationships education will be introduced as mandatory subjects in all state-funded schools from September 2020, alongside sex education in secondary schools. Physical health and mental well-being are included in the new health education curriculum, as well as the importance of physical activity. Many schools already teach PSHE that covers health and relationships, and these new requirements will ensure all schools do this.

For more information, see Department for Education (DfE) (2019) "Relationships education, relationships and sex education (RSE) and health education draft statutory guidance", https://www.gov.uk/government/publications/ relationships-education-relationships-and-sex-education-rse-and-health-education

3.0.11   **The Education Inspection Framework for England (2019)** has four judgement categories: Quality of Education; Behaviour and Attitudes; Personal Development; and Leadership and Management.

3.0.12   The personal development judgement includes:

- *developing students' confidence, resilience and knowledge so that they can keep themselves mentally healthy*
- *developing students' understanding of how to keep physically healthy, eat healthily and maintain an active lifestyle, including giving ample opportunities for students to be active during the school day and through extra-curricular activities.*

    Ofsted (2019) "Education inspection framework (EIF)", https://www.gov.uk/government/ publications/education-inspection-framework

For more information, see Ofsted (2019) "School inspection handbook", https://assets.publishing. service.gov.uk/government/uploads/system/uploads/attachment_data/file/828469/School_ inspection_handbook_-_section_5.pdf

Planning Effective Learning about Safety

3.0.13   This chapter supports the strategic planning of "teaching safety" in schools, and the sections that follow highlight aspects of learning that are relevant to PESSPA. Staff can select and prioritise exemplar learning objectives and outcomes that are relevant to the needs and stages of development of their students.

3.0.14   Learning about how to be safe and healthy is most effective when there is a whole-school curriculum approach. Physical education, the sciences, food technology, citizenship and PSHE can all contribute to students' understanding of this important area of learning.

3.0.15   Staff will always be the responsible "safety managers", but this is a role that does not require them to always be the one making the assessments, devising appropriate management procedures and evaluating their effect. Students learn more effectively when they are motivated, involved, engaged, empowered and trusted. Staff selecting appropriate objectives for the age, ability and previous experience of students will enable them to acquire and develop an awareness of safe-practice principles, to use and apply that awareness, and evaluate and review what is safe and what may be unsafe.

3.0.16   An appropriate response to instructions does not demonstrate that learning has occurred at a deep level. However, students who are questioning, observing, evaluating, taking responsibility for organisation and development, and creating situations where safe-practice principles need to be applied in new contexts are more than likely demonstrating that it has.

3.0.17   Achievement is the result of progressively developing responsibility and providing experiences that appropriately challenge students without placing them at risk of foreseeable harm.

3.0.18   Learning through activity is the premise behind this chapter and contexts are given where it is thought knowledge can best be embedded. Exemplar learning tasks are detailed, together with links to other sources of information and resources. **It is not a scheme of work in any form but has been written to offer a stimulus for further thought. Staff can decide which objectives and outcomes are the most relevant and appropriate for their students, and how to integrate and progress this learning within and beyond PESSPA.**

It is important that learning about safety is planned, progressed and assessed in the same way as other aspects of curriculum learning and that students' prior knowledge is taken into consideration.

For all sessions, it is advised that students wear appropriate clothing and footwear for all activities listed in this chapter. In addition, warming up and cooling down should be standard practice in all sessions. Without an adequate warm-up, muscle tissue injuries may occur.

Section 1: Learning about Safe Exercise Practice

3.1.1   Guidance from the Office of the Chief Medical Officer (CMO) in September 2019 suggests that children and young people (5–18) should take part in moderate-to-vigorous intensity physical activity for an average of at least 60 minutes per day, and engage in a variety of types and intensities of physical activity across the week to develop movement skills, **muscular fitness and bone strength**. Because the CMO's 2011 recommendations on muscle strength did not achieve the recognition they merited, the 2019 report underlines the importance of regular strength and balance activities for all ages.

 To access the "UK Chief Medical Officers' Physical Activity Guidelines" (2019), visit https://assets. publishing.service.gov.uk/government/uploads/system/uploads/attachment_data/file/829841/uk-chief-medical-officers-physical-activity-guidelines.pdf

3.1.2   The first section of this chapter, exemplifying learning objectives and outcomes, focuses on children and young people learning about **safe exercise practice in PESSPA**. The material has been selected to help improve students' **muscular strength and joint flexibility** safely through gymnastics. A high quality curriculum gymnastics programme will not only comprise the development of gymnastic skills and compositional work but also the teaching of safe exercise practice to prevent injury.

3.1.3   Muscle-strengthening activities are important in physical activity and daily life for safety and comfort; for example, lifting heavy objects, standing/balancing on a bus, jumping to reach something, and exiting a swimming pool hands first. Such movements generally require working against a stronger form of resistance. Through learning and practising a wide range of muscle-strengthening activities, children and young people can be helped to understand the importance of working and developing different muscle groups.

3.1.4   Because of their weaker bones and lower mechanical efficiency, children should not perform adult versions of muscle-strengthening activities. Sit-ups, press-ups and circuit training activities performed at speed (eg "How many can you do in 60 seconds?") are inappropriate.

3.1.5   Early Years Foundation Stage (EYFS) and Key Stage (KS) 1 children engaging in hanging and swinging activities, in addition to taking weight on their hands as in bunny jumps, will develop their upper-body muscular strength. Towards the end of KS2, children can benefit from performing simple, low-level strength exercises that involve working against body weight.

3.1.6   Taking part in a high quality gymnastic programme will not only encourage healthy muscular development but also healthy bone growth. Climbing frames and associated linking equipment are essential pieces of gymnastic apparatus for the 21st century child. Growing up in a world of technological devices will strengthen young people's fingers and thumbs but will do little for their back muscles and bones.

3.1.7   While children are growing, bone-strengthening activities will promote healthy bones and reduce risks associated with weak bones, such as sprains or breaks. On a daily basis, children will walk and run much more than they will turn upside down or improve their core strength. It is therefore important to ensure the physical education programme incorporates opportunities for students to take weight on their hands and other parts of the body, other than feet, and to hang, swing and climb on a regular basis. A rich and varied high quality gymnastic programme will contribute to strengthening the body, particularly the upper body, and improve posture.

3.1.8   Students should learn about the principles of safe exercise so that they are able to take part in PESSPA activities both at school and in the community with increasing independence and confidence, and without personal physical injury either in the short or long term.

Learning Objective 1

3.1.9   **Students are learning to take responsibility for developing and maintaining control of their body.**

3.1.10   Students will:

- show increasing "control" when copying and performing simple PESSPA activities/exercises
- talk about what "control" means (ie movements that are "stoppable", not flinging)
- show how a range of simple exercises/activities can be performed with control.

Suggested learning tasks

3.1.11   Students take part in simple movement tasks to help them understand what "control" means:

- Draw big circles with the arms and other body parts and stop on command.

3.1.12   Provide students with a range of alternative exercises, where the body can stop in control on command, to accommodate individual differences in terms of range of motion about joints:

- Travel different ways on the feet, use the whole space and stop on command.

Students are asked

Q: Why is it important to learn to control our body when we are moving?
A: To keep our bodies safe and not get hurt.

3.1.13   Working with a partner, students travel on their feet towards a person some distance away whose back is turned to them. Whenever this person turns around, all students must freeze. If the person sees a student move or wobble, that student returns to the starting line.

Q: How can we stop in control when travelling fast on our feet?
A: Stopping with feet apart will help the body balance; the basic principle for stopping quickly is to take a long stride and lower the body.

3.1.14   Practise bunny jumping with control both on the floor and over benches.

3.1.15   Provide students with appropriate teaching points and clear practical demonstrations that reinforce looking at the hands when the body is upside down.

3.1.16   Encourage students to evaluate the use of control in their own and others' technique when taking their body weight on their hands and running and stopping.

Learning Objective 2

3.1.17   **Students are learning about muscles and joints, and how to exercise them safely.**

3.1.18   Students will:

- describe how muscles can squeeze and relax
- describe which joints are being used
- show what good posture means when sitting and standing.

Suggested learning tasks

3.1.19   Students practise copying simple exercises when warming up, and distinguish between squeezing and relaxing muscles.

3.1.20   Students take part in simple movement tasks when warming up to help them name the joints and decide how they move; for example:

- "Show me how your elbows move."
- "Show me how your knees move."
- "Show me how your shoulders move."
- "Show me how your spine moves."

3.1.21   Students practise moving in physical education lessons, squeezing muscles tight where appropriate (eg as in stretching the legs and arms) and develop a practical understanding of how to demonstrate the teaching points associated with correct joint alignment, particularly in developing good posture.

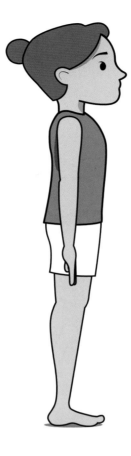

Students are asked

Q: What does standing with good posture mean, and can you show me?
A: Good posture involves correct:
- **knee alignment (feet pointing forward, knees facing forward, knees straight but not locked out)**
- **spine alignment (pull tummy through to backbone, stand/sit tall, slightly squeeze between shoulders).**

Q: Why is it important to keep our backs straight and tall when sitting, standing and travelling on our feet in physical education lessons?
A: It helps us keep good posture and our backs/spine safe.

3.1.22   Students observe and give feedback about correct lifting and lowering of gymnastic equipment, and learn why it is important to lift and lower with good posture.

Q: Why is it important to bend our knees and keep our back straight when we lift and lower portable items of gymnastic apparatus?
A: We might injure our back if we bend it when lowering something heavy. We should keep our back straight and let our legs do the work by bending and straightening.

Learning Objective 3

3.1.23 **Students are learning to take responsibility for maximising the benefits and minimising the risks of high impact activities.**

3.1.24 Students will:
- distinguish between activities in which the whole body leaves the floor and activities in which the whole body does not leave the floor (eg jumping and non-jumping activities)
- show correct jumping and landing technique
- describe the benefits of high impact (jumping) activities (eg strengthen bones and heart).

Staff health and safety knowledge point on high impact activity

3.1.25 High impact activities involve a large amount of force against the floor (eg landing from jumping, springing, leaping activities). Injuries such as shin splints, stress fractures and joint (including back) problems may occur if high impact activities are performed frequently and for long durations.

3.1.26 High impact activities performed with safe technique have many health benefits, particularly in terms of increasing bone strength and developing cardiovascular fitness.

Suggested learning tasks

3.1.27 Students can skip, march, walk and perform jumping jacks.

Students are asked

Q: Which of these activities involves your whole body leaving the floor?
A: Jumping jacks.

265

3.1.28   Students learn how to **land** with safe technique and understand what 'high impact' means.

3.1.29   Success criteria for landing are knees bent, back straight, looking forward with head up, keeping knees in line with toes, using arms to balance, and ball/heel action with feet.

3.1.30   Students learn how to **jump and land** with safe technique and understand what "high impact" means.

3.1.31   Success criteria for jumping are arms back and knees bent at take-off, students looking at their fingertips as they swing their arms into the air and stretch their feet as they push and take off.

Students are asked

3.1.32   With a partner, students evaluate their own and others' jumping and landing technique.

Q: Why does the body need to land in control following jumping activities?
A: There is a large amount of force against the floor so the knees must bend to absorb the impact.

Learning Objective 4

3.1.33 **Students are learning to take increasing responsibility for assessing and reducing risk associated with a range of factors that can impact on their safe participation in PESSPA activities.**

3.1.34 Students will:

- describe what might make PESSPA activities less safe for them (eg being really thirsty and playing in the sun with no hat or sun cream on).

Suggested learning tasks

3.1.35 Students explore safety issues associated with being in hot sunshine through practical physical education lessons.

Students are asked

Q: If you are active outside on a hot and sunny day, what should you do?
A: Put sun cream on and wear a hat.

3.1.36 Students explore safety issues associated with dehydration, being unwell and extreme weather conditions through practical physical education lessons.

Students are asked

Q: If you are thirsty, what should you do?
A: Hydrate yourself by drinking water.

Learning Objective 5

3.1.37 **Students are learning to take increasing responsibility for developing and maintaining appropriate use of control in their own and others' exercise technique.**

3.1.38 Students will:

- make increasingly accurate judgements about the extent to which control is demonstrated in their own and others' exercise technique
- explain the importance for their health and safety of performing exercises/activities with control
- explain the possible risks associated with performing exercises/activities without appropriate use of control.

Suggested learning tasks

3.1.39 Students take part in gymnastic lessons using controlled movements both in the warm-up and main part of each lesson.

Students are asked

Q: Why is it important to use controlled movements in gymnastics?
A: It reduces the stress on ligaments and tendons – frequent/long-term stress on these can result in muscle tears and/or lead to joint problems.

3.1.40   Students observe, evaluate and give feedback about appropriate use of control in their own and others' technique.

3.1.41   Students conduct simple risk assessments of specific gymnastic actions in terms of whether they can be performed with appropriate use of control.

Learning Objective 6

3.1.42   **Students are learning to take increasing responsibility for developing and maintaining correct joint alignment in their own and others' exercise technique.**

3.1.43   Students will:

- explain what joint alignment means (ie moving joints in ways in which they are supposed to move – anatomically correct ways)
- show how the major joints (eg knee, spine) can be moved with correct alignment
- recognise when joints are being hyperextended (locked out) or hyperflexed (fully bent)
- explain the possible risks of hyperextending or hyperflexing joints, particularly when weight bearing or working against resistance (ie stress on ligaments, which can lead to joint problems or poor alignment in other joints)
- make increasingly accurate judgements about the extent to which correct joint alignment is demonstrated in their own and others' technique.

Staff health and safety knowledge point on correct joint alignment

3.1.44   Correct joint alignment is about moving or placing joints in anatomically correct ways (ie as they are designed to work).

3.1.45   Repetitive and/or forced hyperextension (locking out) of joints (eg pressing knees back when standing, locking elbows out when taking weight on hands, extreme/forced arching of the spine or neck) should be discouraged.

3.1.46   Hyperflexion (excessive bending) of joints when performing exercises (eg landing in a deep knee bend from a jump, straight-leg toe touches, forcing chin to chest in a shoulder stand/backward roll) should be discouraged.

Suggested learning tasks

3.1.47   Students develop a practical understanding of joint alignment to keep them safe through learning gymnastic skills and compositional work.

Students are asked

Q: What does correct joint alignment mean?
A: Bend knees (no less than 90 degrees) and keep them in line with toes on landing from a jump and when running or jogging. This will reduce stress on ligaments – frequent/long-term stress on ligaments can lead to joint problems.

3.1.48   Students demonstrate good posture throughout the gymnastic unit of work and know the teaching points associated with correct joint alignment.

3.1.49   Students conduct simple risk assessments of specific exercises or activities in terms of whether they can be performed with correct joint alignment.

3.1.50   Students evaluate correct joint alignment in their own and others' technique.

Learning Objective 7

3.1.51 **Students are learning to take increasing responsibility for maximising the benefits and minimising the risks of high impact activities in their own and others' practice.**

3.1.52   Students will:

- explain how to perform high impact activities with safe technique
- describe the health benefits of performing high impact activities in control (increasing bone strength and developing cardiovascular fitness)
- know the risks associated with performing these activities out of control (eg possible damage to joints and bones)
- describe where mats need to be placed when jumping and landing in gymnastic lessons
- know and understand the success criteria for safe jumping and landing with good technique.

Staff health and safety knowledge point on high impact activity

3.1.53   See **Sections 3.1.17 and 3.1.18**.

Suggested learning tasks

3.1.54   Students perform correct jumping and landing technique throughout their gymnastic lessons.

Students are asked

Q: What are the risks associated with jumping and landing incorrectly?
A: Stress is placed on joints and bones, which can cause injury.

3.1.55   Students observe, evaluate and provide feedback on their partners' jumping and landing technique when jumping from high flat surfaces.

Q: What are the success criteria for safe landings from heights?
A: Knees bent, back straight, looking forward with head up, keeping knees in line with toes, using arms to balance, ball/heel action with feet.

Q: Why and where is it important to place mats when jumping and landing takes place in gymnastic lessons?
A: See Chapter 2, Section 9.

Learning Objective 8

3.1.56 **Students are learning to take increasing responsibility for assessing and reducing risks associated with a range of other factors that can impact on their safe participation in PESSPA activities.**

3.1.57 Students will:

- suggest appropriate action they can take to keep safe in PESSPA situations if they are suffering from mental or physical tiredness
- describe the signs and symptoms of dehydration, and explain how this might impact on their safety in PESSPA situations
- explain how to hydrate appropriately before, during and after participation in PESSPA activities/ sessions.

Suggested learning tasks

3.1.58 Through taking part in physical education lessons, students discuss how tiredness can impact on their safety and performance.

Students are asked

Q: How might tiredness impact on safety in PESSPA situations?
A: The body could get injured more easily.

Q: What should you do if the body feels tired?
A: Stop exercising and rest.

Learning Objective 9

3.1.59 **Students are learning to develop their understanding of safe exercise practice.**

3.1.60 Students will:

- perform physical activities with safe and effective technique
- demonstrate their understanding of back care
- evaluate effective techniques for warming up and cooling down
- select and safely perform each component of a warm-up and cool-down.

Suggested learning tasks

3.1.61 In groups, students design a safe exercise routine that shows control during the warm-up. They demonstrate awareness of keeping legs bent in sit-ups, avoiding exercises where the body bounces during stretching, and dangerous flinging movements where the body is out of control.

3.1.62 In groups, students design a safe exercise routine that shows control during the cool-down.

3.1.63 Students practise their understanding of back care by lifting, carrying and placing equipment with good posture.

3.1.64 Students prepare a practical presentation explaining the value of preparing for and recovering from a specific activity.

3.1.65 Students evaluate these practical presentations that explain the value of preparing for and recovering from a specific activity.

Learning Objective 10

3.1.66   **Students are learning to minimise the risks of high impact activities in their own and others' practice.**

3.1.67   Students will:

- analyse and make increasingly accurate judgements about the extent to which correct jumping and landing technique is demonstrated in their own and others' performance
- analyse and make increasingly accurate judgements about the extent to which the risks associated with high impact activities have been minimised.

Suggested learning tasks

3.1.68   Students practise, apply and improve safe and effective take-off and landing technique in gymnastic lessons.

3.1.69   Students explore and discuss the health benefits and safety risks associated with high impact activities.

3.1.70   Students observe, evaluate and give feedback on their own and others' technique when performing jumping and landing activities.

Learning Objective 11

3.1.71   **Students are learning to reduce risk associated with factors that can impact on their safe participation in PESSPA activities.**

3.1.72   Students will:

- explain how to hydrate appropriately before, during and after participation in PESSPA activities/sessions
- explain how common medical conditions (eg asthma, diabetes) might impact on the safety of individuals in PESSPA situations
- describe the signs and symptoms of common illnesses such as coughs, colds and tummy bugs
- suggest appropriate advice about participating in PESSPA activities/sessions with coughs, colds and tummy bugs
- describe the risks of different weather conditions (eg heat, cold, dampness) when taking part in PESSPA activities/sessions (eg heatstroke, sunburn, dehydration, hypothermia)
- suggest appropriate advice for avoiding such risks.

Suggested learning tasks

Q: Can you name a number of factors that can impact on safe participation in PESSPA activities?
A: Dehydration, common medical conditions and illnesses (eg asthma, diabetes, coughs, colds, tummy bugs), extreme weather conditions.

3.1.73   Students prepare a practical presentation explaining how to assess and reduce the risks associated with a range of factors that can impact on their safe participation in PESSPA activities.

3.1.74   Students evaluate these practical presentations that explain how to assess and reduce the risks associated with the factors identified that can impact on their safety and performance when taking part in PESSPA activities/sessions.

Section 2: Learning about Safety Rules and Procedures

Learning Objective 12

3.2.1   **Students are learning to remember and adhere to simple safety rules and practices.**

3.2.2   Students will:

- suggest kit and footwear that are appropriate for reducing risk in physical education, school sport and physical activity (PESSPA)
- explain the importance of removing jewellery before active participation
- act appropriately when given simple verbal instructions
- accurately recall simple verbal instructions
- describe what might happen if they do not listen to or cannot remember instructions, or do not know what the instructions mean.

Suggested learning tasks

3.2.3   Students learn how to check (under the guidance of PESSPA staff) that their footwear and kit are appropriate, jewellery is removed and hair is tied back for physical education lessons.

3.2.4   Students participate in very simple PESSPA activities that help them, for example, learn how to:

- listen to and carry out instructions
- collect equipment in an orderly manner and only when asked to do so
- stop promptly when asked
- stay inside the boundaries set
- be aware of what is happening around them
- avoid collisions with others.

3.2.5   Students consider what might happen if they do not listen carefully, cannot remember the instructions or do not know what the instructions mean.

Students are asked

> **Q: Why do we change for physical education?**
> **A: To be able to move well, for hygiene reasons, to help control body temperature and avoid clothing interfering with movement.**

3.2.6   When the students are changed and back in the classroom, collate a list of rules on a flip chart and hang this in the classroom to refer to, if needed, during the term.

Learning Objective 13

3.2.7   **Students are learning to take increasing responsibility for checking that their personal space is safe for activity.**

3.2.8   Students will:

- find a space to sit or stand in when requested
- show that they know the boundaries of their activity space
- describe what hazards might make their activity space unsafe
- explain appropriate action they could take if they spot hazards in their activity space.

Suggested learning tasks

3.2.9 Students familiarise themselves with the space they are working in by marking the perimeter with marker spots, lines or cones.

3.2.10 Students are led through a series of activities that require them to travel and/or place themselves around the edges, inside and outside of their activity space.

3.2.11 Students make simple safety checks of their activity space. Is the floor/ground slippery? Are there any sharp or gritty objects on the ground, especially if working in bare feet? Is there anything that might cause tripping, falling or collisions? Are there too many people to work safely in the space?

Students are asked

Q: What hazards might make the activity space unsafe?
A: Leaves on a hard playing surface may cause slipping. There could be food from dinnertime or staple-gun pins from the display boards on the hall floor.

Learning Objective 14

3.2.12 **Students are learning to take increasing responsibility for others' safety by acting responsibly towards their peers.**

3.2.13 Students will:

- identify/describe simple ways in which they can show "good" or "positive" behaviour towards their peers in PESSPA activities
- distinguish between positive and negative behaviour towards their peers in PESSPA situations
- describe PESSPA situations in which it is particularly important to respond positively and responsibly to their peers
- provide appropriate examples of how good or positive behaviour towards others in PESSPA activities/situations can keep them safe.

Suggested learning tasks

3.2.14 Students learn how to collect and share equipment, and take turns when participating in simple PESSPA activities.

3.2.15 Students practise staying inside the boundaries set and stopping promptly on command.

3.2.16 Students adopt good posture when moving and can use space sensibly, avoiding collisions when moving around each other.

3.2.17 Students discuss how good or positive behaviour can benefit their own and others' safety.

Students are asked

Q: What does it mean to behave well in PESSPA situations?
A: Concentrating, listening, being responsible, being sensible, being considerate, being positive, being patient and being careful.

Learning Objective 15

3.2.18   **Students are learning to take increasing responsibility for ensuring behaviour, kit, footwear, personal effects (jewellery, hair, adornments) and personal protective equipment (PPE) meet the health and safety expectations of the PESSPA activity/situation.**

3.2.19   Students will:

- demonstrate and explain how to check and maintain PESSPA footwear effectively
- explain why it is important to tie the laces of PESSPA footwear
- explain the importance of removing jewellery and other adornments before active participation
- explain why any exception to the "no jewellery or adornments" rule must always be sanctioned by PESSPA staff
- make accurate judgements about whether items of PPE offer protection.

Suggested learning tasks

3.2.20   Students discuss the risks of wearing jewellery and adornments, chewing gum and not tying long hair back when taking part in PESSPA activities.

3.2.21   Students discuss why any exception to the "no jewellery or adornments" rule needs to be sanctioned by a member of staff.

3.2.22   Students make accurate, simple checks (under the guidance of PESSPA staff) of their PPE for specific PESSPA activities/situations.

3.2.23   Students make judgements about whether items of PPE offer protection, and check their decisions with PESSPA staff.

Students are asked

Q: What are the risks of wearing jewellery when taking part in PESSPA activities?
A: There could be damage to parts of the wearer's body and possible injury to others.

Q: What are the risks of not using appropriate PPE for specific PESSPA activities?
A: Damage to jaw and teeth (mouth guard), head/brain injury (helmet).

Learning Objective 16

3.2.24 **Students are learning to take increasing responsibility for working safely.**

3.2.25 Students will:

- explain the need for safety rules and practices
- recognise and respond appropriately to potential hazards within and around their activity space
- make appropriate and effective safety checks on their activity space
- describe appropriate precautions for a range of familiar PESSPA activities/situations (eg looking before throwing, kicking or hitting in an activity space)
- make appropriate judgements about when it is safe to throw, kick or hit in specific PESSPA environments/situations
- explain how to check for safety before moving into an activity space
- explain what is meant by "acting responsibly" towards others
- suggest appropriate teaching points for PESSPA activities in which they are taking some responsibility for others' safety.

Suggested learning tasks

3.2.26 Students are given increasing responsibility (with appropriate supervision) for checking that the areas to be used for specific PESSPA activities/sessions have been checked for hazards.

3.2.27 Students take part in practical "games" and activities that require them to look up and show good awareness of their environment and others when running, skipping or walking (eg tag games, dance/gymnastic warm-ups, keeping possession/control of a ball).

3.2.28 Students suggest and discuss safety rules for using specific PESSPA equipment (eg rackets, bats, balls) when working with others in a specific PESSPA environment/situation.

3.2.29 Students discuss what "acting responsibly" towards others means in PESSPA situations (ie making independent decisions that contribute to their own and others' safety).

3.2.30 Students select words or phrases (from those that describe behaviour) that are associated with keeping them safe in PESSPA situations, and explain and discuss the reasons for their choices (eg concentrating, listening, being responsible, being sensible, being considerate, being positive, being patient, being careful).

3.2.31 Students discuss appropriate standards of behaviour for new and unfamiliar PESSPA activities/situations that will affect their own and others' safety.

Students are asked

Q: What does it mean to concentrate? What helps you concentrate well in PESSPA situations?

Q: How can your own behaviour impact positively and negatively on the concentration of others?

Q: Can you identify PESSPA activities/situations that require concentration in order to maintain safety?

Q: What should you do when listening to instructions?

A: Make eye contact and listen carefully so you can accurately recall what has been said.

Learning Objective 17

3.2.32   **Students are learning to analyse the impact of their behaviour on meeting health and safety expectations in PESSPA activities/situations.**

3.2.33   Students will:

- demonstrate their understanding of safe exercise practices (eg tying long hair back and removing jewellery to avoid injury, adopting good posture and demonstrating their concern for back care)
- explain the hygiene implications of sharing PPE, and identify when sharing is not advisable
- make accurate suggestions about what PPE is appropriate for a particular PESSPA activity/situation and when it should be used
- explain why it is important to replace PPE after damage or normal wear and tear.

Suggested learning tasks

3.2.34   Students apply their safe-practice knowledge about not wearing jewellery or adornments.

3.2.35   Students discuss the risks of not using appropriate PPE for specific PESSPA activities.

3.2.36   Students make their own judgements about whether an item of PPE offers protection and fits appropriately.

3.2.37   Students discuss why it is important to know that appropriate PPE reduces, but cannot eliminate, the possibility of injury in PESSPA activities/situations.

Learning Objective 18

3.2.38   **Students are learning to take increasing responsibility for others' safety.**

3.2.39   Students will:

- explain why responding positively and responsibly to their peers can minimise risk in PESSPA activities/situations
- explain why it is important to respect the fact that some peers may feel less confident about the same PESSPA task
- suggest appropriate ways of supporting peers who feel less confident about a PESSPA task
- explain the safety implications of putting peers under pressure to attempt tasks that they do not feel sufficiently confident to try.

Suggested learning tasks

3.2.40   Students participate in practical PESSPA activities/situations that involve them learning how to take "real" responsibility for others' safety (eg performing pairs balances in gymnastics, performing contact lifts in dance, learning to perform a scrummage in rugby, "spotting" in trampolining and supporting in gymnastics).

3.2.41   Students discuss why it is important not to put peers under pressure to attempt tasks that they do not feel sufficiently confident to try.

Section 3: Learning about Safe Warming Up and Cooling Down

Learning Objective 19

3.3.1   **Students are learning that physical activity starts with a gentle warm-up and finishes with a calming cool-down.**

3.3.2   Students will:

- copy simple warm-up/cool-down actions and whole-body stretches
- perform activities that move their joints
- perform activities that gradually raise their body temperature, breathing and heart rate
- perform activities that stretch their muscles
- perform activities that cool and calm the body down.

Suggested learning tasks

3.3.3   Students copy very simple activities that move their joints (eg shoulder/arm circles, shoulder shrugs, giant steps, touching the floor) following demonstrations by PESSPA staff.

3.3.4   Students copy very simple gross motor activities that gradually raise body temperature, breathing and heart rate (eg stepping, jogging, skipping, hopping, follow-my-leader activities) demonstrated by PESSPA staff.

3.3.5   Students copy static whole-body stretches (eg stretching wide and tall while lying and standing, curling up small), held for approximately six seconds, as demonstrated by PESSPA staff.

3.3.6   Students learn to use warm-up/cool-down exercises that are related to the specific activities of the lesson.

3.3.7   Students copy activities that gradually lower their pulse and heart rate (eg static whole-body stretches held for up to 10 seconds) as demonstrated by PESSPA staff.

Students are asked

> **Q: What do we do at the beginning of a physical education lesson to prepare for energetic activity?**
> A: Warm-up.

> **Q: What do we do at the end of a physical education lesson to recover from being energetic?**
> A: Cool-down.

277

Learning Objective 20

3.3.8   **Students are learning to recognise differences in how they feel before and after warming-up.**

3.3.9   Students will:

- recognise and describe the effects of warm-up activities on their temperature, joints and muscles
- perform warm-up activities that make their heart pump faster, make them feel and look hotter, and increase their breathing rate
- describe how warming-up makes them feel.

Suggested learning tasks

3.3.10   Students take part in activities that move their joints, make them warmer and stretch their muscles.

Students are asked

Q: How do you feel before we warm-up?

Q: How should a warm-up make you feel?

Q: Can you show some warm-up activities that are appropriate?

Q: Can you perform activities that make your heart pump faster?

Learning Objective 21

3.3.11   **Students are learning to understand the purposes of warming-up and cooling-down.**

3.3.12   Students will:

- perform simple warm-up activities
- perform simple cool-down activities
- describe the effects of warm-ups and cool-downs on the body
- explain the purposes of warm-ups and cool-downs.

Suggested learning tasks

3.3.13   Students copy and perform simple warm-up activities that:

- loosen the joints (mobiliser)
- gradually increase the heart rate (pulse-raiser)
- stretch the muscles (flexibility).

3.3.14   Taking their lead from PESSPA staff, students perform simple cool-down activities that make them cooler, keep them moving gently, slow down their breathing and heart rate, stretch their muscles and calm them down.

3.3.15   Students discuss the purposes of warming-up before PESSPA (ie preventing injury, preparing the body safely and gradually for activity, "waking up" the brain) and cooling-down afterwards (ie preventing muscle tightness and soreness, helping the body recover from energetic activity, helping the person feel calmer).

Students are asked

Q: Can you explain why we split the warm-up into three parts? Why do we stretch after the pulse-raising activities?
A: The mobilising section loosens the joints, the pulse-raiser increases the heart rate, and the stretching takes place when the muscles are warm to develop flexibility.

Q: How should you feel after an effective warm-up?
A: Warm, loose, ready for action, alert.

Q: How should you feel after an effective cool-down?
A: Cooler, calm, relaxed, recovered.

Learning Objective 22

3.3.16   **Students are learning to perform warm-up and cool-down exercises with safe and effective technique.**

3.3.17   Students will:

- demonstrate correct joint alignment, appropriate control and appropriate use of high impact when performing simple warm-up/cool-down activities
- make increasingly accurate judgements about their own and others' exercise technique when performing warm-up and cool-down exercises/activities.

Suggested learning tasks

3.3.18   Students copy practical demonstrations of warm-up and cool-down exercises, paying attention to correct joint alignment, appropriate control and appropriate use of high impact.

3.3.19   Students make simple judgements about their own performance of warm-up and cool-down activities in terms of correct joint alignment, appropriate control and appropriate use of high impact.

3.3.20   Students observe, evaluate and give feedback on others' technique when performing warm-up/cool-down exercises.

Learning Objective 23

3.3.21   **Students are learning to design effective warm-ups and cool-downs.**

3.3.22   Students will:

- recall and perform exercises appropriate for warm-ups
- recall and perform exercises appropriate for cool-downs.

Suggested learning tasks

3.3.23   Students plan (independently or with others) exercises and components of/a whole warm-up/cool-down for familiar PESSPA activities.

3.3.24   Students plan components of/a whole warm-up/cool-down for new/unfamiliar PESSPA activities.

Students are asked

Q: Can you demonstrate a range of exercises/activities where the joints are specifically being warmed-up?

Q: What is happening in the joints as you mobilise and warm them up?

A: When mobilising the joints, fluid is released, which "oils" the joint and makes it move more freely. The muscles get warm and become pliable, which allows the joints to move more freely and over a larger range. Breathing and heart rate increase to carry more oxygen more quickly to the muscles in order to provide the energy required to do energetic activities. Stretching the muscles prepares them for tightening and lengthening quickly when doing energetic and fast activities.

Q: Can you demonstrate a range of exercises/activities where the body is being cooled and calmed down?

Q: What is happening in the body as you calm and cool the body down?

A: When cooling-down, the body is moving gently to keep blood pumping to the heart and brain. Otherwise, we might feel dizzy or sick. Breathing and heart rate decrease to allow the body to recover. The muscles are stretched to help prevent them feeling tight and sore after exercise. The body feels calm and prepared to go back to the classroom.

Learning Objective 24

3.3.25   **Students are learning to evaluate the effectiveness of warm-ups and cool-downs.**

3.3.26   Students will:

- identify and apply simple criteria to evaluate the effectiveness of warm-ups and cool-downs
- make appropriate adaptations to warm-ups and cool-downs to increase their safety and effectiveness
- explain how warm-ups and cool-downs can be adapted for specific situations (eg adverse weather conditions).

Suggested learning tasks

3.3.27   Students decide on simple criteria to evaluate the effectiveness of warm-ups and cool-downs.

3.3.28   Students lead their peers through components of/a whole warm-up/cool-down that they have planned (independently or with others) for familiar or unfamiliar PESSPA activities.

3.3.29   Students work in groups to evaluate the effectiveness of a warm-up or cool-down.

Students are asked

Q: Can you perform activities that move your joints?

Q: Can you perform activities that make you breathe faster?

Q: Can you perform activities that make you breathe more slowly?

Q: Can you perform activities that stretch your muscles?

Learning Objective 25

3.3.30   **Students are learning to take responsibility for understanding the purpose of warm-ups and cool-downs, and performing them with safe and effective technique.**

3.3.31   Students will:

- identify the value of preparing to take part in, and recover from, exercise/activity
- evaluate their own and others' technique when performing warm-up and cool-down exercises/activities.

Suggested learning tasks

3.3.32   Students perform warm-up and cool-down exercises with good technique.

3.3.33   Students conduct risk assessments of complex and/or new/unfamiliar warm-up and cool-down exercises/activities to check whether they can be performed with correct joint alignment, appropriate control and appropriate use of high impact.

3.3.34   Students discuss the purposes of warming-up before PESSPA (ie preventing injury, preparing the body safely and gradually for activity, "waking up" the brain) and cooling-down afterwards (ie preventing muscle tightness and soreness, helping the body recover from energetic activity, and helping the person feel calmer).

3.3.35   Students monitor the effects of warming-up and cooling-down on their breathing and temperature, and how they feel.

3.3.36   Students discuss what might happen if a warm-up or cool-down was not performed.

Learning Objective 26

3.3.37   **Students are learning to take responsibility for designing, performing and evaluating effective warm-ups and cool-downs.**

3.3.38   Students will:

- analyse and identify the requirements of a warm-up/cool-down for a personal exercise/training programme
- explain the difference between dynamic stretching and static stretching and the appropriate place of each in warm-ups and cool-downs
- distinguish between warm-up and cool-down requirements for activity in general and for specific sports.

Suggested learning tasks

3.3.39   Students distinguish between static and dynamic stretches, and consider the appropriate use of dynamic and static stretches in warm-ups and cool-downs.

3.3.40   Students plan warm-ups for different purposes (eg general activities as in a games lesson and preparation for participation in specific sports).

3.3.41   Students plan independent warm-ups and cool-downs that are specific to a personal exercise/training programme.

Section 4: Learning How the Body Responds to Physical Activity

Learning Objective 27

3.4.1   **Students are learning what happens to the body when it is active.**

3.4.2   Students will:

- describe changes in their breathing, temperature, appearance and heart rate
- demonstrate and explain that being active involves moving joints and using bones and muscles.

Suggested learning tasks

3.4.3   Individually, students walk and gradually increase speed, moving around each other on the playground. They place their hand on their heart when they stop.

3.4.4   Individually, students take part in a range of gross motor activities (eg running, jumping, hopping and leaping) on the playground.

3.4.5   Individually, students perform a range of energetic actions to help them understand the changes taking place in their bodies as a result of physical activity.

Students are asked

Q: How does your heart feel when you are active?
A: My heart pumps or beats faster.

Q: What happens to your breathing when you are active?
A: My breathing is fast and deep. I feel puffed out!

Q: What happens to your temperature and appearance when you are active?
A: My face and skin feel hotter.

Q: Why does the heart beat faster and our temperature increases?
A: The heart beats faster to meet the increased energy requirements of activity, and the body releases the energy as heat.

Learning Objective 28

3.4.6   **Students are learning to understand the short-term effects of physical activity on the body.**

3.4.7   Students will:

- identify the changes to breathing, heart rate and temperature when the body is active
- explain the work of muscles during energetic activity.

Suggested learning tasks

3.4.8   During physical education lessons, which include activities of different intensities, students monitor the effects of exercise on their breathing and heart rate. They learn that both the breathing and heart rate increase so that more oxygen can get to the muscles that are working hard.

3.4.9   Students also monitor the effects of exercise on their body temperature. They learn that this increases because working muscles produce energy in the form of heat, which is transferred to the body surface/skin to control the body's temperature.

Students are asked

Q: The body is using energy all the time. Where does the energy that muscles need come from?
A: Energy comes from the food we eat, the fluid we drink and the air we breathe.

Q: The muscles require more energy when we are active. Where is this energy stored?
A: The energy is stored in the muscles in the body.

Q: What else happens in the body when we are active?
A: The heart rate (the rate at which blood is pumped from the heart) increases to carry oxygen to the working muscles. The breathing rate (the rate and intensity at which a person inhales and exhales) also increases to provide more oxygen to the working muscles. The body temperature also increases as the muscles use up energy during exercise. As a result of the body temperature increasing, heat is produced. The blood vessels widen and get closer to the skin surface to distribute the heat produced by the working muscles. The skin acts as a cooling mechanism to prevent the body overheating.

Q: What are the signs on the skin when heat is transferred from the working muscles to the body surface?
A: The skin feels sweaty/moist.

Q: Why can the skin become flushed or appear red?
A: The blood vessels widen and get closer to the skin surface.

Learning Objective 29

3.4.10   **Students are learning to understand how physical activity should feel for health benefits.**

3.4.11   Students will:

- explain how and why heart rate, breathing rate and body temperature respond to activities of different intensities
- identify which activities feel moderate and which feel energetic.

Suggested learning tasks

3.4.12   During physical education lessons, which include activities of different intensities, students monitor and describe how different activities feel to perform (eg easy, energetic, exhausting).

3.4.13   Students identify the link between how activity feels (eg moderate and energetic) to changes in body temperature, heart rate and breathing.

Students are asked

Q: How does exercise feel if you do it regularly?
A: It feels like it gets easier if the body is exercised regularly.

Q: How should exercise feel for benefits to your health?
A: Moderate activity (where there is an increase in heart rate) on a daily basis (an average of 60 minutes a day) will have health benefits.

Learning Objective 30

3.4.14   **Students are learning about the effects of exercise on the body.**

3.4.15   Students will:
- monitor and explain the short-term effects of exercise
- identify how components of fitness can be improved through specific physical activities.

Suggested learning tasks

3.4.16   While taking part in energetic activities, students monitor and evaluate the short-term effects of exercise on the body.

3.4.17   While taking part in gymnastic activities, students monitor and evaluate the short-term effects of exercise on the body.

3.4.18   Students plan a programme of conditioning activities that will improve muscle tone.

3.4.19   Students plan a programme of whole-body activities that will help reduce body fat.

Students are asked

> **Q: What are the short-term effects of energetic physical activity on the cardiorespiratory system and other parts of the body?**
> **A: Changes in breathing, heart rate, temperature, appearance, feelings, recovery rate.**

> **Q: What are the short-term effects on the musculoskeletal system?**
> **A: Increases in muscular strength, and improved muscle tone, posture and flexibility.**

Section 5: Learning about the Physical Health Benefits of Being Active

Learning Objective 31

3.5.1   **Students are learning to understand how daily physical activity can improve their health.**

3.5.2   Students will:

- explain that being active can make the body healthy
- explain that being active involves moving joints, and using muscles and bones.

Suggested learning tasks

3.5.3   Individually, students take part in a range of gross motor activities on the playground (running, jumping, hopping and leaping, using arms to get height in their jumping and leaping). They place their hand on different body parts when they stop.

3.5.4   Individually, students take part in a range of gross motor activities (running, jumping, hopping and leaping) on the playground to learn about bones and muscles.

3.5.5   Individually, students perform a range of cardiovascular, stretching and mobilising activities to help them understand the working of the joints in the body.

Students are asked

Q: What parts of the body are used when we are active?
A: Heart, knees, feet, legs, elbows, arms and lungs.

Q: Why is being active good for our hearts, lungs, bones and muscles?
A: It helps them grow, get stronger and work well.

Q: What do bones and muscles help us to do?
A: Bones and muscles help us to move.

Q: Where are the joints in our bodies, and what do they do?
A: Joints are where bones meet, and they help us to move.

Q: Can you point to the joints that are moving when running and when throwing a ball?
A: Knees and ankles are moving when running, and elbows and shoulders when throwing.

Learning Objective 32

3.5.6   **Students are learning about the health benefits of being active.**

3.5.7   Students will:
- explain the changes in heart rate, breathing and temperature they experience when they are active
- explain the benefits of physical activity for the heart, lungs, bones and joints
- explain what muscles do
- explain the characteristics, and mental and physical benefits of an active lifestyle.

Suggested learning tasks

3.5.8   Students take part in energetic physical education lessons where activities cause an increase in their heart rate, breathing and temperature.

3.5.9   Students discuss the benefits for their health of being active.

Students are asked

Q: Muscles help us to move by releasing energy. How is energy generated?
A: Energy comes from the food we eat, the fluid we drink and the air we breathe.

Q: The muscles require much more energy when we are active. Where is energy stored until we need it?
A: Energy is stored in the muscles in the body.

Q: What else happens in the body when we are active?
A: The heart rate (the rate at which blood is pumped from the heart) increases to carry the oxygen to the working muscles to meet the increased energy requirements. The breathing rate (the rate and intensity at which a person inhales and exhales) also increases to provide more oxygen to the working muscles. In addition, the body temperature increases as the muscles use up energy during exercise. As a result of the body temperature increasing, heat is produced. The blood vessels widen and get closer to the skin surface to distribute the heat produced by the working muscles. The skin acts as a cooling mechanism to prevent the body overheating.

Q: What are the signs on the skin when heat is transferred from the working muscles to the body surface?
A: The skin feels sweaty/moist.

Q: Do you know why the skin can become flushed or appear red?
A: The blood vessels widen and get closer to the skin surface.

Q: What is happening to your bones and muscles as you exercise?
A: Our bones and muscles are getting stronger.

Q: What is happening to your joints as you exercise?
A: Our joints are working smoothly and developing flexibility of movement.

Q: What are the benefits of being active?
A: With regular exercise, the heart and lungs become stronger, improving their ability to deliver oxygen. The muscles also become more efficient at using the oxygen. A stronger heart means a greater volume of blood leaves the heart with each beat. Therefore, regular exercise improves the efficiency of the heart, lungs and muscles. Other benefits of being active include improved health and well-being, improved body shape, greater capacity to do things without feeling tired, feeling better about yourself, and improved mood and confidence.

Learning Objective 33

3.5.10   **Students are learning about the long-term health benefits of physical activity.**

3.5.11   Students will:

- explain the long-term benefits for health of taking part in physical activity
- describe how activity can enhance mental health, and social and psychological well-being
- explain the importance of building regular exercise into daily and weekly routines and how to achieve this
- explain the benefits for their strength, stamina and flexibility of taking part in a wide variety of physical activities.

Suggested learning tasks

3.5.12   Students select and perform exercises appropriate for developing/maintaining specific components of fitness.

3.5.13   Students take part in a wide variety of familiar and unfamiliar physical activities and identify what they and their peers enjoy (or do not).

3.5.14   Students design and evaluate strategies to help them and others stay motivated to take part in physical activity. They explain how mental health, and social and psychological well-being (eg increased confidence and self-esteem, decreased anxiety and stress, enjoyment of being with friends) can be enhanced through physical activity.

3.5.15   Students discuss how and when to seek support, including which adults to speak to in school, if they are worried about their health.

Students are asked

Q: What are the long-term health benefits of developing and maintaining flexibility, body strength, muscular endurance and cardiovascular fitness?
A: Reduced risk of chronic disease (eg heart disease), reduced risk of bone disease (eg osteoporosis), reduced risk of obesity and back pain, in addition to improved management of other health conditions such as asthma, diabetes and arthritis.

Section 6: Learning about the Role of Physical Activity in Achieving Energy Balance

Learning Objective 34

3.6.1   **Students are learning that their body uses energy all the time, but more when they are active.**

3.6.2   Students will:

- recognise and explain when they are using more energy
- explain what the body uses to provide energy.

Suggested learning tasks

3.6.3   Students take part in physical education lessons and learn about the energy they use when moving.

3.6.4   Students learn through easy, moderate and energetic activities that the body uses food, drink and air as fuel to produce energy for exercise.

3.6.5   Students learn that the body uses **more** energy through energetic activity.

Students are asked

Q: Can you show me an activity that:
- makes you breathe faster
- makes you feel warmer
- moves your joints
- makes your heart beat faster
- stretches your muscles
- makes you use lots of energy
- uses little energy?

Q: How do you feel when you exercise?

Q: What happens to your arms and legs when you exercise?

Q: When are you using lots of energy?

Q: Where do you get energy from when you exercise?

Q: When are you not using so much energy?

Q: How do you take in the ingredients of energy?

A: By eating, breathing and drinking.

Learning Objective 35

3.6.6 **Students learn the importance of energy balance for health.**

3.6.7 Students will:

- explain what the body uses energy for
- explain what happens if a person does not take in enough food and drink to provide the energy they need
- explain what happens if a person takes in more food and drink than they need
- explain what is meant by "energy balance"
- explain the health benefits of achieving energy balance.

Suggested learning tasks

3.6.8 During energetic physical education lessons, students are asked how they are feeling.

3.6.9 During active physical education lessons, students discuss energy and energy balance.

3.6.10 During a cool-down, students discuss the importance of food and drink, and the overall health benefits of achieving energy balance.

Students are asked

Q: What have you done to make sure you have enough energy for today's lesson? For example, have you had breakfast?

Q: How might you feel by break time if you have not had breakfast?
A: Low on energy.

Q: Why does your body need energy all the time?
A: To grow, to breathe, to digest food, to think and to move.

Q: What happens if your body does not take in enough food and drink?
A: Your body will not have enough energy to work efficiently, and you will feel unwell.

Q: What happens if your body takes in more food and drink than you need?
A: The body stores the excess energy as fat.

Q: What does "energy balance" mean?
A: Taking in the correct amount of food and drink to give you the energy you need.

Q: What happens to your body if it remains sedentary?
A: The stored fat is not used, and this may lead to poor health.

Q: Why might someone find it difficult to achieve energy balance?
A: They might not be able to exercise when they go home, or they may eat large portions.

Q: What are the health benefits of achieving energy balance?
A: Feeling well, feeling energetic and maintaining a healthy body composition.

Q: How can energy balance be achieved?
A: By being active every day and through healthy eating.

Learning Objective 36

3.6.11   **Students are learning about energy balance for good health.**

3.6.12   Students will:

- interpret the UK Physical Activity (PA) guidelines to set a personal target to increase/maintain their own participation
- understand that a balanced diet, in addition to exercise, can help maintain a healthy weight
- identify the daily minimum energy intake the body needs to function properly
- understand that strict dieting and excessive exercising can damage one's health.

Suggested learning tasks

3.6.13   Students design and implement an activity plan that increases/maintains their current level of physical activity in accordance with the UK PA guidelines, and evaluate their diet.

3.6.14   Students discuss how increasing activity levels and eating a balanced diet can help maintain a healthy weight (ie energy balance) and how strict dieting and excessive exercising can damage one's health.

Section 7: Learning about the Psychological, Mental and Social Benefits of an Active Lifestyle

Emphasis should be given to the positive two-way relationship between good physical health and good mental well-being, and the benefits to mental well-being of physical exercise and time spent outdoors.

A firm foundation in the benefits and characteristics of good health and well-being will enable teachers to talk about isolation, loneliness, unhappiness, bullying and the negative impact of poor health and well-being.

Department for Education (DfE) (2019) "Relationships education, relationships and sex education (RSE) and health education", https://www.gov.uk/government/publications/relationships-education-relationships-and-sex-education-rse-and-health-education

Learning Objective 37

3.7.1 **Students are learning to understand what it means to feel safe in physical education and at playtimes.**

3.7.2 Students will:
- recognise that being active can produce different feelings
- identify words associated with "feeling safe" in physical education lessons
- explain why it is good to "feel safe" and why it is not good to feel "unsafe" in physical education lessons
- give simple examples of what helps them to feel safe in physical education and at playtimes.

Suggested learning tasks

3.7.3 Students take part in a variety of tag games on the playground after which they link their experiences to positive words/vocabulary associated with feeling safe (eg happy, comfortable, warm, protected, included, being with others).

3.7.4 Staff discuss with students the fact that there is a range of emotions that we experience in relation to different situations (some of us may feel good and some of us may not feel so good), and highlight that this is normal.

3.7.5 Students monitor how they feel during physical education lessons, and select one or more "feeling safe" words (eg happy, comfortable, warm, protected, included) to describe their feelings.

3.7.6 When back in the classroom, students explain how they felt about using the question prompts if needed.

3.7.7 Students discuss and decide sensible rules to help them feel safe at playtimes (eg be aware of others, keep to designated areas, listen to play leaders, try to include others apart from your friends).

Students are asked

Q: How do you feel when you are active?
A: I feel happy/excited/anxious/tired.

Q: How does playing games with others make you feel?
A: I like playing with my friends.

Q: Does everyone feel the same way?

Q: Do you feel safe when you are active and playing games?

Q: What made you feel really safe?

Q: What made you feel less safe?

Q: What might have made you feel safer?

Q: What do you need to do if you do not feel safe in physical education lessons or at playtimes?

Q: Is it safe to play tag games if the playground is very crowded?

Q: What games could you play instead?

Learning Objective 38

3.7.8   **Students are learning to understand how physical activity benefits social and emotional health.**

3.7.9   Students will:

- explain the link between being active and being healthy
- recognise that being active can produce different feelings
- explain when and who they should ask for help if they feel unsafe in physical education lessons or at playtimes
- explain ways in which the adults working with them in physical education and at playtimes can make them feel safe.

Suggested learning tasks

3.7.10   Students take part in a variety of gross motor activities (eg running, jumping, leaping, chasing each other, beating the clock, beating their record) on the playground.

3.7.11   Students describe how being active with others can make them feel good (eg "I feel excited when I chase my friend," "I feel happy when my friend plays with me on the playground").

3.7.12   Staff discuss with students the range of emotions that we experience in relation to different situations (some of us may feel good and some of us may not feel so good), and highlight that this is normal. Generally, if we are enjoying running around outdoors in the fresh air, we can feel good. Staff encourage the students to let a member of staff know if they do not feel so good after exercise/physical activity.

Students are asked

Q: How can physical activity change how we feel?

Q: How are you feeling today?

Q: Can you describe how you are feeling after running around?

Q: Can you explain the link between feelings and being healthy?

Q: What might the adult do to help make you feel better?

Q: Who can we ask in physical education and at playtime to help make us feel safe?

Q: Do you like being active with others?

Q: Do you feel different now than you did before the lesson? How? Why do you think this is?

Q: Can you show me an activity that helps you feel good?

Q: If somebody does not feel so good, what can we do to help them feel better?

Q: Now that we have come to the end of our physical education lesson, how do you feel?

Q: Do you like being active by yourself?

Q: How do you think your feelings might change during your physical education lesson?

Learning Objective 39

3.7.13 **Students are learning to understand what it means to feel safe and talk about their emotions in physical education, school sport and physical activity (PESSPA).**

3.7.14 Students will:

- explain how they can help younger students to feel safe in a play situation
- describe what would be considered violent or reckless play in PESSPA
- explain positive ways of responding to situations where violent or reckless play occurs
- explain how, when and to whom they should report any situations in which they feel threatened or intimidated as a result of violent or reckless play in PESSPA.

Suggested learning tasks

3.7.15 Students discuss safety scenarios while getting changed for PE.

3.7.16 During physical education lessons, students take part in games where competition is encouraged.

3.7.17 While the students are engaged in playing games, staff encourage the teams to work together and take time to discuss safety scenarios.

3.7.18 When back inside the classroom, staff ask the students to think about feeling safe and what they can do if they do not feel safe. Staff explain that there is a **normal** range of emotions (eg happiness, sadness, anger, fear, surprise, nervousness) and scale of emotions that all humans experience in relation to different experiences and situations.

Students are asked

Q: Would it be safe if:
- you were playing tag in the same area as much younger students
- the playground was very crowded?

Q: What is meant by violent or reckless play?

Q: How can you respond positively in PESSPA sessions/situations where violent or reckless play occurs?

Q: What are some possible reasons why violent or reckless play might arise in PESSPA sessions/situations?

Q: How do adults make sure that you "feel safe in PESSPA"?

Q: How might rules and officials prevent and/or stop violent or reckless play?

Q: How might violent or reckless play impact on safety and how you feel?

Q: What can you do if you do not "feel safe"?

295

Learning Objective 40

3.7.19   **Students are learning to understand how different physical activities benefit social and emotional health.**

3.7.20   Students will:

- distinguish between physical activities that make them feel good and those that do not make them feel good
- explain that good health is about "feeling good" as well as being active
- explain the physical, social and psychological benefits of exercise that are most important to them and identify activities that provide them with these benefits.

Suggested learning tasks

3.7.21   Students design and play a variety of tag games, skipping races, ball and bat activities and a variety of other games in groups.

Students are asked

Q: Can you compare your feelings at the beginning of the physical education lesson to how you feel after you have played your games?

Q: Can you describe how you might feel if you were being teased and bullied in a game/ activity?

Q: What are the consequences of this unacceptable behaviour?

Q: Is it fun being active with others? Why is this?

Q: Can you distinguish between activities that make you feel good and those that don't?

Q: Can you describe the characteristics of physical activity that make people feel good?
A: Leading others, being led, being with friends, cooperating with others, working alone.

Q: Can you describe the characteristics of physical activity that make people feel good psychologically?
A: Being successful, winning, feeling more confident, having a good time and laughing with friends.

Learning Objective 41

3.7.22 **Students are learning that different physical activities can provide different health benefits.**

3.7.23 Students will:

- explain the benefits and importance of physical exercise for mental well-being and happiness
- explain the positive associations between physical activity and the promotion of mental well-being, including physical exercise as an approach to combat stress
- explain the benefits of physical, social and emotional health that are most important to them, and identify activities that provide these benefits
- suggest reasons for people having different preferences related to the health benefits of physical activity that are most important to each individual.

Suggested learning tasks

3.7.24 Students take part in a wide range of physical activities, and identify if each activity area provides them with different health benefits.

3.7.25 Students take part in a selected physical activity following an academic examination or test and explain why the activity benefits their "health" (mental, physical, social and psychological well-being).

3.7.26 Students discuss the benefits of physical, social and emotional health that are most important to them, and consider the need to maintain a balance between work, leisure and exercise.

Students are asked

Q: Can you explain the positive associations between physical activity and the promotion of mental well-being, including physical exercise as an approach to combat stress?

Q: Do you feel happier when you are physically active with friends or on your own?

Q: Can you suggest reasons why your friends and colleagues have different preferences about which health benefits of physical activity are most important to them?

Q: What are the benefits and importance of physical exercise for mental well-being and happiness?

Q: Can you identify activities that provide physical, social and emotional health benefits? Which are most important to you?

Section 8: Learning about Back Care

Learning Objective 42

3.8.1   **Students are learning to lift and carry appropriate pieces of equipment in a safe manner.**

3.8.2   Students will:

- demonstrate good lifting, carrying and placing technique
- identify the differences between correct and incorrect body use when lifting and placing equipment.

Suggested learning tasks

3.8.3   During gymnastic lessons, students copy demonstrations of safe lifting and carrying technique provided by physical education, school sport and physical activity (PESSPA) staff.

3.8.4   Students lift, carry and place a variety of appropriate PESSPA equipment under the supervision of PESSPA staff.

3.8.5   Students observe and comment on their own and others' lifting and carrying technique.

3.8.6   Students suggest ways of improving their own and others' lifting and carrying technique.

Learning Objective 43

3.8.7   **Students are learning about the importance of good posture.**

3.8.8   Students will:

- demonstrate good posture when sitting and standing
- identify the differences between correct and incorrect body posture when standing and sitting
- describe how muscles can squeeze and relax.

Suggested learning tasks

3.8.9   Students take part in physical activities where the postural muscles are working (eg tummy curls, back raises, shoulder squeezes, leg raises), and focus on control and alignment when doing the exercises.

3.8.10   Students perform simple resistance exercises that strengthen the postural muscles.

3.8.11   To focus on developing good posture when sitting, standing and moving, students take part in activities where they focus on keeping their back tall, shoulders down, chest out and face forward.

3.8.12   Students practise copying simple exercises and distinguish between squeezing and relaxing muscles. They practise moving with muscles squeezed tight ("Walk stiffly like a robot") and relaxed ("Walk lightly with as little tension as possible").

3.8.13   Students watch each other and improve their own actions through copying others.

Students are asked

Q: Can you locate the postural muscles?
A: In the tummy and backside, along the length of the spine and between the shoulder blades.

Q: What do these important postural muscles do?
A: They keep the spine and back strong.

Q: Can you name five everyday activities that require a strong back?
A: Bending, lifting, sitting, writing and standing.

Learning Objective 44

3.8.14   **Students are learning to make stretched and tucked shapes with their bodies.**

3.8.15   Students will:

- make long/thin shapes and small tucked shapes with their bodies and hold them still for at least three seconds
- explain that their muscles help to keep their bodies still and also help them to move.

Suggested learning tasks

3.8.16   As part of a gymnastic warm-up, students prepare their bodies for the activities to be performed. This includes mobilising joints, pulse-raising activities (eg travelling) and movements that gradually increase the heart rate, as well as stretching the muscles.

3.8.17   Students make long shapes with their body on the floor, close to the floor, standing up and on apparatus. They can stretch their bodies for as long as possible while lying on their back on the floor, focusing on keeping their knees and elbows straight and their backs flat, leaving no space for a hand to go underneath. They also feel if their muscles are held tight. They can try squeezing their knees and feet together, and holding the long pin shape for three seconds. Students can also attempt to hold their body in a front support position like a plank of wood, checking that their backs are straight with their hands under their shoulders.

3.8.18   Students practise standing still with their backs straight and shoulders back.

3.8.19   Students concentrate on maintaining good posture while walking.

3.8.20   In gymnastic lessons, students make small rounded shapes with their bodies both on the floor and on apparatus. They attempt to sit in a small round shape with their feet off the floor and see if they can balance in this tuck shape for three seconds, checking that their muscles are held tight. Students can try squeezing their knees and feet together. They can also consider different ways to make straight and tucked shapes on the apparatus, and focus on what helps them to hold their balances still.

Students are asked

Q: What is helping you to keep your body upright and walk with good posture?
A: Our muscles help us to keep upright and move.

Q: What is helping to keep your body in these still shapes?
A: Our muscles help us to keep still.

Learning Objective 45

3.8.21 **Students are learning to make dish and arch shapes with their bodies.**

3.8.22 Students will:

- show the difference between dish and arch shapes with their bodies while close to the floor and in a standing position
- explain how to make dish and arch shapes with their bodies
- identify the muscles being used when making the shapes.

Suggested learning tasks

3.8.23 As part of a gymnastic warm-up, students prepare their bodies for the activities to be performed. This includes performing energetic movements such as travelling, jumping and stretching.

3.8.24 Students make dish and arch shapes both on the floor and on apparatus. While practising the shapes, they lift their arms and legs off the floor/apparatus. They can attempt dish shapes while on their backs and arch shapes when on their tummies. Students then focus on how they feel when they are making these shapes with their bodies.

3.8.25 If students find it difficult to make dish and arch shapes with their bodies, they can make it easier by keeping their arms by their sides. They can also try starting in tuck shapes on their backs and taking one leg out at a time. If they find it too difficult to hold the dish and arch shapes still for three seconds, students can try holding the shapes momentarily.

3.8.26 Students stand straight with their arms in the air, attempting to be completely straight from their fingers to their feet. They can then attempt to make dish shapes while standing. Students can also pull their arms back past their ears and try making arch shapes with their bodies, checking their hips are pushed forward when making arch shapes while standing on their feet.

Students are asked

Q: What is helping to keep your body in the arch and dish shapes?
A: Our muscles help us to keep upright and move.

Q: Which muscles are helping to keep your body in the arch and dish shapes?
A: Our postural muscles (tummy, back, backside and muscles around our shoulder blades).

301

Learning Objective 46

3.8.27   **Students are learning to combine dish, arch and tuck shapes to perform a short sequence of movement.**

3.8.28   Students will:

- link 2–3 movements together with a clear start and finish
- remember and repeat their short sequence
- explain that gymnastics can strengthen muscles and help with maintaining a good posture.

Suggested learning tasks

3.8.29   As part of a gymnastic warm-up, students prepare their bodies for the activities to be performed. This includes performing energetic movements such as travelling, jumping and stretching.

3.8.30   Students make dish, tuck and arch shapes both on the floor and on apparatus. They create their own tuck starting positions and practise moving from these into long second positions. They can be on their backs or on their tummies. From their second positions, they try to link a third – a tuck or another long position. They focus on moving fluently and smoothly from one position to the next, practising the movements, trying to keep control with strong muscles and making sure they keep their shapes clear. When they finish, they have to remember their sequence so they can repeat it and attempt to improve it.

3.8.31   Students end the lesson by showing contrast between the tensing and relaxing of their muscles.

3.8.32   Students develop their understanding of good posture by watching each other walk with straight backs and arms swinging at the sides of the body.

Students are asked

Q: What do we call the shape when you are on your back?
A: Dish shape.

Learning Objective 47

3.8.33   **Students are learning to combine a range of body shapes, maintaining good posture throughout.**

3.8.34   Students will:

- explain that gymnastics improves joint mobility and muscular strength
- identify which joints are moving when they change from one body shape to the next
- combine a broad range of body shapes with control and stability
- explain the importance of maintaining a strong back
- identify the location of the postural muscles and their purpose.

Suggested learning tasks

3.8.35   As part of a gymnastic warm-up, students prepare their bodies for the activities to be performed. This includes performing energetic movements such as travelling fast, switching from high to low, and large, strong and powerful explosive movements combined with stretching and mobilising joints.

3.8.36   Students copy and recognise exercises to strengthen muscles that support the spine (postural muscles). They learn where these important muscles are and about the need to keep strengthening them to help prevent back pain and make activities easier to perform.

3.8.37   Students make straddle, arch, dish and tuck shapes with their bodies. They demonstrate control and alignment when making the shapes, strengthening the postural muscles and helping to develop a strong back.

3.8.38   Students observe, evaluate and give feedback on each other's shapes, particularly focusing on the work of the postural muscles.

Students are asked

Q: What is the name of the shape where your body forms a right angle between your trunk and the floor, and your feet are stretched? Can you show me this shape?
A: Pike.

Q: Why is it important to sit and stand with good posture, and maintain high quality movement in our gymnastic shapes?
A: To develop strong backs and protect our backbones.

Q: What are the benefits of having a strong back?
A: Everyday activities (eg lifting and sitting) are easier to perform.

Learning Objective 48

3.8.39   **Students are learning about the short- and long-term risks associated with lifting, carrying and lowering with poor technique (eg lower-back pain, knee injuries).**

3.8.40   Students will:

- follow instructions/maps/plans carefully and accurately to set out small pieces of PESSPA equipment
- identify and demonstrate principles of safe and effective technique when working cooperatively with others to lift, carry and place PESSPA equipment
- carry and set out PESSPA equipment independently, maintaining good safety awareness, and safe and effective lifting, carrying and placing technique.

Suggested learning tasks

3.8.41   Students play an active role (under appropriate supervision) in deciding how specific PESSPA equipment is moved and placed.

3.8.42   Students take part (under appropriate supervision) in small group problem-solving tasks that challenge them to plan how to lift, move and place specific PESSPA equipment safely and effectively.

Students are asked

Q: How should you lift equipment safely?
A: Bend the knees, keep the back straight and let the legs do the work. Keep the spine and knees in correct alignment.

Q: How should you place equipment down safely?
A: Bend the knees, and keep the back straight and the weight close to the body.

Q: Why is it important to lift with correct technique?
A: To look after our backs.

Section 9: Learning How to Assess and Manage Risk

Learning Objective 49

3.9.1 **Students are learning to take responsibility for following advice, rules and procedures relating to safe practice.**

3.9.2 Students will:

- recognise and respond appropriately to very simple verbal instructions, written words, signs and/or symbols associated with their safety in physical education, school sport and physical activity (PESSPA)
- listen carefully when receiving information/instructions about safety advice, rules and procedures in PESSPA activities/situations
- recall simple safety rules that PESSPA staff have communicated to them.

Suggested learning tasks

3.9.3 Students learn to respond appropriately to safety commands when involved in PESSPA activities (eg "listen", "look", "stop" and "go" – red and green "traffic light" symbols, written words, gestures, signals or verbal commands can be used).

3.9.4 Students develop a **practical** understanding of safety words associated with specific PESSPA activities/situations.

3.9.5 Students talk about how they and others can successfully follow safety advice, signs, rules and procedures.

Students are asked

Q: What might happen if you do not listen to or follow safety advice, rules and procedures?

Q: Can you remember some simple safety rules that you have learnt in physical education?

Learning Objective 50

3.9.6 **Students are learning to take responsibility for conducting their own risk assessments prior to participating in PESSPA activities/situations.**

3.9.7 Students will:

- explain what it means to get hurt or injured in PESSPA
- describe what might cause them to get hurt in a PESSPA activity/situation or the playground
- make accurate safety checks (under the guidance of PESSPA staff) of their own kit, the equipment they are using and the working area
- make very simple judgements about what is "safe" and what is not "safe" for familiar PESSPA facilities, equipment, activities and procedures
- identify and describe advice, rules and procedures that keep them and others safe when taking part in PESSPA activities/situations.

305

Suggested learning tasks

3.9.8   As they are changing for physical education, students consider how being hurt or injured makes them feel and/or how being hurt or injured stops them being active.

3.9.9   Students identify in **practical** PESSPA sessions/situations (with the help of PESSPA staff) what might cause someone to get hurt (eg bumping into one another, falling over, collapsing equipment), and what has been done to reduce the risk of this happening (eg teacher instructions to look up and watch out for others when running, teacher instructions to check that the floor is clear before playing, teacher checking that the equipment is safe before use).

3.9.10   From very simple safety rules provided by PESSPA staff, students consider and decide on those that are most important for the PESSPA activities/situations in which they are participating. The safety rules can be communicated verbally or through written words and pictures on posters.

Students are asked

Q: How does safe equipment and/or a safe space help to prevent you and/or others from being injured?

Learning Objective 51

3.9.11   **Students are learning to take increasing responsibility for assessing and reducing risks associated with a range of factors that can impact on their safe participation in PESSPA activities.**

3.9.12   Students will:

- describe some common hazards that might occur during any PESSPA activity/situation
- recognise when there are safety issues, using simple criteria provided by PESSPA staff
- describe what might make PESSPA activities less safe for them.

Suggested learning tasks

3.9.13   Students look for specific and very simple hazards during a PESSPA session (eg is the floor clear of any equipment that might make them trip? Is the hall surface clean and dry?).

3.9.14   Students take on the role of "safety officers" in a PESSPA session and have a special responsibility for identifying safety issues.

3.9.15   Students explore safety issues associated with tiredness, dehydration and being unwell through taking part in PESSPA activities.

Students are asked

Q: Can you remember some simple safety advice for when you are physically active in hot sunshine?
A: Wear a hat and put sun cream on.

Learning Objective 52

3.9.16 **Students are learning to take increasing responsibility for following advice, rules and procedures relating to safe practice.**

3.9.17 Students will:

- accurately and consistently follow simple safety rules, signs and procedures in PESSPA activities/situations
- evaluate how successfully they and others are able to follow safety advice, rules and procedures in PESSPA activities/situations
- suggest helpful strategies to ensure that safety advice, rules and procedures are followed accurately in PESSPA activities/situations
- explain the possible consequences of not following safety advice, rules and procedures relating to personal participation in PESSPA.

Suggested learning tasks

3.9.18 Through **practical** PESSPA activities, students compare and discuss the challenges of following written or verbal instructions.

3.9.19 Students consider the appropriate action to take if they have not understood or listened carefully to safety information and advice about PESSPA activities/situations.

3.9.20 As a homework or literacy task, students design "safety rules" posters for specific PESSPA activities/situations.

3.9.21 In low risk practical PESSPA tasks, students monitor and evaluate the extent to which they and others can successfully follow safety advice, signs, rules and procedures.

Students are asked

Q: Why should safety rules, signs and procedures be followed in PESSPA situations?
A: To avoid getting hurt/injured.

Q: What should you do if you feel anxious about a particular activity?
A: Talk to PESSPA staff, who will help you.

Learning Objective 53

3.9.22 **Students are learning to take increasing responsibility for checking gymnastic equipment before and during use.**

3.9.23 Students will:

- explain why checks on gymnastic equipment need to be made, how to make these checks, and the possible consequences of not doing so
- identify any equipment that may be faulty or "broken"
- make observations that are similar to those made by PESSPA staff, when conducting their own equipment safety checks
- describe a range of common hazards relating to equipment that might occur during gymnastic lessons.

Suggested learning tasks

3.9.24   Students work in groups to suggest what gymnastic equipment needs to be checked before and during use.

3.9.25   Students take on the role of "safety officers" in gymnastic lessons and have a special responsibility for identifying safety issues with equipment.

3.9.26   Students get out the full range of gymnastic equipment and arrange it for a proposed theme (eg flight, travelling on all body parts, balance). The number of students required to lift and carry apparatus will vary according to their age, size and strength/ability.

3.9.27   Students check the apparatus for safety; for example:

- Is the apparatus suitable for the theme being taught?
- Is there adequate safe space around the apparatus to perform quality floor work?
- Are all the hooks on the linking equipment fitted correctly to the apparatus?
- Is the portable apparatus stable? Are there enough rubber stoppers on the nesting tables, vaulting equipment etc?
- Is the height of cross poles, ladders and other apparatus applicable to the age range?

Learning Objective 54

3.9.28   **Students are learning to take increasing responsibility for conducting their own risk assessments.**

3.9.29   Students will:

- explain what is meant by harm
- accurately identify what might cause harm in the context of familiar PESSPA facilities, equipment, activities and procedures
- explain what is meant by a hazard
- describe what is meant by a risk
- describe the risks involved in a range of familiar PESSPA activities/situations
- evaluate the likelihood that an identified hazard in PESSPA will present a risk to them and others.

Suggested learning tasks

3.9.30   Students make independent decisions in a range of **practical** PESSPA learning activities/situations about what harm might happen in a particular situation, what might cause this harm, and what can be done to reduce the likelihood that this harm will happen.

3.9.31   As a homework or literacy task, students design posters presenting safety advice, signs, rules and procedures to manage the risks identified in specific PESSPA activities/situations.

Students are asked

Q: What is meant by harm?
A: Injury or damage.

Q: Can you identify what might cause harm in physical education facilities/equipment/activities/ procedures?

Q: What is meant by a hazard?
A: Something that might cause harm.

Q: Describe what is meant by a risk?
A: The likelihood that an identified hazard will cause harm to you and others.

Q: How can we make a situation safe?
A: You can do checks before and during activities, and offer solutions to minimise risks.

Learning Objective 55

3.9.32 **Students are learning to take increasing responsibility for conducting ongoing risk assessment (ie dynamic risk assessment) while an activity or event is taking place.**

3.9.33 Students will:

- describe a range of common hazards that might occur during any PESSPA activity/situation
- accurately recognise when there are safety issues, using simple criteria provided by PESSPA staff
- explain why "ongoing" dynamic risk assessment in PESSPA is necessary.

Suggested learning tasks

3.9.34 At the beginning of a lesson, students are asked to think about what possible hazards there might be/ might occur during physical education lessons.

3.9.35 In **practical** PESSPA sessions, students take on the role of "safety officers" who have a special responsibility for identifying safety issues.

3.9.36 Students discuss and understand the need to check for hazards before and during activities using simple criteria.

Students are asked

Q: What hazards might there be on the playground today after it has been wet and windy overnight?
A: There might be wet leaves on the playground, which could make us trip.

Q: In that case, what should we do to keep everyone safe?
A: Clear the leaves and check the playing area is safe to run on.

Q: What should we check before and during physical activity to ensure we are safe?
A: Kit, footwear, personal effects, equipment, working area and weather.

Learning Objective 56

3.9.37   **Students are learning to take responsibility for using PESSPA equipment in a safe and responsible manner.**

3.9.38   Students will:

- explain how rules and procedures for using specific PESSPA equipment keep them and others safe
- accurately identify when specific PESSPA equipment is not being used appropriately
- explain how concentrating and adhering to instructions, rules and procedures for the safe use of equipment can keep them and others safe
- make accurate judgements about the extent to which they and others use PESSPA equipment in a responsible manner.

Suggested learning tasks

3.9.39   Students discuss the safety implications of using PESSPA equipment inappropriately.

3.9.40   Students discuss what the word "responsible" means in the context of using PESSPA equipment (ie making independent decisions about PESSPA equipment that benefit students' own and others' safety).

3.9.41   Students discuss and decide on appropriate action to take if they see PESSPA equipment being used inappropriately.

Learning Objective 57

3.9.42   **Students are learning to take responsibility for conducting their own risk assessments prior to participating in PESSPA activities/situations.**

3.9.43   Students will:

- explain the purpose of the steps involved in the risk assessment process
- conduct a thorough and accurate risk-benefit analysis for a new or unfamiliar PESSPA activity/ situation or facility
- explain their risk-benefit analysis to appropriately qualified/competent PESSPA staff and make any necessary changes
- explain the importance for their own and others' safety of planning ahead before taking part in PESSPA activities/situations
- explain the significance of being able to conduct effective risk assessments for lifelong participation in physical activity.

Suggested learning tasks

3.9.44   In a variety of PESSPA activities, students work **practically** in small groups to:

- conduct their own risk assessments prior to participation in familiar/unfamiliar PESSPA activities/ situations
- evaluate their own and others' risk assessments
- discuss their risk assessments with an appropriate adult
- make any necessary changes before putting their risk assessments into operation.

3.9.45   Students discuss the importance of conducting risk assessments ahead of participation in PESSPA activities/situations.

Learning Objective 58

3.9.46 **In practical PESSPA tasks, students monitor and evaluate the extent to which they and others can successfully follow safety advice, signs, rules and procedures.**

3.9.47 Students will:

- explain how rules and procedures for using specific PESSPA equipment keep them and others safe
- accurately identify when specific PESSPA equipment is not being used appropriately
- make accurate judgements about the extent to which they and others use PESSPA equipment in a responsible manner.

Suggested learning tasks

3.9.48 In a variety of PESSPA activities, students work **practically** in small groups to:

- evaluate the safety implications of using PESSPA equipment inappropriately
- identify what the word "responsible" means in the context of using PESSPA equipment (ie making independent decisions about PESSPA equipment that benefit their own and others' safety) and decide on the appropriate action to take if they see PESSPA equipment being used inappropriately.

Section 10: Learning How to Get Involved in Physical Activity

Students should also be taught the benefits of hobbies, interests and participation in their own communities. This teaching should make clear that people are social beings and that spending time with others, taking opportunities to consider the needs of others and practising service to others, including in organised and structured activities and groups (for example the Scouts or Girl Guides movements), are beneficial for health and well-being.

Department for Education (DfE) (2019) "Relationships education, relationships and sex education (RSE) and health education", https://www.gov.uk/government/publications/relationships-education-relationships-and-sex-education-rse-and-health-education

Learning Objective 59

3.10.1 **Students are learning to understand when, where and how they can be active while in school.**

3.10.2 Students will:
- explain where and when they can be active in school
- describe how they play safely at playtime
- explain where and when they can be active outside of school
- describe how they play safely out of school.

Suggested learning tasks

3.10.3 Students take part in learning nursery rhymes and other playground games as part of music/dance lessons and are encouraged to play with friends on the playground during breaks and lunchtimes.

3.10.4 Students make up their own games and show others how they are played. They are encouraged to look at the whole playground and see where they can play safely.

3.10.5 Students discuss when and where they take part in physical activities outside of school.

Students are asked

Q: Are you active before school, during break and lunchtimes and after school?

Q: What activities do you play at break and at lunchtimes?

Q: Who do you play with at break and at lunchtimes?

Q: Are you active when you go home?

Q: Where do you go when you are active?

Q: How do you play safely outside of school?

Learning Objective 60

3.10.6   Students are learning to monitor their own activity levels.

3.10.7   Students will:
- describe how physical activity should feel for it to provide physical health benefits (ie "energetic")
- explain the characteristics of "healthy" physical activities (ie they make us huff and puff, they make our muscles work harder, they often involve supporting our own body weight)
- identify "healthy" physical activities (ie that will benefit their physical health).

Suggested learning tasks

3.10.8   Students learn how much physical activity they need to do each day to be healthy (ie at least 60 minutes).

3.10.9   Students take part in activities of different intensities in physical education lessons and learn how physical activity should feel to provide health benefits (ie energetic).

3.10.10   Students create an activity diary for a week and monitor their daily "energetic" physical activity.

3.10.11   Students discuss when, where and how they are active, both in school and outside of school.

Students are asked

Q: How should physical activity "feel" to benefit your health?
A: Energetic.

Q: What are the characteristics of "healthy" physical activities?
A: They make us huff and puff etc.

Q: On what day did you do the most physical activity that benefited your health, and why?

Q: Do you know how many minutes per day you should be active to benefit your health?

Q: What activities give you the most health benefits?

Q: When and where are you most active when at school?

Q: When and where are you most active outside of school?

Learning Objective 61

3.10.12 **Students are learning about which activities they enjoy, and to understand that individuals have different feelings about the types and amounts of activity they do.**

3.10.13 Students will:
- identify their favourite "healthy" activities, and explain why they enjoy them
- understand what encourages them to take part in "healthy" physical activities, and explain what prevents them from taking part in "healthy" physical activities
- explain how to overcome some of the barriers to taking part in "healthy" physical activities.

Suggested learning tasks

3.10.14 Students take part in a range of physical activities, and focus on being active (to benefit their health). They become aware of how much time they spend being "energetic" in lessons, and try to increase the number of minutes they spend being active in subsequent lessons/out of school activities.

3.10.15 Students discuss which physical activities they enjoy and what encourages them to take part. They also analyse what may prevent them from taking part in "healthy" activities. Through this discussion and activity, students learn that everyone has different feelings about the types and amounts of activity they do. Students investigate ways to overcome some of the barriers to taking part in "healthy" physical activities.

Learning Objective 62

3.10.16 **Students are learning how to access information about physical activity opportunities in and outside of school, and how to incorporate them into their lifestyle.**

3.10.17 Students will:
- reflect on their activity preferences
- investigate how and where they can find information about physical activity opportunities available to them
- devise and implement a physical activity schedule that aims to reach the Chief Medical Officer (CMO) recommendations for their age group
- monitor and evaluate their activity schedule, and reflect on their achievements/experience.

Suggested learning tasks

3.10.18 Students reflect on their experience of physical activity, particularly their strengths and preferences.

3.10.19 Students learn where they can access information about physical activity opportunities available at school and also in their local community.

3.10.20 Students examine what changes, if any, they need to make to reach and hopefully surpass the CMO recommendations for "healthy" daily physical activity.

3.10.21 Students design and complete a monthly activity diary, monitoring their personal physical activity levels with the aim of achieving at least 60 minutes of moderate intensity activity each day.

3.10.22 Students reflect on their monthly activity experience and any effects on their cardiovascular and musculoskeletal systems.

Section 11: Learning about the Principles of First Aid

3.11.1 Department for Education (DfE) (2019) "Relationships education, relationships and sex education (RSE) and health education" states the basic first aid knowledge students should have.

3.11.2 Primary students should know:

- how to make a clear and efficient call to emergency services if necessary
- the concepts of basic first aid (eg dealing with common injuries, including head injuries).

3.11.3 Secondary students should know:

- basic treatment for common injuries
- lifesaving skills, including how to administer cardiopulmonary resuscitation (CPR)
- the purpose of defibrillators and when one might be needed.

 To access DfE (2019) "Relationships education, relationships and sex education (RSE) and health education", see https://www.gov.uk/government/publications/relationships-education-relationships-and-sex-education-rse-and-health-education

Learning Objective 63

3.11.4 **Students are learning to take increasing responsibility for keeping themselves safe from danger.**

3.11.5 Students will:

- look and listen carefully for dangers
- accurately spot dangers
- know what to do if they spot dangers
- suggest how to make an area safe.

Suggested learning tasks

3.11.6 Students can access the British Red Cross first aid education website, focusing on the "What is First Aid?" and "Staying Safe" sections. Students can use the website's interactive activities, film scenarios, information sheets and quizzes to help increase their ability, confidence and willingness to give first aid.

 To access the British Red Cross first aid education website, see http://goo.gl/sQYYs7

Learning Objective 64

3.11.7   **Students are learning to take increasing responsibility for keeping themselves safe from danger when giving help to others.**

3.11.8   Students will:

- explain what is meant by risk
- identify school rules about safety
- explain the purpose of having school rules about safety
- explain what could happen if safety rules are not followed
- explain where and how to get help if they feel a situation is unsafe.

Suggested learning tasks

3.11.9   Students can access the British Red Cross first aid education website, focusing on the "Helping Save Lives" and "Emergency Action" sections. Students can use the website's interactive activities, film scenarios, information sheets and quizzes to help increase their ability, confidence and willingness to give first aid.

3.11.10   Students can access the St John Ambulance first aid education website. Its first aid resources and lesson plans cover a range of first aid scenarios and treatments for 7–16-year-olds to learn. The resources include presentations, customisable lesson plans, worksheets and videos.

To access the British Red Cross first aid education website, see http://goo.gl/sQYYs7
To access the St John Ambulance first aid education website, see https://www.sja.org.uk/get-advice/first-aid-lesson-plans/

Learning Objective 65

3.11.11   **Students are learning to take increasing responsibility for acting efficiently and appropriately in an emergency situation.**

3.11.12   Students will:

- explain what an emergency is in the context of first aid
- describe appropriate examples of emergency situations in physical education, school sport and physical activity (PESSPA)
- explain why getting help in an emergency is an important part of first aid
- accurately distinguish between PESSPA situations that are and are not "emergencies"
- show appropriate awareness of who it is safe for them to offer help to in PESSPA situations (ie if they are not with an adult and they don't know the person who is seriously ill or injured)
- check if someone is breathing
- show appropriate awareness of which adults it would be appropriate to ask for help in an emergency PESSPA situation
- explain when and how to call 999
- explain what will happen when they call 999 and what information they need to give the operator.

Suggested learning tasks

3.11.13   Students can access the British Red Cross first aid education website. The site has a range of interactive content, including films, written case studies, photos, animations, role plays and activities. Students can use the website independently or engage with first aid learning through activities facilitated by staff. This flexible approach can be adapted for a range of different ways of learning, settings and abilities.

 To access the British Red Cross first aid education website, see http://goo.gl/sQYYs7

Learning Objective 66

3.11.14   **Students are learning to take increasing responsibility for recognising the symptoms of concussion, and acting appropriately if they recognise these in themselves and others.**

3.11.15   Students will:

- describe what concussion means
- describe how a person might get concussion
- describe possible causes of concussion
- explain why concussion is so serious
- describe and know how to spot the main symptoms and signs of concussion
- suggest appropriate action they would take if they suspect that they or another person has concussion (ie inform a member of staff quickly, "if in doubt, sit it out").

Suggested learning tasks

3.11.16   Students can access the Northern Ireland Council for the Curriculum, Examinations and Assessment (CCEA) concussion website. This website aims to teach about concussion, with a focus on recognising and removing concussion. Activities are appropriate for primary and post-primary students.

3.11.17   Students can watch the "Without your brain, you have no game" animation. Young social innovators from Cashel Community School and LIT Limerick School of Art and Design produced this concussion awareness animation.

3.11.18   Students can access the *British Journal of Sports Medicine* Pocket Concussion Recognition Tool. They can discuss how this would help them to identify concussion.

 To access the Northern Ireland CCEA concussion website, see http://goo.gl/euCFoY
To watch "Without your brain, you have no game", go to https://www.youngsocialinnovators.ie/challenges/without-your-brain-you-have-no-game-step-up
For the *British Journal of Sports Medicine* Pocket Concussion Recognition Tool, see bjsm.bmj.com/content/bjsports/47/5/267.full.pdf

Section 12: Learning about Water Safety

3.12.1 This learning could be delivered through the school swimming programme or within Outdoor and Adventurous Activities, PSHE or Geography.

Learning Objective 67

3.12.2 **Students are learning to understand the dangers of water and how to act responsibly when playing in or near different water environments.**

3.12.3 Students will:

- describe how and where water-based incidents occur
- explain the water safety code.

Suggested learning tasks

3.12.4 Students learn about **how** water-based incidents occur such as:

- falling into water when playing on a footpath
- falling out of a boat
- swimming in clothes
- becoming tired
- sustaining an injury
- being out of one's depth
- hampered by weeds or underwater hazards
- rough water or tides.

3.12.5 Students learn about **where** water-based incidents occur:

- Homes and gardens
- Swimming pools
- Beaches
- Rivers
- Canals and reservoirs.

The Water Safety Code The water safety code is a short, easy to remember guide to acting safely and responsibly around water.
Key safety messages: • Always swim in a safe place • Always swim with an adult • If you fall in: float, breathe, relax • If someone else is in trouble call 999 or 112.

In order to stay safe around water, remember:
 	
1 Stop and Think:
  • Water is always moving
  • The water is colder than you think
  • Edges can be dangerous
  • There may be dangers under water.
 	
2 Stay Together:
  • Never swim alone – stay close to a friend or family member
  • Find a safe place to go – only swim in the sea where there is a lifeguard
  • Plan your activity – check weather, tide times, get local advice and wear the right clothing for your activity.

3 Float:
- If you fall in, float until you feel calm
- Signal for help, raising one hand in the air and shouting for help
- If you can, swim to safety or hold on to something that floats
- Keep warm if you can't swim to safety, using the Heat Escape Lessening Position (HELP) or huddle position.

Call 999 or 112:
- If you see someone else in trouble in the water call 999 or 112
- Never enter the water to save others
- Look for something you can throw to help them float, like a life ring or even a football could help
- Keep watch until help arrives.

Students work in small groups to design a presentation on the dangers in or near water, how to stay safe and what to do if they or others get into difficulty.

Resources to assist delivery of this objective can be obtained from the Canal and River Trust:

canalrivertrust.org.uk/explorers/water-safety

Learning Objective 68

3.12.6 **Students are learning to understand the difference in swimming in outdoor water compared to an indoor pool.**

3.12.7 Students will:

- explain the differences between swimming in open water and a heated swimming pool
- explain how strong swimmers can get into difficulties when the water is cold, unpredictable and deep.

Suggested learning tasks

3.12.8 Students discuss the differences between swimming indoors and swimming outdoors.

Getting in and out of open water is more difficult.

Swimming outdoors can be cold and you need to prepare differently; for example, wearing a wetsuit and swim hat.

In a swimming pool environment there are often steps at the side of the pool which make the entry and exits very easy.

The conditions of open water can quickly change dependent on the weather. You also may not be able to see below the water and spot potential hazards.

Students are asked

Q: Why is it more difficult to swim, breathe and stay alert in cold water?
A: The body temperature drops due to the loss of heat and this causes the loss of energy.

Q: What do you think you should wear to keep warm?
A: Wetsuit and a swim hat.

Q: Why would you wear a wetsuit and a swim hat?
A: To help keep you warm.

Q: How can you keep warm?
A: Act out the HELP and Huddle positions learnt whilst taking part in curriculum swimming lessons.

Q: What happens if you're not prepared to swim in cold water?
A: A natural reaction when falling into cold water is to gasp. This sharp intake of breath may mean water is taken in through the mouth and panic sets in. If this happens, stay calm, keep the mouth clear of swallowing water, take slow deep breaths, float, tread water and signal for help.

Learning Objective 69

3.12.9 **Students are learning to perform water-based safe self-rescue and survival skills.**

3.12.10 Students will:

- demonstrate entering and exiting the water safely
- demonstrate treading water and floating/resting in the water
- understand when and how to perform the Heat Escape Lessening Position (HELP) and the Huddle position (see page 321)
- know how to signal for help
- demonstrate sculling and swimming in clothes whilst practising safe self-rescue and survival skills.

Suggested learning tasks

3.12.11 In the pool, as part of the school swimming programme, students should learn and practise the following:

- entering and exiting the water in different ways
- treading water
- the Heat Escape Lessening Position (HELP)
- the Huddle position
- floating and resting in the water
- attracting attention, sculling and swimming using personal floatation equipment.

Water safety

1. HELP position

    Adopt the 'Heat Escape Lessening Position (HELP) technique' by drawing your knees to your chin, keeping your legs together, pressing both arms against your side and keeping your head out of the water.

2. Huddle position

 https://swimsafe.org.uk/for-schools

Learning Objective 70

3.12.12 **Students are learning to recognise national swimming flags and warning signs.**

Suggested learning tasks

Q: How do you know when it's safe to swim?
A: Know the flags and signs.

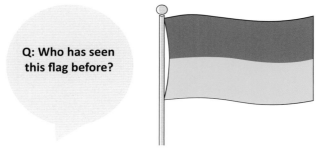

Q: Who has seen this flag before?

Q: What do you think it means?

A: It is a safe place to swim and use body boards and inflatables on the beach. You will often see a lifeguard positioned between the red and yellow flags.

The red flag is a sign for danger and means do not swim. Never go in the water when the red flag is flying under any circumstances. Possible reasons may be fog, large waves or pollution.	
A black and white flag marks the area for surf craft including surf boards such as kayaks, canoes and other craft without engines. Never swim or body board in this area.	
This flag indicates offshore winds blowing out to sea or strong wind conditions – never use an inflatable when the orange windsock is flying.	

Q: Who knows any safety signs you might see at the beach?
A: There are two types of sign:
- **Red round sign with a line through means prohibited**
- **Yellow triangular sign means hazard or danger.**

Resources to Support the Teaching of Safe Self-rescue

1.   **Swim England School Swimming and Water Safety Charter**

- A structured teaching programme that meets government criteria for swimming and water safety.
- Safe self-rescue is embedded throughout the programme.
- Provides resources for teachers to help them deliver water safety lessons in line with the national curriculum.
- Provides resources for students to help them gain knowledge and understanding of the dangers of open water environments.

www.swimming.org/schools/school-swimming-water-safety-charter/

2.   **Curriculum Swimming and Water Safety Resource Pack**

There are eight documents that provide practical guidance on how to plan, deliver and report on curriculum swimming and water safety.

www.swimming.org/schools/resource-pack/

3.   **Swim England and the RNLI 'Swim Safe'**

Swim Safe provides resources to help children stay safe whilst swimming outdoors. During the summer months Swim Safe offers the opportunity for children to put their swimming and water safety skills into practice in open water.

Within the Swim Safe resource there are a range of lesson plans, activity sheets, PowerPoint slides and handouts:

swimsafe.org.uk/for-schools

4.   **The Royal National Lifeboat Institution (RNLI)**

www.rnli.org/youth-education/education-resources

5.   **Royal Life Saving Society (RLSS)**

www.rlss.org.uk/water-safety/water-safety-resources

6.   **Royal Society for the Prevention of Accidents (RoSPA)**

www.rospa.com/waterandleisuresafety/youngpeople/waterresources

7.   **The Canal and River Trust**

canalrivertrust.org.uk/explorers/water-safety

Further Reading

The Association for Physical Education Health Position Paper (2020)

Dr Jo Harris from Loughborough University on behalf of The Association for Physical Education (afPE) updated the Health Position Paper in 2020. This paper outlines physical education's role in promoting active lifestyles and states that curriculum physical education should develop the understanding, skills, confidence and attitudes required for all pupils to be active in their own time. This should include pupils learning about the physical, psychological/mental and social health benefits of physical activity, the physical activity for health guidelines for their age, and how to access the broad range of physical activity opportunities within the school setting and the local community.

http://www.afpe.org.uk/physical-education/afpe-health-position-paper/

Other Useful References

School Sport and Activity Action Plan

Department for Education, Department for Digital, Culture, Media and Sport and the Department of Health and Social Care (2019)

https://assets.publishing.service.gov.uk/government/uploads/system/uploads/attachment_data/file/817093/School_sport_and_activity_action_plan.pdf

Start Active, Stay Active

A report on physical activity for health from the four home countries' Chief Medical Officers (2011)

Department of Health, Department of Health, Social Sciences and Public Safety, the Scottish Government and the Welsh Government

https://assets.publishing.service.gov.uk/government/uploads/system/uploads/attachment_data/file/216370/dh_128210.pdf

What works in schools and colleges to increase physical activity?

Public Health England (2019)

https://assets.publishing.service.gov.uk/government/uploads/system/uploads/attachment_data/file/821463/What_works_in_schools_and_colleges_to_increase_physical_activity.pdf

More Active People for a Healthier World, Global Action Plan on Physical Activity 2018-2030.

World Health Organisation (2018)
World Health Organisation: Geneva, Switzerland

https://apps.who.int/iris/bitstream/handle/10665/272722/9789241514187-eng.pdf

Chapter 4:

Case Law and Frequently Asked Questions

Section 1: Case Law

Introduction

4.1.1   This section outlines some of the case law that has been influential in informing the guidance in this resource. Each case has been cross-referenced **back to** pertinent sections in the previous chapters to demonstrate its application in practice. A reciprocal cross-reference **from** each chapter has also been made to the relevant case.

4.1.2   Within each case law example (which is deliberately brief), the issue concerned is identified along with any key learning points/messages, as appropriate. A review of case law can be particularly useful when drafting internal policies or procedures.

Case Law 1

Cross-reference to **Chapter 2, Section 9: Equipment**
Issue: Inspection of equipment available to the public or vulnerable to vandalism
Steed v Cheltenham Borough Council (2000) (unreported, July 2000, Cheltenham County Court)

4.1.3   The upright of some rugby posts on a public field collapsed, causing the crossbar to hit a boy playing nearby. On inspection, the posts were found to be rusty and deteriorating. Although the posts were inspected regularly during the playing season, they were not inspected as frequently at other times.

4.1.4   The court found that the failure to notice and repair the damaged posts amounted to a breach of the duty of care. Furthermore, there was no justification for the less frequent inspections out of season given the risk of vandalism.

Key learning point

4.1.5   **This highlights the importance of regular inspections by an approved external provider and the need for teachers to monitor the condition of equipment each time they use it. The frequency of inspections must take into account any public use and the risk of vandalism where equipment is permanently in situ.**

Case Law 2

Cross-reference to **Chapter 2, Section 9: Equipment**
Issue: Regular inspection of equipment (goalposts)
Hall v Holker Estate Co Ltd (2008) (EWCA Civ 1422)

4.1.6   An adult was injured during a game of football when he caught his foot in the net of a portable goalpost that should have been pegged into the ground. The goalposts fell forward and hit him, causing facial damage. He claimed the owner of the site should have checked the pegs regularly to ensure the facility and equipment were safe. On appeal, it was held that there was no evidence that the posts were appropriately pegged down as recommended for safe use, nor was there any evidence of a suitable inspection system – both of which amounted to negligence.

Key learning point

4.1.7   **This illustrates the importance of ensuring equipment is regularly inspected and that such inspections are documented. This is particularly important where it is clear the equipment needs to be regularly maintained and properly assembled for safe use, and where it is likely that parts of the equipment are occasionally misplaced or removed, rendering it unsafe.**

Case Law 3

Cross-reference to **Chapter 2, Section 9: Equipment**
Issue: Folding away a trampoline
Clarke v Derby City Council (2015) (unreported)

4.1.8 A 15-year-old student was injured while helping to put away a trampoline at a local authority (LA) school.

4.1.9 The LA denied liability for a failure to supervise the task properly, failure to implement a safe system for it, and causing or permitting too many students to engage in the task. It contended that the trampoline was put away under the teacher's direct supervision and in accordance with the national guidelines – *Safe Practice in Physical Education and Sport* – issued by the Association for Physical Education (afPE).

4.1.10 The LA contended that the teacher was only made aware of the student's injury after the first part of the procedure, which the teacher claimed was carried out without any incident. The LA also claimed that there was no history of any previous similar incidents, and that the trampoline was inspected annually and, at the previous inspection, was found to have been in good working order.

4.1.11 It was further argued that the student's accident was caused by her own negligence in failing to follow the teacher's instructions and to take proper care for her own safety.

4.1.12 At trial, the student alleged that the teacher had been called outside to attend to noisy students waiting for the next lesson. However, there was no lesson after the one in which the student was injured, and the teacher could not therefore have been called outside for the reason claimed. The judge also found significant changes between the student's initial allegations and those made later in court.

4.1.13 The judge said that a failure to supervise was such an obvious complaint that it would have been made at the outset, but that allegation was not initially made. The claim was dismissed.

Key learning point

4.1.14 **This case shows the importance of supervising tasks involving equipment where a foreseeable risk of injury is recognised, following established systems and procedures, and the importance of equipment inspections. In addition, the teacher's comprehensive record of the incident at the time was shown to be of great value.**

Case Law 4

Cross-reference to **Chapter 2, Section 9: Equipment**
Issue: Folding away a trampoline
Greenwood v Dorset County Council (2008) (unreported)

4.1.15 A group of students were involved in folding away a trampoline. One student's arm was fractured when the folding end trapped it. The teacher was judged to have complied with the established code of practice in that she had:

- supervised adequately
- taught the correct process
- regularly reminded the students of the correct process
- provided step-by-step monitoring of the process
- involved sufficient students in the folding process.

Key learning point

4.1.16 **Students are able to assist in assembling and folding away trampolines if they have had sufficient training, and are physically capable and effectively supervised.**

Case Law 5

Cross-reference to **Chapter 2, Section 9: Equipment**
Issue: Removing condemned equipment
Beaumont v Surrey County Council (1968) (66 LGR 580)

4.1.17   A teacher disposed of old trampette elastic in an open bin close to the school playground where students congregated. The elastic was removed by students during break time, and while they were playing with it, another student was hit in the eye.

4.1.18   The court held that, given the likelihood that students would use the elastic for play were they to come across it, the method of disposal was inadequate. Furthermore, while the school operated an adequate method of playground supervision, that had not been in place on the day in question.

Key learning point

4.1.19   **Broken equipment must be removed from use and disposed of in a manner that prevents any further use, whether in the manner intended or otherwise.**

Case Law 6

Cross-reference to **Chapter 2, Section 13: Personal Protective Equipment**
Issue: School notifying parents regarding the school policy on wearing mouth guards
G (a child) v Lancashire County Council (2000)
Source - Lancashire County Council

4.1.20   A student received a serious mouth injury in hockey while not wearing a mouth guard. Although the matter was settled by agreement, the judge commented that it was the responsibility of the school to ensure that where personal protective equipment (PPE) was not mandatory, parents were directly provided with appropriate information in order to understand the risks and to make **informed** decisions regarding their own child. Providing information via students was not sufficient in this case.

Key learning point

4.1.21   **Schools must provide information directly to parents in order that they can make informed decisions regarding supplying discretionary PPE equipment for their child.**

Case Law 7

Cross-reference to **Chapter 2, Section 14: Personal Effects, Clothing and Footwear**
Issue: Barefoot work in gymnastics
Farmer v Hampshire County Council (2006) (unreported)

4.1.22   A Year 1 class (5-6 years old) had been taught by an experienced teacher how to lift, carry and place gymnastic equipment. The class worked in **bare feet**. A girl fractured her toe when a group dropped a low portable beam. A claim for negligence was based on the need for footwear to be worn when carrying equipment. The claim was dismissed on the basis that barefoot work in gymnastics is **normal** where the floor is suitable, the children had been taught how to carry the items, they were closely supervised by the teacher, footwear gives very little protection if a heavy weight is dropped on to the foot, and there is an inappropriate time factor for a whole class to put on and remove footwear during a lesson.

Key learning point

4.1.23   **This case shows the importance of supervising tasks involving equipment where a foreseeable risk of injury is recognised, following established systems and procedures, and the importance of training students to carry equipment safely when working in bare feet.**

Case Law 8

Cross-reference to **Chapter 2, Section 14: Personal Effects, Clothing and Footwear**
Issue: Feet caught in webbing of a trampoline
Villella v North Bedfordshire Borough Council (1983) (Lexis Citation 821)

4.1.24   A young girl trampolining in bare feet caught her toe in the webbing of the trampoline bed, which caused her to fall and fracture her femur. The court held that although there was a difference in the expert evidence with regard to the need for participants to wear socks or trampoline slippers, given the age and inexperience of the student and the size of the gaps in the trampoline bed webbing, an injury of the type that occurred was reasonably foreseeable. A duty was owed to the student to ensure she wore appropriate footwear to prevent such an injury and the failure to do so amounted to a breach of that duty.

Key learning point

4.1.25   **Teachers should insist that students wear non-slip socks in any school-organised trampolining activity.**

Case Law 9

Cross-reference to **Chapter 2, Section 14: Personal Effects, Clothing and Footwear**
Issue: Parents refusing for a student's jewellery to be removed for PESSPA activities
R (ex parte Roberts) v the Chair and Governors of Cwnfelinfach Primary School (2001) (unreported)

4.1.26   The school had a policy that earrings were not to be worn in activity sessions on the basis that they presented a foreseeable hazard to the wearer and other participants. A student was excluded from participation in PESSPA, club and playground activities on the basis that her parents refused to remove her earrings. An action was brought under the Human Rights Act 1998 on the basis of victimisation and deprivation of access to the national curriculum. The court determined that the school was entitled to exclude the student from physical activity on the basis of health and safety. A claim that the exclusion breached the European Convention on Human Rights was rejected.

Key learning point

4.1.27   **Schools are entitled to adopt policies in relation to the wearing of jewellery for PESSPA activities and to enforce those policies where students or their parents fail to observe them. Consideration may, however, need to be given to policy adjustments in the case of jewellery with religious significance.**

Case Law 10

Cross-reference to **Chapter 2, Section 14: Personal Effects, Clothing and Footwear**
Issue: Uniform policy
R (on the application of Begum) v the Head Teacher and Governors of Denbigh High School (2006) (UKHL 15)

4.1.28   The school had a published uniform policy, on which it had consulted widely with the school community, that permitted girls whose religion required modest dress to wear a shalwar kameez. Ms Begum, a Muslim student, who had worn the shalwar kameez for two years, was of the opinion that the observation of her religion required her now to wear the jilbab. The school refused to allow her to attend unless she was wearing the correct uniform, and Ms Begum refused to attend school unless she was permitted to wear the jilbab.

4.1.29   Ms Begum claimed that she had been unlawfully excluded and that the school policy contravened her rights under Article 9 of the European Convention of Human Rights to manifest her religion/religious beliefs.

4.1.30   The court decided that as Ms Begum could attend school whenever she wished provided she wore the appropriate uniform, she was not excluded. Furthermore, her rights under Article 9 were not infringed as she was free to attend another school that would allow her to wear the jilbab. (Although there is a right to education, there is no right to be educated at a particular school or type of school.)

4.1.31   Central to the decision was the extent to which the school had consulted when devising its policy and the efforts it made to bring the issue to the attention of prospective parents and students including Ms Begum.

Key learning point

4.1.32   **While a school has a right to set and enforce a uniform policy, it is important that uniform, including clothing for PESSPA, seeks to respect religious and cultural beliefs without compromising health and safety standards. Where a school wishes to change uniform requirements, it is good practice to consult with the school community first.**

Case Law 11

Cross-reference to **Chapter 2, Section 14: Personal Effects, Clothing and Footwear**
Issue: School policy on the wearing of jewellery for PESSPA activities
Watkins-Singh v the Governing Body of Aberdare High School and Rhondda Cynon Taff Unitary Authority (2008) (EWHC 1865 [Admin])

4.1.33   A claim for indirect racial discrimination was brought against a school because the governors' interpretation of the school's restrictive policy on wearing jewellery prevented a Sikh student attending school wearing the kara (a plain steel band about 5mm in width). The judgement in favour of the student was based on the school's interpretation of the policy being "procedurally unfair" and allowing no exemptions at all.

4.1.34   Consideration of the issue was in the context of wearing the kara in school generally and did not specifically take account of the implications relating to health and safety within PESSPA. However, the student indicated that she was prepared to remove or cover the kara with a sweatband during PESSPA where health and safety was an issue. In his summary of the judgement, the judge made particular reference to her willingness to do this in recognition of health and safety concerns. He thus acknowledged the need for exceptions to be made in specific situations where health and safety concerns are important.

4.1.35   Another important consideration highlighted by the judge was that the restrictive school jewellery policy was formally recognised by the governors only after the dispute had arisen. Prior to that, it was described as being in place but unsigned by the governors, incomplete in content and in a generic form supplied by a neighbouring authority. Every school needs to ensure that **all policies are specific to the school**, appropriately detailed and approved by the governors before implementation.

Key learning point

4.1.36   **While schools are entitled to have uniform policies, they should remain flexible enough to allow appropriate exceptions to be made where it is safe and reasonable to do so.**

Case Law 12

Cross-reference to **Chapter 2, Section 7: First Aid**
Issue: Accident procedures
Felgate v Middlesex County Council (1954) (unreported)

4.1.37   While sitting on the lower of two horizontal bars in a gymnastic apparatus arrangement, a six-year-old girl lost her balance and fell off on to the mats located below, breaking her arm. The teacher, although close by, was assisting a boy climbing a ladder to access the same equipment. The girl's parent alleged inadequate supervision and criticised the post-accident procedures on the basis that the child had been sent to hospital before the parent had been informed of the accident.

4.1.38   The claim was dismissed on the basis that the teacher had adopted a "well recognised practice".

4.1.39   In addition, the judge recognised that where there is a need to seek expert medical attention, this should be prioritised over informing parents.

Key learning point

4.1.40   **While this case recognises that the action taken was appropriate, school procedures in respect of contacting parents should still be adhered to, where possible.**

Case Law 13

Cross-reference to **Chapter 2, Section 8: Facilities**
Issue: Clean and dry flooring
Bassie v Merseyside Fire and Civil Defence Authority (2005) (EWCA Civ 1474)

4.1.41   A firefighter suffered a serious knee injury when he slipped during a warm-up activity prior to training taking place. He was wearing appropriate footwear and the flooring in the room was free of faults. Furthermore, the floor had been swept prior to the start of the warm-up activity but had not been mopped.

4.1.42   It was found that the likely cause of the slip was a fine layer of dust that had been observed on the floor following the accident, which could not be removed by brushing alone. Moreover, the cost of mopping the floor prior to the training was negligible.

Key learning point

4.1.43   **Floors need to be cleaned in an appropriate manner to remove known risks. It is important that schools have risk assessments in place and can demonstrate their cleaning regimens.**

Case Law 14

Cross-reference to **Chapter 2, Section 8: Facilities**
Issue: Inspecting the teaching area
Sutton v Syston Rugby Football Club Ltd (2011) (EWCA civ 1182)

4.1.44   A 16-year-old rugby player was injured during a tag rugby game at his local club, resulting in a knee injury caused by colliding with a partially buried object.

4.1.45   He claimed compensation due to the club's negligence in failing to inspect the pitch. The club argued that while a pitch inspection had not taken place before the match, had it done so, it would only have identified obvious obstacles such as broken glass, not the item that had caused the injury (a partially buried cricket marker stub that did not extend up above the level of the grass).

4.1.46   The judge in the initial trial awarded compensation on the basis that they considered that the site of the accident ought to have been more rigorously inspected than other parts of the pitch. Therefore, had an inspection taken place, the object would have been discovered.

4.1.47   The Appeal Court disagreed, ruling that before a game or training session, a pitch should be **walked over at a reasonable walking pace. This requirement applied** whether the activity was a training session or match, and all areas of the pitch should be treated with the same attention, particularly given that the danger to be avoided (ie falling on to or into foreign objects) could happen on any part of the pitch.

4.1.48   Given this standard, the court concluded that a reasonable walkover inspection of the pitch would not have revealed the stub, and therefore the appeal was allowed.

Key learning point

4.1.49   **Pitches should be inspected prior to each use, and such inspections documented.**

Case Law 15

Cross-reference to **Chapter 2, Section 8: Facilities**
Issue: Managing the teaching space
Jones vs Monmouthshire County Council (2011) (unreported)

4.1.50   Compensation for injury was awarded when a student tripped over a kerb while retrieving a ball from the area surrounding an AstroTurf pitch. The difference in the height of the kerb and pitch was described as being "borderline" as a tripping hazard. The judge determined that if it was recognised as a tripping hazard, something should have been done to manage the hazard. A common-sense solution would have been to remind participants about the difference in height, and monitor that they were paying attention to the task of retrieving the ball sensibly by looking where they were going.

Key learning point

4.1.51   **Known hazards should be brought to the attention of participants, and checks should be made that they are alert to these hazards.**

Case Law 16

Cross-reference to **Chapter 2, Section 8: Facilities**
Issue: Quality of playing surface
Douch v Reading Borough Council (2000) (Zurich Municipal *Court Circular*, April 2001)

4.1.52   A player stumbled and injured himself while running to retrieve a ball during a cricket match, blaming grass-covered humps in the outfield. The judge dismissed the claim on the basis that they were "minor undulations", which were to be expected on such surfaces, with only a remote likelihood of someone falling because of them. It was also accepted that the cost of ensuring professional competition standard surfaces for all players would be prohibitive.

Key learning point

4.1.53   **Although minor undulations may be acceptable, all playing areas need to be regularly inspected to ensure they remain safe to use for the particular activities intended.**

Case Law 17

Cross-reference to **Chapter 2, Section 8: Facilities**
Issue: Inspection of playing surfaces
Taylor v Corby Borough Council (2000) (Zurich Municipal *Court Circular*, May 2000)

4.1.54   While playing a ball game on a grassed recreation area, an adult was injured because his foot went down a 10cm hole that was partially grassed over. Under an existing contract, the area was subject to grounds maintenance 12 times a year, but the contract did not specify that any formal inspections of the playing surface were to be carried out. There was no risk assessment in place, nor were regular checks carried out, although reported defects were addressed.

4.1.55   The court found that the hole had been there for some time and would have been visible to anyone carrying out an inspection. On that basis, the council ought to have had an inspection system in place.

Key learning point

4.1.56   **Some system of regular and documented checks of playing surfaces is necessary, given that it is entirely foreseeable that holes in playing surfaces are likely to cause serious injury.**

Case Law 18

Cross-reference to **Chapter 2, Section 8: Facilities**
Issue: Preparing a long-jump sand pit
Futcher v Hertfordshire LA (1997) (Luton County Court, 1997)

4.1.57   A long-jump participant was awarded damages after they were injured by landing on compacted sand. The area had been raked, but not dug over before or during the competition.

Key learning point

4.1.58   **Surfaces, particularly those that are relied on to minimise impact-related injury, must be properly maintained to ensure they remain effective, with particular attention paid to known hazards.**

Case Law 19

Cross-reference to **Chapter 2, Section 8: Facilities**
Issue: Informing participants of risk
Jones v Northampton Borough Council and another (1990) (Lexis Citation 1876)

4.1.59   In an unusually complex case, a man (the second defendant) hired a sports centre for a game of football on behalf of the social club to which he belonged. He was told by the sports centre manager, who was employed by the council, that the playing surface had a wet patch due to a leak in the roof. He was offered the opportunity to cancel the hiring and rebook at another time. He decided to proceed and asked that the area be mopped.

4.1.60   Although the area was mopped as requested, one player slipped on a wet patch and was injured.

4.1.61   The person who had hired the facility was held to be negligent for failing to inform the other players of the risk even though he was aware of it. He was required to indemnify the council for the compensation they had agreed to pay the claimant.

Key learning point

4.1.62   **Students (and their parents) should be made aware of risks associated with participation in activities. Particular attention should be paid where those risks are unusual or unexpected, such as wet floors.**

Case Law 20

Cross-reference to **Chapter 2, Section 8: Facilities**
Issue: Facility unsafe for participants
Morrell v Owen and others (1993) (Lexis Citation 3341)

4.1.63   A sports organisation hired a hall for a track and field training event. The participants had disabilities but were experienced and proficient in their events. The hall was to cater for two groups – one practising archery and one discus. Those throwing discus did so towards the sports hall netting separating the groups.

4.1.64   The claimant, a wheelchair user, re-entered the hall part way through the session. To reach her position in the archery section, she had to travel along the netting and, once through it, had to wait until all participating archers had finished shooting.

4.1.65   While waiting to proceed, she was hit on the head by a discus that had been thrown towards her position. Although it hit the netting, this failed to absorb the momentum and billowed forward, allowing the discus to hit her.

4.1.66   The court determined that the organisers of the event failed to provide proper or any instruction to participants to avoid injury occurring. They failed to appreciate and plan for the fact that wheelchair users were less ambulant than other participants or that some would need to leave the hall more frequently than other participants. They had, it was said, relied on the fact that the participants were experienced and that they would, in essence, realise the danger for themselves and take steps to protect one another. The court found this to be unacceptable.

Key learning point

4.1.67   **When organising sports events, schools must ensure their plans address the particular needs of the participants and that these plans are communicated to all participants and coaches.**

Case Law 21

Cross-reference to **Chapter 2, Section 8: Facilities**
Issue: Managing the climbing wall
Health and Safety Executive (HSE) v Thornton Grammar School (2014) (unreported)

4.1.68   A Bradford grammar school was ordered to pay £12,500 in fines and costs after the physical education equipment manager fell nine metres from a climbing wall. In his position at the school, he had become more involved in the lessons and "learnt the basics". He was working his way up the wall to rig it for a lesson by threading the rope through anchor points. A colleague on the ground was belaying to provide added rope when needed, but minimising the amount of loose rope, which meant a slip would only result in a drop of a short distance for the climber. However, the technique failed, and the climber fell, hitting the gym floor below. There were no mats or padding, and he was not wearing a helmet. There was no health and safety system in place regarding the climbing wall at all – nothing in writing, no guidelines and no one charged with overall responsibility. The school was found to be in breach of Section 2(1) of the Health and Safety at Work etc Act 1974. The HSE inspector reported:

It is essential that those who provide climbing instructions should themselves be properly trained and certificated. The training and development of staff using the climbing wall at this school was not adequate, and they were allowed to undertake tasks on it that they had not been trained for.

Key learning point

4.1.69   **Schools should develop and document safe systems for the use of inherently risky equipment. Those systems should be communicated to participants and staff alike.**

Case Law 22

Cross-reference to **Chapter 2, Section 16: Transport**
Issue: **Importance of reputable transport companies**
R v Unwin (2011) (unreported)

4.1.70   A coach driver was late to collect a school group from an outdoor activity centre. To make up time on the return journey, he took a short cut that was wholly unsuitable. The teachers complained, and one student received whiplash injuries. The driver had 12 points on his licence already for speeding and driving while using a mobile phone/smartphone but had been spared a ban. He was found guilty of dangerous driving and given a 12-month "alternative to custody" order and banned from driving for 14 months. He was sacked from the coach company the day after the incident.

Key learning point

4.1.71   **There was no reported indication that the coach company was disreputable, but this case emphasises the importance of checking the standards of coach companies. It would usually be sufficient to use a coach company with which the school is familiar and that has a good timekeeping record, along with evidence of good, considerate drivers and well maintained coaches.**

Case Law 23

Cross-reference to **Chapter 2, Section 11: Safe Exercise Practice**
Issue: **Effective management of space**
A (a minor) v Leeds City Council (1999) (Leeds County Court, Zurich Municipal *Court Circular*, September 1999)

4.1.72   An 11-year-old girl was injured during a warm-up activity that involved the class of 25 students running to touch all four corners of the gym before returning to the teacher. The girl was injured as the students criss-crossed on different paths of travel. The claim was upheld. The teacher was considered to be not in control of the exercise and unable to stop a collision once everyone had set off, and such a collision was "foreseeable".

Key learning point

4.1.73   **The responsible adult should ensure that students are able to stop or change direction on order to avoid collisions, and that the group has the ability to stop on command.**

Case Law 24 (Four Cases)

Cross-reference to **Chapter 2, Section 2: Safeguarding**
Issue: **Safeguarding**

4.1.74   The following cases all involve an "abuse of trust". They were brought under the principle of **"abuse of a position of trust"**. It is an offence under the Sexual Offences Act 2003 for a person over the age of 18, such as a teacher, to have a sexual relationship of any kind with a child under 18 where that person is in a position of trust in respect of that child, such as in teaching, even if the relationship is consensual.

4.1.75   **24a: R v Drake (2011) (unreported)**

         A physical education teacher who was also a deputy head teacher was sentenced to six years' imprisonment for maintaining sexual relationships with two 14-year-old students and one 16-year-old student.

4.1.76   **24b: R v Brooks (2007) (unreported)**

         A physical education teacher received a five-year prison term for having an affair with a 14-year-old student.

4.1.77   **24c: R v Thompson (2008) (unreported)**

A physical education teacher groomed a 17-year-old student through texts and telephone calls. He was sentenced to a nine-month prison sentence, to be listed on the sex offenders register for 10 years and is not allowed any unsupervised access to a child under 18.

4.1.78   **24d: R v Lister (2005) (unreported)**

A physical education teacher was jailed for 15 months for using mobile phone/smartphone calls and texts to groom young girls.

Key learning point

4.1.79   **Employer safeguarding policies and procedures should be very clear, and fully adhered to by all school staff.**

Case Law 25

Cross-reference to **Chapter 2, Section 2: Safeguarding**
Issue: Dangerous play/assumption of risk
Hattingh v Roux (2011) ([5] SA 135 [WCC] [2011] ZAWCHC 100; 18650/07 [4 May 2011])

4.1.80   A hooker in the front row of a rugby scrum received a severe neck injury in a school match. The opposing hooker and prop both intentionally placed their heads together in the same gap when engaging in a scrum, instead of interlocking, to exert increased pressure on the opposing hooker. This is **illegal and dangerous**. The judge confirmed that players could not seek to deliberately injure opponents.

Key learning point

4.1.81   **The assumption of risk in sport that is inherently dangerous will not apply to deliberate acts to endanger participants.**

Case Law 26

Cross-reference to **Chapter 2, Section 2: Safeguarding**
Issue: Ensuring fair play
Gravil v Carroll (1) and Redruth RFU Club (2) (2008) (unreported)

4.1.82   A player admitted punching the claimant in an off-the-ball incident following a scrum during a semi-professional rugby match. The injured party needed facial surgery and was out of the game for six months. The offending player was suspended for eight weeks. The injured player alleged that the club (the second defendant) had encouraged aggressive play through a results-based bonus system. The Appeal Court ruled that it was "fair and just" to hold semi-professional and professional clubs liable for their players' illegal or violent actions, establishing "a vicarious responsibility for the injury".

Key learning point

4.1.83   **It is essential for clubs to take steps to reduce the occurrence of foul play.**

Case Law 27

Cross-reference to **Chapter 2, Section 2: Safeguarding**
Issue: Foul play
R v Chapman (2010) (Warwick Crown Court)

4.1.84 During a football match, the injured player, while lawfully shielding the ball, was tackled from behind by the accused with raised studs, resulting in an extremely serious injury. The accused claimed the tackle was not reckless but admitted grievous bodily harm. The judgement referred to the offence as "a very deliberate criminal act". This was the first prison sentence (six months) given for a "reckless tackle".

Key learning point

4.1.85 **Foul play can result in criminal liability.**

Case Law 28

Cross-reference to **Chapter 2, Section 5: Insurance**
Issue: Insurance
Van Oppen v the Clerk to the Bedford Charity Trustees (1989) ([1989] 3 All ER 389)

4.1.86 A student was seriously injured during a game of rugby. The parents sued for negligence, including an allegation that the school had failed to insure students against personal injury or to advise parents of the need to insure their children against the risk of personal injury.

4.1.87 The court held that there had been no negligence on the part of the school in relation to the injury or the issue of insurance. It was established that it is the school's duty to insure against negligence, and it is the parents' responsibility to consider personal injury insurance for their children because it is a matter of choice or discretion.

Key learning point

4.1.88 **Personal injury insurance is a matter for parents.**

Case Law 29

Cross-reference to **Chapter 2, Section 10: Programme Management**
Issue: Risk assessment
R v Ellis (2003) (Manchester Crown Court)

4.1.89 A young boy drowned during a plunge pool activity on an educational visit. Although the teacher had some experience in leading adventurous activities, he failed to take account of prevailing weather conditions that made the activity dangerous. He ignored warnings given by staff with other groups who had decided not to proceed, he failed to ensure safety equipment was to hand, and he failed to give regard to the differing needs of his group.

4.1.90 The teacher was convicted of manslaughter and a breach of the Health and Safety at Work etc Act 1974. He received 12-month and six-month custodial sentences for the respective offences, to be served concurrently.

Key learning point

4.1.91 **Activities should be subject to a dynamic risk assessment, with a "plan B" option where appropriate.**

Case Law 30

Cross-reference to **Chapter 2, Section 10: Programme Management**
Issue: Effective supervision of gymnastic activity
Heffer v Wiltshire County Council (1996) (Devizes County Court)

4.1.92   A student was injured in a gymnastic lesson while attempting a straddle vault over a buck. The class had progressed from performing leapfrog with support to performing the same skill using the buck. Support was withdrawn when using the buck, unless it was requested by the students.

4.1.93   The student in question was hesitant and refused his first attempt, unseen by the teacher. On the second attempt, he managed to clear the buck but used a one-foot take-off, allowing the swing of his leg to dislodge his supporting arm, causing him to fall to the floor and injure himself.

4.1.94   Allowing compensation for the claimant's injury, the court judged that the teacher had been negligent. Although the student was supported throughout the leapfrog activity, that support should not have been withdrawn on the buck. Furthermore, it should not have been left to the student to "opt in" to support as peer-group pressure might have prevented opting in.

4.1.95   The reduction in support was judged to be premature and total, rather than gradual, and it was deemed that progression to the buck constituted a new activity requiring a continuation of support.

Key learning point

4.1.96   **Sequenced progressions should be planned for gymnastic activity, and teachers should move on students when they are judged to be ready. After this decision is made, continuous monitoring and supervision should continue to ensure that students can cope with the new level of challenge.**

Case Law 31

Cross-reference to **Chapter 2, Section 10: Programme Management**
Issue: Students working on activities according to their stage of readiness
Jones v Hampshire County Council (1997) (Lexis Citation 2131)

4.1.97   A vaulting table had been introduced into the school about 3–4 weeks before the incident occurred. The class had not used this equipment before in the way they were being asked to use it during this gymnastic lesson. It was alleged that they were not told precisely what to do with it and that no task had been set.

4.1.98   One student performed a forward roll along the table, and the claimant copied this – twice successfully, but on the third attempt, she fell and broke her arm. The student alleged inadequate instruction and supervision, and an unsafe system being used by the teacher.

4.1.99   The claimant in this case was 24 years old. She was making a claim against this incident that had happened 13 years before, when she was 11.

4.1.100   The Court of Appeal said that "it may be perfectly reasonable for a teacher to allow children to engage in an activity which, on the face of it, is fraught with danger if that teacher has made an assessment of those children and come to the conclusion that the activity is reasonably safe for them". On the evidence provided, no judgement of this nature had been made. The students were "simply left to get on with it".

4.1.101   A breach of duty was evident. The teacher should have seen that the particular activity was beyond the competence of this particular student.

Key learning point

4.1.102   **Teachers should ensure that students are working at the appropriate level of challenge and are not allowed to work beyond their stage of readiness.**

Case Law 32

Cross-reference to **Chapter 2, Section 10: Programme Management**
Issue: Safe practice on climbing walls
R vs Manningtree High School (2013) (Colchester Magistrates Court)

4.1.103   In a prosecution brought by the HSE, a secondary school was fined for safety failings after a 14-year-old boy fell more than four metres from a climbing wall. The teenager was on his first ever "lead climb" – a more advanced rock-climbing technique – during a physical education lesson. He had managed to clip on to three points as he ascended the climbing wall but struggled with the fourth. A fellow student, similarly inexperienced, had been told to belay the rope for the boy. After the climber grew tired, the teacher told him to let go of the climbing wall, which he did. However, instead of being supported by the belay technique, he fell unrestrained and hit the safety mat on the floor, fracturing a heel bone.

4.1.104   The HSE investigation found that, prior to the lesson, none of the students involved were aware of what lead climbing was or the risks involved, and none had been properly trained or prepared for the more advanced type of climbing that was being attempted.

4.1.105   The school failed to have an adequate safety management system in place for lead climbing by failing to adequately protect the students from the risk of falls. In addition, the teacher was not competent to teach or supervise lead climbing.

Key learning point

4.1.106   **Teachers should be deemed competent to teach activities, and able to create and maintain a safe learning environment.**

Case Law 33

Cross-reference to **Chapter 2, Section 10: Programme Management**
Issue: Students working on activities according to their stage of readiness
Anderson v Portejolie (2008) (unreported)

4.1.107   A skier was seriously hurt when taken off-piste during a ski-school lesson. He was successful in claiming negligence on the part of the instructor, arguing that he was not experienced enough to have been taken off-piste and that the instructor should have realised the demand of the task was beyond some in the group.

Key learning point

4.1.108   **Teachers should ensure that students are working at the appropriate level of challenge and are not allowed to work beyond their stage of readiness.**

Case Law 34

Cross-reference to **Chapter 2, Section 10: Programme Management**
Issue: Not using recognised practice
Woodroffe-Hedley v Cuthbertson (1997) (Lexis Citation 3849)

4.1.109   An experienced alpine guide was climbing with a client using an established procedure for ice that included using two ice screws and a running belay. This procedure ensured that in the event of the leader falling, the risk of death/serious injury would be reduced. While acting as the lead climber, the guide abandoned accepted practice and used a single ice screw without the running belay as he wished to proceed to the shelter of rocks without delay on the basis that he feared a rockfall. A sheet of ice gave way under the guide, causing him to fall. The single ice screw did not offer a strong enough anchor point, and consequently, the client was dragged down the mountain after the guide, resulting in his death.

4.1.110   The court found that the risk of the rockfall was not sufficiently immediate to warrant failing to follow established procedure, and as such, this amounted to negligence on the part of the guide.

Key learning point

4.1.111   **Where established and approved procedures exist, they should be followed.**

Case Law 35

Cross-reference to **Chapter 2, Section 10: Programme Management**
Issue: Following regular and approved practice
Shaw v Redbridge LBC (2005) ([2005] EWHC 150 [QB])

4.1.112   The claimant alleged that she had developed a psychiatric illness following an alleged indecent assault that occurred when she was at a school maintained by the defendant LA, which staff did not report to her parents.

4.1.113   The incident was claimed to have been reported to the girl's head of year, who had provided the girl with three options – reporting the matter to the police, reporting the matter to her parents or punishing the boys concerned. The girl said she opted for the boys to be punished.

4.1.114   The teacher concerned denied that he would have left the choice of action in such circumstances to a young girl. He insisted he would, if he felt it appropriate, have reported the matter to the police and/or the girl's parents. In the circumstances, he considered that the incident amounted to little more than horseplay of a type that occurred in schools. While he issued a behaviour sanction, he did not consider the incident to warrant any further action.

4.1.115   Having found the girl's evidence to be unreliable, the court dismissed the claim of negligence because the teacher's action was typical of what would be seen across the profession and judged to be "proper professional judgement", ie regular and approved practice.

Key learning point

4.1.116   **Staff need to exercise proper professional judgement at all times.**

Case Law 36

Cross-reference to **Chapter 2, Section 10: Programme Management**
Issue: Using professional judgement to ensure the activity remains as safe as practicable
Chittock v Woodbridge School ([2005] EWHC 150 [QB])

4.1.117   The claimant took part in a skiing trip organised by the school. As he was a relatively experienced skier and senior student, he was permitted, with a friend, to ski unaccompanied. A teacher observed them skiing off-piste and reminded them that this was not acceptable. When they were observed off-piste on a second occasion, they were severely reprimanded. The teacher threatened to remove their ski passes but did not do so on account of the pair giving assurances that they would not ski off-piste again.

4.1.118   They were next observed skiing on-piste on a run with a narrow section where slower and less experienced skiers were bunched. The claimant's friend negotiated the slower skiers and proceeded down the slope. The claimant attempted to follow but lost control and veered off-piste where he fell, suffering serious injury.

4.1.119   The claim stated that the school were negligent in not removing the ski passes after the second occasion on which the pair had been observed skiing off-piste.

4.1.120   On appeal, the court decided that removal of the ski passes was only one of a range of reasonable options that could have been used to deal with the situation and therefore the teacher had not been negligent.

Key learning point

4.1.121   This case established the principle of a "range of reasonable options" being acceptable in dealing with issues, and recognised that no single response was the correct way to deal with a situation. In other words, some degree of flexibility, according to the circumstances, was more appropriate and responsible.

Case Law 37

Cross-reference to **Chapter 2, Section 10: Programme Management**
Issue: Reintegrating students who have been unable to take part
Moore v Hampshire County Council (1981) (80 LGR 481, [1981] Lexis Citation 1584)

4.1.122   A student who had been excused from taking part in physical education over an extended period for medical reasons eventually persuaded a teacher to allow her to participate.

4.1.123   During her first gymnastic lesson, she fell and broke her ankle while attempting a handstand.

4.1.124   Despite this being the first lesson the student had participated in at the school, the teacher had not supervised her closely. This was the student's introduction to work that the other students in the class had experienced over a series of lessons. The teacher failed to cater for the student's individual needs and background, and further failed to obtain confirmation that she was now formally permitted to take part.

Key learning point

4.1.125   **Students who have missed lessons should be supervised, and provided with a level of challenge appropriate for their stage of readiness.**

Case Law 38

Cross-reference to **Chapter 2, Section 7: First Aid**
Issue: Using professional judgement when supervising lessons
CMG (a minor) v Rhondda Cynon Taf County Borough Council (2014) (unreported)

4.1.126   A primary school student injured her finger in a classroom lesson for which the LA was responsible.

4.1.127   It was alleged that the teacher had told the group to sit on the floor behind a swivel chair on which another student was sitting. The student on the chair leaned over to pass some information to the other student seated behind him. When he was doing this, the chair fell over, injuring the student sitting behind him.

4.1.128   It was alleged that the injured student had complained to the teacher that the student on the chair was deliberately making the chair collide with her. Negligence was alleged on the basis that the teacher was not paying sufficient attention to the student in the chair behaving mischievously, that the class was inadequately supervised, and that the teacher should have known there was a foreseeable risk of injury to students sitting on the floor behind a student on a swivel chair.

4.1.129   The LA denied liability, contending that the floor and chair were fit for their intended purpose, the class was sufficiently supervised, with one teacher for the 11 students in the class, and there was no record of any similar incident in the 12 months preceding the accident. It was also claimed that the injured student had not complained of any injury at the end of the class or during the rest of the day, and the teacher had regarded the accident as so minor, it did not need to be recorded in the school's accident record book.

4.1.130   The judge determined that the chair accidentally fell over when the student in it leaned over. The staff:student ratio was sufficient, and the teacher could not be criticised for deciding not to complete the accident record book as "no real harm" had occurred. The judge also decided that the floor behind the chair was not a dangerous area for students to sit in, and that the **accident** had not been reasonably foreseeable. The judge held this was a pure accident with no one to blame. The claim was dismissed.

Key learning point

4.1.131   **This case illustrates that completing an accident record log for a trivial incident is not always a requirement. The injured student not complaining about any injury during the rest of the day nor leaving school early reinforced the view that the injury was insignificant and therefore required no further action beyond that the teacher had taken – "trust your professional judgement".**

Case Law 39

Cross-reference to **Chapter 2, Section 7: First Aid**
Issue: Keeping accurate records
Liddell v City of York Council (2015) (unreported)

4.1.132   A 13-year-old student attending an extracurricular trampoline lesson alleged that, at the end of the lesson, while she was helping to dismantle the trampoline, she sustained a fractured arm after it became caught in the dismantled bars. She blamed the teacher supervising the dismantling of the trampoline, stating that some students, who were to catch the bars when the trampoline was dismantled, failed to catch them, and that other students, who did catch them, let them go. Her key allegation was that the teacher had instructed her to take the weight of the trampoline alone. In her witness statement, she said she knew she alone was to receive the end section of the trampoline during its dismantling. At trial, she changed this and claimed that she only became aware after her accident that she alone was to receive the end section. The teacher said she gave proper instructions and warnings to the students regarding the correct dismantling of the trampoline.

4.1.133   The court dismissed the claim, finding the teacher to be "conscientious and careful" with regard to health and safety matters, and that the dismantling procedure would have been safe if the students had followed it according to training and instructions. The court said that the student would have been able to understand and follow those instructions.

Key learning point

4.1.134   **This case illustrates the importance of retaining records of accidents involving students at school, and of recording as much contemporaneous evidence as possible at the time of the accident. Where no particular complaint is made by or on behalf of the injured student at the time, as was the case here, this does not necessarily mean that a future claim is not possible. Here, the claim was made seven years after the accident due to the complainant claiming she continued to suffer ongoing symptoms from the original accident.**

Case Law 40

Cross-reference to **Chapter 2, Section 7: First Aid**
Issue: Concussion
School rugby, 2011 (https://www.bbc.co.uk/news/uk-northern-ireland-23943642**)**

4.1.135   A schoolboy died after suffering concussion during a school rugby match in County Antrim in January 2011. He was reported to have been involved in a number of "heavy tackles" during the game and then collapsed afterwards. The coroner explained that the death was as a result of "second impact syndrome" arising from a blow causing swelling to the brain before it had fully recovered from an earlier injury.

Key learning point

4.1.136   **Correct concussion procedures should be rigorously adhered to.**

Case Law 41

Cross-reference to **Chapter 2, Section 12: Group Management**
Issue: Group management in athletic activity
Secondary school athletics, 2015 (https://www.dailymail.co.uk/news/article-3019683/Top-grammar-school-fined-10-000-14-year-old-hit-head-shot-event-calls-ambulance-100m-sprint-student-runs-wall.html)

4.1.137   An experienced teacher took 24 students for an athletic lesson, with hurdles, long jump, triple jump, javelin, discus and shot-put activities going on in a rotational format that had been used regularly by the school in previous years. The arrangement of the activities meant that the end of the landing zone for the shot-put was only about three metres from the end of the triple jump sand pit, where the student was jumping. A whistle was blown to move stations, and the student left the triple jump and went across to the shot-put area to see how far a friend had thrown. At that point, another student launched a shot-put using a turning technique – his back was to the throwing area. The shot hit a 14-year-old student on the head, resulting in life-threatening injuries and requiring emergency brain surgery. He returned to school after being in hospital for nearly a month.

4.1.138   The school's risk assessment for physical education lessons referenced guidance from afPE, but had failed to note and follow their recommendation that such lessons be restricted to a maximum of four activities, with only one to be a throwing event. Six sports with three throwing events was deemed to have significantly increased the risks to students, as did the proximity of the triple jump activity to the shot-put landing area. The HSE inspector said the school put students at serious risk. The school was fined £10,000.

Key learning point

4.1.139   **Students should be carefully managed when teaching athletic activity, with no more than four different activities taking place within the same lesson.**

Case Law 42

Cross-reference to **Chapter 2, Section 12: Group Management**
Issue: Ratios
Jones v Cheshire County Council (1997) (unreported)

4.1.140   An experienced teacher and swimming instructor teacher took a group of 32 children to a swimming lesson. The LA guidelines indicated that the appropriate staff:student ratio for this activity was one teacher to 20 students. During the course of the lesson, the students were split into two groups – one sitting on the side while the other participated in the activity. For the final part of the lesson, all the students were allowed in the pool at once for "free time". A child was injured during the "free time" when he dived into shallow water to swim between the legs of another student and struck the bottom of the pool.

4.1.141   Given the inherently dangerous nature of unstructured free time, the court considered that it required proper instruction with suitable reminders in subsequent lessons. This did not occur, not least because the teacher had not noticed the students attempting the activity. The teacher was held to be negligent both in terms of exceeding ratios determined by the LA and not providing suitable instruction.

Key learning point

4.1.142   **Ratios set by the employer should be adhered to, and students should be effectively supervised at all times.**

Case Law 43

Cross-reference to **Chapter 2, Section 12: Group Management**
Issue: Supervision
McDougall v Strathclyde Regional Council (1995) (unreported)

4.1.143   A teacher advised his students in a class not to attempt any exercise without his assistance if they were not sure whether it could be performed safely. One of the students was about to perform a vaulting exercise, which he had never performed on his own before, with the teacher in attendance. The teacher then moved to assist another student, but the first student went ahead with his performance and was injured. The Appeal Court found that it was not reasonably foreseeable that the student would attempt the exercise without the support of the teacher and that the teacher had not deliberately withdrawn support but had found himself in a situation in which he was required to assist someone else. Therefore, there had been **no failure** of supervision.

Key learning point

4.1.144   **There is a need for very clear teacher instruction.**

Case Law 44

Cross-reference to **Chapter 2, Section 12: Group Management**
Issue: Effective supervision
R v Aberdeen City Council and Aberdeenshire Council (2012) (unreported)

4.1.145   An 11-year-old primary school student attended an open-air pool as part of an educational excursion. During the visit, he became submerged underwater and was recovered unconscious from the bottom of the pool by a member of the public. Cardiopulmonary resuscitation was successfully administered by lifeguards, and the student made a full recovery.

4.1.146   The investigation found issues with staffing levels and lifeguard **positioning** at the pool, as well as with the effective management of educational excursions at the school.

4.1.147   Both parties pleaded guilty to breaching Section 3(1) of the Health and Safety at Work etc Act 1974. Aberdeen City Council was fined £9000 while Aberdeenshire Council was fined £4000.

Key learning point

4.1.148   **Staffing levels and positioning of staff are both essential considerations, including on excursions.**

Case Law 45

Cross-reference to **Chapter 2, Section 12: Group Management**
Issue: Instruction and supervision
Secondary fitness room activities (2011) (unreported)

4.1.149   A 13-year-old student was injured the first time he attended a health-related exercise lesson. While running on a treadmill, the student jumped off, wishing to alter the controls to reduce its speed. Believing he had slowed the speed, he jumped back on, but the treadmill had not slowed down. He lost his footing and fell, trapping his left hand in the treadmill's belt, resulting in friction burns to the hand. The treadmills were fitted with safety clips to be attached to the user's clothing, acting as stop mechanisms in an emergency.

4.1.150   The student alleged negligence on the basis of a failure to instruct him properly in the use of the treadmill, particularly with regard to attaching the safety clip to his clothing, and failing to supervise the class adequately. It was also alleged that a staff:student ratio of 1:12 was inadequate.

4.1.151   The teacher gave evidence that he had instructed the students in how to use a treadmill before any of them began, including a demonstration, and had emphasised that the safety clip must always be properly used. He had also made a detailed record of the accident immediately afterwards, emphasising that tuition had been provided. This record was given significant weight in court as evidence that such tuition had taken place. The judge also accepted that, given the absence of previous similar incidents, the staff:student ratio was adequate.

4.1.152   The judge considered whether the teacher should have seen that the student had jumped off then back on again, that the treadmill was going too fast and that the student had not used the safety clip. The judge held this would place too high a burden on the teacher in these circumstances. There was adequate instruction and supervision, and the claim was dismissed.

Key learning point

4.1.153   **There is a need for adequate instruction and supervision.**

Case Law 46

Cross-reference to **Chapter 2, Section 12: Group Management**
Issue: Supervision
Burton v Canto Playgroup (1989) (unreported)

4.1.154   Adult staffing of a playgroup was supplemented by a **14-year-old helper** who was left alone to supervise a climbing frame. She had been given no training, nor did she have the experience to anticipate the action of a young child who had not been on the apparatus before. The child jumped and injured herself. The playgroup was held responsible for inadequate supervision.

Key learning point

4.1.155   **Staff should always retain responsibility for supervision.**

Case Law 47

Cross-reference to **Chapter 2, Section 12: Group Management**
Issue: Supervision and ratios
Palmer v Cornwall County Council (2009) ([2009] EWCA Civ 456)

4.1.156   One lunchtime supervisor was responsible for about 200–300 students aged 11–15 in a field during lunch break. Her attention was firmly fixed on the younger students, meaning the older students, who were in a different area of the field, were only given an occasional glance. An older student was hit in the eye with a stone thrown by another student who had been enticing seagulls to the field with food to then throw stones at them. The main issues were:

- What should the **proper ratio** of supervisors to students be?
- Would the incident have happened irrespective of the number of supervisors present?

4.1.157   The Court of Appeal held that if there had been proper supervision, no stone would have been thrown, that one person supervising such a large number was **negligent at a management level**, and the purpose of proper supervision is to deter students from dangerous activity and to stop it if it occurs.

Key learning point

4.1.158   **This case highlights the importance of adequate supervision of students in large numbers, and thorough risk assessments, guidance, warnings and training on the supervision of students.**

Case Law 48

Cross-reference to **Chapter 2, Section 12: Group Management**
Issue: Playground management at lunchtimes
Orchard v Lee (2009) ([2009] EWCA Civ 295)

4.1.159   A claim for negligence was dismissed after a student collided with, and injured, a lunchtime supervisor during a game of tag. The students were in a play area, playing the game in a typical manner and not breaking any rules. The court said that the student owed the adult a duty of care, but to establish a breach of that duty, the student would need to have been "playing tag in a way that was to a significant degree **outside the norm** for 13-year-olds", and this was not the case.

Key learning point

4.1.160   **This case shows that the courts remain reluctant to impose liability for accidents in the playground as long as the school has taken reasonable care by applying a common-sense approach with good risk management, including a risk assessment of supervision levels.**

Case Law 49

Cross-reference to **Chapter 2, Section 12: Group Management**
Issue: Playing out of age group
Mountford v Newlands School (2007) (EWCA Civ 21)

4.1.161   A teacher played an **overaged player** in an inter-school rugby match. An opposing player was badly injured when tackled within the rules of the game by this player. The court ruled that the teacher was negligent. In view of the difference in maturity, size and physique (178cm [five feet, 11 inches], 82kg versus 155cm [five feet, two inches], 45kg), the overaged player should not have been allowed to play. Although there is no complete ban on players "playing down" in terms of age group, and rugby is quite clearly a game designed for players of differing sizes and shapes, the fact that the overaged player might cause harm to a far smaller opponent was foreseeable and preventable.

Key learning point

4.1.162   **Teachers should adhere to the regulations laid down by National Governing Bodies for competitive fixtures when children are playing out of their age group.**

Case Law 50

Cross-reference to **Chapter 2, Section 12: Group Management**
Issue: Teacher participation in lessons
Affutu-Nartay v Clark and another (1984) (Lexis Citation 1552)

4.1.163   Students were taking part in a game of rugby during a physical education lesson. As the sides were of uneven number, the teacher who was supervising and refereeing took a playing position on the weaker team. The teacher was a keen rugby player. During the course of the game, the teacher executed a full tackle on a student, which caused them to fall and suffer a serious back injury. Although the court was keen to avoid any suggestion that a teacher should not participate in sport as a means to encourage student enthusiasm and demonstrate skill, it considered that the teacher should have avoided full contact and certainly not have sought to tackle the student.

Key learning point

4.1.164   **Teachers should ensure their involvement in demonstrations does not place students in a potentially harmful situation.**

Case Law 51

Cross-reference to **Chapter 2, Section 1: Qualifications and Professional Learning**
Issue: Competence
Jones v Manchester Corporation (1952) (2 QB 852)

4.1.165　An inexperienced doctor was deployed to carry out a procedure. Due to their inexperience, the doctor failed to properly follow training and miscalculated the appropriate dose of a drug to be given to a patient, which resulted in their death. The court found the doctor to be negligent but also found the employer and their representative, the more senior doctor involved in the procedure, were negligent in deploying an inexperienced member of staff and failing to properly supervise their practice. Liability was assessed on a 20%:80% basis.

Key learning point

4.1.166　**This case established that, where someone is not qualified or competent to undertake the responsibility placed on them but has been placed in that situation by the employer or the employer's representative (eg a head teacher), the employer and manager may be directly liable for negligence.**

Case Law 53

Cross-reference to **Chapter 2, Section 1: Qualifications and Professional Learning**
Issue: Spectators
Wooldridge v Sumner and another (1963) (2 QB 43)

4.1.167　A spectator was injured while filming a competition as a result of a horse running off the course into the course barriers. The spectator had been warned by officials that he should not be in the vicinity of the edge of the course when horses were participating in the event. It was clear that the rider and horse were of an extremely competent standard and that the incident had only occurred at best due to a lapse of skill or judgement by the rider in the course of the competition. The court considered that in the absence of a reckless disregard for the safety of spectators, the participant should not be held liable in negligence for any injury.

Key learning point

4.1.168　**This case reinforced the principle that a spectator injured during the normal course of events in a competition cannot claim negligence on the part of the players, officials or organisers, provided the spectator has been made aware of the need to remain outside the playing area and any run-off zone.**

Case Law 54

Cross-reference to **Chapter 2, Section 1: Qualifications and Professional Learning**
Issue: Competence to teach
Norfolk County Council v Kingswood Activity Centre (2007) (unreported)

4.1.169　An eight-year-old was injured when he fell six metres from a climbing wall. The investigation established that the screw of a karabiner (metal loop) had not been tightened, allowing the karabiner to open and free the safety rope when a weight was applied. It also found that the **training and supervision** procedures were not sufficient for the activities being carried out and were not being routinely followed on the ground. The incident was described as "an accident that could have been prevented had the correct safety procedures been followed and the staff undertaking the activities been trained and supervised".

Key learning point

4.1.170　**Staff leading lessons should be deemed competent to teach the activity that the employer requires them to deliver.**

Case Law 55

Cross-reference to **Chapter 1, Section 4: Parental Consent**
Issue: Duty of care
Woodland versus (1) Swimming Teachers' Association, (2) Stopford (trading as Direct Swimming Services), (3) Maxwell, (4) Essex County Council and (5) Basildon District Council (2011)

4.1.171   In July 2000, a student from an LA school attended a swimming lesson that had been contracted out to a swimming services company [2]. The company hired a pool and provided a qualified swimming teacher and lifeguard [3]. The class teacher and district council swimming staff were also present on poolside.

During the lesson, the student was found 'hanging vertically in the water'. Poolside resuscitation was administered, but the student suffered permanent brain damage. Other students reported seeing the injured student in distress, but any further details or facts were debated.

The claim made was one of inadequate duty of care, and was brought against several of the parties involved.

The school employer, Essex County Council, claimed that duty of care had been delegated to the swimming provider, once the lesson had begun, and that they had no liability for the actions of the commercial company.

The student's father claimed that Essex County Council maintained a **'non-delegable duty of care'** – ie that they remained legally responsible for the outcome despite outsourcing the tuition and water safety to a separate commercial party.

The High Court ruling in 2011 confirmed that Essex County Council was not liable, stating that:

Where a school must take their students to other premises, they discharge their duty of care if they know the premises and if the premises are apparently safe, and if they know that the premises are staffed by competent and careful persons.

This outcome clearly went **against** the long-held common understanding and practice that schools could not transfer their duty of care. In 2012, the Appeal Court upheld the High Court's decision, and it seemed as though this would be the new standard to work to when using external organisations to provide activities off site. However, in 2013, the issue was taken to the Supreme Court, where these original decisions were overturned.

The outcome confirmed that the **school authority** (an LA, a board of governors or a trust) is **responsible in situations where a duty is provided through a third party, whether on or off site.**

This responsibility remains with the school authority because the external agent contracted to provide the service does this **on behalf of** the school authority. Therefore, duty of care remains with the school authority and **cannot be delegated**:

*The **work required to perform such a duty may well be delegable...but the duty itself remains the defendant's**. Its delegation makes no difference to his legal responsibility for the proper performance of a duty which is in law his own.*

This ruling brings the application of duty of care for schools back to the long understood standard. As the highest court in the land has made **this decision, it is now common law**. It impacts on all maintained schools, including LA schools, academies and free schools. Fee-paying schools perform similar functions under contract rather than common law.

Key learning point

4.1.172
- **Employers remain liable for any negligent act relating to their services and programmes, including where these are contracted out to a third party to use technical expertise not necessarily available within the direct workforce of school staff.**
- **Where the external agency is found to be negligent the school authority would be in breach of its duty of care to the students.**
- **The school must continuously monitor and manage so that whoever carries out duties on its behalf does so without fault, and not simply rely on pre-check competence.**

(Based on summary of case by Peter Whitlam, afPE project manager for health and safety, November 2013.)

Section 2: Frequently Asked Questions

Introduction

4.2.1   This section outlines some of the most frequently asked questions (FAQs) raised with the afPE health and safety team. Also included are some very specific questions that necessitate a more detailed response. Cross-references back to the relevant section of the resource are given to help with understanding the background to the answer provided, along with any key learning points.

FAQ 1

Cross-reference to **Chapter 2, Section 9: Equipment**
Issue: Using wall bars and climbing equipment

Question

4.2.2   At what height is it safe to allow my year four students to work on the climbing equipment?

Answer

4.2.3   The type of climbing equipment most commonly found in primary schools ranges in height from two to three metres (six feet, six inches to 10 feet). This presents a range of options with regard to how high students climb. There will be a number of factors to be considered in making this decision:

- Prior learning – have the students regularly worked on the equipment since the start of Key Stage 1?
- Quality of teaching – have the students been progressively taught correct climbing technique in order to ascend and descend safely?
- Competence of the member of staff – is the staff member sufficiently confident and competent to supervise and manage students on the climbing equipment effectively?

4.2.4   Where the answer to any of these questions is "no", the member of staff may feel a need to restrict the height at which the students work. A lack of training in correct climbing technique can mean that some staff members are reluctant to use the equipment with students, and this needs to be addressed so that it is not used as a reason to restrict students' learning.

4.2.5   Setting restrictive heights is not recommended, and a risk assessment approach is preferred, using questions such as those suggested above. Staff are encouraged to pursue additional professional learning where required so that they can enable students to fully develop these skills. As with all practice, any relevant employer's guidance should be followed.

Key learning point

4.2.6   **Both students and teachers should know correct climbing and dismount techniques.**

FAQ 2

Cross-reference to **Chapter 2, Section 9: Equipment**
Issue: Use of mats in gymnastic activity

Question

4.2.7   Should I place mats at the base of the gymnastic climbing equipment?

Answer

4.2.8   Students should understand the purpose and limitation of gymnastic mats, and appreciate that it is
safe practice and good technique that will prevent them from falling. Although it is common practice
to see mats at the base of climbing equipment, these mats may have limited potential to reduce the
impact of a low-level accidental fall, and cannot be considered adequate in preventing head injury and/
or concussion. Their primary purpose is to provide an area to extend a sequence on to the floor, or to
indicate the planned area for dismount from the climbing arrangement. Care should be taken to ensure
that mats do not present a tripping hazard in other areas of the activity space.

4.2.9   Staff working in gymnastics need to feel competent that they can teach safely. Where this is not the
case, they should make this clear to their line manager. Until sufficient training has been completed, they
should only use low-level equipment in lessons.

Key learning point

4.2.10   **Mats are useful for assisting in sequence work, not for preventing falls from height.**

FAQ 3

Cross-reference to **Chapter 2, Section 13: Personal Protective Equipment (PPE)**
Issue: Use of mouth guards in hockey sessions

Question

4.2.11   Should the school make the wearing of mouth guards for hockey compulsory?

Answer

4.2.12   Wearing mouth guards for hockey at all levels is highly recommended. A hockey stick in the hands of a
beginner has the potential to do considerable damage to other players if poorly controlled.

4.2.13   If considering this course of action, you will need to inform parents in the first instance. You may suggest
that the school provides all students with their own mouth guard, and following this, students will need
to purchase a replacement if they lose theirs. Alternatively, if you ask parents to purchase the mouth
guard, the school may decide to source them in bulk.

4.2.14   If the decision to make the use of mouth guards compulsory is implemented within the school term, a
letter communicating the proposed change to the parents of students affected is sufficient. However,
in the longer term, the details should be included in the physical education, school sport and physical
activity (PESSPA) kit policy, and communicated through the normal channels, such as the school
newsletter, prospectus and website.

4.2.15   Staff will need to check who has their mouth guard at the start of each lesson, and in cases where
students do not have their mouth guard with them, the member of staff needs to manage the situation
in order to make the activity safe for all participants. Students should not be completely excluded on
the basis of not having the required equipment. In such circumstances, their participation should be
modified for the lesson, but they should still work towards the same outcomes (eg in a coaching role).

Key learning point

4.2.16   **Schools should have a clear policy on the wearing of mouth guards.**

FAQ 4

Cross-reference to **Chapter 2, Section 4: Parental Consent**
Issue: **Parental consent for out of school activities**

Question

4.2.17   I will be taking a group of students from my school to compete in a school sports tournament next week. The organisers of the tournament have provided consent forms that they would like the parents of students taking part to sign and return. I think this is not necessary for my students. My school collects consent from parents at the start of each year to cover all trips and activities that the students may be involved in during that year. On the basis of this, can I inform the tournament organiser that all consents have been received?

Answer

4.2.18   Yes. If the school has already requested this information for each student, then details can be passed on to the tournament organisers, thus avoiding the need for additional consent forms to be sent out, completed and signed. As part of your preparation for this event, you should have sent information about the tournament to the parents of students involved, informing them about arrangements in place (eg methods of transport being used, finishing time and arrangements for collection either at school or from the event). On receiving this information, if a parent does not wish their child to take part, they can make this known to the school.

4.2.19   Existing paperwork can be used to suit the requirements of a variety of contexts if it covers what is required. There is no need for a specific form for every activity. The event organiser may want to remind the school that parental consent needs to be confirmed, but the responsibility to do this remains with the school.

Key learning point

4.2.20   **As long as parents are kept informed, well written parental consent paperwork can apply to a variety of contexts, reducing staff workload.**

FAQ 5

Cross-reference to **Chapter 2, Section 8: Facilities**
Issue: **Use of school facilities by external organisations**

Question

4.2.21   A community gymnastic club has approached us and asked if they can hire the school sports hall to run public gym sessions. We are happy to do this, but what is the best way to arrange it?

Answer

4.2.22   Community use of school facilities is something that is very much encouraged. Many school facilities are unused in the evenings and at weekends, while clubs and organisations struggle to find suitable venues.

4.2.23   As the host for the venue, the school should draw up a contract of hire, the conditions of which need to be agreed with the users. This contract should state that the school will "hand over" the facility to the community user in a condition that is safe and fit for purpose. The community user will need to check the facility on arrival and report any concerns about its condition to the host, ideally before the session starts.

4.2.24   Terms of use may include the host stipulating items/equipment within the facility that should not be used by the club (eg the school trampoline) and also areas of the facility that should not be accessed (eg the school storage cupboard). The community club would be responsible for ensuring that its members and spectators respect these conditions.

4.2.25   The school will also need to check that the club organisers hold the necessary insurances, such as their own public liability insurance. The school's public liability insurance should only be required if a person linked with the club is injured as a result of an issue with the facility itself (eg a tripping hazard on stairs or a wet floor) where the school is seen to be at fault. The school would not be liable for claims made by those associated with the club concerning the activities of the club.

4.2.26   The school employer should be agreeable to any such arrangements, and professional advice should be sought with regard to the contract. The user should understand that they become the temporary occupier and would have legal responsibility for use of the facility.

Key learning point

4.2.27   **Schools intending to hire out their facilities should ensure they are up to standard, and all pertinent information should be contained in a contract of hire.**

FAQ 6

Cross-reference to **Chapter 2, Section 7: First Aid**
Issue: EpiPens

Question

4.2.28   I have been told that it is compulsory for me to undertake training in the use of an EpiPen. Is this correct?

Answer

4.2.29   In the past, it was a requirement that in order to use an EpiPen/autoinjector, the user had to have received training. Under the revision of the Medicines Act 2012, this is no longer the case, and any layperson can administer adrenaline through the use of an EpiPen/autoinjector.

4.2.30   However, if there is a high probability that an autoinjector will have to be used, staff should have training in this procedure, especially if working with individuals who carry one with them at all times in case of anaphylaxis.

4.2.31   As a generalised approach, a first aid training provider could tailor the first aid courses they deliver to include slides and demonstrations on this subject so that all staff members have a baseline knowledge of it. This will typically need to be discussed with the first aid training provider prior to delivery of the course.

Key learning point

4.2.32   **Schools should ensure EpiPens can be administered, and training on this procedure for school staff is good practice.**

FAQ 7

Cross-reference to **Chapter 2, Section 3: Special Educational Needs and Disabilities and Chapter 2, Section 16: Transport**
Issue: Wheelchairs

Question

4.2.33   Who can push a wheelchair?

Answer

4.2.34   There is no legal age limit for being able to push a wheelchair. Where appropriate, students can be taken through basic safety points to enable them to push their peers safely in wheelchairs. Experienced adults who have completed manual handling training should have covered safe handling of wheelchairs to enable them to carry this out, and can be asked to share this knowledge with students.

4.2.35   A risk assessment to decide who should push a wheelchair should be completed considering all of the following:

The Wheelchair User	The Person Pushing the Wheelchair	The Environment
Their: • ability to communicate • weight • ability to bear weight • ability to cooperate and follow instructions • physical conditions that affect their mobility (eg spasms and muscle tone or fatigue may necessitate monitoring of wheelchair users for enjoyment and safety) • behaviour.	Their: • sensitivity in speaking to the wheelchair user, encouraging them to voice any concerns, and not speaking for them unless required • individual capability and strength • condition that might affect their capability, such as pregnancy or injury • training needs (any student given responsibility for pushing will also require guidance and oversight by a trained adult) • level of competence.	The: • space constraints • floor or surface quality • movement restrictions caused by the layout • inclines that may be present.

Key learning point

4.2.36   **A risk assessment should be conducted to help decide who can push a wheelchair.**

FAQ 8

Cross-reference to **Chapter 2, Section 11: Safe Exercise Practice**
Issue: **Safe exercises for students**

Question

4.2.37   Is there a list of exercises that are "unsafe" for students in schools?

Answer

4.2.38   No. The reason for this is that it would be impossible to decide which exercises should be included. Assessing the risks associated with a specific exercise depends on a range of factors, including:

- who is performing the exercise (eg their physical maturity, experience, capability)
- whether the exercise complies with the principles of safe exercise practice, ie control, impact, alignment and developmental appropriateness
- how well the exercise is taught
- how well the exercise is performed
- how frequently the exercise will be performed.

4.2.39   It follows that if there was a list of "unsafe" exercises, an exercise not on the list could become high risk (eg if it was performed with incorrect technique).

4.2.40   It is the responsibility of PESSPA staff to make their own risk assessments of the exercises they wish their students to perform using the principles explained in **Chapter 2, Section 11: Safe Exercise Practice**. This will involve:

- clarifying the purpose of the exercise they wish to use with their students
- completing a risk assessment of the exercise using the principles of safe exercise practice (**Table 13, page 173**).

Key learning point

4.2.41   **Risk assessments should be conducted before making a decision about which activities students can engage in, and school staff should keep their knowledge and practice current through regular upskilling.**

FAQ 9

Cross-reference to **Chapter 2, Section 11: Safe Exercise Practice**
Issue: **Warm-ups**

Question

4.2.42   Should I include static or dynamic stretches in warm-ups?

Answer

4.2.43   Static stretches involve stretching a muscle and then holding it still in a stretched position (eg static calf stretch or hamstring stretch). Research about the benefits of static stretches within warm-ups is largely inconclusive. It suggests that while static stretching might not be helpful in terms of preparing for highly dynamic performance, there are few indications that it is physiologically harmful as a component of a warm-up. Static stretches in warm-ups can be very useful in an educational context for helping students to learn about how to stretch, to identify where they can feel muscles stretching, to locate and/or name the muscles involved and to develop correct alignment in their technique.

4.2.44   Dynamic stretches involve active movements of muscles that cause them to stretch (eg lunges dynamically stretch quads and hamstrings). Dynamic stretches in warm-ups can be helpful, especially directly preceding very dynamic participation. It is advisable for dynamic stretches to be performed slowly and over a smaller range in the early stages of the warm-up. The speed and range of dynamic stretches should increase gradually and carefully as the warm-up progresses. Correct alignment of joints and appropriate use of control are requirements for safe and effective dynamic stretching, which is why they are more suitable for older students. Ballistic stretching, which involves bouncing while a muscle is at the end of its range, should be avoided due to the high risk of soft tissue injury.

Key learning point

4.2.45   **School staff should remain up to date on the latest research into the most appropriate types of warm-ups.**

FAQ 10

Cross-reference to **Chapter 2, Section 11: Safe Exercise Practice**
Issue: The appropriate age at which to educate students about warm-ups and cool-downs

Question

4.2.46   My year two class seem flexible enough. Do they need to stretch in warm-ups and cool-downs?

Answer

4.2.47   You are correct in your observation – younger children are indeed more flexible than adults. While the benefits of stretching for this age group are debatable, it is beneficial to keep the messages about how to warm-up and cool-down consistent throughout their learning.

4.2.48   Whole-body static stretches held for about six seconds can be used with younger children. A good time to start learning some simple stretches for specific muscles might be towards the end of Key Stage 2.

Key learning point

4.2.49   **It is good practice to teach students at an early age about warming-up and cooling-down.**

FAQ 11

Cross-reference to **Chapter 2, Section 5: Insurance**
Issue: Extracurricular activity insurance

Question

4.2.50   As a physical education teacher, I have been asked to take a group of students to a sports event on a Saturday. Does my school insurance cover me to do this?

Answer

4.2.51   If this is a school-organised and approved activity, then the employer is expected to provide sufficient and appropriate insurance to cover staff for the range and type of activities they might be asked to carry out within their contract of employment. Where it is commonplace for teachers to lead fixtures and activities on a Saturday, it is likely that the employer has included cover for this, but this should be confirmed.

4.2.52   Academies and free schools are responsible for arranging their own insurance. Those sourcing insurance cover therefore need to be clear about exactly the extent of cover required, ie including weekends if the employer requires attendance at events then by teachers.

4.2.53   Where the event or activity is not organised and approved by the school (eg it is a request by parents), if the teacher decides to go ahead, they must make their own insurance arrangements.

Key learning point

4.2.54 **Assumptions should not be made about insurance cover. The extent of existing cover needs to be carefully checked before engaging in an activity.**

FAQ 12

Cross-reference to **Chapter 2, Section 6: Digital Technology**
Issue: Photographing and filming students

Question

4.2.55 We are running a large school PESSPA event and want to adopt a correct and manageable approach to photography. What should we consider?

Answer

4.2.56 In most cases, schools will already hold permissions or rejections for their students to be photographed or filmed, and should be able to inform the organisers of the event, which will avoid the need for the organisers to request duplicate information. As set out in the Data Protection Act 2018, parents attending the event are able to take photographs or video of their child when it is for personal use.

4.2.57 Where official photographers are used for the event, a procedure should be agreed with the organisers. This could include issuing coloured bands or stickers to students without consent to be filmed, and ensuring that the photographer respects these. Both schools and organisers, however, will need to clarify to parents that at such large events, the possibility of a student being photographed without consent can, at times, be unavoidable. Where this happens, every step should be taken to prevent the picture being printed. Where pictures are printed, they should not include individual names.

4.2.58 Although parents/observers may be able to film without breaking data protection regulations, it is important that schools develop and apply their own rules. Safeguarding policies should also ensure that any information used should not allow students to be identified.

Key learning point

4.2.59 **Permission to film or photograph students should be obtained before any image of them is used.**

FAQ 13

Cross-reference to **Chapter 2, Section 10: Programme Management**
Issue: Applying sun cream

Question

4.2.60 I have heard that school staff should not assist students with applying sun cream. Some younger students struggle to manage this on their own. Should they be helped?

Answer

4.2.61 School policy on the use of sun cream often specifies that students must apply their own, or that the parents should do so before the child arrives at school. The Health and Safety Executive (HSE) suggests that the real issue to address is about teaching young people at an early age how to take sensible precautions against the sun, which is learning they can make use of throughout their lives. The HSE does not consider it helpful or proportionate for schools to insist on students wearing long sleeves and sun hats as some students will find this very uncomfortable. The HSE also clarifies that **there is no legal obstacle to school staff helping children to apply sunscreen**. Schools are able to make their own decisions about this, and where they do decide that staff can assist students, all staff should observe correct procedures regarding physical contact at all times. Whichever route a school decides to take, as with all policy, it should be clearly communicated to all staff, students and parents.

Key learning point

4.2.62 **Schools should establish their own policy on applying sun cream, and staff should adhere to this.**

FAQ 14

Cross-reference to **Chapter 2, Section 7: First Aid**
Issue: Concussion

Question

4.2.63   Do schools need to have a specific policy about concussion?

Answer

4.2.64   If schools already have protocols and procedures **for head injuries** as part of their whole-school first aid and emergency treatment policy, including guidance regarding concussion, a separate policy is not required. Subject leaders should check that this policy covers specific guidelines about concussion in PESSPA contexts. Where this is not the case, they can develop these as part of PESSPA policy and procedures using the information provided in **Chapter 2, Section 7: First Aid**, and the suggestions listed below:

- Ensure that the well-being and safety of students are paramount above all else.
- Understand that symptoms can be delayed for up to 48 hours, and recognise the need for monitoring anyone with possible concussion over that period.
- Apply the whole-school policy at all times.
- Know how to recognise, assess and treat possible concussion injuries (a copy of the Pocket Concussion Recognition Tool for all staff would be helpful).
- Understand what second impact syndrome (SIS) is and how critical it is that such situations are avoided.
- Have their own knowledge and understanding about concussion assessed when they first enter school.
- Risk assess where such injuries may arise within their individual teaching, supervision or management contexts.
- Record any and all possible concussion occurrences within a whole-school register of incidents.
- Ensure parents are made aware of any such situation their child has experienced.
- Be in a position to advise parents that recreational activities such as prolonged reading, television, computers, video games, smartphones, exercise and sport should be avoided until a gradual return to full health is achieved.
- Follow up post-incident, within established whole-school procedures.
- Ensure that parents are aware that it is a parental responsibility to obtain confirmation from a recognised medical source that their child is fit to participate in a gradual return to full learning and activity sessions.
- Develop students' understanding about concussion, how it may occur, how it may be recognised, and what safe practice outcomes are essential to mitigate such an injury.
- Communicate with other staff who teach a student who has been diagnosed as being concussed so that this is taken into consideration in lessons, with any impact on studies noted and referred if necessary.
- Be aware that concussion will impact on academic learning and that adjustments need to be made during convalescence and a gradual return to full involvement in school activities, such as by applying a "no homework" rule.

4.2.65   Select from this list – and add to it where appropriate – according to the organisation of your school and structure of its policies.

Key learning point

4.2.66 **Guidance on procedures surrounding potential concussion should be outlined in school policy and regularly updated, and all staff should apply this as required.**

FAQ 15

Cross-reference to **Chapter 2, Section 12: Group Management**
Issue: Arrangements for transgender students – below are three common questions around this emerging and important issue

Question 15a

4.2.67   How do I manage sleeping arrangements on my sports tour when I have a transgender young person in the group?

Answer

4.2.68   Schools must not discriminate against a trans young person because of their transgender status. Every school authority should have an equalities policy that includes information on how off-site visits will be carried out so that all young people can participate equally. Parents can be offered copies of the equalities policy and an opportunity to speak individually with the visit leader or a member of senior management if necessary. Where a sports event involves transgender participants, you should consider any individual needs and any reasonable adjustments that may be required.

4.2.69   Do not make assumptions – speak with the transgender person and their parents to find acceptable solutions. Each visit and young person should be considered on an individual basis.

4.2.70   Overnight stays may involve the most significant issues around accommodation and showers/toilet facilities. Many variables will affect the event, including the age, sexual maturity and gender identity of the individual and where they may be in any transition process.

4.2.71   It is important that you do not make uninformed decisions about someone's gender when making accommodation, changing, toilet and showering arrangements. A solution should be agreed with the individual young person prior to departure.

4.2.72   Practical arrangements may include:

- access to gender neutral toilets
- showers of the identified gender used by agreement at alternative times
- a separate bedroom (although this may introduce other safeguarding/safety issues that will need to be fully considered)
- a shared bedroom with other transgender young people or with friends where there is trust and understanding
- sensitivity around organising changing areas.

4.2.73   If parents of other young people taking part in the visit express concern, you should explain that the establishment is following the school authority policies, which are sensitive both to individuals and to the welfare and safety of the group. Parents can be offered copies of the school equalities policy and the opportunity to speak individually with the teacher leading the sports tour or a senior teacher. You should, however, also be aware of the need for confidentiality.

4.2.74   In conclusion, decisions should be made on a case-by-case basis, taking account of the areas highlighted above, and any other individual factors. Schools should always work from a position of inclusion.

Question 15b

4.2.75   If a young person asks for support with gender identity issues, how should I respond?

Answer

4.2.76 Every young trans person is different – there is no script. It is important that the student's gender identity is respected so listen to what they say, and do not lead the conversation. In supporting students, you should make clear that you are unable to keep things to yourself and will need to inform other people in line with school policy. The following questions may help in your discussions with the student:

- How can we best help you?
- Have you spoken to anyone else about your feelings or gender identity?
- How do you wish to express your gender identity?
- Which name and which pronouns do you wish to be known by/called at school?

4.2.77 Try to allow the student to express how they identify in a way they find comfortable, and keep an open mind, taking care to find out what their needs are and how they want to proceed.

4.2.78 If they are looking for medical help with their transition, then their GP is the first port of call. The GP should at least be able to refer the young person to Child and Adolescent Mental Health Services (CAMHS) so the young person or their family can have their questions answered.

4.2.79 Writing an action plan may be the next step if the student is intending to transition while at school.

Question 15c

4.2.80 We have a student transitioning from boy to girl, and we allowed them to compete in the girls race on sports day. This young person duly won and broke the school record. The parents of the runner-up complained, and it has caused an issue in school.

Answer

4.2.81 Parental complaints and concerns should be dealt with in accordance with the school's adopted complaints procedures. It may be possible to resolve such issues informally, but where this is not possible, complainants should be encouraged to submit their complaint formally to the head teacher (HT)/chair of governors as appropriate.

4.2.82 The exemption within Section 195 of the Equality Act 2010 makes it lawful to restrict participation of transsexual people in competitions where physical strength, stamina or physique are major factors in determining success or failure, if this is necessary to uphold fair competition, but not otherwise.

4.2.83 If the physical strength, stamina or physique of the average student of one sex would put them at an advantage compared to the average student of the other sex as a competitor in a sport, game or other competitive activity, it is not unlawful for those arranging the event to restrict participation in the activity to students of one sex. Sports that come under this heading are referred to in the Act as a "Gendered Activity".

4.2.84 If you are likely to be involved in the above situation as a teacher or subject lead, it is recommended that you seek legal advice from whoever provides this for your school authority.

Key learning point

4.2.85 **Schools should develop their own policies which ensure that the needs of transgender students are met and these should be understood/applied by all school personnel.**

FAQ 16

Cross-reference to **Chapter 2, Section 12: Group Management**
Issue: **Staff v student activity**

Question

4.2.86   At the end of term, we like to raise money for charity by having a staff v students sports event. How is this practice viewed?

Answer

4.2.87   Staff taking part in PESSPA activities should be limited to demonstration and learning purposes only. Participation should be generally static, or used in a controlled manner to provide a visual interpretation of the information being taught. The potential differences in ability, size, weight and experience between students and adults are further exacerbated when a "competitive" element is introduced, such as in staff v student games. While students find such events entertaining, it is highly recommended that they do not take place. An alternative could be considered (eg staff v staff with students as the audience). On such occasions, the staff taking part would do so with their own consent (at their own risk). Any liability arising from personal injury would not be pursued through the employer, other than that arising from the facility used not being fit for purpose, unless this was considered to be a school-organised event, and the staff involved were "at work".

Key learning point

4.2.88   **The risks outweigh the benefits in this type of activity, and it should be avoided.**

FAQ 17

Cross-reference to **Chapter 2, Section 10: Programme Management**
Issue: **Trampoline parks**

Question

4.2.89   Can I take students to trampoline parks?

Answer

4.2.90   Trampoline parks are large warehouse units, similar to soft play centres, with a number of trampoline beds linked together in a "patchwork" arrangement both on the floor and the walls. Many have additional facilities incorporated into or around the trampoline area, such as climbing walls, basketball courts and trampettes with large inflatable landing areas that encourage participants to try somersaults. Such facilities have become very popular for young people, and provide opportunities for high energy activity. However, given sessions are generally open to large and diverse groups from the very young to adults, they can be chaotic environments. It may be appropriate for staff to seek a private session where possible.

4.2.91   As outlined in **Chapter 2, Section 1: Qualifications and Professional Learning**, staff teaching trampolining to students at school are recommended to have a formal qualification, and to develop the skills required progressively and safely. While centres provide staff to monitor activity, many do not have formal qualifications, nor do they engage in developing skills in a controlled manner.

4.2.92   Most centres require participants to sign waiver forms to absolve the centre of liability in the event of an accident. The extent to which such waivers would be effective is debatable. However, staff are not able to sign such forms on behalf of students, nor can students under 18 years of age sign their own waivers. The waiver will also not act to absolve the school of liability in the event of an accident.

4.2.93   Bearing in mind the nature of such parks, staff must consider the educational objectives of any visit. In a private, controlled session, parks can offer opportunities for younger students or those with additional needs to develop balance and coordination skills in line with curricular requirements.

4.2.94   Given the particular issues that trampoline parks present, some employers have taken the view that they are inappropriate for the purposes of educational visits. Staff must therefore be aware of and follow their employer's policy on the matter.

Key learning point

4.2.95   Staff should follow their own employer guidance on this type of activity. If they go ahead with such an activity, staff should satisfy themselves that the visit has been thoroughly risk assessed, including consideration of all the issues outlined previously.

FAQ 18

Cross-reference to **Chapter 1, Section 6: Policy Writing for PESSPA**
Issue: Withdrawing students from physical education lessons

Question

4.2.96   We have noticed that a number of students are being withdrawn from lessons and school activities by their parents, including compulsory parts of the curriculum such as swimming. Governors are concerned about the implications of failing to provide students with the full curriculum. What are the actual rights of parents in this situation?

Answer

4.2.97   While schools that are obliged to follow the national curriculum must offer certain subjects, there is a limited right for parents to withdraw their children from some of those subjects. In particular, parents may withdraw their children from religious education, and sex and relationship education. Parents may also withdraw their children from the daily act of worship, which in many schools takes place during whole-school assembly. This right may be exercised at any time without the need to provide a reason, and may be exercised at both faith and non-faith schools.

4.2.98   However, there is no right to withdraw children from physical education, including swimming. Nevertheless, schools may need to be mindful of their responsibility to make reasonable adjustments with regard to required PESSPA kit to take account of some students' religious beliefs, in accordance with the Equality Act.

4.2.99   Furthermore, the right to withdraw students from religious education, and sex and relationship education does not extend to other parts of the curriculum that may discuss similar themes. For example, there is no right to withdraw a student from science lessons where reproduction is covered.

4.2.100   If students feel the need to withdraw themselves from lessons (perhaps using their parents to support this), discussing the reasons and barriers with the individuals could prove helpful in re-engaging them. Sometimes, the issues are easily resolvable, but the students have not had the confidence to raise their concerns.

Key learning point

4.2.101   Access to the physical education curriculum is a student right, and students should not be withdrawn. Staff should work with students to resolve any barriers to participation.

FAQ 19

Cross-reference to **Chapter 2, Section 1: Qualifications and Professional Learning**
Issue: Qualifications for working in a fitness suite

Question

4.2.102   I am a qualified secondary physical education specialist. Do I need a formal fitness industry qualification in order to teach my students in a fitness room facility?

Answer

4.2.103   No. Full qualified teacher status (QTS) and a specialism in physical education are sufficient to be able to teach your students in a fitness room, although additional professional learning is recommended. As a member of staff teaching or supervising in this environment, you should be competent to do so. An assessment of such competence should confirm that you are:

- well informed and up to date in terms of knowledge about safe exercise practice for young people
- sufficiently experienced and confident in using a range of fitness room equipment
- able to lead, demonstrate, observe and correct safe exercise technique
- able to manage group circulation and practice within the facility.

4.2.104   If a teacher needs to further develop/update any of these competencies, it is recommended that additional appropriate professional learning is undertaken, such as a Level 2 gym instructor qualification (eg http://www.ymcafit.org.uk/courses/gym-instructor) or appropriate training course.

Key learning point

4.2.105   **There is no single award that will qualify staff to work in fitness rooms. A risk assessment should identify if staff are competent to lead activities in these facilities. Where any need is identified, further training should be undertaken.**

FAQ 20

Cross-reference to **Chapter 2, Section 1: Qualifications and Professional Learning**
Issue: Non-QTS staff teaching physical education

Question

4.2.106   Can a higher level teaching assistant (HLTA) or cover supervisor teach a practical physical education lesson?

Answer

4.2.107   If an HT makes this decision, they must be satisfied that the HLTA or cover supervisor is competent to teach such a lesson. A competence assessment needs to be undertaken to ascertain whether the HLTA or cover supervisor is sufficiently competent to teach the **specific PESSPA activity** required. This assessment will consider aspects such as qualifications, experience, reputation and knowledge of the children, and should include the member of staff being observed teaching the class.

4.2.108   If an accident were to occur during a PESSPA lesson that the HLTA or cover supervisor was leading, the HT would have to be satisfied that they could justify their decision that allowed this to happen. The HT would do this by presenting evidence that a thorough and accurate positive competence assessment had been carried out that reported the HLTA or cover supervisor as a competent deliverer, and that the students in their sessions were achieving and making progress. This type of evidence would then be considered. If they cannot justify their decision, then the situation should not continue.

4.2.109   The National Agreement of 2003 covering England and Wales, and related to regulations made under Section 133 of the Education Act 2002, places a duty on HTs to ensure that each class or group timetabled for core and foundation subjects, and each class or group in the foundation stage has a qualified teacher assigned to teach it. Provided this requirement is met, an HLTA or cover supervisor performing the role of a teacher can be a long-term arrangement.

4.2.110 If the class being covered is accommodating the class teacher's planning, preparation and assessment (PPA) time, the responsibility for the class must be transferred to another qualified teacher or to the HT.

Key learning point

4.2.111 The HT should ensure that they are satisfied of the competence of any member of staff leading a physical education lesson, and be confident in defending this decision if challenged.

FAQ 21

Cross-reference to **Chapter 2, Section 15: Sports Fixtures, Festivals, Tours and Club Links**
Issue: Off-site fixtures

Question

4.2.112 I understand that I need to carry out a risk assessment for away sports fixtures with other schools. Is it necessary to do this for every fixture?

Answer

4.2.113 Decisions regarding when and how risk assessments should be carried out depend to a large extent on the requirements of the employer. While employers are tasked to undertake risk assessments under the Management of Health and Safety at Work Regulations (1999), the type and frequency of these is generally a local decision. Guidance provided by the Department for Education (DfE) suggests a measured approach to risk assessment and that "sensible management of risk does not mean that a separate written risk assessment is required for every activity".

DfE (2014) "Health and safety: advice for schools", https://goo.gl/oyHvHU

4.2.114 The above information is relevant to daily school sports fixtures, and as such, it is considered acceptable for one risk assessment to cover all fixtures for the year unless the risk assessment needs to be reviewed following an incident or change of circumstances. In contrast, where a school decides to enter an off-site tournament in which they have not previously been involved, it would be wise to risk assess this activity separately.

4.2.115 In all cases, the employer needs to decide which approach is to be taken. It is important to note that separate risk assessments may be necessary for some young people who are participating in the event, ie children with additional needs.

Key learning point

4.2.116 Risk assessments can cover all fixtures if there is nothing different about the fixtures. The employer policy must be followed.

FAQ 22

Cross-reference to **Chapter 2, Section 2: Safeguarding**
Issue: Disclosure and Barring Service (DBS) requirements

Question

4.2.117 I currently teach in a secondary school and am moving to a new post in further education. Will I need to have a new DBS check carried out?

Answer

4.2.118 If you signed up to the DBS update service when your previous DBS check was carried out, your new employer should be able to access and check, with your permission, your existing DBS certificate online. The process is outlined overleaf.

4.2.119   Since 17 June 2013, the DBS has offered the DBS update service in conjunction with the single certificate process. Applicants who have a check can voluntarily sign up to this scheme at a cost of £13 per year.

4.2.120   If a school has an applicant who has signed up for the update service, before undertaking a status check, it must obtain permission from the applicant to carry out this check.

4.2.121   The school must also see the original certificate in order to check that it is the same level as the required level (ie standard, enhanced or enhanced with a children's/adults'/both barred list check).

4.2.122   When it sees what, if any, information is revealed about the applicant, the school must consider this as part of its recruitment process.

4.2.123   If the original certificate is not available, a new check must be completed.

4.2.124   As outlined above, employees need to show their new employer their original certificate so they can take the necessary details from it. This is possible as long as the employee is moving within the same workforce, and the type and level of check required are the same.

4.2.125   When the new employer checks the certificate with the online service, they should be able to satisfy themselves of the employee's eligibility to work within the terms of the new post, provided that the certificate does not reveal any criminality or barring information and remains current, ie there is no outstanding information to be added to it.

Key learning point

4.2.126   **The update service is designed to reduce the need to apply for additional DBS checks. If employees do not sign up to the service, repeated checks are likely to be required, although some employers may insist on fresh DBS checks.**

Index

Notes